Heretic Queen

Heretic Queen

QUEEN ELIZABETH I
AND THE WARS OF RELIGION

Susan Ronald

ST. MARTIN'S GRIFFIN
NEW YORK

www.stmartins.com

The Library of Congress has cataloged the hardcover edition as follows:

Ronald, Susan.
    Heretic queen : Queen Elizabeth I and the wars of religion / Susan Ronald.—1st ed.
      p. cm.
    Includes bibliographical references and index.
    ISBN 978-0-312-64538-0 (hardcover)
    ISBN 978-1-250-01521-1 (e-book)
    1. Elizabeth I, Queen of England, 1533–1603—Religion. 2. Reformation—England. 3. England—Church history—16th century. 4. Great Britain—History—Elizabeth, 1558–1603. I. Title.
  DA356.R577 2012
  942.05'5092—dc23   2012010248

ISBN 978-1-250-03150-1 (trade paperback)

First St. Martin's Griffin Edition: August 2013

10 9 8 7 6 5 4 3 2 1

For my mother

CONTENTS

Part III: The Years of Religious Terror, 1580–1591

Part IV: A House Divided, 1591–1603

ACKNOWLEDGMENTS

All authors have a team of active and apparently silent supporters that help to make their books possible. My outstanding agents, Peter Robinson and Michael Carlisle, stand in the first row of those who must be thanked, followed closely by my U.S. editor, Charles Spicer, my excellent copy editor, India Cooper, and the entire team at St. Martin's Press.

I am enormously grateful to the bishop of Coventry for our illuminating chat at Stratford-upon-Avon about the similarities and differences between Roman Catholicism and the Elizabethan settlement. I also thank Alan Brooke, Lady Antonia Fraser DBE, Sarah Gristwood, Alex Hoyt, Chris Laoutaris, Hugh Van Dusen, Alison Weir, and the teams of librarians at the University of Oxford's Bodleian Library, the London Library, and the British Library. Above all else, I thank my long-suffering husband, Doug Ronald, for his forbearance and unswerving support and to my mother for her belief in me. I dedicate this book to you, Mom.

AUTHOR'S NOTE

Religion was high politics in the Elizabethan era. From the time of the Lollards in the fifteenth century, religious tensions steadily rose in England and elsewhere, resulting in the Reformation—that smooth, seamless expression that most of us feel we understand. What is clear to me is that the Reformation was the biggest social, political, religious, and even economic change to hit European civilization, ever.

In our increasingly secular age, it is difficult for us to imagine just how much was demanded of the average English person living then. A stark choice between allegiance to the monarch or to the church and your immortal soul was laid before you. Patriotism and survival in this life or religious belief, custom, and the hereafter became the battleground for the hearts and minds of every English man, woman, and child. This invidious choice led to a series of wars—some hot, others cold—that were waged on battlefields and the high seas; in the countryside, cities, and towns; from church pulpits and places of work; at court and most especially in the home. It led to a new concept—patriotism. It affected everyone living then, and the outcome made England, the rest of Britain, and the Elizabethan and Jacobean colonies in North America what they were to become.

Elizabeth's middle way—neither Catholic nor Puritan—was a solution that pleased very few. Yet it was a solution that she maintained throughout her forty-five-year reign. For a queen renowned among her advisers for prevarication for its own sake, Elizabeth's Anglican vision shows her remarkable tenacity. She knew in her heart and mind that any wavering might mean civil war. After all, during her reign France was plagued with over thirty years of civil wars, and the Netherlands began its civil war to protect its ancient religious privileges—a war that lasted eighty years. Elizabeth believed that if she gave in to the reforming "godly" Puritans or Presbyterians on the one hand, or her Catholic population on the other, civil war could not be far behind. So she held fast.

Heretic Queen will bring new people and faces from the Elizabethan era to populate its pages. Some familiar names like Mary Queen of Scots are central characters, though in Mary's case, I stress her links to France as a crucial part of the story. William Cecil (Lord Burghley), Robert Dudley (first Earl of Leicester), Francis Walsingham, and others will appear in their usual leading roles as privy councillors. Yet they will also wear new faces and don new clothing in their roles within the Catholic, Protestant, and Puritan leaderships. Foreign places and wars not often thought of as "Elizabethan" are also present, most notably the troubles in France and the Netherlands. These had a great bearing on Elizabeth's domestic, foreign, and religious policies. The generally unremarked turning point in Elizabethan international religious affairs was the arrival of the Duke of Alba in Brussels in August 1567, ostensibly to quell Philip's rebellious Calvinist subjects, but in effect to wage holy war. The background to this is essential to understanding the rest of the story.

What you, the reader, should try to do is to suspend the stereotypes of Tudor film and literature, and allow yourself to drift back to a time when religion was everything. Imagine yourselves in a world where before having breakfast you would have prayed once already. Imagine a daily routine based on religious rules and habits: a world where even the art on your walls—whether a cheap "stained" cloth or a ballad torn from a book or an expensive tapestry—had a religious theme; a world where your reading recreation was the Bible or a cheap chapbook that gave you access to the spellbinding sermons of Thomas Cartwright or Edward Dering; and a world where holding a different belief and preaching it could end very badly. Ultimately, it was a world where if you plotted against the queen's vision for England—even for the salvation of your soul—you would be imprisoned and probably executed on the grounds of treason.

One of the most graphic ways in which religion was high politics relates to the date. In 1582, Pope Gregory XIII introduced the Gregorian calendar that is still in use today. In October 1582, all Catholic countries of Europe moved their dates forward by ten days, which is sometimes termed New Style by authors, with the Julian calendar dates termed Old Style. By 1587, most of Europe used the Gregorian calendar. England, however, remained steadfast to the Old Style due to continued papal meddling in its internal affairs; that is, until 1752, when Britain finally accepted the change to the Gregorian calendar. While New Year's Day was on March 25 in Elizabeth's time, in the book New Year's Day is January 1 for ease of understanding. Also, from 1587, I've converted New Style dates to Old Style where necessary since the primary action takes place in England. Spelling has been modernized for ease of reading, into American English, save in the titles of books. People who were ennobled are known afterward by their new titles; for example, Sir Robert Dudley becomes the Earl of Leicester, or simply Leicester.

Heretic Queen is the result of my historical study into the complex and fascinating issues surrounding religion and its influence on the politics of the day—fundamental issues that are not terribly different from those facing our world now. Those who thought they were "freedom fighters" were viewed as "terrorists" by governments throughout Europe, be they in England, Ireland, Scotland, France, the Netherlands, Germany, Italy, or Spain. Tolerance was an alien notion to all but the Dutch and would remain so until the eighteenth century. Ultimately there was right and wrong on both sides.

What made the choices so stark came down to two main and juxtaposed belief systems. The Puritans believed that the Lord's Word was precise and that there were only black and white in the broad spectrum of color that the Christian faiths were rapidly becoming. The absence of the notion of "tolerance" in the Elizabethan era made the religious settlement that the queen strived for a dream of a utopia yet to exist. Elizabeth effectively attempted to establish a tolerant regime that would not "make windows into men's souls"; her solution proved imperfect, yet inspired for her day. It was a valiant attempt at creating a tolerant society, swimming against the tide of religious fundamentalism to the right and left.

A century later, Charles II would try to create a tolerant regime commencing with his Declaration of Breda just before he was restored to England's throne, and he failed as well. The issue of a Protestant or Catholic England rumbled on well into the nineteenth century. The fault was not in the flawed philosophies or policies of either Elizabeth I or Charles II but rather in the fundamentalist creeds of the English on both sides of the divide.

We all have different histories and biographies depending on who is looking at us and how the author chooses to write about us. My last book, *The Pirate Queen: Queen Elizabeth I, Her Pirate Adventurers, and the Dawn of Empire,* concentrated on how a genuine, terrifying domestic need for cash generated a swashbuckling foreign policy that gave birth to the British Empire. This existed alongside the burning religious issues of the day, with virtually all of the swashbucklers and their courtly patrons leaning toward the Puritan persuasion.

In *Heretic Queen,* I show how religion was high politics and how domestic policy was ruled by the religious imperatives of the Reformation, often overruled by other monarchs and a temporal papal authority beyond England's shores. I continue to explore how Elizabeth coped in a man's world, how she ruled so successfully, what motivated her, and in fact, what has made Elizabeth so unique in our hearts and minds for the past four-hundred-plus years. Above all else, *Heretic Queen* is the story of a monumental struggle of ideology and survival on all sides. Together these two books form my single biographical history of Elizabeth's reign.

It is my sincere hope that you will see Elizabeth better as a result. I also hope you can get a sense of what it was like to live in Elizabethan England through a new looking glass, offering you a fresh perspective of our now distant ancestors. It was an extraordinary period, not so different from our own. Above all, I do hope you enjoy the book.

Of course, any errors contained herein are entirely my own.

—SUSAN RONALD
Oxford, April 2011

Heretic Queen

The Sacrificial Priest

The London of Mary Tudor's reign—like most times past—
was truly another country. Rich woodlands and coppice
woods of lime, ash, oak, elm, holly, beech, hornbeam, and
maple carpeted the capital's county of Middlesex, stretching
northward nearly twenty miles to the Essex and Hertfordshire borders.
Some of these highly prized woods had belonged to the Oxford and Cambridge colleges ever since the universities had been founded hundreds
of years earlier. Others, equally well maintained, had been the property of
Westminster Abbey or St. Paul's Cathedral or other church establishments.
That is, until the time of King Henry VIII. With the dissolution of England's monasteries under Henry beginning in 1536, all the valuable woodland that had once belonged to the Catholic Church reverted to the crown.
Since then, much of England's managed woodland had been passed on to
Henry's nobles, in thanks for their help in plundering and destroying papal
monetary authority in England.

Yet it was the yeoman tenants and peasants of the woods who
"farmed" these as renewable sources of fuel and building timber. At the
autumn coppice harvest, the wood gatherers would cut the poles, or new
shoots, trim and divide these into one- or two-inch bundles of a hundred

evenly sorted sticks called fagots, tie these together, and bring them to the woodmongers for sale. Though fagots were mainly used for kindling in small kilns, they were an essential part of the wood trade: literally fueling homes, bakeries, forges, and brewhouses. That is, until February 4, 1555.

Woodland, coppice, heresy, and treason were linked for the first time in Queen Mary's reign on February 3, 1555, when an eight-foot solid oak stake around ten inches in diameter was driven into the ground at Smithfield Market just outside the city walls. Long known as the place of execution for traitors, Smithfield offered particular benefits to Queen Mary's advisers, as it was close enough to the Thames to haul such timber from the Essex borders at an advantageous price. Yet whether the oak stake or the fagot bundles originated from royal forests or former church lands remains a mystery. Whether the ten bundles of fagots needed to carry out the dastardly deed were all brought to Smithfield on the same "shout," or riverboat, we shall never know.* Whether the oak stake or the fagots had been stored at the wharves at Queenhithe or Timberhithe or at the ones just below London Bridge near Wood Street was never recorded.[1]

What mattered for the people was that the "whispering times" had returned. No one dared speak out openly against the imposition of the English prayer book in the previous reign, or the seizure of local chantries. The "old blindness" of Catholicism among the family elders had been restored with Mary's reign, and the younger generations would soon discover, just as their elders had done, that it was dangerous to meddle in God's word, or the word of their anointed monarch.[2] For those who had any doubts that the "whispering times" were back, the local criers shouting out that an execution for heresy would take place the following day at Smithfield convinced them. The victim's name shocked everyone and made them wonder if anyone could be truly safe again.

---

*In the fifteenth century, those people who brought the fagots to the heretics' fires were granted forty days of pardon from the fires of purgatory by the Roman Catholic Church. Burning at the stake for heresy was first instituted in 1401.

Even the choice of Smithfield Market as a place of execution was an inspired and elegant one. The fact that Wat Tyler, leader of the Peasants' Revolt in 1381, had met the boy king Richard II at Smithfield and that John Forest, prior of the Observant Convent at Greenwich, was caged like a wild animal and roasted alive there in 1538 by Henry VIII resonated in the people's minds. To them, these were fables from another world, another country, that was both "rich and strange."[3] These historic events held a symbolism that Queen Mary's councillors sought to drive home, striking terror into the hearts of her people. It would be this fear that would transform the once beloved queen's fledgling reign, for ill and forever.

It took three men to dig the hole in the frozen February ground that day, and three more to raise the oak stake while the others secured it. Four armed guards were ordered to stand watch around the stake overnight— in case some unrest should be fomented. The ten bundles of one hundred sticks of kindling each would be placed around the stake on the morning of the execution. These were held under lock and key overnight in a rick-cart nearby.

What was most striking to average Londoners was the name of the victim. They were simply incredulous. Surely it could not be true that such a holy man as he would meet his death by burning at the stake? Not since the time of Mary's father had there been such widespread alarm. It was the kind of fear that confirmed to them that, if a man or woman spoke contrary to the new articles of religion, even if they were entirely ignorant of the charge against them, they would be condemned to death and suffer their due pains as appointed by law.[4] The "whispering times" had indeed returned.

Seemingly, no one attempted to persuade Queen Mary—England's first anointed queen regnant—that this execution was anything except righteous in the eyes of the Lord. Even Mary's husband, Philip II of Spain, had believed that executions for heresy in England could only bring misfortune upon his wife's rule, but Mary and her closest advisers, who included the papal legate, knew best. After all, it was the Privy Council, headed by Mary's bully-boy Stephen Gardiner, Lord Chancellor and bishop of Winchester, that had interrogated the unfortunate sinner. It was Gardiner and the archbishop of Canterbury who were closeted with the queen to determine the just punishment for his crimes. It was the bishop of London who raised his hand high to become their instrument of torture for future heresies in the city. The more reasoned council voices grew mute and obeyed their dread queen's wishes.

Mary, by now visibly swollen "with child" in the first of her phantom pregnancies, had already become mistrustful of her large council. Though fervently believing that the execution of heretics was the right path to follow, she feared the displeasure of her people. Still, above all else, the law must be seen by the people to be served. At the outset of her reign in 1553, Mary had plainly instructed her council:

> that good preaching may overcome the evil preaching in time past,
> and that no evil books be printed, bought or sold without punish-
> ment. I think . . . punishment of heretics ought to be done without
> rashness.[5]

Nonetheless, London was a particular worry to the queen. It was London that held the mood of the country and the will of the people. It was essential that those living in the capital feel that Mary was acting justly—not only according to the laws of religion but also according to the laws of the land. "Especially in London I would wish none [heretics] to be burnt without some of the council's [sic] presence," Mary ordered, "and everywhere good sermons at the same [executions] . . . So I account myself bound to show such example that it may be evident to all this realm how I discharge my conscience."[6]

With this message foremost in her mind, councillors were selected to report back from Smithfield on the public reaction—whether the outcry would be favorable to the heretic or to her. The most trusted comptroller of the queen's household, Sir Robert Rochester, along with Sir Richard Southwell, both of whom were also sheriffs, fit the bill.

. . .

So, on the wintry morning of February 4, 1555, under heavily laden clouds, the rick-cart dragging the ten bundles of fagots was taken from the nearby warehouse by two unnamed men and wheeled to the site of execution. They were surrounded by the queen's men on horseback to guard against the threat a spontaneous riot. The pyre was built on a bed of straw and dried twigs, to help it catch fire more readily, with the fagots stacked upright around the oak stake at a ninety-degree angle. Men on horseback wearing the queen's livery policed the crowd, while the queen's guard, armed with pikes, lined the avenue through which the sinner would walk to the stake. When the condemned man appeared, the crowd's whispers rose in a groundswell of incredulity: So the rumors were true, they muttered to one another. See how thin this man of the cloth, this "sinner," had become, others lamented. Surely he had been tortured . . . surely there must be some mistake?

None the less, there was no mistake. The unrepentant priest walked calmly in his long, soiled shirt to the stake, chanting the *Miserere*. Mary's bishop of London began his short sermon while the sinner was tied to the oak post. The queen's guard formed a tight circle around them to prevent any members of the public interfering with the execution. When the sermon was finished, the bishop nodded to the executioner to set the fagots alight. The queen's mounted men closed in to control the crowd. Rushing around the pyre, the poor executioner touched his torch to the straw, to ensure that when the flames reached the condemned man, they would consume him evenly. Then, as the fire spread, he poked at the burning straw with his pike, so that the fagots would catch fire quickly. It was the only act of mercy the executioner would be permitted to give. Yet when the flames licked at the sinner's feet, the condemned priest smiled. Minutes later, he was dead, burned at the stake for his belief in the Protestant faith.

The root cause of the priest's execution could be traced back to the beginning of Mary's reign. In the seventeen months since Mary had become queen, she had had to wrest her throne away from the teenaged usurper Lady Jane Grey; then, within five months, in February 1554, shortly after Mary's Spanish marriage had been proclaimed, the queen was forced to subdue a southern rebellion led by Sir Thomas Wyatt and his Kentish followers. Both her half sister the Lady Elizabeth and the young usurper Lady Jane Grey were implicated as the Protestant heirs to Mary's throne. Still, Mary proved herself worthy of the Tudor name, winning the hearts and minds of Londoners with her stirring speech, described as a miracle of "good kingship." As a result Wyatt failed to penetrate London beyond a tavern at Ludgate Bar.

The first casualty of the Wyatt Rebellion, as the insurgency later became known, was Lady Jane Grey. Blindfolded, the poor, innocent pawn tragically sought the block upon which to lay her head for the executioner to sever. She was only seventeen.

Lady Elizabeth, only three years older than her cousin Jane Grey, was no innocent and quite rightly feared the same end. When Gardiner questioned her during her virtual imprisonment at Whitehall, she held her nerve, claiming she knew nothing. Mary, naturally, didn't believe her. Elizabeth was ordered to the Tower, charged with treason for her alleged part in the rebellion. Hoping she could make Mary see reason, she wrote a long pleading letter to the queen. Yet despite all her efforts to avoid the infamous "one way" journey taken by so many others in the reigns of her ancestors, Elizabeth entered the Tower precincts by water the following day from Tower Wharf, amid the terrifying screams of the castle's exotic menagerie of beasts and the roar of its lions. In a streak of wickedness, Mary had insisted that Elizabeth be placed in the generous accommodation that their father had renovated for Anne Boleyn's coronation.

Though Mary was never called the "queen of tempests," hers was a reign that would be recalled by many as a veritable storm of discontent and mayhem. Wyatt was beheaded on the morning of April 11, 1554. Hours later, his body had been quartered, its bowel and private parts burned. His head was parboiled and nailed to the top of the gibbet at St. James's. Within the week Wyatt's head had been spirited away by one of his loyal followers.[7]

Three weeks later, on May 4, Sir Henry Bedingfield was appointed constable of the Tower. His first act was to raise one hundred troops, making Lady Elizabeth fear that she would play her part on the same block as Lady Jane Grey. Instead, on May 19, 1554, Elizabeth was removed to house arrest a safe distance from London, arriving some days later at the Palace of Woodstock in Oxfordshire. Bedingfield wrote to the queen that "men betwixt London and these parts be not good and whole in matters of religion . . . be[ing] fully fixed to stand to the late abolishing of the Bishop of Rome's authority."[8] Equally, he was tormented by Elizabeth's evident popularity on their progress to Woodstock. People lined the streets in villages and towns, giving her flowers, herbs, and expensive spices and wishing her "God speed" and good health. It was not a good sign for Mary's fruitful reign.

Worse was yet to come.

Seven months later, the endgame for the unrepentant vicar John Rogers had just begun. On December 2, 1554, the bells of St. Paul's Cathedral rejoiced for England's long-awaited spiritual peace. Queen Mary—the first anointed Tudor queen of England, France, and Ireland—was presiding over the reconciliation of the Church of England to Rome. Already Mary could have been forgiven for thinking that she had been a mere "queen of tempests" and not the queen of a wealthy, green, heavily forested and pleasant land.

It was on this especially wintry December day that John Rogers also listened to the bells of St. Paul's peal in celebration of England's spiritual return to Rome. He was at home, as he had been for the past five months, under house arrest. Rogers had become the vicar of St. Sepulchre Church in London in May 1550, only four and a half years earlier, during the reign of Mary's little brother, Edward VI. The following August, Rogers received the prebend (stipend) of St. Pancras in St. Paul's Cathedral. He could be forgiven if he reflected that in the reigns of Edward VI and his sister Mary I, his much-admired career some four years distant was now an unrecognizable foreign world.

His personal descent into his private hell had begun on the very day Mary Tudor had grabbed back her throne from the Duke of Northumberland's puppet, Queen Jane.[9] Rogers was unceremoniously attacked as a seditious preacher by Mary's religious examiners and stripped of his livelihood.[10] Undaunted, he remained steadfast to his beliefs. Yet the moment the papal legate had been welcomed back to London a few weeks earlier, John Rogers had known that all his years of devotion, sacrifice, and religious study were at an end.

Of course, he knew that he had broken no laws and that the queen had acted prematurely against him. In Mary's eyes, in July 1553, she was merely consolidating her hold on her troubled country. She had not yet been able to convene Parliament, much less change the laws reconciling England to Roman Catholicism. So while the hapless vicar had committed no offense other than to preach the official religion of the realm, an Anglicized version of Lutheranism, Queen Mary could not stomach sanctioning such preaching, albeit temporarily, during her rule.

As Mary swept to power in July 1553 on a wave of popularity thanks to the wrongs she had been made to endure, foremost in her mind was her solemn quest, bordering on delusion, that as the granddaughter of Queen Isabella of Spain, who had driven the Jews and Moors out of the Iberian Peninsula, she would drive the Protestant specter from England. She had been deeply scarred by the battle of wills with her father and Thomas Cromwell, who had forced her to sign the Oath of Succession renouncing her obedience to Rome in 1535. Within the year, she had applied to the pope for absolution for what she felt had been her most heinous sin.[11] The establishment of the Church of England had been, to her mind, solely for the purpose of setting aside the marriage of her mother to her father. Now that she was England's queen, Mary was determined that it would be *her* vision for England's collective soul and conscience that would prevail.

Knowing this to be true, seventeen months later, in December 1554, there was little doubt in John Rogers's mind that he would become a martyr to his religious beliefs. Despite claims that would be made by his inquisitors to the contrary, Rogers's real crime was not in preaching the *new* religion so much as in saving William Tyndale's religious work from destruction by Roman Catholic interests in Antwerp. His crime was translating the Bible into English as the "Thomas Matthews" edition of the holy book, preserving much of Tyndale's exceptional language.[12] Miles Coverdale, who had also been at the English factory in Antwerp when Tyndale was betrayed and seized, had taken the "Thomas Matthews" edition and revised it several times thereafter, until it had become the Great Bible that had been put into every church in the country. Rogers would never know that his masterpiece would become the foundation of the 1611 version of the King James Bible that would endure for over three and a half centuries.

Within a month of that December 2 morn in 1554, the Holy Roman Emperor's envoy wrote home that "another bill has been brought forward, a measure for the punishment of heretics that had already been through Parliament under Henry IV and Richard II," as a means of expediting the return to Catholicism and punishment of its black sheep.[13] The reinstatement of laws dating from the late fourteenth and early fifteenth centuries smacked of a messianic desperation to brand heretics by the tried and tested definitions of yore, long before Martin Luther had pinned his ninety-five theses to the door of Wittenberg's church a hundred or so years later.

There were other controversial bills brought before Parliament at that same session as well. The most notorious of these provided for Philip's sovereignty during Mary's confinement for childbirth. Another provided for who would have the right to act on Philip's behalf should the queen be incommoded while he was absent from the kingdom. Given the dangers of childbirth, a bill was also tabled to agree that Philip could remain king even in the event of Queen Mary's death. It was hoped the measure would be regarded as a precaution to ensure the succession. The Holy Roman Emperor's envoy, Simon Renard, believed that the bill regarding the heretics would be passed but doubted that the upper house of Parliament would accept Philip as king in his own right, any more than it would vote in favor of the bill of "bastardy" against Elizabeth Tudor in the current session.

• • •

Nevertheless, with the legalities of the return to Rome finally resolved in the queen's mind, and the ancient laws regarding heresy back on the statute books, an intelligent and pious man like John Rogers knew that his end was near if he did not conform. His wife, Adriana, had long been "more richly endowed with virtue and soberness of life than with worldly treasures," as were their eleven children. He had been incarcerated for over a year without trial, deprived of his stipend illegally, and his family was literally starving. It was for them that he, along with other political prisoners, wrote to the queen, to protest the illegality of their imprisonment and to demand their release or their right to trial.[14]

Yet release had never been an option. On January 22, 1555, the queen's elder statesman, the overwhelming bishop of Winchester and chancellor, Stephen Gardiner, ordered the trials for heresy to begin in the presence of the Privy Council.[15] Rogers was brought before the royal commission to face his inquisitors. Chief among them was Edmund Bonner, bishop of London, who would be remembered by history as "bloody Bonner"—the man who ordered the burnings of 232 "heretics" of the total of 282 burned at the stake during Queen Mary's reign.

Though weakened by a long term of imprisonment without trial, miserable living conditions, and lack of proper sanitation and hygiene, Rogers stood tall before the council declaring, "That which I have preached I will seal with my blood!" The Lord Chancellor then asked, "Wilt thou return to the Catholic Church and unite and knit thyself with us, as all the Parliament House has done?" Rogers replied, "I have never did nor will dissent from the Catholic Church." It was an irate Lord Chancellor who fired the next salvo at Rogers, "But I speak of receiving the Pope to be Supreme Head." Rogers's response was eloquent: "I know of no other head of the Catholic Church but Christ. Neither will I acknowledge the Bishop of Rome to have any more authority than any other Bishop has either by the word of God or the doctrine of the Church."[16]

Despite the constant harangue from his inquisitors, Rogers remained steadfast and declined to recant. It was too late to turn the clock back; too late to reinsert a supreme head of the church between a bishop and

Christ. At the end of his interrogation, Rogers even prayed for the pope and his cardinals, as well as the souls living in purgatory, begging the Lord to pardon them for their sins. Of course, a guilty verdict of the court had been a foregone conclusion.

So John Rogers was brought on Monday, February 4, 1555, to his place of execution, the market at Smithfield in London. The disbelieving crowds gathered around, some to enjoy the ghoulish spectacle, others wondering what evil omen the execution of a vicar portended, still others horrified and knowing that there would be worse to come. As John Rogers passed through the onlookers, a groundswell of cheers rose from the people, reaching a crescendo when he walked calmly onto his pyre and was tied to its stake by his ankles and chest.

As the fagots of wood were set alight around his feet, Rogers seemed renewed, almost free. He murmured his prayers until the fire had taken hold of his legs and shoulders. Then, as if to mock his tormentors, Rogers committed the ultimate insult. He washed his hands in the flames as if they had been cold water and he was purifying his soul, then lifted his blazing hands up to heaven. Rogers had vanquished his captors with this final act of simple defiance. He yielded up his spirit into the hands of his Heavenly Father and showed the way for the 281 Protestant martyrs to follow him in the remaining three years of "bloody" Mary's reign.

The next day, the panicked Holy Roman envoy, Simon Renard, wrote to Philip, "I do not think it well that your Majesty should allow further executions to take place unless the reasons are so overwhelmingly strong and the offences committed have been so scandalous as to render this course justifiable in the eyes of the people . . . The watchword should be *secure, caute et lente festinare.*"[17]

Security, caution, and hasten slowly.

PART I

A Wounded and Divided Land, 1558–1566

They would secretly seek to inflame
our realm with firebrands.

—Elizabeth I to the Spanish
ambassador de Spes

ONE

The New Deborah

A princess who can act any part she pleases.
—Lord Burghley, of Elizabeth

The reign of Mary I ended on November 17, 1558, and that of Lady Elizabeth began. No longer disinherited and demoted, Elizabeth had miraculously survived to become queen. By the time of Elizabeth's coronation in January 1559, life in Mary's reign was decidedly another country.

As the procession for Elizabeth's coronation began, snowflakes danced on the air, bowing and sweeping as if upon a stage in deference to the earsplitting cheers from their adoring audience. The cries of joy were not for the flakes or their thin white blanket that spread itself like a gossamer veil over the city. All those who huddled together by the quayside rejoiced for the tall, slender woman with red-gold hair.

Queen Elizabeth had suddenly appeared on the privy stairs of White-hall Palace in a flurry of activity, cocooned by her entire court of barons, knights, and ladies. As she stepped forward, she nodded slowly, perhaps knowingly, at her people in the distance. To all eyes, the new queen made her way down to the awaiting barges with a regal grace not seen since the times of her father, King Harry. To all fluttering hearts, the rekindled joy was palpable.

It was two o'clock in the afternoon, and the flood tide had turned. The

River Thames waited for no one, not even kings or queens. Still, Elizabeth paused before taking the boatman's outstretched hand. She raised her chin skyward, allowing the snowflakes to fall upon her upturned face, and smiled. Did she silently rehearse the prayer she would utter aloud two days later, "O Lord, Almighty and Everlasting God, I give Thee most hearty thanks that Thou has been so merciful unto me as to spare me to behold this joyful day"?

Perhaps not. Still, she was evidently savoring the moment, as she would each of the unfettered moments in the days to come. The years since her mother's execution had been fraught with hardship, disillusionment, and downright abuse from those closest to her. In the twelve years since Henry VIII's death, Elizabeth had danced on many a high wire, with countless onlookers praying she would fall and break that handsome neck of hers. Though she had come close on two occasions, Elizabeth had survived.

Perhaps that was in part due to her father's last queen, Catherine Parr, who had made certain that Elizabeth received a first-rate education. This, along with the friendship of key individuals, the instincts of a survivor, and the genetic makeup of the daughter of Anne Boleyn and Henry VIII, had ensured that she would reach this day. Yet Elizabeth, as a fervent follower of the new religion, took no credit for "God's work."

On this day—Thursday, January 12, 1559—she would reenter the Tower of London precinct as England's queen. More than any other royal palace, the Tower held terrible memories for the last of the Tudors. Of course, it was there that her mother, Anne Boleyn, and her cousin Catherine Howard were beheaded for their "treason" against her father, the king. It was at the Tower, too, that only four years earlier she had been held prisoner by Mary, fearing for her very life. Yet it was the way of the kings of England that they would sojourn at the Tower for two nights before their coronations, and Elizabeth Tudor was not about to break with tradition.

As the galleys and barges glided eastward down the Thames, the queen's barge with its rich cochineal red Flemish tapestries could be clearly seen. Elizabeth herself glittered with jewels and was warmed by her rich furs.

She sat cosseted at the rear of her long galley rowed by forty men. There was no doubt that she was the main reveler in the spectacle, sparkling at her own good fortune. A band of musicians swathed in the queen's crimson and black livery played their shawm, sackbut, and drums with "a great and pleasant melody playing most sweet and in a heavenly manner."[1] She was England's angel in her gilded galley slicing crisply through the water, oars rising and falling to the rhythm of the drums and the awe of her people.

Meanwhile, the Lord Mayor and his aldermen followed closely behind in their highly decorated vessels. The court and the city fathers accompanying her fanned out across the Thames, like hundreds of peacocks in great array, aboard their silver galleys and brigantines, their colorful banners streaming, proclaiming their ancient mysteries, or crafts. The procession made a choreographed spectacle quite unlike any other along London's busy waterway, with hundreds of barges in the royal entourage rowing in unison toward a single and singular purpose.

Il Shifanoya, the Venetian observer in London, reported to the doge that it reminded him of Ascension Day at Venice, when the Signory goes to espouse the Sea.[2] There was no mistaking the queen's naval progress from the other ships plying their trade along the Thames. Wherries crowded in as near as they dared while their occupants waved, throwing their hats in the air, hailing Elizabeth, and wishing her "God speed!"

When the royal barges emerged through the treacherous eddies at London Bridge and came into sight of the Tower, the captain of the guard ordered the artillery to be fired in honor of their lady. The roar of the guns echoed above the waterway, a signal to the entire capital that Her Majesty had neared the first stop on her journey to become the country's anointed monarch. A few moments later, the royal barge docked at the sovereign's private stairs. In keeping with tradition, Elizabeth crossed into the Tower by a small bridge and disappeared into her royal apartments. Naturally, these were far removed from those that had once been her royal prison. It was only much later that Elizabeth would reveal that her enforced stay in the Tower at the hands of her sister remained an ever present memory.

• • •

Though Friday the thirteenth had been upheld as an unlucky day since the Lord Jesus dined at his Last Supper with his twelve apostles, England's queen celebrated it all the same in the great tradition of her ancestors. Her Knights of the Bath were created on that day at the Tower in preparation for the coronation ceremony. Elizabeth was making a point of disregarding superstition: Religion—whether Protestant or Catholic—abhorred superstition, and as England's temporal leader (for Catholics) or putative head of the church (for Protestants), she would guide *all* her people by example. It was a beautifully understated piece of spin to demonstrate her leadership and bravery to her predominantly illiterate subjects. Besides, Dr. John Dee had cast her horoscope, with royal consent, of course, and had determined not only the most propitious date for the queen's coronation but also the schedule of events leading up to the day. In another finely tuned act of symbolism, her father's own Master of the Revels, Sir Thomas Cawarden, was appointed to supervise the coronation celebrations.[3]

Even the death of Cardinal Pole, the papal legate, on the same day as that of Queen Mary had played in Elizabeth's favor, or so it seemed. Ten Catholic bishops had died since October 1558, leaving an unprecedented opportunity for the head of the church in England to name their replacements. It had already been whispered that the queen planned to take on the role of Supreme Governor, leaving the Marian religious settlement and the return to Rome in tatters.

Fearing what was to come, the remaining bishops made a pact of solidarity, declining to officiate at the coronation ceremonies in the vain hope that Elizabeth would see that they still wielded power both as the religious figureheads in their bishoprics and as the Lords Spiritual in the House of Lords. Notwithstanding this, through the assiduously applied coercion of her privy councillors, the archbishop of York, Owen Oglethorpe, was at last persuaded to do the honorable thing. Though the disobedient bishops had nearly succeeded in making a sham of the coronation ceremony, the issue of disciplining them would be best left for the forthcoming Parliament.

• • •

While Elizabeth's court prepared for the state entry into London, the city sprang into action. Scaffolds had been built and strategically placed throughout the city since Christmas week. The streets where the queen would pass were quickly covered in fresh gravel and tamped down. The light snow had made the way muddy, so the gravel was laid to ease Elizabeth's passage with her royal entourage. It also made it easier to roll the pageant carts into position.

Saturday, January 14, 1559, would be the City's day to revel. Coronation Day would be celebrated in Westminster at its abbey on Sunday. Across the country, London's activity was mirrored by great celebrations and outpourings of thanksgiving. Queen Elizabeth craved the love of her people, and without their sharing equally in her joy, the coronation ceremony would have been like an actor performing to an empty theatre.

That morning, as if by royal command, the snow stopped. At two o'clock in the afternoon, the spectacle of coronation began. As the Most Dread Sovereign, Lady Elizabeth, by the grace of God Queen of England, France, and Ireland, Defender of the Faith, et cetera, marched forth from the Tower, she raised her eyes to heaven in much the same way she had done at Whitehall and proclaimed,

> *O Lord, Almighty and Everlasting God, I give Thee most hearty thanks that Thou has been so merciful unto me as to spare me to behold this joyful day. And I acknowledge that Thou has dealt as wonderfully and as mercifully with me, as Thou didst with Thy true and faithful servant Daniel, Thy Prophet, whom Thou delivered out of the den from the cruelty of the greedy and raging lions: even so was I overwhelmed, and only by Thee delivered. To Thee therefore only be thanks, honour, and praise, forever. Amen.*[4]

Then, as suddenly as the sun peeks out from behind a cloud, the solemnity of the moment passed, and Elizabeth climbed gracefully onto her litter. The dazzling court, accompanied by a thousand jeweled horses, wended its way through Blackfriars to St. Paul's and on toward

Westminster. All the houses lining the way were hung with brightly col-
ored banners, their inhabitants leaning precariously out of the penthouses
to glimpse their queen. Merchants and traders pressed against the wooden
barricades and crowded into the narrow streets. Each was dressed in his
long black and crimson cloak; each sported the ensign of his own trade
and carried his trade's standard high. They made, so everyone said, a fine
show. The blindingly bright ray of hope that Elizabeth symbolized after
the dark final eighteen months of Queen Mary's reign shone from every
house, each shop, and all faces. Elizabeth owed her very popularity to their
hope for a better life and, in her mind, a return to the reformed church. Not
only had 282 "heretics" been burned at the stake in those dark eighteen
months in 1556–57, but England had been led into a fruitless war against
France at King Philip's behest, lost its ill-defended staple town of Calais, and
emptied its coffers.

When the queen's trumpeters blasted their great fanfare to proclaim the
approach of Queen Elizabeth, the crowd threw their hats in the air for
joy. Many bystanders craned their necks to see beyond the heralds so they
could glimpse their young and handsome queen. When, at last, Elizabeth
passed in her open litter trimmed down to the ground in gold brocade
with a raised pile, all those who lined the roads let out cries of sheer joy.
Surely if ever there was a glorious queen, it was she, the last of King Harry's children.

Official accounts record that the handsome mules that carried Elizabeth were also clothed in gold brocade and wore jeweled harnesses. They
speak of a veritable sea of footmen in crimson velvet jerkins studded with
the queen's initials, *ER*, in raised gilt silver, a white and a red rose on their
breasts and no hats upon their heads. These men heralded the queen's arrival. At Elizabeth's side walked her Gentlemen-Pensioners of the Axe,
all clad in crimson damask, also without hats, despite the cold. Elizabeth's devilishly handsome Master of the Horse, Sir Robert Dudley, was
mounted on a magnificent charger. He led a white hackney covered in a
cloth of gold followed by the queen's Lords of her Privy Chamber.[5] Yet
the most significant part of the procession went unrecorded. When Eliza-

beth passed through London's streets, spectacle and spectator had become one.

The Passage of our Most Dread Sovereign Lady, Queen Elizabeth, through the City of London to Westminster, the day before her Coronation, dated January 23 "cum privilegio," records with the reporter's eye how Elizabeth Tudor made her entrance as England's queen that day in a costume of a royal robe of very rich cloth of gold with a double-raised stiff pile, a coif of cloth of gold, and a plain gold lace crown upon her reddish-gold hair, which hung loose. She was bedecked with jewels in her hair and wore necklaces but had no jewels on her long, slender white fingers, which held her jeweled gloves. It exclaims at length that when the queen entered the City of London, surrounded by the nobility of her realm, the "people received [them] marvelous entirely, as appeared by the assembly, prayers, wishes, welcomings, cries, tender words, and all other signs, which argue a wonderful earnest love and most obedient subjects toward their sovereign." Elizabeth declared in return that she was "no less thankful to receive her people's good will, than they lovingly offered it unto her."[6]

These were more than mere words. Elizabeth wanted to confirm to her people with a gesture, a word, and later with many good deeds that she held their love above all others. When commoners pressed themselves forward to hand Elizabeth flowers, she showed her most gentle deference to them by pausing to listen to their requests, then blessing them with her royal touch before she moved on. To the journalist's eye, "he could not better term the City of London that time, than a stage wherein was showed the wonderful spectacle, of a noble-hearted Princess toward her most loving people, and the people's exceeding comfort in beholding so worthy a sovereign, and hearing so prince-like a voice."[7]

After so many years in the wilderness, alienated from the royal household, Elizabeth Tudor had at last taken her rightful place center stage. She had used those years wisely to fine-tune her performance. While still a princess-in-waiting, Elizabeth had resolved to hold her subjects in awe with her majesty and delight them with her common touch. On this day, she succeeded.

Similarly, her people had clear and concise—if religiously allegorical—messages for their new sovereign. These took the physical form of triumphal arches strategically placed on pageant wagons along the queen's route toward Westminster. At Fenchurch, a "scaffold richly furnished, whereon stood a noise of instruments, and a child in costly apparel," welcomed the Queen's Majesty on behalf of the city.

At Gracechurch Street, in front of the sign of the Eagle Inn, the city had erected a sumptuous three-story triumphal arch depicting Elizabeth's right to the throne. On the lowest stage were King Henry VII—the first Tudor monarch—and his wife, Elizabeth of York, daughter of Edward IV. Henry's descent and right to the throne were depicted in the Red Rose of Lancaster. Elizabeth of York, the queen's paternal grandmother, clutched her White Rose of York in one hand with her scepter, while the other rested on Henry VII's hand. Out of the roses sprang a branch that led the eye upward to the second story, where a richly clad King Henry VIII bestrode the platform with his queen Anne Boleyn seated at his side. Another branch wound its way upward to the third story, where a likeness of Queen Elizabeth sat on her royal throne. The queen hardly needed anyone to interpret the meaning behind the triumphal arch or its stated desire for "quietness to increase."

They processed to the far end of Cornhill, where the pageant devised by the city depicted the queen seated in the "seat of worthy governance" with the virtues of "Pure Religion, Love of Subjects, Wisdom, and Justice" seated beside her. Under their feet, "Pure Religion treads upon Superstition and Ignorance; Love of Subjects did tread upon Rebellion and Insolence; Wisdom did tread upon Folly and Vainglory; and Justice did tread upon Adulation and Bribery."[8] This pageant above all others during her reign was highly representative of the medieval style of drama and allegory Elizabeth had inherited from her sister's short years on the throne. It was a realm brimming over with spiritual messages.

The pageant at Soper Lane was again like the medieval mysteries, with the eight Beatitudes sending their message from innocent children's mouths to the queen. Elizabeth listened to a child's soliloquy and thanked her people with great sincerity. Every moment among them was joyful, and each moment was stored away as a reminder not only of their love for her but also of their need to be governed with her love.

When the litter stopped at the Standard in the Cheap to great fanfare of trumpets, Master Ranulph Cholmeley, recorder of London, presented a purse of crimson richly wrought with gold filigree filled with a thousand marks in gold. Taking it as a most generous and valuable gift with both hands, Elizabeth said:

> I thank my Lord Mayor, his Brethern and you all. And whereas your request is that I should continue your good Lady and Queen, be ye assured, that I will be as good unto you as ever Queen was to her People. No will in me can lack, neither do I trust shall there lack any power. And persuade yourselves, that for the safety and quietness of you all, I will not spare, if need be, to spend my blood. God thank you all.[9]

Had the City known that the crown had been virtually bankrupted by Queen Mary and her Spanish husband in fighting his French wars? The city fathers certainly knew that war was bad for trade, and the loss of Calais devastating. Elizabeth may have pondered this question, though she had already set in place a means to cure her relative penury. Still, it is more likely that she simply enjoyed her moment of triumph and brushed aside the business of the realm that would crash down upon her soon enough.

As the royal procession pressed forward through the throng to Little Conduit in the Cheap, the trumpeters fell silent, and the roar of the crowd became a whisper. There the aldermen and the recorder of London readied themselves for their personal message to their new sovereign. When the northern side of the fourth pageant, entitled "Ruinosa Respublica" or "A decayed Commonwealth," came into view, complete with cave, withered and dead trees, and craggy, barren rocks, the queen deduced long before she was told that this represented the past. This was the realm bequeathed to Elizabeth by her sister, Mary, Mary's husband, Philip, and the papal legate, the archbishop of Canterbury, Reginald Pole.

The southern side of the pageant, entitled "Respublica bene instituta" or "A flourishing Commonwealth," was depicted with green grass, fresh, beautiful flowers, and a rich, luscious tree. An old man with a scythe and wings, said to be "Father Time," came out of a hollow on the pageant wagon, leading his beautiful daughter, "Truth," clad in white silk. Elizabeth could be in no doubt as to their message. In the child's hand was a book on which was written in Latin *Verbum Veritatis,* or "The Word of Truth." The book was taken through the crowd and given to Elizabeth. As soon as she saw that it was the Bible written in English—the same Bible written by the martyred John Rogers to speak God's Word to the masses— she kissed it and held it up to her people with both hands before clutching it back to her breast. Elizabeth gave thanks to them and said "she would often read over that book."[10] Her gesture was clear: The new Queen of England wanted Christ's Word to reach them in English. Their Elizabeth would preside over a Protestant realm, and a veritable swoon of adoration flowed from the crowd in response.

At last, the royal procession came to the boundary between the City of London and Westminster at the River Fleet and Fleet Street. Upon the pageant stage there was a great palm tree under which sat a "meet personage" in "Parliament robes" with a scepter in her hand and a golden crown upon her head. Above her head was inscribed "Deborah the judge and restorer of the House of Israel, Judic. iv." Again, Elizabeth could be in no doubt as to her subjects' message: She was the new Deborah, responsible for judging wisely while rebuilding her House of Tudor and the commonwealth over which she reigned.

The message in each pageant built upon those that had passed before. The people had spoken. As Albion's Deborah, Elizabeth would rebuild their common house, bend it to her will, and rule with the love of her people. Yet to do that, she would need to dissimulate—to act as a player upon a stage. It was the only way she could marry the disparate religious and political wills of her court to her people, confused by twelve years of religious extremism inflicted on the realm by her royal siblings. It was the only way she could assuage the French, the Spanish, and the pope into believing that she meant them no harm. It was how she would remain mistress of her own and her people's destinies.

It was the task that Elizabeth Tudor was born to undertake.

TWO

The Realm and the Ministers of Lucifer

*The Wolves be coming out of Geneva and other places of
Germany and hath sent their books before,
full of pestilent doctrines, blasphemy, and heresy,
to infect the people.*

—Bishop White of Winchester, January 1559

The pomp and ceremony of Elizabeth's coronation festivities painted a fragile veneer over the serious problems facing her realm. The queen was in no doubt that the country had been brought to misery in the preceding reigns and that England's very survival depended on her successes in the first months of her rule. In the twelve years since her father's death, neither Edward's nor Mary's reign had redressed the damaging effects of Henry's Great Debasement of English currency. Nor had her siblings sought to enhance England's credibility or credit with merchant bankers or princes abroad. Calais, that cornerstone of the English wool industry—the country's number one export—had been lost. Instead, both her siblings had been concerned with saving English souls, allowing English purses to fall into decay.

For Edward VI, "soul saving" meant the nation's conversion to a Lutheran style of Protestantism. Mary, naturally, had to set this to rights. Within three months of Cardinal Pole's arrival in London, Mary and Philip wrote to the saber-rattling Pope Julius III that they had repealed all

Henry VIII's and Edward VI's laws and had returned her people to the true faith.[1] Recognizing the danger of disobeying Mary's zealous Roman Catholic—called "popish"—religious reform, even Elizabeth had been forced to conceal her Protestant convictions. As queen, she was well versed in the traumas and trials of someone who had to dissemble, and she would soon avow that she wished to spare her people a similar fate.

For Elizabeth, who had also known life as a political prisoner suspected of treason, the issue of religion needed to be resolved in a way that would unite her people behind her while allowing them freedom of conscience. Part of the problem was that tolerance was a revolutionary concept and an adventurous and uncomfortable step into the unknown, and the more Elizabeth displayed tolerance, the less it was understood. Some would conclude that Elizabeth had little religion; others that her flexible attitudes meant she had little conviction. Both were far from the truth.

Their confusion was understandable. In her sister's time, Cardinal Pole and Bishop Bonner had enforced the papal will with iron fists, under the guiding influence of Philip's bishop, Bartolomé Carranza.[2] It had been Carranza who infused Mary Tudor's reign with the blood of her fellow Englishmen and -women, and Carranza who had insisted on executing Archbishop of Canterbury Thomas Cranmer for heresy.[3] England, under the sure Spanish hand of Carranza—nicknamed "the black monk"—had donned the mantle of Roman Catholicism uncomfortably.

Yet Elizabeth felt that regardless of the individual will of her people in matters of religion and worship, the English had been cowed into compliance. The sway held by Philip's Spanish clerics over English affairs had been bitterly resented. Hundreds of Tudor "new men" and their families had exiled themselves in the Low Countries, Germany, or Switzerland rather than conform to Mary's Catholic vision. Others, like Sir William Cecil, conformed outwardly but refused to make themselves available to the crown as ministers of state. Had Cardinal Pole persuaded the monarchy to recover church lands from those who had benefited from the Dissolution of the Monasteries, surely they "would rather get themselves massacred than let go [of their properties]," the imperial ambassador affirmed to Philip.[4]

Now these very men were returning to Elizabeth's England in droves. In the time they had been away, poverty had risen sharply, and with it, so had crime and vagrancy. The "sturdy beggar" had become a common feature of urban and rural life. Poor harvests and recurrent bouts of plague and the "sweating sickness" had decimated the country.[5]

For the largely illiterate rural population, the worlds of the "new" religion and the "old" had become confused. The country customs of maypoling, wise women, the alehouse, the cunning-man, ballads and broadsides, dancing, Sunday sports, tabling and dicing, bowling and cards, and cakes and ale stood to be lost to Protestant ministers of the Good Book with their solemn Sabbath observance, sermon-gadding and repetition, sobriety, chastity, respectability, and thrift. In effect, magic, the supernatural, and the "old" Catholic religion had become intertwined with these essential country pastimes.

If Elizabeth's England were to move forward with the new religion again, the queen would have to ensure that her people appreciated that being Protestant did not mean that they would lose their cherished touchstones.[6] What Elizabeth understood all too well was that the rhythm of life had become dependent not only upon the seasons and weather but also on the vagaries of a weakened economy, the social inversion brought about by the Tudor new men, confusion and lawlessness, a dread of change, and a realm divided by religious schism.

The other bogey of English life, xenophobia—always a concern for peace at home and trade abroad—was rife. With most of the returning English having adopted Continental ways in their worship, these loyal subjects of Elizabeth's seemed foreign to those who had stayed at home. While England had just shed its Spanish king, albeit as Mary's consort, the wounds were still raw.

Yet England was heavily reliant on overseas trade for the sale of its number-one finished exported product: broadcloth. France had overrun Calais in the recent war, and Elizabeth needed to find a new staple town quickly. With no peace agreed, the French king's claim of friendship to Elizabeth on December 30, 1558, might have been welcomed, if it had been heartfelt:

> *She knows how sincere and perfect is the amity and affection which he always felt towards her, of which she has already had sufficient*

proof and security. This friendship and esteem which he has had
during his whole life has been nothing diminished by the war which
to his great regret had sprung up between the late Queen of England,
her sister, and himself, and by the great and incredible damages he
had received from her.[7]

However, it was a sham. While begging pity and understanding from Elizabeth, Henry II made an official plea to his friend Pope Paul IV to recognize his daughter-in-law Mary Queen of Scots as queen of England, too. Paul IV, who was always willing to strike a blow against Philip II for trying to block his election, was sanguine.[8] He wrote in the papal diary that same December: "The French in view of the Queen of England's death [Mary Tudor] grew lukewarm about the peace and hopeful of detaching that kingdom from King Philip or uniting it with that of Scotland, and (among other means to that end) were instant [sic] with the Pope that he should declare Queen Elizabeth illegitimate, and as it were, of incestuous birth, and consequently incapable of succeeding to the throne, whereby they pretend that the crown would belong to the Queen of Scotland."[9]

Clearly, Henry II was playing a double game. He hoped that if he could get the pope to agree to Elizabeth's "illegitimacy" and put forward his daughter-in-law as the only surviving legitimate Tudor heir to the throne, he could gain suzerainty of England without bloodshed.[10] In fact, his machinations were hardly necessary. Henry VIII's 1544 statute declaring Elizabeth illegitimate still stood. Naturally, Mary Tudor had left this section of the act active, since she had always maintained that Elizabeth was the offspring of a marriage the Catholic Church regarded as incestuous. Until and unless Elizabeth called her first Parliament and had the act struck off the statute books, Mary Queen of Scots already had the best legal claim to England's throne as the great-granddaughter of Henry VII.[11] Both Elizabeth and Philip II of Spain were acutely aware of this.

From Philip's perspective England's monarch was a matter of utmost significance. He, of course, was no longer king consort of England. He had had a long and bloody rivalry for French territories in northern France and a prior history over Naples with Henry II and the Vatican. Pope Paul IV had excommunicated him in 1556 over the Naples debacle. By the end of 1557, the war with France had caused Philip's first bankruptcy, compelling him to come to the bargaining table with Henry II for peace talks at Cateau-Cambrésis. Despite their mutual Catholic affinity—for Philip had been endowed with the title of "His Most Catholic Majesty" and Henry "His Most Christian Majesty" by the Vatican—neither monarch had much cause to trust the other.

For Philip, any official union between Scotland and England, in conjunction with Mary Stuart's undoubted role as France's future queen, was an absolute anathema. Elizabeth had become, as a result, his most important potential ally in northern Europe. Without her friendship and protection, and England's, the sea route to his tremendously wealthy colonies of the Low Countries could be cut off. Inevitably, with this at the forefront of his political thinking, Philip had cast himself in the role of Elizabeth's—and England's—protector from the moment he realized that his wife, Queen Mary, would never conceive. Somehow, Philip would have to reconcile his vision for the Spanish Empire with his title of "His Most Catholic Majesty" and make Elizabeth his de facto ally. Simon Renard's warning to Philip four years earlier, in 1554, *"secure, caute et lente festinare"*—security, caution, and hasten slowly—remained his watchwords.

Renard's cautionary words also applied to Elizabeth. Death had fortuitously silenced English Catholicism's most eloquent spokesman, Cardinal Pole, and his queen, Mary Tudor, on the same day. Furthermore, the hated Spanish influence on English religious affairs in the previous reign had done much to muddy the religious and political pictures in the people's minds, making Mary Tudor less popular with each passing day. Notwithstanding this, Elizabeth knew that the people loathed change and was cognizant of the many dangers in making any dramatic changes in the religious practices of her realm. Besides, that was what both France and Spain had anticipated, and Elizabeth meant to confound their expectations.

The queen saw herself as the monarch of all her people and equally knew that fully satisfying the extreme right or left in the religious spectrum—a kaleidoscope of Christian beliefs, which now included not only the broader terms of Roman Catholic and Protestant but also Zwing-lian, Calvinist, and Lutheran, among others—would alienate the majority of Englishmen, who placed their beliefs in the Christian middle. Though she would never have used the word "tolerance," preferring the less contro-versial term "compromise," tolerance was at the outset the cornerstone of her decision to walk a middle road.

To implement her vision, Elizabeth needed to carefully select her min-isters who could carry the day for her in the Commons and the Lords. The most enduring and important of these was Sir William Cecil. Like the queen, Cecil was a moderate Protestant; and, like Elizabeth, he was against forcing England's Catholic population into an unpalatable solution. As her principal secretary, and later Lord Treasurer as Lord Burghley from 1572, Cecil would become Elizabeth's "significant other" in politics throughout her long reign. Their remarkable relationship would last, if not always flourish, until Cecil's death in 1598.

Sir Nicholas Bacon, Cecil's brother-in-law, a great believer in mass ed-ucation, became the queen's Lord Privy Seal in January 1559. Sir William Paulet, Marquis of Winchester and Lord High Treasurer, and Lord Wil-liam Howard, first Baron Howard of Effingham—both good Catholics—remained privy councillors as they had been in Mary Tudor's reign. In maintaining some of her sister's more gifted advisers, Elizabeth had inti-mated how she wished to govern: There would be no new brooms to sweep Mary's Catholic advisers from power. Talent and loyalty alone would bring advancement.

Meanwhile, Elizabeth sought other learned opinions with regard to the religious settlement she knew she would have to impose as soon as practicable. Sir Nicholas Throckmorton, an old hand at Tudor politics who was also held prisoner in the Tower after the Wyatt Rebellion, wrote to the queen that she must "succeed happily through a discreet beginning . . . to have a good eye that there be no innovations, no tumults or breach of orders."[12] Throckmorton's advice was echoed by Armagil Waad—a Tudor diplomat who had served both Henry VIII and Edward VI—in his paper *The Distresses of the Commonwealth, with the Means to Remedy Them.* Waad began with the most succinct assessment of Elizabeth's position when he wrote, "The Queen poor; the realm exhausted; . . . division among ourselves; wars with France and Scotland; the French King bestriding the realm, having one foot in Calais and the other in Scotland; steadfast enmity but no steadfast friendship abroad." Elizabeth, he warned, would need great powers of dissimulation and cunning if she were to succeed in religious reform while maintaining unity among her people. Waad recommended "that you would proceed to the reformation having respect to quiet at home, the affairs you have in hand with foreign princes, the greatness of the Pope, and how dangerous it is to make alteration in religion, specially in the beginning of a prince's reign."[13]

Others advised a revolutionary blow to the Marian religious solution: to call Parliament forthwith and set up a national church complete with its own Protestant prayer book, admonishing that "the sooner that religion is restored, God is the more glorified, and . . . will be more merciful to us and better save and defend her Highness from all dangers."[14]

Elizabeth had already given her people a clear sign of her Protestant intentions on Christmas Day when she ordered Archbishop Oglethorpe *not* to elevate the host at Mass in accordance with the Catholic rite. His refusal to obey his queen resulted in Elizabeth storming out of the service immediately. Two days later, though she hadn't had the authority to do so, she issued a proclamation permitting certain parts of the service in English after the Protestant fashion but forbidding all preaching and teaching as a restraint on the most vocal of the "ministers of Lucifer"—as the Catholic bishops called the Protestant Marian exiles.[15]

So, while Sir William Cecil gathered up all advices from both Protestants and Catholics, privy councillors and burgesses, and port towns and the City of London and compiled the first of his many "memoranda of lists" of pros and cons, Elizabeth ordered him to issue the writs summoning Parliament for its first session on January 23, 1559. On February 9, the "Bill to restore the supremacy of the Church of England &c. to the Crown of the realm" had its first reading in the Commons. Where Mary had bulldozed through her "Act of Repeal in restoring Papal Authority in England to the House of Lords," Elizabeth had to be more circumspect, channeling her proposals through the Commons. Despite those ten seats left vacant by bishops who had died in the autumn of 1558, a large minority of the upper house still wore the purple gowns of Catholic bishops. If the bishops opposed the anointed monarch, Elizabeth preferred that the confrontation take place between the Commons and the Lords, not the monarchy and the Lords. In the event, it was the Commons that would prove to be the trickier of the two houses.

A second bill was drafted for "Royal Supremacy over the Church," with the queen as its head. At the same time, Elizabeth tried to calm the Spanish Ambassador, Count de Feria, over any perceived changes away from Mary's religious settlement. He wrote to the Vatican pretending to know that Elizabeth was "resolved to restore religion as her father left it," meaning effectively as an Anglican form of Catholicism albeit with the monarch as head of the church.[16] Whether this was cunning political maneuvering to bring the more moderate Catholic bishops to her side in the struggle ahead is rather difficult to say, but it would have been a masterstroke of both political and religious unity if she could have engineered it. The Catholic bishops could have preserved Elizabeth from a heavy reliance on the Protestant hard-liners, or "hot gospellers," allowing the queen to tread her middle way. Instead, England and Elizabeth came a poor second for the bishops.

With a core of around a quarter of the members of Parliament being Marian exiles, men clothed in what would become known as "Puritan gray," Elizabeth found that the House of Commons would represent a formidable force for reform, despite her wishes. The radical leaders—men like Sir Anthony Cooke, Cecil's father-in-law, and Sir Francis Knollys, Elizabeth's cousin by marriage—apparently swept aside the weakened Catholic opposition in the Commons and added another bill "for the order of service and ministers in the church." The following day, yet another bill, "The book for the common prayer and ministration of the sacraments," put forward by both Cooke and Knollys, was entered in the Commons Journal.[17] The Protestant "ministers of Lucifer" were in firm control of the Commons, aiming to put forward an extreme solution to the religious question with their own radical bill and prayer book. Cooke and Knollys led the Commons in the prolonged debate that ensued, aimed at tagging on these two bills to the Supremacy Bill that had already gone up to the Lords.[18] Their action was tantamount to bringing the religious settlement back to the days of Edward VI and the 1552 prayer book that had been such an abomination to Catholics.

This was a most unwelcomed maneuver from the "ministers of Lucifer," hateful to Elizabeth and absolutely contrary to her policy at this most sensitive moment. Naturally the amended Supremacy Bill was in trouble in the Lords. Catholic voices were raised to a fever pitch against it. Bishop Scot of Chester delivered a long-winded speech, effectively saying he was opposed to the queen as head of the church. The archbishop of York, Nicholas Heath, gave a rather more succinct account of why the queen could not be "Supreme Head of the Church of England, immediate and next unto God." Parliament had no right, he believed, to grant any spiritual role to her, particularly as she was a woman and incapable of fulfilling Christ's injunction to Peter to feed his flock. St. Paul, he quoted, had placed an obligation on women to be silent in church and not to "lord it" over men. Paradoxically, this was the same argument used by the Presbyterian "hot gospeller" John Knox in his tirade against the "monstrous regiment of women" that had so offended Elizabeth. Common ground had been struck by extremists on both sides.

The Commons at last understood that they would never get their amended bill through the House of Lords. With Easter looming on the calendar—Sunday, March 26—a compromise needed to be made for the holiday or the Catholic order of service would stand, with the pope as head of the Church of England. Either the Commons would accept the Lords' amendments and lose the Protestant prayer book or reject them and retain the pope. The compromise—which pleased none—was that Elizabeth would become Supreme Head of the Church of England. On March 22, the queen made it known that she intended to give her assent to the Act of Supremacy "in the present last session of Parliament" reviving the statute of Edward VI for Communion in *both kinds*—meaning both Protestant and Catholic.[19] The "ministers of Lucifer" glowered with rage at the compromise. In the words of the Spanish ambassador two days later, "I see that the heretics are very downcast in the last few days."

• • •

What the Spanish ambassador hadn't known was that Elizabeth had made a complete volte-face on her "hasten slowly" policy. On Palm Sunday, March 19, the queen received word that a peace treaty had been signed at Cateau-Cambrésis between Spain, England, and France. Relieved of the uncertainty regarding the peace negotiations, William Cecil made his true feelings known to Elizabeth and, along with Sir Nicholas Bacon, Sir Francis Knollys, and others advising the Privy Council persuaded her that now was the time to strike in *all* religious matters—including the uniformity of churches in England and their prayer book. What most likely sealed their success was the argument from Cecil that though history repeats itself, it seldom does so in precisely the same way. The challenges that Elizabeth faced differed from those in her father's or her brother's or her sister's reigns and needed to be treated with an independent solution. The following morning, Elizabeth gave her assent to a disputation between nine Protestant and nine Catholic divines to determine the questions of supremacy and uniformity.

With only days to go before the originally intended deadline of March 24, Elizabeth ordered instead that Parliament be adjourned until after Easter, when the disputation could take place. Of the nine Protestant voices, only one had not been exiled during Mary's reign. As feared, pandemonium broke out, and the disputation was adjourned. The clerk of the Commons made only one entry in his *Journal* noting that some members of the House met, read part of a bill, and "adjourned to hear the disputation between the bishops . . . and other Englishmen that came from Geneva."[20]

Timing in the religious settlement was everything. Elizabeth had been won over to the Protestant side by an improvement in her international fortunes, irrespective of the debates in Parliament. The Commons, in the main the strong Protestant voices of the "hot gospellers," charged forward and appended another bill to restore to the crown any monasteries or chantries revived under Mary. The only point on which both sides of the religious divide were united was that a woman could not be the Supreme Head of the Church. Elizabeth gave an indication of royal assent if the Commons would consider a compromise. The "hot gospellers" assented, and Elizabeth agreed to adopt the title of Supreme Governor of the Church of England instead. Both sides were relieved and further agreed quickly on one final amendment: that nothing done by this particular Parliament should be judged heresy or schism later. The bills as amended passed the Lords with all the Catholic spiritual peers and one lay peer dissenting.[21]

By Easter 1559, England had a combined Act of Supremacy and Act of Uniformity, and a legitimate queen. Only time would tell if Elizabeth—naturally imperious, formidable, self-willed, and calculating, but nonetheless a politically untested twenty-five-year-old woman—would prove a strong enough sovereign to bring England through its social, economic, political, and religious crises with any degree of diplomacy, vision, and aplomb.

Few outside the corridors of power understood Elizabeth's need to have her people obey her command regardless of their religious beliefs and for no other reason than they were loyal English men and women. Even fewer understood that she valued freedom of speech in Parliament and elsewhere.[22] From Elizabeth's viewpoint, the outpouring of love expressed by Londoners during her coronation procession had made it clear that they saw her as the Protestant savior providing the nation with new hope, prosperity, and independence from the foreign influence that rankled so during her sister Mary's reign. To succeed in their expectations, she would need all of the powers of diplomacy, tact, and even dissimulation that she could summon.

Failure was simply not an option.

THREE

Determined to Be a Virgin Queen

*It is hoped that the Queen will not long continue to
temporize so much in regard to her marriage, and many think
that she will not be so very uncompliant with the wishes of
the King [of Spain] who greatly fears lest your Holiness should
make some pronouncement [of bastardy] . . . against the said
Queen to the advantage of the King of France.*

—Coded intelligence from London to Pope Paul IV,
April 24, 1559

Hand in hand with the Act of Uniformity was the preoccupation that haunted the entire Tudor dynasty: the succession. Elizabeth's advisers were frankly stumped as to who would make a suitable husband to strengthen the Protestant settlement. Love, of course, never entered into the equation. The issue of who would be England's monarch after Elizabeth, and whom she could marry to give England the son and heir to ensure a *Protestant* succession, was a top state priority. Ancillary worries like what would happen if she died while that son was in his minority or, worse, if she, too, only gave birth to a girl, were not foremost in the minds of those urging her to wed. Yet despite the huge significance surrounding the succession, Elizabeth herself seemed to be uninterested in the marriage question at all.

By the spring of 1559, Elizabeth had bestowed her distinct favor on her dashing Master of the Horse, Sir Robert Dudley. Elizabeth had known Dudley most of her life, significantly sharing her time with him while they were both prisoners in the Tower, where their bond of friendship grew. However, as the son and grandson of men who had been executed as traitors, and the brother-in-law of poor Lady Jane Grey, executed by Mary for usurping her throne, Lord Robert could have only been termed, at the best of times, a poor choice of consort. Dudley was further disqualified as a possible husband on other, more substantial, grounds. He was already a married man. His wife of some years, Amy, was safely tucked away in the country reportedly dying of a "lump in her breast."

Count de Feria wrote to Philip II that spring, "Lord Robert has come so much in favor that he does whatever he likes with affairs, and it is even said that her Majesty visits him in his chamber day and night. People talk of this so freely that they go so far as to say that . . . the Queen is only waiting for her [his wife] to die to marry Lord Robert."[1]

Never one to be deterred from a desire to control Elizabeth, and thereby England, de Feria suggested to Philip that it might "be well to approach Lord Robert on your Majesty's behalf, promising him your help and favour and coming to terms with him."[2] What terms, if any, could those possibly be?

When William Cecil got word of de Feria's plotting, he was livid. He had been bewildered by the queen's sudden girlish flirtation with Dudley and was determined to get her married off and into safe hands before it was too late. Memories were long when it came to certain matters, and none had forgotten that while still a princess, Elizabeth had nearly lost her reputation and perhaps more through her scandalous association with Thomas Seymour, her stepfather. It was one thing for a young princess to act flirtatiously but quite another matter altogether for a queen of England to behave so indecorously.

Still, Elizabeth was queen and felt that Cecil was the one behaving unreasonably. Given Elizabeth's lifelong expertise at playing one faction against another, it's quite possible that the more Cecil protested, the more she sought to bring him to heel by ignoring him, but that is not to take anything away from what would become a deep and lasting devotion to Dudley. Her daily outings with her Master of the Horse, hunting from morning until night, were the steamy stuff melting all diplomatic missives. The French, Venetian, Spanish, and papal envoys speculated madly, and incorrectly, about Elizabeth's intentions. It seemed to Cecil that the longer the affair continued, the less marriageable Elizabeth would become, potentially endangering her reputation and the realm beyond repair.

So Cecil gambled that he knew the queen's mind. He prompted her directly and obliquely that the people looked upon her relationship with Dudley as unsuitable. When that didn't work, he threatened to resign unless Elizabeth came to heel. Just in case she didn't believe him, Cecil announced his purpose to anyone who would listen, including the notoriously loose-lipped Spanish envoy de Feria. Unless Cecil could wrest Elizabeth away from the clutches of Lord Robert, he predicted, "the extreme injury of the realm" and the ruination of the young queen would ensue.

Nonetheless, Elizabeth was not prepared to have her secretary of state dictate terms to her. Though Cecil admired the queen in many ways, in keeping with the times, he regarded Elizabeth in biblical terms as a "weak and feeble woman" unable to govern a vulnerable England on her own. There was nothing astounding in this condescending attitude to the queen for a Tudor man. It was simply the honest truth as known in their day, and as her first minister and secretary of state, it was his duty to limit the queen's exuberance (as he saw it) for her Dudley. Cecil felt duty bound to draw the proverbial line in the sand where the queen's potential loss of reputation weakened England's already fragile political and spiritual position. So he spread the word that he would resign, even if it meant being sent to the Tower. He let it be known that England by and large was outraged by any proposed match with Dudley. He even went so far as to say that such a marriage could lead to deposition of the queen or revolt, and that the French would aid such civil unrest. Naturally, his intention was that this would shock Elizabeth into seeing reason and thereby abandoning her Dudley.

Cecil's ploy wasn't as big a gamble as it might seem. He knew Elizabeth craved the love of her people more than anything else. He had been advising her on her landholdings since she was in her teens and knew just how far he could push her. No matter how much she claimed she didn't want to marry for reasons of state, the fact remained that it was expected of her. After all, her half sister, Queen Mary, had accepted this reality, reasoning that the only way to keep England in obeisance to the Holy See of Rome was to have a child and heir.

Yet despite all the gossip and Elizabeth's evident desire to simply amuse herself with Dudley, there is every indication that she had no intention of marrying, ever. For Parliament and the Privy Council, it was simply unthinkable that England's twenty-five-year-old handsome, inexperienced, and fiery queen not only desired but actively sought spinsterhood—particularly in light of the Dudley scandal that was brewing.

In part this was because in Tudor England, all men believed that women lived for the estate of holy wedlock, and it was disbelieved that a queen of England would set herself above this rule of God. Procreation was their reason for existence, so the Bible taught. "Eve" was the root word of "evil," and Eve the cause for the downfall of Man from the Garden of Eden. Religious thought and marriage were dangerously intertwined among all Christians, with muddled belief systems about women permeating popular art and literature. Women were sometimes portrayed as maternal, while at other times they were seen as a wicked source of disease and the cause of the sexual debasement of society.[3] After all, hadn't Henry VIII himself become the victim of the charms and bewitchment of women—most notably Elizabeth's own mother—who had debased his reign?

Since the beginning of the sixteenth century, there had been a male fascination with the female form; a male need to understand the maternal body's secrets and how a woman could represent both the innocent nourishment of maternity and man's bestial sexual desire. Anatomists like Charles V's physician, Andreas Vesalius of Brussels, tried to explain this dichotomy by stealing the bodies of prostitutes or female criminals in direct violation of religious decency and papal decree. It was only by dissecting the female body that he could reveal the secrets it held, Vesalius claimed.

Yet the anatomist himself became like a man possessed in his quest, frequently allowing himself to be locked out of the city gates to "look for the bones" of executed criminals. Vesalius's own account of his body-snatching borders on the sensual: "So great was my desire to possess those bones that in the middle of the night, alone and in the midst of all those corpses, I climbed the stake with considerable effort and did not hesitate to snatch away that which I so desired."[4]

Significantly, in Vesalius's *Letter on the China Root,* published in 1546, he waxes lyrical on the lasciviousness of the monks and how the monasteries are a microcosm for the corruption within the Catholic Church. At the heart and soul of the monk's fall from grace is the female form—the nun whose virginity cannot be taken on trust unless "anatomized."[5] Even earlier than Vesalius, the charismatic and libidinous scoundrel Pietro Aretino (1492–1556), who popularized erotic poses of lovemaking, reveled in clerical and political gossip among the literati close to the papacy by making the rich and famous "infamous" with his observations on the papal sex scandals of his day.

In fact, the popular trend to anatomize, or dissect, the female form in print was well established by the beginning of Elizabeth's reign. The title page of Vesalius's *De humani corporis fabrica,* first published in 1543, shows a dissection of a woman posing as if in a pagan sacrifice. Yet the female form was only one feature of a woman's imperfections, and queens, so it seemed, were no exception.

The woman's mind was not highly valued either. In his influential work written in 1528, *The Book of the Courtier,* Baldesar Castiglione explains that men steadfastly held the view that women were "the most imperfect creatures, incapable of any virtuous act, worth very little and quite without dignity compared with men."[6]

Imperfect or no, being an effective woman ruler was a nearly impossible task when viewed through the eyes of Tudor man. To marry and have children—heirs—unlocked her realm to the unwanted interference of the husband or king consort, just as it had done with Mary I and Philip of Spain. To not marry opened a queen regnant to possible scandalous criticisms by religious extremists that she sought to satisfy her sexual desires outside of wedlock, as with Elizabeth and Robert Dudley.

Tudor men hardly considered that having children held its own risks, though childbirth itself claimed both mother and child in alarming numbers until the twentieth century. Besides, marriage was no guarantee of giving birth to a boy. What if the queen could only give birth to a girl? Then, even if she had a son, would that son—and Elizabeth—live until he was old enough to rule? Even well-loved heirs, too, could drain power away from a reigning queen, just as Elizabeth had done with her sister. Would Elizabeth's heir do the same to her? Muddying the picture even more was the added complication of Elizabeth's parentage and moves by the French king to have her declared a bastard by Pope Paul IV.

As the daughter of Henry VIII and Anne Boleyn, Elizabeth was despised as the offspring of an "incestuous" marriage and suffered at the hands of those who should have cared for and loved her.[7] Elizabeth knew the twisted fate of most women and had known a husband's cruelty through a daughter's eyes: witnessing Henry VIII's fifth wife, Catherine Howard, pulled from the palace by her hair and fearing the demise of Henry's last wife, Catherine Parr, over the writing of her Protestant religious tracts. Elizabeth had seen male domination at close quarters throughout her life. She had experienced the terror of the unknown that pregnancy represented, as in the case of her sister's phantom pregnancies or the deaths of two of her stepmothers after childbirth.

Yet when it comes to her most private reasons for steadfastly refusing marriage—despite playing along with the pretense of it myriad times in her life—we shall never truly know if she ever held hopes of a husband and family. Was her enforced celibacy because she could never marry the one man she surely loved, Robert Dudley? Or did she regard the overzealous need for her to conform to the image of a queen as conceived by Parliament—to beget an heir—tantamount to an anatomization of her body and soul? Did she fear being unable to conceive a child, like her sister? Did she fear dying in childbirth? Or giving birth to a deformed child as her mother reputedly had done? Or did she see her own imagined child, the beloved and coveted heir apparent, as stealing away the prerogative that she had at long last inherited?

Perhaps she saw a husband—who must dominate her because he was a man—as an unnecessary by-product and the ultimate usurper of her own newfound power? Or did Elizabeth simply seek from the outset to create a pure, chaste image of herself not only as queen but as virgin queen, defying popular literature and art; to be loved as England's mother, freeing it from the bewitchment and superstition of the Catholic Church? Perhaps at different times it was all these things. Then again, perhaps not. It is a secret that Elizabeth took with her to her grave.

Though Elizabeth eventually gave in to Cecil's blackmail, she would have recalled the evangelizing voices of the Calvinists through the words of the fire-breathing Scots vicar John Knox, who had already blown a steady tempest against all women—and women rulers in particular. Having returned to Scotland in the spring of 1559, Knox had to face the great displeasure of England's new queen for his *First Blast of the Trumpet Against the Monstrous Regiment of Women*, published in Geneva a year earlier. Elizabeth refused to see Knox or admit him to her realm. William Cecil tried to make Elizabeth see the political imperatives of remaining on friendly terms with the pugnacious Scot and the significance of the Scottish Protestant movement Knox represented, particularly in light of the French king's unreliable friendship, but Elizabeth was not for turning.

Knox protested in writing that he was not Elizabeth's enemy, nor the enemy "of the regiment of her, whom God hath now promoted." His tract of the previous year had been directed against Mary Tudor, Mary Stuart, and her mother, Mary of Guise—all of whom had had devastating effects on Scotland, he claimed. While mildly conciliatory, Knox couldn't help but stick his proverbial foot in it with a letter to Cecil, directed at Elizabeth. "If," Knox droned on, "Queen Elizabeth shall confess so that the extraordinary dispensation of God's great mercy maketh that lawful with her which both nature and God's law doth deny all women, then shall none in England be more willing to maintain her lawful authority than I shall be. But if, God's wondrous works be set aside, she ground, as God forbid, the justness of her title upon consuetude [custom], laws and ordinance of men, then as I am assured, that evil foolish presumption doth greatly offend God's supreme majesty, so do I greatly fear that her ingratitude shall not long lack punishment."[8]

Despite her anger with Knox over his interpretation of women as "the weaker vessel," Elizabeth stayed focused on the political imperative dictated by the signing of the peace treaty at Cateau-Cambrésis in the spring of 1559. She knew full well that this treaty wasn't so much a declaration of peace as a "time-out" from active combat. Mary Tudor had lost England's staple town of Calais needlessly in what Elizabeth and the country viewed as the king of Spain's war to none other than France's commander of the action, the warrior Francis, Duke of Guise—uncle of Mary Queen of Scots. The loss of Calais alone made England economically vulnerable.

For William Cecil, an alliance to the right man through marriage could serve to protect England's interests abroad. Such an alliance, Elizabeth thought, needn't take the irrevocable step into marriage. After all, France, not Spain, represented the greatest threat to England's security. There were thousands of French troops massing on England's northern borders with Scotland. Elizabeth's cousin Mary, since the age of one week Mary I of Scotland, had been a creature of the French court since she was six years old, transforming Scotland into almost a vassal state of France.[9]

Indeed, Mary had taken her first husband just a year earlier, on April 24, 1558, amid tremendous splendor and fanfare in Paris. The Scottish queen—one of the most "imperfect creatures" in so many ways—had wed the sickly Francis of Valois, the dauphin of France. Mary was only fifteen years and four months of age. This marriage, carved from the model of so many medieval child marriages among royalty, allied her impoverished realm to one of the most glorious in Europe. Although the young Scots queen knew she was marrying for the good of her realm; nonetheless, to observers she seemed simply ecstatic.

Had Elizabeth looked on in wonder from her exile at Hatfield then, envying Mary, who had been compared to Helen of Troy in beauty, the fabled Lucrece in chastity, the Athenian goddess Pallas in wisdom, Ceres in riches, and Juno in power?[10] Or did Elizabeth take good heed of one of the wedding eulogies by Estienne Perlin dedicated to the French king's sister, the Duchess of Berry, observing, "How happy oughtest thou to esteem thyself, O kingdom of Scotland, to be favored, fed and maintained like an infant on the breast of the most Magnanimous king of France . . . for without him thou would'st have been laid in ashes, thy country wasted and ruined by the English, utterly accursed by God"?[11]

There were plenty of women in history, from Eleanor of Aquitaine four hundred years earlier up to Mary's wedding day, to show Elizabeth to beware of a groom. So, in her speech delivered to the House of Commons on February 10, 1559, Elizabeth clearly stated her marital intentions for her reign:

> And albeit it might please almighty God to continue me still in this mind to live out of the state of marriage, yet it is not to be feared but He will so work in my heart and in your wisdoms as good provision by His help may be made in convenient time, whereby the realm shall not remain destitute of an heir that may be a fit governor, and peradventure more beneficial to the realm than such offspring as may come of me . . . And in the end this shall be for me sufficient: that a marble stone shall declare that a queen, having reigned such a time, lived and died a virgin.[12]

Though frequently accused of inconstancy and vacillation by the men surrounding her, ultimately Elizabeth remained steadfast to this stated aim. While the full-blown "Cult of Elizabeth" was some years off, Elizabeth clearly sought to confound everyone's notions of womanhood, and most particularly of her. She would play off one faction of men against the other with a studied system of male favorites throughout her reign. She would keep her councillors guessing with her infuriating prevarication and dissimulation designed to make her mistress of all she surveyed. Above all, she would create her own image of what she thought a queen should be.

Though it would be another twenty years before she was called "Gloriana," the seeds for the Cult of Elizabeth were planted at the outset of her reign. She would start as she meant to go along. In the English translation of *The Book of the Courtier* by Sir Thomas Hoby in 1561—two years after Elizabeth's affirmation to Parliament—the character Magnifico takes up the cause of women at court as enlightened, seeking education, magnanimity, temperance, and virtuousness, before going on to ask, "Don't you think that we might find many women just as capable of governing cities and armies as men?"[13] This was the way Elizabeth was determined to be known and remembered, not as some Jezebel, brood mare, or harlot.

Consequently, before the ink was dry on the treaty parchment of Cateau-Cambrésis, Elizabeth apparently complied with Cecil's ultimatum and sent word to King Henry II of France that she favored a French match. His second-eldest son, also Henry, was a mere child, but that didn't seem to matter to either side. As Philip II had recently married Elisabeth of France, daughter of Henry II, conforming to the treaty of Cateau-Cambrésis, something had to be done to prevent a Franco-Hapsburg alliance against England, even if it meant pretending to be interested in marrying the French child and heir.

Naturally, the prospect of acquiring England through marriage proved too tantalizing for Henry to resist. Elizabeth welcomed the French envoys with jewels and gifts and pomp and ceremony when they came to discuss the match in May 1559. If the match couldn't be concluded, then Henry could always contemplate Mary's own fair claim to England's throne. Either way, Henry felt he had a strong hand.[14]

So, where did the papacy stand in this power struggle in northern Europe? While the pope, as the head of a disintegrating Catholic Church, wielded secular power in Italy through the Papal States, which had fought Philip unsuccessfully in a fruitless war only a few years earlier, the pope was in a relatively weak position to rule on Henry's demand to declare Elizabeth illegitimate. Philip of Spain was against it, so the pope prevaricated.

Since Paul IV believed there was little hope of the return of the Protestants to the Catholic fold, alienating Elizabeth mattered little to him. Still, he owed a great deal to the kingdoms of France and Spain, which had been battling for supremacy with the papacy for hundreds of years. To make matters worse, the Spanish and French kings guarded their titles as "Most Catholic" and "Most Christian" kings jealously as treasured tokens of their own place in the hierarchy of Christendom.

Paul IV knew from bitter experience that it did not pay to cross these mighty monarchs. When Pope Clement VII vexed the Holy Roman Emperor, Charles V (Philip's father), he paid for it dearly. Charles's army occupied Rome from 1527 to 1528, sacking and burning the city repeatedly. Even the pope's protectors—the famous Swiss Guard—seemed to turn against the papacy by deserting Catholicism for one of the newer Protestant sects. France's king, then Francis I, Henry's father, offered the papacy safety at Avignon, which Pope Clement VII knew he'd have to refuse.[15]

Paul IV held a vivid recollection of these events and, as a native Neapolitan, felt that the Spanish remained an occupying force in Naples. Even more galling, Paul personally loathed the Spanish king, feeling that Philip had slighted him when he had served as legate in Castile. It was this loathing that led the pope into one of the many Franco-Hapsburg wars on the side of the French, later known as the Carafa War of 1556–57 (Carafa was the pope's family name). The pope ill-advisedly invaded Naples, and papal forces were roundly defeated by Spain's viceroy and Europe's best military commander, the Duke of Alba. All this meant that while Pope Paul IV's heart told him to issue the bull against Elizabeth as Henry II requested, he could ill afford to alienate the Spanish king yet again.[16]

So Henry II failed to oust Elizabeth as England's just ruler in the eyes of Catholic Europe. Henry also failed to understand that the alleged great claim of his daughter-in-law to England's throne was suspect. As a "foreigner," despite her assertion as next in line for the throne, Mary was not eligible to become queen of England under English common law without an act of Parliament, something Elizabeth was hardly prepared to approve. Even more damning for Mary's claim was that she had been excluded from the succession by Henry VIII's will, which had been passed by an act of Parliament.[17]

Though these impediments were seen as an adequate safeguard for England's new Protestant ruling classes, England's Catholics who were still loyal to Rome promoted an alternative view: Mary was the granddaughter of Henry VIII's older sister, Margaret, and the great-granddaughter of Henry VII. Mary had not been born of an "incestuous" marriage as Elizabeth had been. Henry VIII's self-proclaimed divorce from Catherine of Aragon had never been recognized by the Catholic Church, and as Catherine was still living when Elizabeth was conceived and born, she was a "bastard" to all who continued to believe in papal authority in England.

For all these negatives, even Elizabeth's shortcomings could be overlooked if she took the right husband. For Catholic Europe, the most obvious candidate was England's former king consort, Philip of Spain; or at least, so he thought. As early as the end of 1558 Philip's emissary in England, de Feria, had written to the Spanish king urging him to propose marriage to Elizabeth. It was in Philip's interests to remain king of England as a counterbalance to the French Guise interests in Scotland. Certainly his policy of containment of the French would be easier if Elizabeth Tudor would have him. So Feria wrote to Philip on November 20—only three days after his wife, Elizabeth's half sister, died—affirming:

> I therefore wish your Majesty to keep in view all the steps to be taken on your behalf, one of them being that the Emperor should not send any ambassador here to treat of this . . . even if he took the tidbit from your Majesty's hand, but . . . I know for certain they will not hear the name of the duke of Savoy mentioned as they fear he will want to recover his estates with English forces and will keep them constantly at war. I am very pleased to see that the nobles are all beginning to open their eyes to the fact that it will not do to marry this woman in the country itself.[18]

While de Feria's intelligence pandered to the king's ego, he was right in one respect. The Holy Roman Emperor, Philip's uncle Ferdinand, also had thought Elizabeth Tudor a prize worth having. Ferdinand had proposed his younger son, the Duke of Savoy, as a prospective bridegroom but tried to dress up the match in other ways as recompense. Still, as a younger son who had little money and less land, the duke was not deemed to be of sufficient standing for the queen of England, particularly as he was a good Catholic to boot. His only redeeming feature, so it seemed, was that he was not Spanish.

Despite talk of her "incestuous" parentage, other kings and noblemen sought Elizabeth's hand as a gilded prize, too. Prince Eric of Sweden had proposed marriage. His main attraction was that he was Protestant. Still, Parliament had voiced a desire for Elizabeth to marry an Englishman— but not Dudley, and preferably the Earl of Arundel or her father's courtier Sir William Pickering. While they all bickered, Elizabeth cavorted with her handsome Master of the Horse; studiously setting aside any plans others had for her to wed.

So when, in March 1559, Henry II wrote to Elizabeth officially proposing his second son, Henry, Duke of Anjou (later Henry III of France), as her groom, Elizabeth, inexperienced though she was, saw the perfect way to halt this barrage of suitors and get what she wanted. It would be years before Henry of Anjou would be old enough to wed, and by then, so much else could happen.

Without her usual prevarication, Elizabeth wrote to Philip advising him of the French offer, tacitly asking for the Spanish king's protection against Valois threats, expressed or implied. Naturally, the last thing that Philip would have wished was for the English queen to marry one of the Valois heirs and create a union between France and England—between the second in line to the throne and a queen regnant. So Philip acceded to Elizabeth's requests for protection, pledging his loyalty to her and his former realm of England before quickly agreeing to the most significant condition of the Treaty of Cateau-Cambrésis. The Spanish king took his third wife, Elisabeth of France, daughter of Henry II, as a safeguard against future French aggression.

It was a veritable whirlwind of marriage proposals, refusals, and counterproposals—all happening in the spring of 1559. Where did the outcome leave England in the rapidly changing political landscape? Precisely where Elizabeth wanted: living off the prospect of marriage without ever delivering the promise. As hard as it was for the men surrounding her to believe, Elizabeth had actually meant what she had been affirming for years already: that she was happy in the estate of spinsterhood. Unlike the men advising her, Elizabeth knew full well that should she marry, her husband would become the focus of power, draining it away from her as surely as if he had opened her veins. Given Elizabeth's determined character, this would remain the ever constant cornerstone of her personal rule.

Nevertheless, having a queen lead the "kingdom of England relapsed into schism and heresy" was not a matter that Pope Paul could leave to fate. A scheme was hatched and presented to him in the early days of summer 1559. A trusted intermediary to deal directly with the queen for her return to the Holy See was proposed in the person of Sir Francis Englefield, who planned to spend that winter at Padua, through another sympathetic Englishman, whose name was George "Nevel":

> They might be commissioned to impart the Pope's good intention to the said Inghilfeildt [sic], for his encouragement to persevere in the true religion, and that he may keep up the spirits of the Catholics that are still in the kingdom. And likewise he might be authorized to tell "Inghilfeildt," that, if he should be minded to apprise his Holiness, by writing or messenger, of the course of affairs, there is a person at this Court with whom he may communicate without risk of being discovered and incurring the displeasure of the Queen. Nevel, who is just about to join "Inghilfeildt," is a worthy gentleman and a kinsman in some degree of Cardinal Pole.[19]

The scheme to provide Pope Paul with intelligence from England continued by proposing that "certain Catholic prelates and priests who have been deprived of their churches and benefices for refusing to follow the new religion" and were in need of funds should be provided for from revenues of the English Hospital in Rome.[20] Such priests would undoubtedly show their gratitude in some way in the years to come, the letter implies.

Then, quite abruptly, the political and religious landscape veered off course again that summer. The French king was killed in a jousting accident, dying ten days later on July 10. Pope Paul IV followed to his own grave on August 18. By the time the new Pope Pius IV was elected by the convocation of cardinals, it was Christmas Day 1559.[21]

Mary Queen of Scots was now queen of France. By Christmas Day, Mary and her husband, Francis II, had amassed some thirty-five thousand troops on the Scottish borders. The Scottish Protestants who had refused to fight for Mary of Guise as early as 1557 had now taken up arms against her French troops on the open fields between Edinburgh and Leith. Their rout could only mean one thing: invasion of England.

The temporal world seemingly couldn't wait for a new pontiff to be elected and spiraled ever closer to either world domination by Spain or another war with France. How odd, Cecil mused, that the choice of the next pope was perhaps the only hope of averting any of these unpalatable outcomes for England.

FOUR

Many an Uneasy Truce

*The injurious pretenses made by the Queen of Scots to
this realm proceed from the principals of the house of
Guise, who now have the chief governance of the crown
of France . . . and that neither the French king . . .
nor the Queen of Scots, his wife . . . have imagined
such an unjust enterprise.*

—Proclamation by Queen Elizabeth, March 24, 1560

The conclave that elected Gian Angelo de' Medici as Pope Pius IV took place once peace had been restored to the eternal city of Rome. His predecessor, Paul IV, had been hated almost as much as he loathed those around him. On Paul's death, violence broke out, with the headquarters of the Roman Inquisition destroyed by rioters and its prisoners released. Jews who had been isolated in the ghetto in Rome were allowed at last to reintegrate into society. However, peace could only return once the Vatican took its retribution against the papal nephews for their sins. Accused officially of heresy and murder, they were tried by a commission of eight cardinals and executed in the Castel Sant'Angelo. Philip II of Spain looked on with grim satisfaction at a most fitting end to Paul's anti-Hapsburg regime.[1]

In the absence of a legitimately elected pontiff, the proposed "intelligence use" of English Catholic exiles by the papacy was usurped by Philip himself, who set up Sir Francis Englefield and others at Louvain in the Low Countries. Sir Francis had, of course, been known to Philip as one of his dead queen's privy councillors, and the Spanish king claimed a loyalty to the exiled Englishman for that reason alone. Still, the truth was far more sinister.

Philip had inherited one of Europe's premier university cities in Louvain. Rising high above the River Dyle in Flanders, Louvain's four colleges that comprised its university were a magnet for all scholars who sought an academic life, regardless of nationality, so long as they espoused the Roman Catholic faith. By the 1530s, the general college, known as the Castle, attracted students for the study of medicine, canon law, civil law, and theology. The likes of the great mapmaker Mercator, Charles V's physician Vesalius, Mary Tudor's beloved teacher Juan de Vives, and the politician-turned-theologian Antoine Perrenot de Granvelle all studied there. By 1560, when Philip II of Spain had the brain wave to use Louvain to his own ends, the university had already celebrated its one hundredth anniversary.[2]

This "Belgian Athens," as Louvain was sometimes called, was so sought after that only Paris could rival it in its voracious quest for top professors, and in the 1560s, English professors were the flavor of the moment for Louvain's putative benefactor, Philip of Spain. Through the good offices of Sir Francis Englefield, Louvain's ranks swelled with Catholic professors from Oxford and Cambridge, one of the most notable of whom was Oxford's professor of Hebrew, Thomas Harding.[3] These English Catholic exiles, who nicknamed Louvain the "Catholics' Oxford," would serve their new master Philip in many ways. Often they kept tabs on the thousands of young, troublesome intellectuals speaking every European language crammed into Louvain's city walls and reported their gossip back to their master. Sir Francis was particularly well qualified to carry out this task. After all, while Englefield was a privy councillor in Mary Tudor's reign, he learned from Nicholas Bacon's template* how to improve universities and create an education system for the masses.[4]

Understandably, England's Catholic professors were more than happy to answer Englefield's call. His star recruit, Thomas Harding, had written *An Answer to Master Jewell's Challenge* in response to the bishop of Lon-

---

*Nicholas Bacon was by now Elizabeth's Lord Privy Seal.

don's Easter sermon at St. Paul's Cross that year. This was the first of dozens of religious tracts intended to stir the English masses and Europe's leaders into action against the slanderous activities of the new Anglican Church. In fact, many of Harding's words found their way into official correspondence between Philip II and his ambassadors throughout the 1560s. These stirring words had little impact inside England, however, for Cecil ensured that "no such book written in English by the Catholic party should be received and read in England under great threat of punishment."[5] Yet before his death in 1572, Harding would prove invaluable to the Catholic cause in helping a little-known priest, Father William Allen, establish the English College at Douai in the Low Countries.

Well aware of the development of these university seminaries, Elizabeth and her Privy Council saw that their best weapon of defense against the Catholic backlash would be a broad policy of educating both England's children and, more significantly, its adults. It would no longer suffice for average English people to rely on their local church as the primary source of knowledge about the world, as the vicars could not always be trusted to convey the dangers that faced them from Catholic Europe. Thus Bacon's original plan to teach the basics of reading and writing to the masses, proposed during Elizabeth's sister's reign, was once again considered.

Naturally, Philip lamented the censorship of fine Catholic sentiments in England while applauding the ban on the dissemination of heretical Protestant texts in his territories. His bitter enemy, the recently deceased pope, had had still other views on how to spread "the Word." The pope had shown his mistrust of Philip's motives, recognizing the Spanish king's desire to dominate in nearly every sphere, just like his father. In fact, while Philip's father, Charles V, still ruled the Holy Roman Empire as well as Spain and her colonies, Cardinal Carafa—as the pope was then known—had been feared by even the most highly regarded of Catholic ministers. Ignatius Loyola, founder of the Jesuits, had fallen out with Carafa when the cardinal was the Inquisitor of Venice. "Every bone in my body trembles," Loyola avowed, "at the news of Carafa's election [as pope]." Carafa was so fierce an opponent of any who stood in his way that it was widely rumored "sparks flew from beneath his feet as he walked."[6]

It is little wonder that Philip vowed not to leave anything to chance on Carafa's death in August 1559. While pope, Paul had blocked Philip's reconvening the Council of Trent, abandoned since 1545, for fear that if such a council were geographically remote from Rome, papal authority would be usurped by secular voices—meaning Philip's. The pope's solution for the reunification of the church was to set up a reform commission of sixty bishops under direct papal authority. This would have the effect of isolating Philip from any decisions regarding the Catholic Church. Paul's sudden death therefore proved a godsend to the Spanish king. Under cover of the violent outbursts that erupted in Rome with the pontiff's demise, Philip began to weave his magic. Through bribery, blackmail, and coercion the Spanish ambassador let the conclave know that if it wanted cooperation with the breadbasket of Rome—meaning Philip's kingdom of Naples—as well as Spain's protection from the Ottoman Turk in the Mediterranean, there would be a significant price to pay. Only those cardinals whose names appeared on Philip's approved list could be put forward for election as pontiff.[7]

With little pretense of resistance, the conclave accepted the Spanish king's terms. It was into this brave new world that Gian Angelo de' Medici was elected and took the name Pius IV. In the absence of a papal nuncio to England and the exchange of an English ambassador to Rome, Elizabeth could only look on, hope for good intelligence, and pray for wisdom in keeping Philip as her friend, when in fact she suspected he was her most intransigent enemy.

Though Pius was acceptable to Philip, he was nonetheless something of a throwback to a bygone era. He would be one of the last popes to acknowledge paternity of his children and felt that what he lacked in common sense and diplomacy he could make up for in bluster. His Italian power base was due, in large part, to the fabulously wealthy Farnese family, but he longed to show his worth in the international arena. If it meant that he must toe the line—for a little while—and accede to Philip's wishes to become the favored candidate for the papacy, then so be it. After all, a pope who could be sympathetic to the Spanish king was a thing of considerable value, and Pius IV knew it.

Philip's own brand of messianic imperialism was just beginning to flower. Soon he would be known as "holier than the pope." In a few years he would preach to the Holy Roman Emperor that "to believe that a passion as great as the one which surrounds the choice of religion . . . can be settled by gentleness and concessions, or by other means that avoid firmness and punishment, is to be greatly deceived."[8] The Catholic faith, and its sustained influence in the world, was at the heart of all that Philip held dear. Catholicism and conquest, or perhaps conquest for Roman Catholicism, became the main driver for his own forty-three-year rule.

Notwithstanding this, the Protestant Elizabeth represented a very useful counterfoil to French influence on the Continent and, of course, in Scotland. If Philip had to bend his short-term view of the English and Scottish Protestant threat to contain the imperialistic inclinations of France's king and queen, not to mention Mary's Guise uncles, then he would.[9] While Philip's Spain only experienced six months without war in his long rule, he had resolved on a diplomatic solution to masterminding the changing, and at times unknown, forces in Europe at the end of 1559. After all, he was marrying the young and pliable Elisabeth of France, the fourteen-year-old daughter of Catherine de' Medici and sister of Francis II. By keeping on good terms with France *and* Elizabeth of England, he could at a stroke neutralize Mary Queen of Scots and France and placate his increasingly hostile Protestant subjects in the Low Countries.

That was a longer-term strategy, though. In the autumn of 1559, Philip needed to turn his attention to the papacy and the Italian peninsula. A "General Visitation" of his three Italian possessions was ordered, cataloging, mapping, and capturing on canvas all that he owned, while the cardinals continued to bicker over who would be the next pope able to satisfy the Spanish king's commands.

Feeling the force of Philip's power in neighboring Naples could only serve to remind the conclave that Spain had long held a unique position within the Roman Catholic world. When Charles V (Philip's father) had been king of Spain, his boyhood tutor had become Pope Adrian VI. In thanks for his advancement, purchased dearly by Charles, of course, Adrian had granted Spanish kings from 1523 the right to appoint all bishoprics within his realms.[10] The arrangement had been reached on the understanding that it would avoid corruption within the church and eliminate half the bribery for offices. In a final grab for power from the church, Charles V had also agreed with the pope that the king of Spain could scrutinize any papal bull in advance of its publication in perpetuity, ostensibly to avoid the embarrassment to both parties should these documents contradict the laws and customs of Spain. This would become a crucial concession within the first twelve years of Elizabeth's rule.

Still, for all his unbridled inherited power, Philip respected the office of the papacy, after his own personal fashion. This was best manifested through his use of religious monies collected. The *subsido,* or subsidy, came from rents of church lands and buildings or any other form of income enjoyed by the Spanish clergy—all of whom had been appointed by the Spanish king, and not the pope.[11] The *cruzada* was an agreed form of taxation on the church and its revenues conceded to Ferdinand and Isabella in the late fifteenth century in their crusade that drove the Moors—and the Jews—from Spain.[12]

Though seen as a "national" levy, it was the *cruzada* that effectively held the greatest sway Philip wielded with the papacy—as well as with his uncle Ferdinand, Holy Roman Emperor. While many Moors had been driven from Spain, and the Inquisition continued to ensure *la limpia de sangre,* or "the purity of blood," of the Spanish people, the threat of the Ottoman Turk remained a clear and present danger in the Mediterranean and held the awesome menace of knocking on the gates of Vienna itself. It was the Ottoman threat that gave Philip his real leverage with Rome. A crusade against "infidels" slowly became an all-inclusive blunt instrument used by both the papacy and Spain for the next forty years against all breakaway sects of Christianity in addition to Jews, Moors, and Ottoman Turks. This naturally included the English church. Of all the Catholic heads of state, only Philip held the power to engage in this "crusade" militarily on a massive scale. So whatever opposition Rome, or for that matter any other country, voiced against Philip, the might of Spain remained in high demand by the Vatican.[13]

Nowhere is this uneasy relationship as obvious as in the early days in the proposed reconvening of the Council of Trent for the reformation of the Roman Catholic Church. The newly elected Pius IV believed that any such council, if held outside of Rome, must reopen all issues on reformation in order to attract the breakaway Christian "sects" back to the Roman Catholic fold. Philip disagreed. For him, any new council must only be a continuation of the one adjourned in 1545, during which it had been decided to take a hard line with any country that did not recognize the supremacy of Rome and the Catholic faith. Pius IV, for all his good intentions to remain independent, would soon realize that despite being head of the Church of Rome, he would need to placate the Spanish king.

Their first crossing of swords occurred on May 4, 1560, over the choice and timing to send a papal representative to Queen Elizabeth. Pius, who had only been in the job for five months, decided in clear defiance of Philip's wishes to appoint a nuncio to invite the queen of England to a completely new Council of Trent. Outraged, the cardinal archbishop of Milan (who had hoped to be elected pope himself) wrote to the papal nuncio in Spain that

> you must know that the Pope has resolved to send a nuncio to the Queen of England, to try to bring her back to the bosom of the Church and the obedience of the Holy See; for the garboils [tumult or confusion] in which the Queen at present finds herself afford him hope that the enterprise may be honored by success. For this purpose, his Holiness has selected Abbot Parpaglia, whom he has already furnished with money for the journey . . . His instructions are to travel through France, and do all . . . to procure from their Majesties all such assistance as he may deem most serviceable in the affair.[14]

Abbot Parpaglia did in fact travel through France to the Low Countries to advise Margaret of Parma, Philip's half sister and governess of the

Spanish Netherlands, of his mission. When the pope called in Spain's ambassador, Francisco de Vargas, to make him aware as well, the obvious but undesirable result occurred. While Pius continued his diplomatic conciliatory efforts with Elizabeth, Vargas brewed his own brand of poison by letter to Philip. Within two weeks of the pope's initial decision to send Parpaglia to England, two papal newsletters declared "it is not yet decided who is to go to England in place of the Abbot . . . who some think, may after all be sent, as the Pope does not consider the objections of Vargas sufficient for his unfitness for the mission."[15] By June 29, such was the power of the Spanish king that all had been resolved to Philip's satisfaction. "As to Abbot Parpaglia, the Pope has taken his Majesty's observations in good part," the missive begins, "and has forthwith sent word to the Abbot that, if he have [sic] not already crossed to England, he must await further orders; and if he have [sic] . . . he is to enter upon no negotiation without the participation, consent and approval of his Catholic Majesty's ambassador in that kingdom."[16]

It is little wonder that Elizabeth and her councillors remained ever vigilant of Philip's actions and seemed, at the very least, to give the appearance of cooperating with him whenever they could without compromising England's position at home or abroad.

Yet France remained England's main preoccupation. With thirty-five thousand French troops on the borders of Scotland and the Protestant Lords of the Congregation in open revolt against Mary of Guise, Elizabeth was urged to act rather than seek a diplomatic solution. Time had finally run out. The Scots had sent the young William Maitland of Lethington, secretary of Scotland, to meet with Cecil as they acknowledged "how far everyone of them is bound to him [Cecil] for the great favours shown in the furtherance of this their common cause which they have in hands, as also some of them in particular for the benefits received at his hands."[17]

The same day, Cecil received a missive from his envoys that the Scots Lords were at Linlithgow, vowing to "retain their soldiers in wages, and to levy more men to be revenged on the French. It is like they will send for money from the writers [Sadler and Croftes] which they think not good to deny them, and yet would thereupon know the Queen's pleasure."[18]

What could Elizabeth do? The only thing standing between England and a French invasion from Scotland was the Protestant Lords of the Congregation. Elizabeth had written to the Scots to remain in "quietness" a week earlier, but news on November 10 also told of more skirmishes and even greater preparations for war. Mary of Guise had taken up residence at Edinburgh Castle and wrote to Elizabeth reminding her "of a former letter requesting that no aid should be afforded to the subjects of Scotland" as they were rebellious, which hinted that she knew Elizabeth had provided them with money.[19]

Not only had Mary Stuart and her husband, Francis II, quartered the arms of England, but their Guise family advisers in France had sent a dangerous number of French mercenaries to Elizabeth's northern borders ostensibly to quell the Scottish Protestant Lords of the Congregation. To boot, it was costing her a fortune to defend England's borders with her army at Berwick. She had been queen for just over a year and was again facing the same enemy with whom she had made peace only nine months earlier. The relationship with France could, at best, be described as an uneasy truce.

By the end of November, Elizabeth had maneuvered enough behind the scenes to write boldly to Mary of Guise that "respecting the conservation of amity between the two realms . . . she thinks . . . her doings shall be always constant and agreeable . . . For her mind to peace, she affirms that she is as well inclined to keep it as she ever was, and will be most sorry to see any occasion given her by the Dowager to the contrary."[20]

On receipt of Elizabeth's provocative letter, Mary of Guise, awaiting overdue succor from her brothers in France, made for Edinburgh's port of Leith. Meanwhile, the court of Francis and Mary traveled to Blois for their first resplendent Christmas as king and queen of France. The queen mother, Catherine de' Medici, was on her way to the Spanish border, accompanying her young dark-eyed daughter Elisabeth to meet her groom,

Philip of Spain. Elizabeth's general, the Duke of Norfolk, readied the Army of the North for battle against the French at Berwick. Unsurprisingly, all the while, Elizabeth fumed in London about the senselessness and expense of war.

No one, not even the Duke of Norfolk as commander, had been prepared for the first English stealth naval attack. His instructions to William Winter, a colorful rapscallion adventurer who would later be knighted for his derring-do, were clear: "He [Winter] shall aid the Queen's said friends and annoy their enemies, specially the French, without giving any desperate adventure; and this he must seem to do of his own head as if he had no commission of the Queen or of the Duke of Norfolk."[21]

Winter's tactics on the icy December seas were a masterstroke of seamanship. He drove back the French ships filled to the gunnels with victuals and soldiers all the way to the Spanish Netherlands for shelter. As the French crew and soldiers clambered ashore, they were robbed by waiting pirates. By New Year's Day 1560, Winter had sailed into the Firth of Forth at Leith, cutting off the French army at Fife. The French abandoned their weapons, many fleeing for their lives.

This left Mary of Guise bereft of reinforcements and victuals. She was fighting two enemies—her own people and the English—and had been denied relief from her brothers and daughter in France. Posturing against international criticism, Elizabeth set about justifying herself to both Spain and France for her preemptive strike against the Scots regent. To Philip, she sent an ambassador to Margaret of Parma in the Low Countries. Margaret feigned not to understand what all the fuss was about. After all, hadn't Elizabeth continued to bear the title of queen of France, defunct for over a century? What did it matter if Mary called herself queen of England? Where Margaret was perspicacious was in her assessment of the queen regent's plight: She had "no garrisons, no money, no troops." Furthermore, though Elizabeth had now written to Philip asking him to remain neutral, it was England's queen who had begun hostilities without having previously written to let him know her intentions. Nonetheless, Margaret reasoned, it might be best to tell the French that they would make Philip "jealous" if they occupied England.[22]

• • •

Incredibly, by the time Philip had received Margaret's letter, the dour Spanish king was utterly besotted by his new bride, declaring his complete happiness at long last. Yet unbeknown to Philip, Elizabeth, or Margaret of Parma, the teenaged femme fatale was receiving weekly instructions from her mother. Catherine de' Medici hoped to transform Spanish foreign policy in France's favor and one day oust her daughter-in-law's Guise uncles from their preeminent position behind the throne. Philip did promise to protect France, yet events would soon outpace any action Philip might have wished to take.

In the chill of that February 1560, rumors began to fly of a secret plot against the Guise family in France. Seemingly, the French Protestants wanted to lash out at the grave injustices and hostility of the administration led by the cardinal of Guise. In fact, it was whispered that the French Protestants wanted to seize the cardinal and his brother, put them on trial before a kangaroo court, and liberate the young king and queen from their nefarious influence. Catherine de' Medici herself could not have written a better script.

The only problem was, who could lead such an insurrection against the omnipotent Guise brothers? The king of Navarre, Antoine, was seemingly unable or unwilling to decide which side of the fence he was on, despite being a Protestant and the Bourbon heir to the French throne after Catherine de' Medici's three sons.[23] So the rebels turned to Antoine's younger brother Louis de Condé as their putative leader.

Of course, Condé could not be seen to rebel personally against the House of Guise, so he in turn intrusted the role of leader to a local nobleman, the Seigneur de la Renaudie. Condé could not have made a worse choice. La Renaudie held a grudge against the Guise brothers and had, in fact, once been a client of theirs. He had converted to Calvinism in Geneva after fleeing the employ of the Guise, but even John Calvin wanted nothing to do with him. Nonetheless, La Renaudie met with the plotters at the port of Hugues on the evening of February 1, 1560, and it was agreed that their leader would secretly send out five hundred agents to recruit mercenaries.[24] Even Queen Elizabeth was approached for money and arms. The date for the insurrection was set for March 16, some six weeks later.

With one of the worst-kept secrets of its day whispered on every street corner, it is little wonder that the plot failed. When the English Catholics teaching in Louvain heard of it, a letter was hastily penned to the cardinal of Lorraine, Louis of Guise. La Renaudie boasted what he intended to do to a Paris lawyer. A German prince wrote to the bishop of Arras about the audacious plot. Everyone, it seemed, had this fabulous secret he was simply dying to tell. In the event, it was La Renaudie's Paris lawyer, fearful of being implicated, who revealed the ringleader's identity. Still, La Renaudie was a small fry, and it did not suit the cardinal of Guise to expose some harebrained scheme hatched by a local Frenchman. No, instead it should be a grand plot on a grand scale. The cardinal would establish the rumor that this plot was the doing of the heretic English queen. Of course, Catherine de' Medici became alarmed, writing to her daughter, "We have been warned that from all directions men are marching towards Blois."[25]

Three weeks after this first "Huguenot" meeting, the cardinal of Guise ordered the king, the queen, and their entire court to be removed to the medieval Angevin stronghold at Amboise. The spectacular château, built in the thirteenth century, rises steeply above the town just at a bend in the Loire River, jutting out on a high promontory. Amboise was where Francis's grandfather had been born and where Leonardo da Vinci had died. Catherine's children had spent much of their childhood here, as it was deemed impenetrable. It seemed a perfect place to avert disaster.

Slowly Catherine became convinced that it was not Elizabeth behind the plot but rather the enemies of the current French regime. She insisted that Admiral Gaspard de Coligny—a Protestant—be brought in to provide the young king and queen with advice, and perhaps also act in extremis as a hostage. Meanwhile the cardinal sent out scouts to comb the countryside for the insurgents. Catherine, looking more to protect her son than anything else, redoubled her efforts to placate the French rebels, eventually resulting in the Edict of Amboise. This gave an amnesty for all past religious crimes but failed to offer religious freedom. Some religious dissenters were released from prison, but no one came forward with further information against the rebels or proof that Elizabeth had been involved.

The next weeks passed in a nerve-racking calm. Some foreign informant warned that the leader of the insurgents was "a great prince." Catherine now suspected Louis de Condé, who had suddenly arrived to join the beleaguered court. Condé's Protestant sympathies were known to everyone, making him the most likely ringleader. In a truly Machiavellian maneuver, Catherine appointed Condé to be her son's chief bodyguard, thus forcing the unlucky prince to remain at the castle by the king's side and unable to instruct his rebels when to strike. It had the other added benefit of seeming to convey great honor on Condé while effectively holding him prisoner.

For the next ten days—between March 6 and 16—a number of rebels and insurgents were captured in the woods surrounding Amboise. Then finally, the captain of the guard came to confess to the queen mother that his role had been to seal off the king's apartments to separate Charles from the Guises. La Renaudie wasn't discovered until March 19, again in the woods surrounding Amboise. He was killed by a single shot, summarily executed. The so-called Tumult of Amboise, allegedly financed by Elizabeth, was over before it had begun.

Not, however, for Francis, Duke of Guise. Summary justice would be meted out. Any rebel found would be killed on the spot. Shooting was reserved only for rebels of "standing." Their followers would be bound and sewn into sacks before being dumped into the Loire River to drown. Still others were hung from high in the towers of the château in full view of the town. Before long, the battlements, acting as makeshift gibbets, became heavily festooned with body parts for all to see.

Condé witnessed the carnage and smelled the decaying bodies on the wind. When a large crowd gathered in one of the château's courtyards, Condé sat with the royal family as they watched fifty-two nobles executed by decapitation on the block. Francis of Guise directed the gruesome proceedings on horseback, unflinchingly enjoying himself. He ordered the condemned to sing psalms while they awaited their fate. Unable to avert her gaze, Catherine remained erect and transfixed. Condé's only comment seems to have been "If the French know how to mount a rebellion, they also know how to die."[26]

Mary Queen of Scots and France was at Amboise during the bloodletting, yet her whereabouts are not recorded. She had a healthy dislike for carnage, and chances are she excused herself from the "entertainment" on the grounds of ill health. Still, with a large body count and her uncles directly implicated in the bloodbath, Mary cannot have failed to know about the events.

It was against this background that Mary received word of the death of her beloved mother at Leith. By the time Admiral Coligny had undertaken an enquiry into why these "Huguenots" had rebelled, peace between Scotland and England was agreed. The Treaty of Edinburgh provided for the withdrawal of all but a minimal French force in Scotland, bringing France's active role in Scottish politics to an abrupt end. Mary and Francis were to abandon quartering the English arms, though Francis—and later Mary—refused to give in. To do so would be to admit that Mary was not the legal heir to Elizabeth's throne, they claimed.

Within months, two deaths and a pregnancy further changed the course of English and French history. On September 8, Robert Dudley's long-suffering wife, Amy, was found dead in suspicious circumstances at the foot of the stairs in their Cumnor home near Oxford. Dudley was immediately exiled from court, awaiting the outcome of the legal inquiry. Only Cecil—Dudley's longtime adversary—extended the hand of friendship, which Dudley grabbed on to willingly. Whether it was an accident, suicide, or even murder, we shall never know for certain, but Amy's death of a broken neck was highly significant in English affairs. Despite Elizabeth's evident affection and love for Lord Robert, even she recognized that this "stain" on his character could never be erased. Dudley had become unmarriageable. Cecil would write the English ambassador Throckmorton that he was certain that the queen would never be disposed to marry.

While Dudley was exiled from court awaiting the outcome of the inquest into his wife's death, Francis II, king of France, breathed his last on December 5, 1560. He died of an abscess on the brain. Mary Queen of France was now merely Mary Queen of Scots, dowager queen of France. Her little brother-in-law, Maximilien-Charles, became Charles IX. Catherine de' Medici proclaimed herself regent with the blessing of the king of Navarre, since she had agreed to return Navarre's younger brother Condé to him unharmed. The reign of terror of the Guise brothers was, so Catherine believed, at an end.

Mary was just eighteen, a former queen of the only country she could remember and the unwanted queen of the Protestant country of her birth. She had two obvious choices ahead of her: to remain in quiet retreat in France for the rest of her days or return to Scotland. Despite trying to create a third choice—marrying the imbecile and dangerous son and heir of Philip II—Scotland beckoned loudly. Mary's natural half brother, James Stewart, Earl of Moray, had come to France ostensibly on behalf of the Protestant Lords to discuss what might happen if Mary chose to return to Scotland.

Unbeknown to him, one tidbit of gossip he conveyed from the English court would determine that Mary must return home: Catherine Grey, the putative heir from the English Suffolk line to the succession, had married the Earl of Hertford in secret, and she was expecting their first child. Moray elaborated that Elizabeth, outraged that her semiofficial heir should marry without royal consent, had ordered Catherine and Hertford sent to the Tower until further notice.[27]

This made any indecision Mary might have felt evaporate. If Mary wanted to claim the throne of England, she would need to visit her cousin Elizabeth and charm her, just as she had done with everyone she met. Mary resolved to come to England to prove that she was not only the rightful heir to the throne but also a most fitting one.

FIVE

The Battle for Hearts and Minds

For this is man's nature, that where he is persuaded that
there is the power to bring prosperity and adversity,
there will he worship.

—George Gifford, A Discourse of the Subtill
Practices of Devilles by Witches and Sorcerers

I f Elizabeth understood one thing above all else, it was that both she and England were in mortal danger. The apparently innocent appeal of the young Queen Mary to return to Scotland through England seemed to be the most natural and innocuous of requests, but Elizabeth, despite pressure from nearly all her councillors, was not budging. For her, to have the very queen who refused to sign the Treaty of Edinburgh travel the length and breadth of England with her mostly French royal train was a threat she simply was not prepared to take. To have the Scots queen charm England with her beauty, her youth, her French courtly ways, and her silver tongue rankled in every fiber of Elizabeth's body. Eventually Cecil was compelled to write that Her Majesty could "in no wise consent . . . Why should the Queen show any such courtesy considering she [Mary] hath not kept promise in any one thing but always said well and done nothing?"[1] Even had Mary not been a serial breaker of promises, to allow a Catholic queen to travel unchecked among an English population who had not necessarily declared itself either in favor of or against the Elizabethan religious settlement was simply too great a risk.

To make matters worse, Elizabeth saw plots and counterplots within her own nobility and among her councillors. The Suffolk heir to the throne, Lady Catherine Grey, never a favorite of Elizabeth, had been suspected for some while of allowing herself to become embroiled in Spanish plots to overthrow her. In fact, the Spanish ambassador wrote to Philip, "I try to keep Lady Catherine very friendly," as early as November 1559. "And she has promised me," Ambassador de Feria reported, "not to change her religion, nor marry without my consent."[2]

Alas, Catherine Grey did not keep de Feria and his successor, Alvarez de Quadra, informed of her crucial decisions in matters of either religion or the heart. To compound her offenses when they were discovered, she had even managed to foil Elizabeth's own plan to marry her off to Scotland's Earl of Arran in 1560. The queen had opened negotiations with the Scots Lords of the Congregation in the hope of uniting Scotland and England on Elizabeth's own death by marrying the two rival claimant lines to England's throne.[3] Instead, after a clandestine courtship, Catherine Grey married Edward, Earl of Hertford, son of the disgraced Lord Protector Seymour from the reign of Edward VI. To the Elizabethan mind, "the purpose of the toils and perils of lovers should have as their principal aim the conquest of a woman's soul rather than her body."[4] As a queen who had declared that her woman's body was quite separate from the body politic over the Dudley affair, Elizabeth read her own mortal peril into Catherine's marriage to Hertford.

Elizabeth was incandescent. Hertford had escaped to France months earlier, most likely in fear of what would happen once it was discovered that his wife was "with child." When Catherine was eight months pregnant, she was thrown unceremoniously into the Tower of London, where she soon gave birth to her son, Edward, named after his father. However, it would be wrong to think that Elizabeth's harshness to Catherine was just some petty act of vengeance against her putative heir.

Nagging uncomfortably at the back of the queen's mind was whether her nobility—or worse still, Cecil—had had a hand in the match. The Spanish ambassador, de Quadra, was of the opinion that Cecil had been behind Catherine's clandestine marriage and made no secret of his feelings to Elizabeth. Yet there were so many whispered intrigues surrounding

Lady Catherine that the only sensible course of action from Elizabeth's viewpoint was to have the marriage to Hertford annulled by the archbishop of Canterbury and place Catherine in the Tower indefinitely.

Though the "Hertford Affair" had happened months earlier, in Elizabeth's meeting with the Scots ambassador Maitland in September 1561 in London, she reiterated her fears about naming a successor: "So long as I live, I shall be Queen of England. When I am dead, they shall succeed me that have the most right . . . I know the inconstancy of the people of England, how they ever mislike the present government and have their eyes fixed upon that person that is next to succeed. *Plures adorant solem orientalem quam occidentalem.*"[5]

The Latin text holds the key to her thinking. It translates as *More worship the rising than the setting sun.* In this one phrase is encompassed all the scheming and plotting that surrounds a hopeful heir, whose youth, vigor, and vitality pose a threat to the reigning monarch. Elizabeth would never waver from this viewpoint and actually made it illegal to mention the succession in 1571. It seems incredible that her council and nobility refused to take her at her word on this absolutely fixed point.

Still, the succession mattered, not only to those at court but also to the people at large. They were being asked to accept rapid changes thrust upon them by the Act of Settlement and Uniformity in religious matters, where the monarch reigned supreme over church as well as state. This meant, of course, that the monarch affected each and every life with her whims and fancies and demanded her subjects' utter loyalty. Loyalty, however, depended in large part on the individual's religious convictions, status in society, and geographical location.

The nobles were fairly easy for Elizabeth to comprehend, just as it was reasonable to expect them to accept whatever the queen decided. It was, after all, the way of life at court. Though the Tudors were noted for their recognition of service by merit—often rewarding the Tudor "new men"—

their nobility represented only a very small fraction of society. Many followed Elizabeth's itinerant court between her palaces. The queen knew full well that they all sought preferment and that their oaths of allegiance tripped as easily off the tongue as silent conspiracies could be hatched. They simply needed watching, and Cecil had already made a start on what would become the longest surviving of the Elizabethan secret services, with many eyes and ears strategically placed to pick up the slightest whiff of a plot against her.

The English merchant classes were another matter entirely. Most of the royal palaces were situated in and around London, which increased trade significantly in the capital and helped maintain it as the realm's largest city, with the Thames as its major thoroughfare.[6] City life created new opportunities for advancement either at court or in trade, but London remained rife with disease and criminality. Even the Puritan "godly" worshipping at St. Paul's were not immune from the sacrilegious goings-on within its walls. In 1561, "the south alley" so scandalized a provincial bishop that he wrote home that it "is used for popery and usury, the north for simony, and the horse fair in the midst for all kinds of bargains, meetings, brawling, murders, conspiracies, and the font for ordinary payment of money, as well known to all men as the beggar knows his bush."[7] The foremost house of prayer in the City was a house of worship as much as it was a den of iniquity and home to booksellers touting clandestine censored books as well as ballads, pamphlets, and holy hymn sheets licensed by the Stationer's Register.

Though still a walled city, London had long before spilled out beyond its protective gates: to the north, east, and west were Aldersgate, Cripplegate, Moorgate, Bishopsgate, and Aldgate, with the royal palace of the Tower of London to the south, bordering the Thames. When the Bow Bell sounded, the gates creaked shut and the bellmen set out on their patrol, calling out the hour with the warning:

> *Remember the clocks,*
> *Look well to your locks,*
> *Fire and your light,*

And God give you good night
For now the bell ringeth.[8]

Yet most English men and women lived in the countryside, the bulk of them yeomanry or peasants. Most of them were removed from much of the hurly-burly of England's larger regional cities. They lived according to the agrarian calendar, often buffeted by the winds. Their country traditions had long been muddled between pagan ritual and ecclesiastical rite, with saints' days rather than the day and the month holding more meaning to the average Elizabethan. "St. Hilarytide" meant January 13, just as "St. Georgetide" indicated April 23. "Whitsuntide" was both a pagan holiday and the festival commemorating the mystery of Pentecost and the descent of the Holy Ghost, and while it remained a solemn celebration for the religious, Whit Sunday, fifty days after Easter, was also a time of community merrymaking and feasts for reveling, with Whitsun church cakes and ales served.

Though outlawed with the Elizabethan religious settlement, telling the time of year by saints' days remained the common practice. Days that were pagan in origin, like Midsummer Day, sometimes called St. John's Day, on June 24, had been masquerading as holy days for over a millennium. In Elizabeth's England, they came under government scrutiny as an unacceptably pagan solar festival in Romish disguise. Barnaby Googe attacked the St. John's Day festivities of "bonfires and floral garlands . . . as popish relics."[9]

Ecclesiastical holy days—or red-letter days in the calendar—were struck off at a stroke with the Elizabethan settlement, with the result that the days off from work were reduced by nearly half. "Our holy and festival days," according to the Elizabethan chronicler and country parson William Harrison, "we had under the Pope four score and fifteen called festival, and thirty *profesti* [minor festivals], beside the Sundays, they are all brought unto seven and twenty; and with them the superfluous numbers of idle wakes, guilds, fraternities, church ales, help ales, and soul ales, called also dirge ales, with the heathenish rioting at bride ales, are well diminished and laid aside."[10]

All too soon, the preferred country way of celebrating just about anything in the calendar with cakes and ale would become abhorrent to the new Protestant pious, as Shakespeare's memorable line in *Twelfth Night* reminds us: "Dost thou think, because thou art virtuous, there shall be no more cakes and ale?"[11] In some parishes, maypoles were relegated to an ignominious reuse as parish ladders. Garlands remained unpicked in the meadows. Still, despite official censure of the custom of merrymaking with cakes and ale, as well as loud fireworks (the louder the better) and bonfires, these would remain steadfast features of country life, just as the hills and valleys remained constant in the landscape.

Along with the country ways went magic and superstition. The English read their weather from the behavior of the animals, from the turning color of the leaves, and from the skies and stars. Astrology was a booming trade, with local astrologers charging their townspeople as much as a shilling to foretell where a lost cow or mare had strayed off to. Everyone looked to the stars to help decipher the uncertain future, and many believed in a harmonious "music of the spheres" where, unlike in Shakespeare's *Hamlet,* the time was *not* out of joint.[12] For the average Elizabethan, if there was discord in the planets, life on earth would become most distinctly "out of joint."

All these long-held belief systems did not sit easily with the new religion Elizabeth sought to give her people. Though outwardly everything seemed to be the same, within the church, life was different. Vicars and bishops inveighed against the seasonal rituals and feasts as heathen practices, spawned by the bishop of Rome, the Antichrist. Papists, as the Roman Catholics were called by the Tudor Protestants throughout Elizabeth's reign, blamed the age-old pagan customs for the poor morals of the people. "I never commanded," preached William Keth from his parish pulpit in Dorset, "your candles at Candlemas, your popish penance on Ash Wednesday, your eggs and bacon on Good Friday, your gospels at superstitious crosses decked like idols, your fires at Midsummer, and your ringing [of church bells] at Hallowtide for all Christian souls."[13]

What Elizabeth had sought to create was security and stability through the Protestant faith that would replace all the controversy and rhetoric of the previous fifty years. However, this stability was bought at the cost of local customs and generations of homegrown magical ways of making sense of the world in which the English lived. The change, if it was to be successful, she believed, would need to be swift, like the removal of a bandage from an oozing sore.

Visitations of parish churches by bishops were well under way within a year of the religious settlement passing into law. The "visitors" would ask the local parish vicar "whether any holy days or fasting days heretofore abrogated . . . be superstitiously observed." Moving on from there, they inquired if there was any "superfluous ringing on All Saints' Day at night, or on the following day, of old superstitiously called All Souls' Day." Ministers answering yes would find themselves censured as surely as if they allowed licentious church ales to continue unabated.[14]

Altars were stripped, their rood screens demolished, and the saintly images painstakingly painted onto the walls of every church and set into stained glass wherever possible were erased with lavish coats of whitewash. Liturgical vestments and ornaments were burned or smashed. Commissioners ensuring that the realm's parishes complied with the Act of Settlement of 1559 were sworn in. Presiding in the county of Lincoln, Bishop Nicholas Bullingham ordered his commission to visit 180 parishes in the months of March and April 1566. The records of these visitations survive to this day. What emerges is a litany of rampant destruction, the fate of every image, book, vessel, and ornament used in Catholic worship being accounted for. From the rood and altar stones down to the cruets and towels, everything was punctiliously inscribed. Even the names of those attending the visitations were noted down. What emerges from the Lincolnshire visitations some eight years into Elizabeth's reign is a reluctance of the inhabitants to abandon all their touchstones of Catholicism coupled with a lack of enthusiasm for the process of reform. At Ashby near Horncastle in Lincolnshire, the parish proved exceptionally recalcitrant in "defacing of all papistry" until absolutely forced to do so by Bishop Bullingham, when he "caused his men to rive . . . in pieces" all manner of books and candlesticks.[15]

As late as 1568, the rood lofts still stood at Chichester, or were laid by in readiness to be reconstructed. All "trifling trumpery for the sinful service of the popish priest . . . feigned fables and peltering popish books" were targeted for mass destruction, and yet the "old ways" prevailed without the benefit of their accoutrements.[16] The men carrying out the visitations could take away the objects, but they couldn't stop the people from retaining an element of the pagan or Catholic magical past.

One of the sticking points in the minds of the English was that the Anglican Church denied the claim disseminated by Roman Catholicism that God's grace could be manipulated for earthly causes. "That which we call fortune," wrote Thomas Cooper, an Elizabethan bishop, "is nothing but the hand of God, working by causes and for causes that we know not. Chance or fortune are [sic] gods devised by man and made by our ignorance of the true, almighty and everlasting God."[17]

Lay people persisted in the mingling of Catholic magic and its supernatural miracles with special divine providences as taught by the new Anglican Church. Their social belief systems were based on an uneasy mélange of superstition, witchcraft, philosophy, and the new science of medicine. The clergy frequently lamented that it was "scarce credible" how miserably "our common ignorants are besotted" with the opinions of "charmers, fortune-tellers, wizards and cunning men" and "how pitifully they are gulled by their damnable impostures, through their own foolish credulity."[18]

Any parish worth its salt had its own miracle worker, wise woman, white witch, or astrologer—all of whom claimed that they could "cure" what ailed body or soul. With many of these practitioners claiming to have derived their powers from Adam or Moses or the Archangel Raphael, thereby linking themselves to the ancient religious past, they gained common and easy currency in the eyes of the people. After all, the old Roman Catholic Mass with its healing power of the saints and their relics had long performed a magical repertory for the faithful, and the people had been robbed of its enchantment by the Protestant Reformation. These "cozeners," or deceivers, gave comfort and a necessary link to the past that the Elizabethan settlement strove hard to sever. If Elizabeth's church was to win the hearts and minds of her people, something needed to be done.

. . .

Somehow Elizabethan clergy had to unite the notions of popular magic into religion through the worship of God and prayer, rather than allow the common "charmers" to hijack the people's need to worship with superstition. Essentially, they needed an improved education system; and it was the Lord Keeper and Lord Privy Seal Sir Nicholas Bacon, William Cecil's brother-in-law, who devised the solution and set it into practice. Bacon had been excluded from meaningful office during Mary I's reign due to his Protestant leanings. By the time Elizabeth ascended the throne, he had become absorbed in the benefits of educational planning, scientific and literary patronage, and classical studies. These would continue to be his primary interests beyond his fully active political career until his death in 1579.

What Bacon recognized was that "the chief thing . . . in wardship is the ward's mind."[19] Bacon had originally submitted his plans for educating young wards who came under the influence of the Master of the Court of Wards to Sir Francis Englefield under Mary, but it was only when Cecil held the post in 1561 that the mass education plan for "the better sort" was accepted.

Under Bacon's plan, all male wards whose lands were worth in excess of £100 annually and who were at least nine years old were to be enrolled into an academy, where they would be taught Latin, Greek, French and other modern languages, music, and physical education and practice regular Christian devotions. Throughout their twelve years at the academy, these boys would learn the fundamentals of common law, martial arts, horsemanship, and the other social requirements for young gentlemen.

Yet, his plan didn't stop there. Bacon recognized that many of these elite young gentlemen neglected their studies, not seeing how very lucky they had been. The yeomanry in the countryside craved the same opportunities but had been denied them. His solution was to establish a grammar school at Redgrave in Suffolk, where he lived, specifically to meet the needs of the young country lads. Though far less was expected of them than of the young gentlemen, Bacon was explicit that students should be firmly taught to read and write in English and Latin and that they would benefit from a firm hand. The same level of Christian devotions was expected of these boys as of the wealthier wards, though training in horsemanship and weaponry was vastly scaled down to the proper use of the longbow. Naturally girls were excluded from the plan, as what they needed to learn for a fruitful life could be taught in the home.

Bacon went on to refound the grammar school at Bury St. Edmunds, supervise the founding of a new grammar school at St. Albans, and endow Corpus Christi College at Cambridge with six scholarships and money for the college chapel. The intent was for his grammar school boys to be elevated to the new vision for England, as expressed by the new Anglican Church, and to spread the word among their fellow parishioners. In other words, Sir Nicholas believed that by mass education, at home and within the parish as well as at universities, superstition and Roman Catholicism could be eradicated at a stroke. What Bacon did in East Anglia was replicated by other privy councillors throughout the land, most notably by Robert Dudley in the Welsh Marches and the Midlands, where he was the chancellor of the University of Oxford.

Of course, mass education took a long while to take hold, and it was still limited to boys, and further to boys from yeoman families "in good standing." Still, it was a beginning.

Near the beginning of Elizabeth's reign in 1561, it is estimated that as much as 85 percent of the population could neither read nor write. This meant Elizabeth and her clergy were well aware that although the new Book of Common Prayer was placed in every pew that year, few could read the words, much less understand their meaning. The government's solution to the literacy problem came in the unusual guise of Foxe's *Acts and Monuments*, which recounted the tales of the Protestant martyrs. It became the duty of those who were fortunate enough to have been taught to read to ensure that those who couldn't would be able to hear them recite the tales aloud instead. Every parish church held several copies, and this little book alone, which touched people's everyday lives, became the cornerstone of literacy throughout the realm. By the end of Elizabeth's reign in 1603, literacy would reach levels never before thought imaginable, with some communities boasting a literacy rate in excess of

60 percent. While the queen maintained that she did not wish to make windows into men's souls, she was determined to fill their minds with the words she wanted them to hear.

Over the ensuing years, the common peddler, or "chapman," became a familiar sight trudging along the highways and byways of England, selling wares from linen to ballads and chapbooks. These were essentially pamphlets printed cheaply and destined for the masses. Those who bought them learned the ballads sung to familiar tunes of old about social ills or reform or godly works and often hung them on their walls as decoration. The image of the Protestant martyr, unsurprisingly, was among the most popular ballads, as it repeated the images engraved into the public psyche by Foxe's *Acts and Monuments*.

Yet in the 1560s, both ballads and chapbooks were fast becoming a blunt instrument written by rural dissenters claiming that the Elizabethan settlement hadn't gone far enough to eradicate "popery." Surprisingly, it was from the voices of the Protestant dissenters that the next unseen threat to Elizabeth's England would arise.

Still, in the fast-changing landscapes of 1562, Elizabeth's main task remained far more complex than a reeducation of the English to win their hearts and minds. Peace at home and the security of the realm depended on her ability to play off the powers of the papacy, Spain, France, and Scotland against one another rather than allowing them to join forces against England. By January that year, Pope Pius IV had caved in to Philip II's demands that the Council of Trent should be a continuation of the abandoned council of 1545, rather than a new council that would give Protestant states a clearer voice in a reconciliation of the Christian faiths. In February, the archbishop of Milan wrote to the Holy Roman Emperor's nuncio that "the decision come to by the Assembly of France . . . to allow the Huguenots no more respite, and not to suffer them to preach in walled towns, albeit they say they must needs connive at their conventicles outside the cities," making for grim reading when intercepted by Cecil's spies.[20]

By March a call went out from the pope to Europe's monarchs for their representatives at the Council of Trent to make their way there. This would be the council's third sitting, which would eventually welcome over two hundred bishops.[21] That same month, Elizabeth sent an ambassador to Paris with a message to Catherine de' Medici offering her support and her good offices as mediator between the Catholic Guise faction, the young king's and Catherine's loyal supporters, and the Huguenots. When Pius IV heard of Elizabeth's offer, he penned a consiliatory letter to Catherine. In it, the pope begged the dowager queen to give guidance to England's heretic sovereign. Surely, if Elizabeth sought mediation between the Christian faiths, he added pursuasively, the English queen could only achieve her ends by sending a representative to Trent. While Pius IV awaited news of his entreaty, the cardinal archbishop of Milan wrote to the papal legate in France that "England remaining thus oppressed by the heretics, it is to be feared that there will be constant correspondence between them and the rebels and heretics of France and other neighboring countries, whereby heresies and rebellions will be propagated in all the surrounding states."[22]

Elizabeth responded to the papal request by asking for a prorogation of the council. She claimed to be "excited by the opinion expressed" and "waxed much more ardently" about how she needed the prorogation in order to organize representation there.[23] In fact, Elizabeth was merely playing for time.

Word had reached Elizabeth that Lady Margaret Douglas, Countess of Lennox, was militating for her son Henry, Lord Darnley, to marry the Scots queen. In Lady Margaret's view, as the daughter of the eldest sister of Henry VIII, the marriage of her son to Queen Mary would create an undeniably strong entitlement to succeed to the English throne. Naturally, Elizabeth was apoplectic with rage, ordering Cecil to quash without delay any claim Lady Margaret's descendants could possibly make. Cecil dutifully wrote to Lord Randolph, the Scottish Protestant leader, to obtain the proof "bearing upon the papal annulment of the marriage between Lady Margaret's father and mother."[24]

At the same time, Cecil persuaded Elizabeth that she should attempt a rapprochement with Mary. Talk of "an interview" between the cousins was first mooted from Scotland at the end of 1561, after the first proposal of marriage by Lady Margaret on behalf of her son to Mary. While the English response is missing from the archives, Cecil wrote on New Year's Eve that he found "a great desire in both these Queens to have an interview, and knowing the diversity of both their intents, although I wish it yet I think it dangerous to be any singular dealer therein."[25] In other words, he smelled a double-cross.

He wasn't the only one. The Scottish Protestant Lords were unhappy to learn that their queen was sending a number of prelates to the council at Trent without "the concurrence of the realm, which is indeed wholly alienated, insomuch that Mass is said nowhere except in the Queen's own house." In fact, the papal newsletter of April 6, 1562, goes on to state that Mary "will certainly send thither someone to represent herself, and testify at least to her good intention of living in the religion of her forefathers, which cannot fail to be a great help towards the more ready settlement of the affairs of that kingdom."[26] The papal view was that as Mary was firmly ensconced on her Scots throne, she should "take for her model Mary Queen of England, of pious memory, and she will receive all the support that the Pope and the Catholic Princes can render her."[27]

Meanwhile, Catherine de' Medici was facing a direct challenge to her young son's rule. The Guise faction was now backed by Philip II. The Spanish king disapproved of Catherine's earlier attempts at reconciliation with the Huguenots through the Colloquy of Poissy the previous summer, and he feared that Protestantism was gaining ground in France. As Philip stepped up his campaign for Catherine to clamp down on the rampant spread of Protestantism, Louis de Condé was the first to lead the Huguenot noblemen to treat Catherine as "our Queen" and make countless professions of loyalty to her and the child king, Charles IX.[27]

Then something entirely predictable, yet unexpected, happened. The Duke of Guise rode out with his armed escort on the morning of Sunday, March 1, to hear Mass in the town of Vassy, which belonged to his niece Mary Queen of Scots. While at Mass, the sound of voices singing from a nearby barn within the town could be heard through the stone church walls. Unlike the approved Mass he heard, the voices wafting to his ears sang the illegal and forbidden Protestant service. As the voices of the Protestant psalm singers rose, so did the duke's temper. Though he later claimed that he had not instigated hostilities, the duke and his men were clearly the aggressors. The only survivors of the "regrettable accident" were, of course, Guise and his followers, who stated that angry words flared into a violent struggle between the Huguenots and his men. Seventy-four Protestants were killed and over a hundred wounded. Women and children were slaughtered. Guise himself received a cut across his cheek that scarred him for life. The "regrettable accident" became known as the Massacre of Vassy, and it would spark off the first religious war in France, a war that would embolden Elizabeth to try to retake Calais.

SIX

Untrustworthy Allies

❦

*England remaining thus oppressed by the heretics, it is
to be feared that there will be constant correspondence
between them and the rebels and heretics of France
and other neighboring countries.*

—Charles Borromeo, archbishop of Milan, to the
French legate, March 1562

Before word of the atrocity at Vassy reached Catherine de'
Medici, civil war in France was on everyone's lips. The outspoken English ambassador, Nicholas Throckmorton, urged
English intervention on the side of the Huguenots to Cecil, particularly as Spain had removed most of its troops from the Netherlands
to fight the greater threat of the Ottoman Turk in the Mediterranean the
previous year. His letter to Cecil of April 10, 1562, ordered, "Besides severe
looking to the subjects at home to cut off and prevent practices and conventicles, you must animate and solicit the Princes Protestant with speed
by all means you can not to suffer the Protestants to be in this realm
[France] suppressed."[1] Throckmorton urged an English intervention, particularly since a new, effective leader of the Huguenot faction had
emerged, a prince of royal blood—Louis, Prince de Condé, battle hardy
and able to pursue the French Protestant cause by force of arms.

Within two weeks of Throckmorton's letter, Condé sent an envoy to
England, Monsieur des Sechelles, an ardent, Bible-bashing emissary with
pressing letters for Cecil. Des Sechelles's prime purpose in coming to En-

gland was to invite Elizabeth's intervention in the Huguenot struggle on
Condé's behalf. The Frenchman argued that the cost of English support
of Condé's cause would be a mere snip at a hundred thousand crowns.
There would be no need for an English army to support them, at least not
yet. Oddly, no minutes of the high-level meetings with des Sechelles were
taken, nor is it known who was in attendance. The mission was shrouded
in the utmost secrecy. Cecil broke his silence, writing to Throckmorton
on April 24 that he was hoping to send an English emissary to broker a
peace between Condé's elder brother, the king of Navarre, and the queen
mother of France. Nonetheless, Cecil added, he held out little expectation
of Elizabeth's compliance with the plan.

Then suddenly, four days after Cecil sent his letter, Sir Henry Sidney,
Robert Dudley's brother-in-law, was dispatched to France to negotiate a
peace. That Sidney had been selected for this highly sensitive mission was
no quirk of fate. He had been specifically chosen by Sir Robert Dudley
with the personal blessing of Elizabeth. Dudley's interest in French affairs
was part of a much larger, complex puzzle of bluff and double-bluff with
the Spanish ambassador, de Quadra, who had been working as Dudley's
hopeful puppet-master. It was de Quadra's primary objective to "turn"
Dudley to betray the English Protestant cause if the Spanish king would
favor him as Elizabeth's husband. However, de Quadra hadn't reckoned
on a betrayal within his own household by his secretary, Borghese Venturini, instigated by Cecil.

There are two versions of the tale: the first from de Quadra to Philip II
and the Duchess of Parma; the second from Cecil to Thomas Chaloner, the
English ambassador in Spain. In Cecil's version to Chaloner, Borghese Venturini betrayed his master because he believed that de Quadra was dedicated to international Catholic interests rather than Spain's. In other words,
de Quadra set the pope above Philip. De Quadra's version of events makes
more sense: Borghese loved living extravagantly, and his loyalty was purchased by Cecil, who was prepared to support that lifestyle. What Borghese "sold" was how the Spanish embassy in London functioned: who
precisely attended Mass at the embassy on Sunday; who came and went on
state business; what the latest Spanish thinking was; and most significantly,
how de Quadra was inciting English Catholics to rise up for the Spanish

cause. Lastly, Borghese told Cecil about de Quadra's long and intricate intrigue with Dudley to obtain England's throne as Elizabeth's consort.

This revelation should have sent Dudley to the Tower and had de Quadra recalled. Yet nothing of the sort happened. There were no letters of admonition from Cecil against Dudley, no urging by Elizabeth to have de Quadra recalled. There were some raised voices, barely cries, over de Quadra's meddling with English Catholics, but nothing more. Most telling, de Quadra alone was discredited.

This curious espionage episode had several noteworthy outcomes. The first concerned Dudley. Since he was not cast out of Elizabeth's inner circle, as had been the case after his wife's mysterious death, we can only assume that Cecil and the queen had been party to Dudley's alleged flirtation with Catholicism and de Quadra's clumsy attempts to "turn" him to Spain's advantage. The second outcome was that by keeping de Quadra in place as the enemy the Privy Council knew, they had utterly neutralized him and his policies. The third outcome was to make Cecil the putative head of a fledgling Elizabethan secret service. This "secret service"—one of several in the years that lay ahead—would become the principal tool in unmasking all manner of threat against the crown.

On a personal level, Cecil could lay to one side any pretense that de Quadra was his friend. In the revelations by Borghese, all of de Quadra's poison against "the heretic" Cecil had also been laid bare. Cecil wrote to the Spanish ambassador that "as an Englishman sprung from no ignoble race," he would "by every lawful means uphold his own dignity." Not only was Cecil defending himself against de Quadra's slurs, but he also upheld the dignity of Robert Dudley and Elizabeth.[2]

Consequently it was against the backdrop of this intrigue by the Spanish embassy in England that an emboldened Sir Henry Sidney met the English ambassador in France at the beginning of May 1562. His mission, as laid out by Cecil, was simple. The queen's purpose was strictly to restore the peace, and in the event that there was any meddling of foreign princes in France's internal affairs, she would protect England's position by force of arms. The threat was clear. If Catherine allowed Spain to intervene on behalf of the French crown, England would retake its former staple town of Calais. Robert Dudley's message to Throckmorton put this French spin on Elizabeth's interest in country's misfortunes when he wrote, "She [Elizabeth] doth not so much measure common policy as she doth weigh the prosperity of true religion, as well to the world as for conscience sake."[3] Politics was, as ever, about religion.

Sidney's mission would reinforce this. He made no headway at court, perhaps because of Throckmorton's outspoken viewpoint that the English should mount an armed intervention in France. By the time the mission was over, Sidney's contacts with the Huguenot leaders had become solid, even cordial. When Sidney returned a month later, Throckmorton's favored plan of sending men to Newhaven (Le Havre) or Dieppe to assist Condé militarily against a future exchange for Calais had become Dudley's favored course of action, too.

The letter from Throckmorton to Cecil of May 2, 1562, is more significant for its foresight twenty years into the future than for wise counsel at the time:

> She [Elizabeth] must ally herself with the Protestants in every country through the bond and contract of religion. And when she shall have in this country [France] as many well-willers for religion and ability then her Majesty is one of the best assured and established princes in her state and therewith one of the strongest in Europe.[4]

Catherine de' Medici saw all overtures of "peace" through Elizabeth's good auspices as a trap. Though the queen mother tried to restore the peace by republishing her Edict of St. Germain on April 16, 1562, allowing the Huguenots to preach wherever they liked—albeit not within a league of Paris—she soon found that this solution was obnoxious to the papacy and Spain.[5] Like Elizabeth, Catherine wanted to find a middle way to make peace with her warring people. Unlike Elizabeth, she had failed to grasp the harsh reality that Protestant reformers had categorically rejected the two principal tenets of the Roman Catholic Church: the Eucharist and papal authority.

Pope Pius IV, meanwhile, fretted that an English intervention in France would tip the scales in Condé's favor. This possibility, combined with Elizabeth's steadfast refusal to name Mary Stuart as her heir, compelled Pius to write through the archbishop of Milan to the Guise faction:

> *England remaining thus oppressed by the heretics, it is to be feared that there will be constant correspondence between them and the rebels and heretics of France and other neighboring countries, whereby heresies and rebellions will be propagated in all the surrounding states . . . [Therefore] His Holiness will not fail to support the Queen of Scotland's claims to the succession to the throne of England by all such means as shall be deemed necessary to the end that the Catholic religion may be re-established in that kingdom.*[6]

Louis, cardinal of Lorraine, one of Mary's uncles, hastened to Rome after the papal will had been made explicit by this letter. Shortly after his arrival, a report was received that Lyon had fallen to the Huguenots and that a thousand Catholics had been slaughtered in the churches in which they had taken refuge. Days later, word of another atrocity reached the pope: The Huguenots had taken Rouen and unroofed the church. The lead used to cover the ridges and valleys of the roof would be sold off, so the papal legate wrote, for some 20,000 francs in order to pay for the Huguenot wages and arms.[7]

Elizabeth, counseled by Dudley, sent Edward Horsey back to France to see if there was any mileage in assisting the Huguenots in securing the key port towns of Newhaven and Dieppe from the French crown.[8] The roads and waters to Newhaven were blocked by royal troops, so Horsey diverted to Dieppe, arriving safely in June 1562. One of his agents, the resourceful Peter Adryan, headed inland to Rouen, where Condé claimed he was in sore need of relief. Horsey reported back to Elizabeth that Condé only wanted money and that he remained confident he could maintain Newhaven and Dieppe without foreign intervention. Adryan thought that Rouen was in the greatest danger of falling, but Horsey concluded that the city was too far inland to serve England's purpose.

Both men had assessed the situation clearly. By late June, Condé pressed his request for a 100,000-crown loan from England once more, this time acknowledging that he needed men as well. Sir Thomas Wroth was sent to Germany "with speed" to raise an army of mercenaries, stipulating that the German princes should contribute men and arms paid for by England. Elizabeth agreed. She could support Condé and his Huguenots with cash while appearing not to meddle. It was a formula she would employ many times in the years to come.

Meanwhile, de Quadra, bereft of influence and intelligence, reported that Elizabeth had called an emergency meeting of her Privy Council on July 17 to discuss the worsening situation in France and the intervention of the English navy with troops into Normandy. No such meeting was ever reported to have taken place, yet Cecil did issue a memorandum of that same date. In it, he makes England's intention to go to war clear. Local justices of the peace were warned to guard against uprisings; southern and eastern counties were ordered to levy troops; merchant ships were called upon to provide transport; a general at the head of an army of ten thousand men was to be appointed, and another envoy was dispatched to Germany. Three days later, Cecil issued another memorandum, entitled *The Perils Growing upon the Overthrow of the Prince of Condé's Cause*:

> The whole regiment of the crown of France shall be in the hands of the Guisans; and to maintain their faction they will pleasure the King of Spain in all that they may. Hereupon shall follow a complot betwixt them two, to advance their own private causes; the King of Spain to unable the House of Navarre for ever from claiming the kingdom of Navarre; the House of Guise to promote their niece, the Queen of Scots, to the crown of England . . . and . . . the realm of Ireland to be given in a prey to the King of Spain.
>
> In this meantime all the Papists in England shall be solicited not to stir, but to confirm their faction with comfort, to gather money and to be ready to stir at one instant when some foreign force shall be ready to assail this realm or Ireland. Whosoever thinketh that relenting in religion will assuage the Guisans' aspirations, they are far deceived.[9]

For England, it was an invidious situation. To do nothing was not an option, and to venture forward was extremely risky. When Condé's envoy arrived in July 1562 to plead for ten thousand men this time, the choices available to England were narrowed. Besides, Throckmorton had become a liability in Paris with his undisguised hawkish behavior and was recalled at the end of the month. He was replaced by the diplomat Sir Thomas Smith, who was far better at keeping his own counsel. By the end of August, a "secret" course of action had been decided upon. The Earl of Warwick, Robert Dudley's elder brother Ambrose, would lead a fighting force of six thousand footmen to help the beleaguered Huguenot forces at Newhaven, leaving Admiral Coligny in charge of Dieppe.

Yet throughout this fraught period of negotiation and soul-searching, one thing was evident: Elizabeth now favored direct action. According to the ubiquitous de Quadra, "The Queen was quite furious at the Council, and replied to some of those who opposed the expedition that if they were so much afraid that the consequences of failure would fall upon them she herself would take all the risk and would sign her name to it."[10]

Of course Condé dangled the possibility of England's regaining Calais, but that was secondary. Elizabeth feared a Catholic or Guise victory in France would lead to an emboldened English Catholic population, just when the first green shoots of her religious settlement were becoming apparent. Religious unrest in France was tantamount to a clear and present danger within England itself.

The triumvirate that would dictate English policy until peace could be secured would be Queen Elizabeth herself, Sir Robert Dudley, and William Cecil. Dudley and his brother Ambrose would provide the military "expertise," Cecil the administrative backup, and, of course, the queen would mastermind the foreign missions—both official and unofficial. It fell to Cecil to watch and neutralize the inveterate conspirator de Quadra. Once again, the Spanish ambassador would fare rather badly in his next brush with Cecil's fledgling secret service.

It was a combination of De Quadra's natural arrogance and Cecil's bravura that led the events in the autumn and winter of 1562–63. Starved of firsthand information from the battlefront in France, de Quadra hungered to become the focal point of his king's attentions once more. Most of our knowledge of what transpired at the English court in this period comes from de Quadra's angry dispatches to Spain and how he presented Philip's strongest protests against Elizabeth's invasion of France. He harangued Cecil repeatedly that England's only interest in French affairs was Elizabeth's desire to regain Calais. Cecil replied angrily that England would have never lost Calais in the first place if Philip hadn't prevailed on his lovelorn wife, Mary, to support his own wars in France in 1557–58.

None of this is surprising, but what happened in January 1563 is.

De Quadra gave refuge to the would-be assassin of an Italian officer at the Spanish embassy, then at Durham Place on the Strand in London. Somehow de Quadra himself became involved in a street brawl as his servants locked the doors of the embassy behind the assassin and drove the crowds away. Meanwhile, the fugitive was directed to the water gate of the embassy opening out onto the Thames and escaped by boat. Unfortunately for de Quadra, the man was captured a short time later. Within hours the incident was reported to Elizabeth personally, who ordered the locks on the water gate changed and the only set of new keys brought to the Queen's Keeper.

On January 7, de Quadra lodged a complaint before the Privy Council. The Duke of Norfolk presided, and the Spanish ambassador remained confident that his complaint would be upheld. Cecil replied on behalf of the queen. He pointed out that the would-be assassin had been a constant visitor to the Spanish embassy, had often received his meat and drink from the ambassador, had attended Mass there as many foreign Catholics did, and, most importantly, while in hiding in the embassy on the day of the attempted murder, held a private audience with de Quadra in his private chambers. Cecil went on to explain how the Spanish embassy made use of its private water gate to create mayhem in the city, with the perpetrators escaping through the embassy and onto the Thames. He read out a litany of known and notorious traitors and conspirators against the queen, including the most recent attempt against Elizabeth's life by Arthur Pole, the unfortunate nephew of Cardinal Reginald Pole, who proclaimed himself king of England as a direct descendant of Edward IV's brother the Duke of Clarence. Cecil, though never saying as much, had evidently placed a number of people within the Spanish embassy to spy on the ambassador.

Even if Norfolk had been sympathetic, with such overwhelming evidence against de Quadra, he was left no alternative but to do as the queen wished in the circumstances. The Spanish ambassador was offered suitable quarters—without a water gate—elsewhere in London, while Elizabeth wrote a scathing letter recounting the whole disgraceful affair to Philip. She demanded he either put a stop to de Quadra's ceaseless plotting or recall him at once. It had taken three separate incidents to completely neutralize the Spaniard: the pseudo-Catholic plot of Arthur Pole in 1562, the affairs of Borghese Venturini, and, finally, the refugee assassin.

For the sin of having been discovered and humiliated, Philip made the uncharitable decision of leaving de Quadra in London but without further pay. When the Spaniard died in August 1563, he was so heavily in debt that local tradesmen took possession of the body, refusing to release it until they were paid. Two years after he died, his body was secreted back to Spain for burial.

While Cecil was unmasking the Spanish ambassador in the autumn of 1562, the news from France was bleak. Rouen was in danger of falling, and Dieppe's weak fortifications meant that the likelihood of its holding out was remote. All Huguenot efforts would be reduced to the sole stronghold of Newhaven, where the English reinforced Coligny's men. Throckmorton had entered Condé's service, allegedly as a free agent, but reported back to Elizabeth in December that "the Prince is weary of warfare and inclineth wholly to the Queen Mother's affections."[11]

Elizabeth ordered that Warwick and his men must remain within the walls of Newhaven, since if they were to break out and relieve Dieppe or even Rouen, it could be construed as an overt act of war against an anointed king, Catherine's young son, Charles IX. So that her intervention should not be misunderstood, Elizabeth sent word to her ambassador in Spain, Thomas Chaloner, to explain to Philip II England's worries and why she had been obliged to intervene in French affairs.

Then disaster hit. Elizabeth was struck down with smallpox. For three weeks she hovered between life and death. To the entire court's distress, she named Robert Dudley as Lord Protector in the event of her death. So they prayed for her survival. While she personally believed in and felt his loyalty, others in power remained extremely doubtful. The English people, too, held bad memories of "protectorship" at the hands of Dudley's father, Northumberland. They, too, prayed loudly for the queen's full recovery. For the English, it was their act of faith and prayer that allowed Elizabeth to survive unscathed.

By the time the queen had recovered, relations between the allies were near breaking point. The Huguenots had finally lost Rouen during her illness, and they blamed Elizabeth personally for her impossible order to keep her forces within Newhaven's city walls. Both Condé and Coligny turned against the garrison. They looked to Catherine de' Medici to sue for peace. Abandoned by their untrustworthy allies, the English were left to face an exceptionally harsh winter under constant threat of attack from disgruntled Huguenot forces or the French, both funded by the king of Spain.

Then the Battle of Dreux took place. The Prince of Condé was taken prisoner along with the former ambassador Throckmorton. Command of the Huguenot forces fell to Admiral Coligny, who was a far superior soldier to his predecessor. He persuaded Elizabeth in short order to supply more money and men, and this time, Elizabeth agreed immediately. However, by the time the money to pay Coligny's mercenaries arrived in February 1563, it was all over. The leader of the Catholic forces, Francis, Duke of Guise, had been assassinated by a Huguenot sympathizer named Poltrot de Mérey, who may well have been in the pay of Coligny.[12]

...

The political, if not religious, landscape had changed. Catherine de' Medici was doing all in her substantial power to woo the Huguenots back to the crown of France without the able command of Francis of Guise. On March 10, Condé, while still a prisoner of the French crown, came to terms with the queen mother, ignoring all that Coligny hoped to achieve, and leaving the English in charge of the fortress town of Newhaven, uncertain of their role.

Elizabeth eventually ordered Ambrose Dudley to surrender, but only if England could regain Calais. By June, even that bluster was nothing but a hollow threat. Plague had struck the garrison, and the English were dying at a rate of seventy-five men a day. They were out of food, and their communications to the rest of France had been cut off. A rescue by sea had been hoped for but never came. Finally, on July 27, Elizabeth authorized Warwick's surrender. The French allowed him and his surviving men to return home. Though abandoned by the Huguenots and decimated by plague, the English had held out, but their return would spread the plague along the south coast of England up to London as if by some divine retribution for the invasion of France.

From London, Elizabeth composed her "Prayer Wisdom in the Administration of the Kingdom" in which she begged the Lord to "send therefore, O inexhaustible Fount of all wisdom, from Thy holy heaven and the most high throne of Thy majesty, Thy wisdom to be ever with me, that it may keep watch with me in governing the commonwealth, and that it may take pains, that it may teach me, Thy handmaid, and may train me that I may be able to distinguish between good and evil, equity and iniquity."[13]

Elizabeth had learned the most valuable lesson of her reign. Wars were costly in men, money, and matériel and were to be avoided at all costs. Most importantly, their outcome could never be reliably predicted.

SEVEN

Christ's Soldiers

The Pope is so affected by the pitiable plight of the Catholics
of England that the greater are the persecutions which they
suffer, the more he is moved to compassionate [sic] them, and
desire to succour and aid them by all possible means.

—Cardinal archbishop of Milan to the papal nuncio in Spain

While Elizabeth's eyes were turned toward the Catholic threat symbolized by the papacy, France, and Spain, another home-grown menace emerged. Scorned as "precisians," "gospellers," "scripture men," or even "saints," these men and women are branded "Puritans" by history. All these epithets were hurled at them by a Christian community that derided their chosen path. The common complaint against these "godly people" is best expressed by sayings like "I perceive you are a Puritan outright: you are one of these new men that would have nothing but preaching." Then there was the alternative exclamation "It was never a merry world since that sect came first among us."[1]

In the 1560s, the godly, or "professors" as they liked to call themselves, were a minority of Protestants in England. Like their French counterparts, the Huguenots, they were seen as a troublesome sect on the rise whose evangelistic message would no doubt rock the fragile religious boat with Catholics and Protestants alike. They were heavily reliant on pastors capable of enthralling and preaching the Word, breathing hellfire and damnation. Demographically, the godly were sprinkled lightly in rural areas with the mainstay of their strength in the populous regions of London, Essex, East Anglia, and the Weald of Kent—in other words, in the areas that held the greatest power in the realm.

The poor, uneducated and disenfranchised, sought whatever religion they could from their local customs, which were more akin to magic than religion. However, the profile of the godly, or Puritan, is more diffi-cult to assess. Generally, they derived from a broad cross-section of society that was in the main economically independent. Minor courtiers, aristo-crats, aldermen, and merchants could be counted among the elite Puritan brethren. They shunned the alehouses—"a little hell" to them—as well as bowling alleys and bearbaiting. Later in the reign, they would embark on an all-out war against the theater.

Their leisure time was devoted to religious "exercises" where like-minded godly folk gathered together across parishes as "gadders" to hear sermons. These exercises became so prevalent that "the preaching might be only upon the Sabbath day," one Essex man complained, "but now they run in the week-days and leave their business and beggar themselves."[2] Soon, their gatherings would spill out of churches into house-meetings, which became known as "night conventicles," where the great Puritan writers of the day would engage them in discussion of the proper way to celebrate the Sabbath.

It was these Puritans who held the strongest prejudices against Eliza-beth's desire to please all her people. They railed against the continued use of the surplice in the Church of England, known as the Vestments Contro-versy. Edmund Grindal, bishop of London, when licensing ministers to preach, asked them to "exhort the godly so to frame their judgments that they conceive no offence." However, it was the Puritans' mission to pros-elytize that saved England's wayward flock, so they believed, and Grindal's instructions were ignored. For them, the English were doomed to an eter-nity in purgatory, unless they mended their ways. "There is but one way to prevent the danger that may be feared from this generation and their practices," John White, an outspoken Lancashire preacher, wrote, "that sin be severely punished and a preaching ministry settled, as much as pos-sible, in all places of the land, and painful preaching effectually main-tained against the manifold discouragements of this iron age."[3]

Even if the licensed preachers hadn't ignored Grindal, by the mid-1560s the godly Puritans had begun to abandon England's churches for the meetinghouses "to turn to the Lord in all sincerity." The family home was rapidly becoming the new Puritan parish, out of reach of the authorities. Within twenty years, Robert Browne and his small sect of Brownists would take this to an extreme and find themselves exiled in the Low Countries.

Still, the most dangerous of the godly Puritans to the Elizabethan settlement were not mere merchants, aldermen, aristocrats, or lesser courtiers but rather the godly members of Parliament like Paul Wentworth and his elder brother Peter. Paul, the more outspoken of the two, became troublesome to Elizabeth in her Parliaments of 1563 (reconvened in 1566) and 1572. For him, the 1560s was a pivotal decade. The early part of the decade had been devoted to the Elizabethan settlement, the counterattack by the papacy at the Council of Trent, and the proliferation of English seminaries on the Continent. Like-minded godly professors, including the Wentworth brothers, believed that Elizabeth had ignored the great Catholic threat. The Catholic nations had convened their Council of Trent, to which England and other Protestant nations sent no representative. When it was suspended in December 1563, it was, of course, no closer to a solution regarding schism. So Puritan voices rose ever louder in alarm. Indeed, the battle lines had been drawn, with each side of the religious divide working ceaselessly to promote its own interests. As the decade progressed, the sense of general unease grew, along with the Wentworths' earnest Puritan zeal for England.

At the same time, Trent debated the issues surrounding schism and heresy, Elizabeth convened her Parliament of 1563 to fulfill its primary function: the granting of much-needed money following the debacle at Newhaven. It was a heated session, with Elizabeth steadfastly refusing to countenance marriage or discuss the succession, as "there is no need to prate about my death," she said.[4] The fact that she had come perilously close to death the preceding year had been quite forgotten by the queen. However, the Commons was determined that Elizabeth should name either Catherine Grey, still imprisoned for marrying without royal assent, or the Scots' queen, Mary, as her successor. The Puritan faction strongly favored Mary.

Though surprising, it did make sense. Scotland had officially become a Protestant realm when the edict of Parliament was passed at Edinburgh in August 1560. By the time Mary returned to Scotland, being a Roman Catholic had become a dangerous thing. The proselytizing, godly John Knox grudgingly agreed to tolerate Mary, as "content to live under Your Grace as Paul was to live under Nero." Knox knew he held great sway over the hearts and minds of the Presbyterian Scots with his ubiquitous sermons repeated in print and on the lips of the devoted. On meeting Mary, Knox recognized a shrewd and calculating mind. He told his friends that "if there be not in her a proud mind, a crafty wit and an indurate heart against God and His truth, my judgment faileth me." At least, that's what he wrote to Cecil.[5]

Knox was intolerant, but he saw at once Mary's ability to master the ungovernable. He could not fail to be impressed with Mary's desire to tame the "wild Scots" of the Highlands and understand the workings of Scottish society. In fact, she had learned a great deal about her kinsmen in precious little time. The swaggering Scots magnates; the feudalistic notions of kinship and clans; the "manrent" of formal bonds between the population and their lairds, who granted protection in exchange for service; primitive communications; widespread villainy and piracy; and a land divided by geography and language with wild Highlanders speaking Gaelic—"that language of savages"—all conspired to make Scotland virtually ungovernable for any monarch, much less a young woman who had only lived in the country as a toddler. Naturally, when an opportunity arose to gracefully "export" some of her troublesome clansmen to Ireland, Mary showed herself a master of Machiavellian politics. Of course, there was a dual benefit to the maneuver: She would be rid of the clansmen in Scotland while destabilizing Elizabeth's troubled province of Ireland.

𝒯𝒽𝑒 𝒮𝒸𝑜𝓉𝓈 𝑒𝓃𝓉𝑒𝓇𝑒𝒹 Ireland fomenting their own brand of lawlessness in Ulster, but this most remote part of Elizabeth's realm had always harbored a troubled soul. Only five years earlier, when Philip of Spain was also king of England, the first plantations in Laois-Offaly, comprising Englishmen and Anglo-Irish settlers, were reported to be at peace. This was considered quite a coup as the chaos of the Irish clan system (known as "septs"), and in particular the O'More and the O'Connor clans of the region, had continually wrought havoc. Even in the previous year, the Lord Lieutenant of Ireland, Thomas Radcliffe, Earl of Sussex, claimed smugly that "all the rebellions which I found in Ireland be now subdued, the knots and maintenances broken, the principal persons of the realm brought to acknowledge such obedience as heretofore they have not done, and all the realm remains in quiet."[6] Nothing could have been further from the truth.

Sussex had erased the "bad boy" of the Irish chieftains during this period, Shane O'Neill, from the picture. When Shane's father died in 1562, he was elected "the O'Neill"—head of the Ulster clan—but did not receive his father's English title of Earl of Tyrone. Ambitious and hungry for power, Shane viewed the withholding of the English title as an intolerable slight. He also knew that so long as Sussex remained Lord Lieutenant, he would never receive it. After all, Shane had been inciting trouble with his allies, the Scottish "redshanks" MacDonald and McDonnell clans, in the province since 1548.[7]

In an attempt to circumvent Sussex, O'Neill wrote to Elizabeth that his "rude uncivil and disobedient people will fall to civility and hereafter be faithful obedient and true subjects" should England's queen recognize his power through the granting of his father's lapsed English title.[8] Sussex, however, argued strongly against him and prevailed. He convinced Elizabeth that Shane was a villain who sought to turn the Gaelic chieftains in Ireland against her, but it was Sussex's argument that Shane could equally employ the strength of the Catholic Church and Europe's Catholic monarchs against England that finally won over the queen.

This made the daunting task of ruling Ireland all the more difficult for Elizabeth. Shane O'Neill, for all his bravura, bullying, and murderous ways, was no less an exceptionally capable leader of men and outstanding military strategist. He transformed his lordship of the sprawling and most Gaelic of Ireland's provinces, Ulster, into a battleground in the coming years that employed thousands of Scots mercenaries. Shane's capture of the O'Donnell chieftain and his family allowed him to extend his stronghold into Tyrconnell. Once the province was captured, Shane summarily divorced his own wife and forced O'Donnell's daughter, Mary, into a vile marriage that was only cemented by the threat of torturing and killing her parents if she did not accede to his every wish, which included maintaining Mary's mother, Katherine, as his mistress. Sussex was apoplectic with rage and made the subjugation of Shane to the English crown his overwhelming priority.

Shane, too, was outraged. "You began with a conquest in my land without cause," Shane wrote to Sussex. "And so long as there be any English man in my country against my will, I . . . will send my complaint in another way to the Queen's Majesty to declare unto Her Grace how you interrupted my going."[9] Sussex's reply to Elizabeth warned, "If Shane be overthrown all is settled, if Shane settle all is overthrown."[10]

Yet Elizabeth saw the bigger picture. With Mary freely exporting her own troublesome clansmen to Ireland as mercenaries, Ireland was becoming an unbearable threat to England's security from its western back door, or, as Elizabethans called Ireland, "the postern gate." It was more important to have Shane openly submit to Elizabeth's will than to withhold the title of Earl of Tyrone he so coveted. Sussex, she reasoned, would need to be overruled. Cecil suggested that the queen have the Earl of Kildare treat with Shane to broker a settlement. It was reached at a cost of the earldom and £2,000 to defray the expenses of his journey to court and a pardon with safe conduct.

When, at last, Shane and his "Gallowglass" warriors appeared at court, their presence caused quite a stir, "with their bare heads, ash-coloured hanging curls, golden saffron undershirts, if not the colour of infected human urine, loose sleeves, short tunics, and shaggy lace."[11]

Yet, true submission to England was far from the Irish chieftain's mind. While Shane put his case for his Earldom of Tyrone to the queen, he mingled with the archplotter de Quadra and openly worshipped at the Catholic Mass held in the Spanish embassy. On learning of his treachery, Elizabeth and her councillors deemed O'Neill to be nearly more dangerous in London than he had been in Ireland.

While Elizabeth ascribed to the school of "keeping her friends close and her enemies closer," O'Neill was proving an elusive man to pin down. It was one thing to have Mary's bellicose clansmen fighting as mercenaries for O'Neill and quite another to have him plot with de Quadra and the might of Spain. With Sussex also present at court declaiming labyrinthine conspiracies throughout the troubled province of Ireland, Elizabeth concluded her interview with Shane O'Neill prematurely, before the matter of his true allegiance and the Earldom of Tyrone was resolved. Shane vowed revenge.

On his return to Ireland, unrestrained feudal warfare broke out between Shane and the clan chieftains who were "infringing" on his proclaimed territories. The Earl of Ormond (the Butler family) and his clients—all of whom were Anglo-Irish—ostensibly fought on behalf of the English crown against O'Neill. In reality Ormond and his men were hoping to manipulate his bitter enemy, the Earl of Desmond, and his "Geraldine" followers, who fought alongside the treacherous Shane. As few locals hadn't aligned themselves with the various feuding lords, a state of virtual civil war gripped Ireland. Shane laid waste to much of the country—burning crops, butchering Irish men, and raping Irish women. Pius IV, Philip II, and the Scots queen watched and waited in dismay.[12] Shane's scorched earth policy, though, directly affecting only Irish affairs, would later be held up to Irish Catholics as a sign of Irish barbarity.

While Shane pretended that his outrage was religious, it remained a purely sectarian struggle for power against the crown. Fortunately, Elizabeth saw the endgame in Ireland clearly. Where English Catholics had been forced into submission by the Act of Settlement with further legislation rammed through the Parliament of 1563 for their reticence to adopt the Anglican Church, Ireland had by and large escaped the same scrutiny. The perception at court was that the Irish remained lawless and that governance of the land by England's Lord Lieutenants was akin to moving in "a dark and dangerous labyrinth."[13] Even the Catholic Church feared to tread into the Irish "Wild West" replete with adventurers, scoundrels, and thugs who masqueraded as either Anglican or Catholic clergy as suited their personal agendas.

Nonetheless, Pius IV dipped a toe in the water, perhaps not believing the outpourings of lawlessness he had heard, and carelessly appointed the flamboyant Miler Magrath as archbishop of Down and Connor. Within no time, Magrath would change sides and become Elizabeth's eyes and ears as her Anglican bishop in Cashel, riding in full body armor, carrying a skull on a tall pole as his trademark, and trailing an army of outriders behind him.[14]

With characteristic political blindness, Pius IV wrote to Shane O'Neill as Prince of Ulster on July 14, 1564, commending him in "his indefatigable zeal and steadfast courage" in the defense of the Catholic faith. The papacy, still believing in its temporal role outside of the Papal States, had joined battle directly with England's postern gate of Ireland. The Antichrist, as Elizabeth's godly ministers called the pope, must be stopped.

EIGHT

Mary Stuart, the Great Catholic Threat

꡴

The Pope greatly deplores that the peace of the Queen, the
Cardinal's niece, and her realm should be thus broken, but
he trusts in God that the authors of the mischief will
pay the penalty of their rashness.

—Pope Pius IV to Charles, cardinal of Lorraine,

October 1565

Within the year, trouble brewed between Elizabeth and Mary. Robert Dudley had been elevated to the rank of Earl of Leicester and was offered to Mary as a handsome bridegroom to seal amity between England and Scotland. Mary famously shunned Elizabeth's dashing Master of the Horse. Instead, Mary had, it seemed, settled on a far worthier English subject, Henry Darnley.

Darnley had been put forward as a potential husband for Mary years earlier by his scheming mother, Margaret Douglas, Countess of Lennox. The countess, the daughter of Henry VIII's elder sister and Elizabeth's cousin, had been on the wrong side of Elizabeth's temper once before. In 1562, the Lennox claims supposed that their son's marriage to Mary of Scotland would ensure young Darnley's accession as king of England in his own right. After all, Henry Darnley was the great-grandson of Henry VII.

Yet despite Elizabeth's understandable concern at Margaret's overt scheming, resulting in both the Earl and Countess of Lennox being thrown into the Tower suspected of treason, in 1565, Elizabeth allowed the Earl of Lennox and Darnley to pass into Scotland to save their family's substantial lands from falling into untrustworthy hands.

Elizabeth had made a dire mistake. Still, it was an error undertaken with the full knowledge and blessing of both her most trusted advisers, William Cecil and Leicester. But why? Leicester later avowed his own distaste for his proposed marriage to the Scots queen claiming that "the invention of that proposition proceeded from Mr. Cecil, his secret enemy."[1] Cecil, for his part, must have preferred an English subject to any foreign prince as Mary's husband and connived with Leicester for Darnley's "one month sojourn" to Scotland in the hope that Darnley could become a replacement for the hapless Leicester. No wonder Elizabeth couldn't bear the sight of either Leicester or Cecil for a while—it must have dawned on her that she had been well and truly hoodwinked by them both.

Darnley and his father wasted no time in inserting themselves into Mary's court in Edinburgh. At first Mary seemed indifferent to the handsome boy. Yet when Darnley came down with measles, Mary nursed him back to health. Suddenly, Mary became besotted by the tall, dashing, and athletic Darnley.

What is unclear is if Cecil had expected that the rambunctious Scots lairds and courtiers would rise up against the likely Darnley marriage. Darnley was a Catholic, too, and in the lairds' eyes, should the couple wed, this could only spell the doom of the fledgling Protestant Presbyterian realm of Scotland. Eventually, they enlisted the aid of their unflinching John Knox to preach against this ill-starred match from the pulpits. The English ambassador, Thomas Randolph, who had been a reliable, if gossipy, source of information about life at Mary's court, asked to be recalled. Randolph sensed civil war on the wind. Mary's two most trusted and influential ministers, Sir William Maitland and her half brother the Earl of Moray, took the Protestant line and let the queen know their feelings. Still, Mary chose to ignore them, sending Maitland south to London for Elizabeth's obligatory permission to marry the English nobleman Darnley.

When Maitland arrived in London on April 15, 1565, he and Cecil conferred privately for three weeks. No correspondence survives outlining the specific nature of those meetings, only whisperings picked up from the dispatches of the French and Spanish ambassadors. Naturally, Maitland asked Elizabeth for her permission for the match; she declined to respond directly, stating instead that she would send Sir Nicholas Throckmorton to Edinburgh with her reply. By May 21, Throckmorton delivered Elizabeth's message taken down at the Privy Council meeting that a marriage with Darnley "would be unmeet, unprofitable and perilous." The same letter also confirmed that there was "no place left to dissolve the same [the Darnley match] by persuasion or reasonable means otherwise than by violence."[2] Catherine Grey's marriage to Hertford loomed in Elizabeth's mind; with Darnley, like Catherine's bridegroom, out of reach.

She was right to fear the worst. Mary had decided that she didn't really need Elizabeth's approval to wed Darnley after all. On July 22, Darnley was granted the coveted Scots title Duke of Albany. On July 28, he was proclaimed Prince Henry, to be styled "king of this our kingdom" of Scotland. On Sunday, July 29, the couple was married by Catholic rite. Mary's wild infatuation with Darnley would prove her eventual undoing.

All the while, disquiet was souring into open revolt in Scotland. Moray had spread rumors that the Catholic Lennox faction had planned to assassinate him. The Lennox party claimed that Moray planned to kidnap Lennox and Darnley and take them back to England to face Elizabeth's displeasure. By July 1, 1565, Moray had asked Randolph for a subsidy of £3,000 from Elizabeth to suppress this overt threat to the Protestant religion in Scotland and to further an English alliance. Yet somehow, no one seemed to notice that Darnley's Catholicism was plainly fashioned from convenience rather than faith. Hadn't Darnley readily listened to John Knox sermonize at St. Giles Church in Edinburgh? Hadn't he avoided the nuptial Mass at his own wedding?

By August 6, Moray was "put to the horn," or outlawed, for refusing to explain his behavior to his half sister Mary. When he had heard Elizabeth's warning against the Darnley marriage, Moray declared himself "the sorrowfullest man that can be," for he knew he had failed to align the Scottish Protestant cause against the Scottish queen. For Moray, there was no doubt that rebellion was the only solution.

Moray was outmaneuvered, on all counts. On August 11 Mary sequestered his substantial properties along with those of his followers Rothes and Kirkcaldy. A week later, she proclaimed her intention to march against the rebels and ordered a muster of troops, paid for by the time-honored tradition of pawning her jewels. Mary secured the wild north of the country by making the Earl of Atholl her lieutenant against the expected insurgency of the Earl of Argyll, then led her army westward to face Moray. Yet battle was not joined.

Moray, with the Scots Lords Châtelherault, Rothes, and Glencairn, had slipped southward, entering Edinburgh without a fight on August 31. Moray was shocked to discover that Mary had claimed his rebellion was merely a laird's attempt to snatch the crown, when he had believed he was raising a civil war to maintain Protestant liberties. Still, he found that both Catholics and Protestants in the capital had little appetite to put themselves "to the horn." Even the ubiquitous John Knox expressed a newfound admiration for Mary, whose "courage increased man-like" and who sported a pistol thrust into her saddle, outriding her ladies in the face of danger.[3] From Glasgow, Mary issued another proclamation, promising a definite settlement of the religious question. Sir William Maitland straddled the fence, declining to join Moray or throw his weight behind his queen. Six weeks later, Moray was ensconced in exile at Elizabeth's pleasure in Newcastle-upon-Tyne, a pariah for his rebellion, which had been derided in Scotland as the "Chaseabout Raid." Only help from England could reverse their collective fortunes.

Previously, in June 1565, Elizabeth had decided to lock up Mary's future mother-in-law in the Tower of London once more for her meddling in the English succession. Elizabeth had warned Mary through Ambassador Randolph that to go ahead with the marriage was "unmeet and perilous" and that waging war against her old and tried councillors could only end in tears. By October 13, the Venetian ambassador in France reported back to the Signory that Moray had had the "secret support" of the English queen. If the Venetian ambassador to France reported this, then Elizabeth's position could hardly be a secret from Catherine de' Medici and Mary's uncle the cardinal of Lorraine in France, or the Vatican or Spain.

A week before the Venetian ambassador's report, Moray had fled across the border into England just as Mary prepared to attack. Elizabeth had tried in the previous month to broker a deal between the two sides in the interest of peace, and most particularly to prevent Mary from appealing to her uncle of Lorraine or the Vatican for support of money or men-at-arms. Mary's reply was categorical: She would not tolerate Elizabeth's meddling in Scotland's affairs. The same day, the French ambassador in London, Paul de Foix, received another letter from Mary claiming that Elizabeth was attempting to make her renounce the Catholic faith. Elizabeth had paid, so Mary claimed, 6,000 crowns to the rebels. "God forbid," Elizabeth responded disingenuously to the Spanish ambassador, Guzman da Silva, later, "that I should help disobedient subjects."[4]

Whilst Moray was called to London to receive a public upbraiding, Cecil concentrated on what mattered most to the Privy Council. Mary had breached faith with Elizabeth by failing to consult with her as she had promised to do regarding her marriage. Mary had assisted the Irish rebels against their anointed queen, and Mary was conspiring with the pope against Elizabeth. Moray had reported these transgressions and more, but Cecil, at the time, lacked written proof that Mary had enlisted the pope in her troubles. The council concluded that war with Scotland should be averted, unless and until proof of Mary's treason against England could be obtained by "all good means of mediation" by Elizabeth's command. Cecil could hardly know that on the same day the French ambassador wrote of the Scottish rebellion, Pope Pius IV penned a letter to Mary's uncle Louis, cardinal of Lorraine:

> *Having heard that . . . some will do their utmost to procure such*
> *terms of pacification as may be very far from advantageous, nay ac-*
> *tually ruinous to the Catholic religion, he [the Pope] has deemed it*
> *his duty to exhort the Cardinal to do his utmost to deter the King*
> *and Queen [of Scotland] from making such a composition; which*

> would . . . be utterly repugnant to the office and dignity of Catholic
> Princes . . . and most grievously offend God, the Pope, and all good
> men.[5]

Pius IV immediately wrote to Philip II and the archbishop of Milan, who held sway with Philip's uncle Holy Roman Emperor Ferdinand. Philip's reply was a resounding endorsement of Mary, promising money and men should England support the rebels or if "the Queen of Scotland should assert by force of arms her pretensions to the succession to the English throne."[6] Philip's lengthy reply also advised Mary that "she must needs to be at pains to retain the servants she has gained in England, and also to gain all such others as she can, without letting it be known . . . and still, as ever it will be necessary to keep alive the negotiation with the Queen of England for her designation of the Queen of Scotland as her successor." As if his advice to deceive Elizabeth were not enough, Philip concluded, "I entreat his Holiness to direct that the like correspondence be had with me on his part, that we may proceed in the business in such concert as it demands, and carry it to the proposed end."[7]

On December 9, Pope Pius IV was dead. His successor, Michele Ghisleri, took the name Pius V. With his election came the enthronement of the Papal Inquisition and a stated aim for the utter extinction of so-called Christian heresies. A former Dominican monk, Pius V sought to make asceticism a way of life at the Vatican, naturally making powerful and rich enemies amongst the nobility. There would be a tightening up of laws long ignored, a hatred of accepted papal nepotism, and an unabashed attempt to bring sobriety to Rome. Prostitutes were expelled, profanity and animal baiting banned, nuns and monks compelled to live in the strictest seclusion according to their vows, and a new catechism instructed. Far from Pius V offering an olive branch to the beleaguered Protestant countries like England, this was a fire-breathing pope who saw Roman Catholicism as his country, disregarding all national boundaries and the desires of those who ruled them.

...

Meanwhile, for Mary, the future seemed bright. The popes—both old and new—had provided her with emotional succor and financial aid; her people had rallied to her; Philip II had planted both feet firmly in her camp, and she was expecting her first child. It hadn't mattered to her that there had been no time for a honeymoon. Mary had relished grabbing hold of the reins of power, assessing who could be trusted and who might turn against her.

Still, she hadn't noticed that governing was an anathema to her husband. Darnley's sole interest as king was the official bestowal of the "crown matrimonial" that would allow him equal status with his wife and strengthen his claim to England's throne. Frustrated by his desire, he was frequently seen about the town, drunk and in the company of commoners. At other times, Darnley processed through Edinburgh with lighted tapers, in an ostentatious Catholic gesture, asking others if they would be content to go to Mass with him. In fact, Darnley's whereabouts became so unreliable that Mary was obliged to cast an iron stamp of her husband's signature in order to avoid delaying affairs of state. Hunting, hawking, and other manly pleasures occupied his days and nights. The iron stamp, once made, was entrusted to the custody of David Rizzio, Mary's secretary.

It was Rizzio's service that became the focal point of Darnley's jealousy. Sir William Maitland had miraculously found his way back into Mary's service without demur. Yet in Maitland's absence, David Rizzio, an ambitious and talented Italian musician, had been catapulted to power as Mary's private secretary, gaining the queen's entire trust. Rizzio, a Catholic, was believed to be a papal agent to Pope Pius V, who had, in turn, urged Mary to weed out "the thorns and tares of heretical depravity."

In no time at all, rumors swirled about that Rizzio was more than a secretary to Mary, much more. Darnley himself, in a fit of rage, publicly accused his wife of lying with the dwarfish man and Rizzio of being the father of the child in Mary's womb. The more Darnley railed against Rizzio, the more dear Rizzio became to Mary. By March 1566, this Italian Catholic was undoubtedly the most powerful man in Mary's government.

There were already plots afoot to dislodge him from Mary's favor. Maitland wrote to Cecil that unless matters changed, he saw no way forward but to "chop at the very root" of the problems that were bound to face Mary in the weeks ahead. To discuss these issues, Maitland sent Robert Melville to Cecil on an extraordinary mission: to officially warn that the English ambassador, Randolph, had been suspected by Mary of assisting the Chaseabout rebels. In fact, Melville conveyed the extent of Maitland's double-dealing as being more labyrinthine than originally suspected.

Before Cecil could act, Maitland had Randolph ejected from Scotland. When Randolph wrote to Cecil, he confirmed that Darnley's father, the Earl of Lennox, was now conspiring with the former rebels to oust Rizzio, providing that they would support Darnley's bid for the crown matrimonial.

It hardly came as a shock a week later when both the Earl of Bedford and Randolph wrote in a joint communiqué to Cecil from Berwick that "a great attempt [is] to be made by such advice as the Lord Darnley hath gotten of some noblemen in Scotland whereby he thinketh to advance himself unto that which by other means he cannot attain unto." These most trusted English diplomats urged that only Elizabeth, Leicester, and Cecil should know of the contents of the letter, since "you have heard of discords and jars between this Queen [Mary] and her husband . . . He is himself determined to be at the apprehension and execution of him whom he is able manifestly to charge with the crime."[8] The "him" referred to was David Rizzio, and Darnley himself was now part of the plot to murder Rizzio in exchange for the Protestant Lords' cooperation in bestowing upon him the crown matrimonial. The most extraordinary part of the whole adventure was that only four months earlier, these same Protestant Lords had risen in revolt against Mary for wedding Darnley, and once

Parliament was convened on March 7, 1566, their lands would be confiscated under a bill of attainder for their actions.

On a personal level, it was tragic. Though Mary was six months pregnant,
she rarely saw Darnley. The bloom of her infatuation had wilted. For
company, she replaced him with other courtiers like Rizzio and the "vain,
glorious, rash and hazardous" James Hepburn, Earl of Bothwell, to whom
"his adversaries should have an eye," in the words of Nicholas Throckmorton. Only a month earlier, Mary had given Bothwell's bride, Lady Jean
Gordon, eleven ells of cloth of silver for her wedding dress and joined in
the sumptuous celebrations. Yet Lady Jean had no illusions about her new
husband, or indeed about herself. She had married him loving another
man, Alexander Ogilvy. Lady Jean knew that Bothwell had always been a
man with an eye to the main chance. The queen, well aware that Bothwell
and her half brother Moray were bitter enemies, advanced Bothwell to a
position on her Privy Council, in part as a sign of favor, in part for her
physical protection. Bothwell had been at Mary's side during the Chaseabout Raid and had made himself invaluable in organizing her motley
army.

Then, as expected, when Parliament convened on March 7, Mary failed to
put forward Darnley for the crown matrimonial. Two days later, on Saturday, March 9, the plotters struck. Their targets were David Rizzio,
Bothwell, and Bothwell's new brother-in-law and friend, the fifth Earl of
Huntly. Darnley entered the queen's supper chamber through the privy
stairs of his apartments to see Huntly, Bothwell, David Rizzio, and Mary's
ladies at the supper table with the queen. Mary, outraged at his presumption to come to her rooms unannounced, was soon stunned to see some
of the Chaseabout plotters enter behind him. The most unsavory of these
men, Patrick, Lord Ruthven, launched into a sordid tirade about Mary's
supposed relations with Rizzio, while five more of his fellow conspirators
followed closely, wielding pistols and daggers. Rizzio grabbed hold of

Mary's skirts, pleading for his life. Ruthven wrenched the diminutive Italian away from her while another of the plotters steadily pointed a pistol at her swollen belly. Rizzio screamed and kicked, begging for his life to be saved, but to no avail. According to the various accounts of Rizzio's murder, his body was stabbed between fifty-three and sixty times. Darnley's own dagger was used for the bloody deed to ensure his loyalty.

Yet somehow in the melee, Bothwell and Huntly had escaped through a back window. The queen's attendants fought to enter the suite of rooms to protect Mary, but to no avail. They swiftly alerted the people of Edinburgh that there had been an almighty disturbance at the Palace at Holyrood and the queen needed help. The city's alarm bell sounded, and the people rushed into the grounds of the palace.

Seeing the swelling crowd, Darnley coolly stepped up to the balcony window of the room where the slaughter had taken place moments before to reassure the people that the queen's "attackers" had been dealt with, that all was again well, and that they should return to their homes. Mary grasped how dire her situation was and so, stifling her revulsion at what had just transpired, played up to Darnley. He was a drunk and a weakling in her eyes, having taken her enemies as his friends in the murder of poor Rizzio—only to gain the crown matrimonial.

Mary set about persuading Darnley that his "friends" had effectively succeeded in a coup d'état that would leave him just as vulnerable as she. Before daybreak, Darnley had seen the error of his ways. What Mary hadn't known at this juncture was that Moray had been involved in the plot as well.

At midnight on the second evening after Rizzio's murder, Mary and Darnley quietly made their way down the same privy staircase by which the plotters had entered the supper room. They were met outside by Lord Erskine and two or three loyal soldiers with horses, in the shadow of Rizzio's newly dug grave. Under the cover of a cloudy night, they made good their escape to Dunbar Castle in a furious five-hour ride. Despite the shock of the attack, Rizzio's murder, and the helter-skelter ride, Mary showed no signs of miscarrying.

On March 15, Mary wrote an impassioned letter to Elizabeth about her ordeal. She described the butchery of David Rizzio before her very eyes and appealed to Elizabeth to beware of such unforeseen betrayals herself. Meanwhile, Bothwell and Huntly joined the queen and Darnley at Dunbar along with Atholl and other loyal noblemen. Two days later, she had four thousand men at her command. By the time Mary retook Edinburgh at the head of an army of eight thousand men on March 18, 1566, Darnley rode beside her, reduced to the standing of a surly cipher. The murderers fled for exile in England. Sir William Maitland, who had known everything in advance but said nothing, made for Dunkeld. The fire-and-brimstone leader of the Scottish Kirk, John Knox, exiled himself to Ayrshire, for fear of being cut down in the swathe of retribution which he was sure must follow.

Yet in a stunning tour de force, Mary decided to pardon all rebels who had lined up against her in the Chaseabout Raid. Moray, too, was forgiven despite Mary's previous intransigence. Only Darnley would have a fitting end reserved to him for his treachery. As Maitland reported in October 1566, "he [Darnley] misuses himself so far towards her that it is an heartbreak for her to think that he should be her husband."[9]

PART II

The Catholic Ascendancy,
1566–1580

NINE

Betrayal amid Dreamy Spires

*I feel by myself, being also here wrapped in miseries and
tossed . . . in a sea swelling with storms of envy,
malice, disdain, suspicion.*

—Sir William Cecil to Sir Henry Sidney, 1566

It seemed that everyone besides Darnley knew his days were numbered. Undoubtedly, the situation in Scotland also played a discordant tune to Philip II's and Pius V's ready ears. Still, just how the Scottish affair would end—and when—was a mystery, one that England would need to watch closely for its own security. Though Mary claimed to her subjects that Moray's rebellion had not been religiously inspired, she had been quick to demand aid from the pope on religious grounds. The murder of Rizzio, whether a papal agent or not, fueled Pius's ire against Elizabeth for the simple reason that the perpetrators (save Lennox and Darnley) were Protestants.

That June, through their own secret channels, Elizabeth and her councillors were made aware that Pius V had sent "a Nuncio to Scotland and ample aid in money to enable the Queen to cope with the insidious designs of her rival of England and to keep the realm Catholic."[1]

England itself was in turmoil, too. That same spring of 1566, dissent had been rife. London's godly had drawn a line in the sand, refusing to accept Elizabeth's decree, or advertisement, on clerical dress. The demand was simple enough to her clergy. Wear conforming dress, which included the surplice. London's preachers and bishops had rebelled, breaking "the gracious knot of Christian charity" at their Convocation of 1566. The English church had developed a well-organized left wing that was bent on having its own way. The previous Christmas, London's pulpits swayed with preachers attacking the decking of churches with holly, cardplaying, and overindulgence in food and flesh on fish days. At St. Peter's Cornhill, John Gough preached that it was wrong "to do also what we lust, because it is Christmas." He preached abstinence, for if we "give but an inch, they will take an ell."[2]

Just before Holy Week, the Archbishop of Canterbury Matthew Parker gave these rebellious preachers an ultimatum: Conform or be suspended. Thirty-seven declined and were duly punished. Without the Word to stir up emotion, it was hoped that the revolt would soon lose its impetus. Neither Parker nor Elizabeth had expected that the wayward preachers would publish a tract entitled *Briefe discourse against the outward apparel*— the first Puritan manifesto. Nor did they believe that Robert Crowley, the printer of *Piers Plowman*, would join forces with John Philpot and John Gough to preach to London's multitude in the open air when they were deprived of their churches.

An official reply was prepared, *A briefe examination . . . of a certaine declaration*, most likely written by Archbishop Parker himself, in which he referred to the situation as "superfluous brawling of men perverse in heart, from whom the truth is withdrawn." Crowley was determined to have the last word and published *An answer for the tyme to the examination*.[3]

More tracts followed from one side, then the other. Cries of "repentance" and "deformation of the English Church" or shouts against "this filthy ware" (meaning the surplice) were bandied back and forth between England's men of the cloth in pamphlets, broadsides, and ballads. Two Oxford preachers, Laurence Humphrey and Thomas Sampson, wrote pleadingly to the Puritan divine Heinrich Bullinger in Switzerland, but they were given short shrift as harboring a "contentious spirit under the name of conscience."[4]

Elizabeth was left little alternative. The order went out to Archbishop Parker and the church commissioners to end the discontent forthwith. Parker acted swiftly, exiling the agitators from London and scattering them around the country like seeds on the wind. Robert Crowley was sent to the bishop of Ely in Cambridgeshire. Gough and Philpot were exiled to the Diocese of Winchester. Miles Coverdale, to whom the Reformation in England owed so much, resigned his living. Others went back to whence they had come. Without their rebellious leaders based in London, the movement seemingly crumbled.

Having won the battle, the queen judged that the time was ripe to enshrine the church vestments into a new law. Yet however much the Privy Council and Elizabeth may have wished otherwise, the only way to achieve this was to reconvene her troublesome Parliament prorogued in 1563. The same men who had proved so reticent to accept the royal will with respect to the succession and the settlement of the Church of England three years earlier would once again stand judge over her.

Times were hard. Aside from the controversy over church vestments, harvests had been poor and the previous winters bitterly cold. Shane O'Neill's rebellion in Ulster continued unabated and had already cost the treasury some £26,000 in the previous two years alone. A fresh Irish policy by England to settle the northeast coast of the country was seen as "the surest and soonest way" to handle the mercenary Scots and to "inhabit between them and the sea whereby . . . all hope of succor may be taken from them." There was a palpable dread among the privy councillors that the unstable Scottish situation would spill over into England's realm of Ireland.

To make circumstances worse, English shipping had been curtailed for "quarrels of matters of religion without cause." English merchants stood accused of unprovoked attacks against Spanish shipping on the high seas in response to the "strange and pitiful" treatment of Englishmen in Spain. It seemed trade with the English, who were now branded as *Luteranos,* had ceased to be a respectable affair. From Spain's viewpoint, the English had infringed on the seventy-five-year-old Spanish and Portuguese division of the world granted by Pope Alexander VI by the Treaty of Tordesillas, which divided the New Worlds yet to be discovered between them. For Philip, England was nothing more than an interloper.[5]

In an effort to help calm all nerves, Elizabeth pulled out her well-worn marriage card once again in favor of the Archduke Charles, the third son of the Holy Roman Emperor, and an Austrian Hapsburg. She hoped that this would head off any rumblings Parliament might wish to make over her marriage plans and issues touching the succession, as well as calm Philip and Pius V. Over the summer, negotiations were reopened, and Parliament was notified that it would officially reconvene in September.

Meanwhile, the queen would also put her summer progress to good use and observe the state of the realm. With so many godly ministers dispersed back to the countryside, Elizabeth needed to ensure that her nobility would remain watchful for signs of seditious preaching. She was well aware that some of these troublesome preachers had found their livings and solace in her nobles' and merchants' homes as the doors to the parish churches were closed to them. There, in the privacy of the domestic setting, they not only found sanctuary but also circumvented the queen's will. "London is a city," Elizabeth complained, "where every merchant must have his schoolmaster and nightly conventicles, expounding scriptures and catechizing their servants and maids," so that servant girls could "control learned preachers and say that such a man taught otherwise in our house."[6]

Since many of the Puritan preachers exiled from the capital had been trained at either Oxford or Cambridge, it made sense to include the most troublesome of these cities on her progress. Though it was not previously on her route, Elizabeth decided she should visit the university city of Oxford, ostensibly to show her support for its educational prowess. In fact, it was to gauge the mood of the students and their masters and allow them to see firsthand the magnificence and munificence of their anointed queen, particularly since two of the rebellious preachers who had recently been denied their benefices in London had just come down from Oxford. Besides, the Earl of Leicester had confirmed privately that there were other contentious souls to be found. Elizabeth's decision to travel there was not so much a whim as a matter of state security.

· · ·

Early in Elizabeth's reign, the mayor of Oxford had advised the Privy Council that "there were not three houses in [Oxford] that were not filled with papists." He was admonished by the queen's councillors and told never to repeat such malicious gossip. Yet the mayor knew that at the Mitre Inn on the High Street and at the Catherine Wheel and the Swan Inn, Catholics swarmed into their cellars to meet secretly to celebrate forbidden Catholic rites.[7]

Like London, Oxford had always been a reluctant follower of the Elizabethan settlement; hence Elizabeth had the Earl of Leicester appointed as its chancellor. Trusted eyes and ears were required in every corner of the realm, but nowhere more than in Oxford and Cambridge, and who better to keep a watchful eye in these university cities than Leicester in Oxford and Cecil at Cambridge? Besides, Leicester had been responsible for the promotion of at least eight of Elizabeth's most outspoken émigré bishops from Geneva and Frankfurt and had been instrumental in making her vision for the Anglican Church a reality. Though the appointments of these bishops had run counter to the queen's conservative instincts, Elizabeth was hardly in a position to be choosy at the outset of her reign. With most Marian bishops refusing to confirm their acceptance of the Act of Settlement, her selection list was rather slim.

Still, Leicester was not the only privy councillor to put forward former exiles to carry out Elizabeth's wishes in her new church. Sir Nicholas Bacon was equally involved in attempting to tame these Continental firebrands. Archbishop of Canterbury Parker lamented that Bacon "intruded into such room and vocation" as to finally break down his own reluctance to conform. Bacon found a willing helpmate at home with his second wife, Ann, who was also the sister of Cecil's equally godly wife, Mildred.[8]

Yet Oxford, having suffered the Elizabethan purges of Puritan radicals and popish priests, remained a city of decidedly Catholic leanings. Though the "secret and forbidden" Mass was not heard in the city's cathedral or churches, word of its hidden adherence to the "old faith" had spread widely. Heinrich Bullinger, the Swiss Protestant divine activist, had been told that the university was "as yet a den of thieves, and of those who hate the light," and so declined to send his son there. The bishop of Salisbury, John Jewel, lamented that only two of the university's colleges were of "our sentiment." Nicholas Saunders, a fellow of New College, claimed that the college failed to ask for the Oaths of Supremacy and Uniformity required of graduates due to the overwhelming number of dissenters among its fellows.

Oxford's headmaster was a Marian survivor who eventually became a casualty of the Elizabethan "visitors." At Corpus Christi, Magdalen, and Trinity, the bishop of Winchester, who had acted as their visitor, knew that a blind eye would be best for implementing the observance of the Elizabethan settlement. There was much "winking" among visitors at Oxford's transgressions. Even more worryingly, it had been noted by Leicester that there was a steady exodus of Oxford's students and its masters to other Catholic seminaries overseas.[9]

Elizabeth had tried to visit Oxford two years earlier, but an outbreak of plague prevented her at the last minute. Now, with the world situation in turmoil, London in a Puritan mood, and her closest advisers questioning whether Catholics or the godly were the enemies of the state, it was essential for the queen to lay on a charm offensive to woo Oxford's troublesome university population.

So, on Saturday, August 31, in the late afternoon, the royal procession was heralded into the city. The Earl of Leicester, in his gowns as chancellor of the university, and then the mayor and his aldermen led the queen's procession. As Elizabeth entered the medieval city, her magnificence seemed heart-stopping to onlookers:

> *Her head-dress was a marvel of woven gold, and glittered with pearls*
> *and other wonderful gems; her gown was of the most brilliant scarlet*
> *silk, woven with gold, partly concealed by a purple cloak lined with*
> *ermine after the manner of a triumphal robe. Beside the chariot rode*

*the royal cursitors, resplendent in coats of cloth of gold, and the mar-
shals, who were kept busy preventing the crowds from pressing too
near to the person of the Queen . . . The royal guard . . . were about
two hundred . . . and on their shoulders they bore . . . iron clubs like
battle-axes.*[10]

Leicester was Elizabeth's host for the week's disputations and debates.
While most monarchs would have shuddered at the prospect, Elizabeth
shared her councillors' love of learning and was keen to see Oxford again
at the vanguard of education alongside the Italian universities. Seventeen
hundred students attended the week's intellectual deliberations. In keeping with the royal favor Elizabeth was bestowing, prizes were offered to
the most worthy of the disputants. On Tuesday, September 3, a young
man from St. John's College triumphed over his opponents when he argued that the tides are caused by the moon's motion. He had no idea that
within fifteen years, Elizabeth herself would be worshipped as Cynthia,
the goddess of the moon, the "wild ocean's empress." Nor could he have
known that Sir Walter Raleigh would compose the *Book of the Ocean to
Cynthia* portraying his agonizing relationship with the queen. The young
man so warmly favored by Elizabeth was immediately offered patronage
of both Cecil and Leicester. His name was Edmund Campion.

On Thursday, the Divinity Disputation took place. Elizabeth's council
selected the rather hot topic of "Whether subjects may fight against
wicked princes?" in the hope that dissident students could be weeded out.
It would have taken a foolhardy student to compare Elizabeth to a wicked
prince, particularly when examples in Scotland were so fresh in their
minds.

By the end of the disputations, Edmund Campion won his court pa-
tronage, while Tobie Matthew of Christ Church won the coveted Queen's
Scholar prize. Matthew would eventually become archbishop of York.
Campion would become a traitor.

Yet the term "traitor" had come to mean something of a movable feast in
the previous twenty years. In Mary I's reign, Henry VIII's archbishop

Thomas Cranmer had been burned at the stake in Oxford for "treacherous heresy." St. Mary Hall's college head, Dr. William Allen, described Cranmer as a "notorious perjured and oft relapsed apostate recanting, swearing and foreswearing at every turn."[11] As university proctor, Allen had been deeply involved in the Marian purges at the university in 1556–57 against the "new religion." This made him a traitor in Elizabeth's time.

By 1561, William Allen had exiled himself from the university he so adored, for fear of meeting the same fate as those he had purged. He drifted with other English Catholics to the Low Countries and the University of Mechlin, continuing his theological studies there. Allen supplemented his meager income as a private tutor to a young Irish nobleman. Yet when Allen returned briefly to his family in Lancashire due to illness, he was appalled to see how many "good" Catholics attended church services and conformed outwardly to the Elizabethan settlement.

A brief stint at Oxford before returning to the Low Countries in 1565 converted Allen to activism for the preservation of English Catholicism. Ordained in the priesthood at Mechlin that year, Allen published *A Defense and Declaration of the Catholike Churchies Doctrine, Touching Purgatory* in response to Bishop Jewel's *Apology*.[12] It was a work that had already singled him out for the Elizabethan regime's special investigations by the time Elizabeth visited Oxford.[13]

Allen, far from being "exiled" and bereft of like company, found himself in the middle of a thriving English Catholic diaspora. Over a hundred senior fellows and masters from Oxford alone were dispersed throughout the Low Countries at its universities, particularly at Louvain and Douai. Still, Allen fretted that their lack of a proper English institution to afford them the "regiment, discipline and education most agreeable to our Countrymen's natures" was a terrible burden. These thoughts, echoed in his *Apologie*, gripped Allen in the autumn of 1566. While Elizabeth was at Oxford, Allen resolved to redress this wrong. He would establish a truly English Catholic seminary on the Continent.

Still, there were other Elizabethan traitors in Oxford's midst who remained unknown to the queen. The university would produce thirty-seven seminary priests in the years to come. One of them, Gregory Martin, would become the translator of the Rheims-Douai Bible of the 1570s. Two months after Elizabeth left Oxford for the battles that lay ahead with her Parliament, Magdalen College would take on a new, seemingly unremarkable tenant in the shadow of Oxford Castle at number 3 Castle Street. The tenant was a twenty-six-year-old carpenter named Walter Owen, accompanied by his wife and young family. His four sons would eventually join the mission to save England for Catholicism. His toddler son, Nicholas Owen, would die taking the secrets of his most enigmatic craft of "hidemaking" for Catholic priests to the grave.

Their roles in this history were still far in the future. After Elizabeth's Oxford visit that autumn, Parliament was duly convened, and the anticipated revolt of godly members in both houses occurred. Not only did the Commons refuse to consider the Act for Apparel, addressing the existing sumptuary laws as well as church ornaments and vestments; they refused any action whatsoever until they had the queen's solemn reassurance that she would marry. They were deeply suspicious about the seriousness of the planned marriage to Archduke Charles, a Catholic and a Hapsburg. Besides, the Commons felt it held the whip hand to force Elizabeth into action regarding a lasting solution to the succession by withholding a sizable parliamentary subsidy until its demands were met. They had not reckoned on the queen's iron will and anger. Elizabeth lashed out at them and forbade any further discussion about the private matter of her marriage.

By November, Elizabeth struck at the House of Lords for allowing the Commons to run roughshod over them, calling those members of both houses who tried to dictate to her "those unbridled persons whose mouth was never snaffled by the rider." Foremost among these "unbridled persons" was the godly Paul Wentworth. On the day Parliament convened following her interdiction to speak about her marriage, he rose to ask three questions: "Whether Her Highness' commandment, forbidding the lower house to speak or treat any more of the succession and of any their excuses in that behalf, be a breach of the liberty of the free speech of the House or not?" The second question asked "whether her ministers, in pronouncing her commandment to the house in her name are of authority sufficient to bind the House to silence in that behalf." Finally, he asked if her commandment was not in breach of the liberty of the House or sufficient to bind the House, then "what offence is it for any of the House to err in declaring his opinion to be otherwise?"[14]

Paul Wentworth was alarmed. By not discussing Elizabeth's marriage plans and thereby the succession, the Protestant settlement, imperfect though it was, remained too precarious. He decided to use democratic reasoning to try to keep the issue under debate, calling upon the "liberties," or freedom of speech within Parliament, when addressing the queen. Other godly voices were raised in support of Wentworth's reasoning as well. For the first time, a new voice was heard on the side of the godly: Francis Walsingham. It was a grueling session and, despite all the heartfelt arguments, ended in stalemate.

Elizabeth's Bill on Apparel aimed at closing all discussion about church vestments was withdrawn. She had browbeaten the Commons into voting her two-thirds of the subsidy for the good of the realm, without designating her successor in the event of her death. The burning matter of her marriage was declared by Elizabeth as being personal and therefore closed. She fulminated at her privy councillors, including Leicester and Cecil, who had been part of the "godly conspiracy," and she refused to allow them in her sight. The drama ended with her reassurance to the House on the prickly issue of the succession, with Elizabeth uttering the sour words that she would "deal therein for your safety," making her anger known in no uncertain terms when she added, "For it is monstrous that the feet should direct the head."[15]

Elizabeth, disgusted and enraged, dissolved Parliament on January 2, 1567, with a devastating broadside aimed at members and her Privy Council:

> I love so evil counterfeiting and hate so much dissimulation that I may not suffer you depart without that my admonitions may show your harms and cause you shun unseen peril. Two visors have blinded the eyes of the lookers-on in this present session . . . Under pretense of saving all they have done none good . . . They have done

their lewd endeavor to make all my realm suppose that their care was
much when mine was none at all.[16]

From Elizabeth's perspective, only she could protect her people against the armed insurrections that plagued her neighbors. Her steadfastness against the adversities ahead changed England forever.

TEN

The Iconoclastic Fury

If the Low Countries are lost the rest of
the Monarchy will not last long.
—Governor of Milan to Philip II, 1566

A week before Elizabeth entered Oxford, and only months after the murder of Mary's secretary, Rizzio, the Low Countries were once again in a state of open revolt. This province of the Hapsburgs, stretching from modern-day Belgium and Luxembourg to the Northern Netherlands, had come to Philip through his inheritance as Duke of Burgundy. A hodgepodge of languages, customs, and natural borders, it was also the economic powerhouse of northern Europe. Only twenty years earlier, the Low Countries had been amalgamated into one administrative province from seventeen smaller ones by Philip II's father.

Charles V had also revamped the States-General (the representative assembly) comprised of the great nobles from each smaller province to self-rule, subject, of course, to the king's will. Unwittingly, Charles had taken a disparate, often quarrelling multilingual group of provinces and molded them into a fledgling nation in the name of easing his personal administrative burden. Within a few years, the Netherlanders spoke of their *patrie* (fatherland) rather than the town or province they hailed from. When Charles had the States-General pass the "Pragmatic Sanction" in November 1549, ensuring that on his death or abdication the provinces would continue to obey his chosen heir under the same central institutions of his reign, he had also enshrined the Netherlanders' "ancient rights" forever.[1]

By 1566, the Low Countries had undergone a remarkable transformation. Densely populated, with some three million people to England's five million, covering an area a bit larger than England and Wales, the country was renowned for its exceptional artisans, particularly weavers, and abilities to create enormously profitable commerce as middlemen. So when, in Philip's eyes, Elizabeth infringed on his right to dominate trade in the Baltic and the Caribbean, he sparked off a trade war with England, temporarily closing off the staple market of Antwerp to the English. Elizabeth sought another staple town at the Hanseatic town of Emden, but it was always a pale and poor alternative to Antwerp.

The heartland of the Netherlands was the provinces of Holland, Zeeland, Flanders, Brabant, and Hainault, where the population was at its most dense in the large towns of Antwerp, Ghent, Brussels, Lille, Valenciennes, and Amsterdam. As India would one day become the jewel in the British crown of empire, so the Low Countries had already become the glittering prize in Spain's. These provinces were known for the beauty of their cities and architecture, incredible engineering feats in holding back the seas by an intricate system of dikes, and artists and musicians far ahead of their time. Yet the Spaniards most appreciated the Netherlanders for their ability to generate vast sums of money through commerce to help Charles, then Philip, in their holy wars against the enemies of Roman Catholicism—be they Protestant or Muslim.

In the 1560s, the regent in the economic powerhouse of the Netherlands was Margaret of Parma, Philip's half sister, aided by his trusted minister, Antoine Perrenot de Granvelle. Nonetheless, Granvelle was an untrustworthy pair of hands to hold such a jewel. Philip, long ensconced in Spain, had forgotten about the deal struck for "ancient rights" by his father. He was angered by the blackmail extorted by the States-General where in return for a loan of 3.6 million ducats to fight the Ottoman Turk in the Mediterranean, Philip would agree to remove three thousand of his crack *tercios* troops from the country.[2] Worse still, Philip allowed the poisoned pen of Granvelle to further color his thinking.

On Granvelle's advice, Philip responded to the Netherlander arrogance by working tirelessly with the pope on a secret plan to redraw the religious map of the Low Countries. With the administration of the heartland of the States-General in the hands of just three men dedicated to the Netherlanders' ancient rights—Stadtholders William of Orange, the Count of Egmont, and the Count of Horn—it was a dangerous policy for Philip to pursue, much less administer. Elizabeth, as ever kept abreast of events by her able factor to the Low Countries, Sir Thomas Gresham, prayed for peace. Emden could never replace Antwerp, and without peace in the Low Countries, returning there would be impossible.

It was a vain hope. The heavy hand of Rome fell hard. The pope published the new religious map of the Low Countries, augmenting the bishoprics from four to fourteen following linguistic borders. He made the archbishopric of Mechlin the most powerful and wealthy of them all. Naturally, the papal appointment for Mechlin went to Cardinal Granvelle. Of course, the exiled English Catholic community, including William Allen of Oxford, was at Mechlin at the time.

The new religious map thinly disguised Philip's endgame: to bring the Inquisition to the Low Countries. Antwerp was the first to rise up, threatening the prosperity of the entire Netherlands. Granvelle became the hated "king's man," for his falsity in pretending to be on the Netherlanders' side. After these first uprisings, Granvelle wrote to Philip that "people here universally display discontent with any and all Spaniards in these provinces."[3]

Elizabeth and her councillors were utterly dismayed. She had already forged strong links with Protestants in the Netherlands, Sweden, Scotland, and France, as well as the Lutheran princes and electors in the German lands. Secret diplomatic correspondence was replete with references to her exiled English Catholics and their efforts on behalf of Catholicism. She especially noted wisely that William of Orange had married Anna, daughter of the Lutheran elector of Saxony, and that Philip had clearly opposed the match. Though Orange remained Catholic and had no plans to change faiths, his religious outlook was more akin to Elizabeth's than

Philip's, seeking to unite his people through religion rather than divide them. Even Orange, however, was powerless to stop Philip and Granvelle in their first onslaught.

The feared Inquisition came, and thousands of Dutch citizens fled to England, where they were welcomed. These were no poor immigrants but skilled merchants and artisans and could only add to the wealth of the realm. Naturally, Orange, Egmont, and Horn sent an ultimatum to Philip, explaining that his Inquisition was impoverishing the Netherlands and demanding the removal of Granvelle. If Philip refused, they would resign from the States and the council.

While this seemed appealing, Philip knew nonetheless that these three men had been maintaining law and order in both the States and the council previously. So Philip hesitated. It was Horn who forced the situation. A member of the French Montigny family, Horn decided on a solemn league against Granvelle, suggesting that each member—whether nobleman or servant—should dress himself in a livery of a single color with the badge of a fool's cap and a bell, parodying the cardinal's hat. They held a number of outrageous meetings and banquets with Granvelle as the brunt of their joke, demanding that he leave the Low Countries at once. The cardinal seemingly retaliated, branding them all "Beggars"—*les Gueux*. Their "beggarly" insult soon became their battle cry, and all who followed Horn became known as "Beggars."

Eventually, Philip refused, and as threatened the three noblemen replied in July that they would stay away from court in Brussels. At the same time, the States of Brabant refused to pay their taxes to their Spanish king until Granvelle left the country. Margaret of Parma knew that rebellion was in the air and tried to persuade Philip to recall Granvelle, sending her secretary to Spain to plead with him. If he removed the cardinal, she argued, the king would remove the symbol of the hated Inquisition, which would bizarrely allow them to get on with their work of eradicating heresy.[4]

Still, the Beggars were not Granvelle's only enemies. Spaniards vying for Philip's favor in Madrid finally broke the king's will. Granvelle was recalled from Brussels on March 13, 1564, never to return. With his departure, the incorporation plan of the various bishoprics was dropped, as was the Inquisition. The 700 persecutions against heretics in Flanders alone fell to 250 that year, then down to 175 six months later.[5] The Beggars again took up their natural roles at the States-General and at court, working closely once more with Margaret, who praised their cooperation repeatedly in her letters to her brother. In fact, they were so cooperative that the Brussels government was able to impose an open-ended ban on the importation of English goods until such time as Elizabeth controlled her piratical rovers in the Channel. Elizabeth hadn't foreseen that result, especially in light of their shared Protestant views held with the Netherlanders.

Meanwhile, there were hotter wars in the Baltic that threatened English trade with other Protestant countries. Denmark had declared war on Sweden and the Hanseatic towns, decimating England's remaining staple trade at Emden. Poland and Russia soon joined in the fray, and the Baltic was essentially closed to the English.

That winter of 1564–65 was one of the harshest of the sixteenth century. Widespread starvation and unemployment were rampant. The Dutch artist Pieter Breughel painted his masterpiece *Hunters in the Snow* with its evocative background depicting the vast frozen wastes and icebergs blocking the port of Delfshaven on the Maas, a centuries-old reminder of the desperate times.

The harsh winter was followed by a ruined harvest. In Catholic Ghent, the magistrates recorded that "the evident danger from the dearth of corn and the large number of paupers, coupled with the arrival in this town of about 300 people from the region of Armentières who, it is feared, are infected with heresy" spoke volumes. Farther north in Holland, people were "murmuring and voicing criticisms which might tend towards sedition, and also singing songs with the same end." As in England, ballads spread the word. In the south at Brussels, a government minister wrote, "If the people rise up, I fear that the religious issue will become involved."[6] The link between hard times and the rise of Protestantism is unmistakable.

• • •

The Netherlands had adopted Calvinism as its favored form of Protestantism. Calvinism, as opposed to the English Puritanism or the German Lutheranism, arrived late in the Netherlands but spread like a ferocious fire. With the outbreak of the first religious war in France between Huguenot and Catholic, thousands of Huguenot refugees had poured across the frontier to the Low Countries or across the seas to England for protection. There they preached and taught their coreligionists the Word according to John Calvin. "Heresy grows here," Margaret of Parma wrote, echoing Elizabeth's fears, "in proportion to the situation in our neighbors' countries."[7] It was the Huguenots who gave the necessary instruction in the dogma of the Reformed faith, and the English Puritans who gave them their first churches in London. From England, the Dutch exile Guy de Brès learned how to organize the Reformed Church back home.

Meanwhile, Calvinism evolved rapidly into the Dutch Reformed Church. Debating chambers of rhetoric and amateur dramatic societies were used as meeting places to give voice to their ideas. Prominent Protestants belonged to these, as did Marrano Jews who had fled the Spanish Inquisition.[8] Many of these Marranos who had been quietly allowed to observe Judaism for over a century became sympathetic to the Protestant dilemma and joined the Calvinist Reformed Church. With their membership came new ideas on the art of avoiding detection and persecution.

Still, the religious situation was intolerable. The States met in the spring of 1565 and settled on sending Egmont to Spain to discuss revising the heresy laws. When he returned at the end of April from his mission, Orange was speechless with outrage. Not only had Egmont failed in his mission, but he had been utterly charmed by Philip. When official instructions arrived a week later, Philip made his policy clear. Heresy would not be tolerated in the Low Countries. Only the regent, Margaret of Parma, could call a council of bishops. A new education policy would be implemented to stamp out Calvinism, as the heretics had "usurped the sovereign control of all business."[9]

Then, in June, Fernando Álvarez de Toledo, third Duke of Alba, who had been out of favor and a strong supporter of Granvelle, was suddenly back in good odor.[10] Alba accompanied the Spanish queen to visit her mother, Catherine de' Medici, at Fuenterrabia on the border with France. There, Alba held secret discussions with the leading French councillors of state concerning the "heretical threats" to their kingdoms behind the innocent cloak of a family reunion.[11] The result was a series of vicious documents known as "the letters from the Segovia Woods"—written by Alba but signed by Philip—directly challenging the Netherlander nobles and their Protestant cause. Either they would obey their king and enforce the laws against heresy or they would be accused of treason. The choice was theirs.

Margaret of Parma delayed in publishing Philip's orders until two days after her son's wedding on November 11 to Maria of Portugal, giving the Council of State until November 30 to consider the full impact of the king's orders. Only on December 20 was a proclamation made to all provincial authorities to enforce the new heresy laws.

Even before the proclamation had been published, Orange, Egmont, and Horn had decided to withhold their cooperation and maintain their solemn league against the heresy laws, which were a direct contravention of their ancient privileges. Their stance shocked Elizabeth. These men were Philip's peacekeepers, not some evangelical preachers. This was Philip's aristocracy who were near revolt. By January 1566, as many as four hundred signatures of noblemen and administrators were sealed on what became known as the Compromise of the Nobility demanding a confederation against the Inquisition. Missing from the Compromise were the signatures of the three most powerful men in the country: Orange, Egmont, and Horn. They had no need to sign, they argued. They simply refused to carry out the king's orders in their provinces.

When Margaret pressed Orange to obey, he asked to be relieved of all his governorships. The great nobles met at Orange's home at Breda and eventually sent their "Request"—presented to Margaret on April 5—setting out reasons for their noncompliance. They knew full well that without them there would be no government in the Low Countries. Margaret had no alternative than to circulate her own orders conceding defeat to all magistrates and provincial seats of government on April 9.

Just as Elizabeth's attempts at moderation pleased few, Margaret's undertakings failed to win the support of the court opposition, in the persons of Orange, Egmont, and Horn, and the fundamentalist Calvinists. Orange announced he would abandon the Netherlands and the service of Philip II for his family home in the German territory at Dillenburg. Egmont and Horn followed suit. Margaret was thrown into a virtual state of panic. She begged the three men to remain at their posts until she could arrange for further concessions from Philip, vowing that everything "should be done by the Council of State, morning noon and night."[12]

Before the royal messengers had left for Spain, the Calvinists stepped up their resistance. To sit idly by and wait for what they feared would be an inevitable violent reply from Philip was simply not an option. By June a steady stream of exiled Netherlanders was returning home from England and France, armed with their Bibles and the ability to reach out to their countrymen with Christ's Word. The first public Calvinist service took place in Zeeland on June 30, followed two weeks later by the first service in Holland. Within two months Calvinist worship was organized throughout the western Low Countries, aided by the good weather and long evenings. By July a slow trickle of people listened to their open-air sermons preached in town squares, outside city walls, on the land of the nobility or by hedgerows. Before the month was over, it had increased to thousands. One man observed that around thirty thousand people attended Calvinist meetings in the Antwerp area alone. More shocking still, it was rumored that Calvinists attended their open-air meetings fully armed. The awesome nature of these "conventicles," as they were called, is captured in Breughel's contemporary painting *The Preaching of St. John the Baptist*. Women, children, and artisans, along with people from all walks of life, are crammed together in the painting to hear the Gospel and sing psalms.

It was the armed nature of the meetings that worried both the nobility and Margaret. The Council of State discussed the dangers of an armed mob as early as July 9, 1566. Only three possible actions seemed open to them to maintain law and order. At an emergency meeting of the States-General, bishops and clergy were instructed to exhort their flock to pious works and civil obedience. Margaret pinned her hope on prevailing with the Beggars.

All of this happened before Margaret had had Philip's response to the "Request" signed by Orange, Egmont, and Horn. Even worse, by the end of July the Beggars, too, had lost control. Only the Calvinist pastors seemed to have any impact on the people, making hundreds if not thousands of converts each day of ordinary people who had held their prior beliefs for a lifetime. More Calvinist preachers poured in from Geneva, France, Germany, and England, many wearing the blue leggings of the Calvinist "hedge preacher." One of the returned Netherlander exiles from England, Sebastian Matte, a hatmaker turned preacher, appeared beneath the walls of Veurne with two thousand armed Calvinists from Ypres, attempting to make the town a fortified base for his operations.

Though the attempt failed, Matte remained undaunted. On August 10, his sermon near the monastery of St. Laurence at Steenvoorde led to the first smashing of Catholic images by approximately twenty members of the congregation. Three days later the same group preached a rabble-rousing sermon at the St. Anthony monastery at Bailleul. At its conclusion, the monastery was sacked. The next day, the same was repeated at Poperinghe, only this time, a hundred people joined in the smashing of idols, with over half of the people newly returned from England. The "iconoclastic fury" had begun.

The Calvinists preached that many of the Netherlanders' woes were due to their impure churches, defiled by Catholic unholy images. Idolatry was an insult to God, and the images must be removed before more harm came their way. It was, in effect, the sacred duty and right of every Calvinist to purify their churches just as the English, French, and Scots had done before them. A government minister from Kortrijk reported that summer that "the audacity of the Calvinist preachers . . . has grown so great that in their sermons they admonish the people . . . to remove all idolatry from their hearts . . . and must also remove it from their sight . . . They will soon commit some shameful pillage of the churches, monasteries and abbeys; some of them are already making boasts about it."[13]

All trade had trickled to a virtual halt. Elizabeth, along with other foreign debtors, had had repayment of her debts prolonged. Though payment was due in August, the situation was so fraught that a second suspension of debt repayment was anticipated.[14] Philip's most loyal councillor, Viglius, wrote on August 2 to a friend in Spain that "the fire, once lit, will spread, and that, since trade is beginning to cease on account of these troubles, several working folk—constrained by hunger—will join in, waiting for the opportunity to acquire a share of the property of the rich."[15]

As Viglius so rightly predicted, it did not take long for the real trouble to begin. On August 21 at Ghent, grain prices remained at an all-time high. It was the last market day of summer, and the desperate poor and hungry people rioted, placing their own prices on the grain to be sold. The next day, the Calvinist preachers entered Ghent and sacked the churches and convents in the city. Everything—from the stained glass to all other articles of Roman Catholic worship—was destroyed. Antwerp, Middelburg, Mechlin, Amsterdam, Delft, Utrecht, The Hague, Leiden, Eindhoven, and other cities followed. The burgher guard stood by idly—fully armed—and did precisely nothing. They later told their magistrates that they would not fight their people for the church, the pope, or their monks. The Low Countries were in a state of civil war.

In the towns where the burgher guard obeyed orders—as in Lille, Bruges, or Leuven—there was no iconoclasm. Appeals from Margaret or Orange, Egmont, or Horn were of no avail. A small determined group of zealots—no more than a hundred men newly returned from England—had rampaged at lightning speed through the country, bringing total anarchy to the communities through which they passed. Despite the unremitting destruction, few raised a hand against them, even Catholics. The English Catholic diaspora watched and waited in dismay.

There was a distinct condoning of the attacks against church property. In spite of the real hardships facing the people, the church continued to prosper. It failed to offer alms or relief to the most needy. Its role as provider of charity and salvation had been replaced in the minds of many by that of a greedy landlord and tithe collector. Philip's institution of the new bishoprics only enhanced this view. The fear among the ruling classes, whether Netherlander or Spanish, was that the riots would not be confined to the churches.

Finally, on August 23, Margaret of Parma conceded freedom of worship to Protestants wherever it was already in effect. Still, the apparent agreement of the nobility and the Calvinists to Margaret's "Accord" fooled no one. The violence continued in the north of the country throughout September. Farther south, consistories sprouted all over Holland, Hainault, Flanders, and Limburg, with substantial congregations. By autumn, Orange had received word that the vengeance of the Spanish king was near. The Duke of Alba was on his way with a large force of Spanish troops—men hardened in the all-consuming battles against the Ottoman Turk—to teach the Netherlanders a lesson they would never forget.

"The army His Majesty is raising . . . is thought certain to consist of ten thousand Spaniards," Horn wrote to Orange on October 4. "Eight thousand veterans from Italy and two thousand recruits . . . six thousand Italians, twenty-four thousand Germans, two thousand light cavalry, one thousand men-at-arms and five thousand heavy cavalry . . . I can assure you that it is a long time since a Christian prince was better supplied."[16] An appalled William of Orange reported this to his council, adding, "We shall soon see the prologue to a high tragedy."[17]

Even as Orange uttered these words, the spread of Protestantism in northern Europe faced a new danger. The pope's legate to Scotland had given vast sums to Mary to reestablish Catholicism there. Within the month, word was sent to the pope of "the Queen's discontent with the King, her husband, who, seeing that the Queen will not allow him the authority that he had before the last turmoils of the realm . . . bade adieu to all the Lords of the Council with the intent to embark in a ship that he had ready."[18]

The ship made ready by Darnley would reportedly head for Flanders, into the midst of the Netherlanders' civil war, with Spanish troops closing in. Elizabeth and her privy councillors waited nervously, unable to influence events in the Low Countries or its closest neighbor, Scotland.

ELEVEN

Two Murders and Mayhem

Oculos habent et non vident.
Eyes have they but they see not.
—William Cecil to Henry Norris, November 1567

Soon enough, Elizabeth had a new worry in Scotland. Queen Mary had become embroiled in one of the great conundrums of the century that would set in train the circumstances of her own demise: the murder of her husband, Henry, Lord Darnley. Just as Mary had become quite ill in November 1566, so Darnley was reported to be suffering from smallpox early in the new year. Despite the reports, it seems more likely that Darnley, aged only twenty-one, was already seriously ill with tertiary syphilis.[1] Surprisingly, Mary resolved to nurse her husband back to health.

What made the sequence of events even more incredible was that everyone knew Mary and Darnley loathed the sight of one another. Had Mary been influenced by Bothwell and others loyal to her, who only a month earlier thought to be rid of Darnley "by other means" without implicating the queen? Why was there this "rapprochement" when rumors that Darnley wished to harm their son, Prince James, were so widespread? After all, Mary had snatched James away from Stirling Castle to bring him to the safety of Holyrood only days earlier. Whatever her motivations for wishing to play nurse to Darnley once more, we may never know them.

Mary ordered for hasty preparations to be made to remove Darnley from his Glasgow hide—and the company of his Lennox Stewart companions—to Edinburgh. In her capital, Mary could surround Darnley with men of her own choosing—Bothwell's men—ostensibly to prevent her husband from plotting against her. What, if anything, Darnley had been scheming again remains a mystery. What mattered was Mary's all-consuming belief that Darnley had instigated the murder of her secretary, David Rizzio, and that he had intended to kill her as well. These facts alone were sufficient for what followed.

So Darnley was brought from Glasgow to Edinburgh. Mary visited her husband regularly, their relationship seemingly improved, and he slowly recovered. On or before February 8, 1567, a cache of gunpowder was placed at Darnley's lodgings at the old provost's at Kirk o'Field by men loyal to Mary. The Scots queen, who had spent the early evening with Darnley, recalled at the last minute that she had to attend a masque in honor of a nobleman's marriage and bade her husband farewell. Darnley expected to return to the marital home at Holyrood Palace the next day. At some time around two o'clock in the morning of February 9, an explosion rocked Edinburgh. The provost's lodgings were blown to smithereens. Darnley's body was found in the gardens, mysteriously strangled.

When William Cecil received the news, he was worn out after the months of wrangling with the Commons and Elizabeth. He spoke longingly of resignation and wearily of his gout. In his letters to his old friend Sir Henry Sidney, now in Ireland facing the wrath of Shane O'Neill, Cecil wrote that "my body [is] well but my sinews . . . by their weakness I am as a dead body."[2] Within days of composing the letter, Cecil learned privately from his northern commanders and spies, followed by Mary's emissary, Robert Melville, two versions of the lurid affair of Darnley's murder. According to Sir William Drury, the English commander at Berwick, placards had been posted throughout Edinburgh charging the Earl of Bothwell with the murder of their king, naming Mary as his accomplice. This account matched the gossip that had been circulating at court and in London's streets. Mary's version proclaimed that she was entirely ignorant of the plot and that had it not been for a quirk of fate, she, too, would be dead.

Elizabeth listened to both sides of the story. Her letter to Mary frostily addresses her as "Madame" instead of her usual salutation of "*ma chère soeur.*" It opens with a sentence filled with shock and awe that can still be felt across the centuries: "My ears have been so deafened and my understanding so grieved and my heart so affrighted to hear the dreadful news of the abominable murder of your mad husband . . . that I scarcely yet have the wits to write about it." A few sentences along Elizabeth is blunt: "However, I will not at all dissemble what most people are talking about: which is that you will look through your fingers at the revenging of this deed, and that you do not take measures that touch those who have done as you wished, as if . . . the murderers felt assurance in doing it."[3]

Nine days after the Darnley murder, the Spanish ambassador to London, Guzman de Silva, wrote to Mary on the order of Philip II that he "had been told of the bad offices of her husband [Darnley] in writing against her to His Majesty, the Pope and other Princes in the matter of religion."[4] The Venetian ambassador reported to the doge that Darnley's murder had been the work of heretics. Still the open question remained: Did Mary know about the plan to murder her husband?

Naturally, Darnley's outraged father, Lennox, begged Cecil for Elizabeth's assistance in punishing the murderers, especially Mary. Meanwhile, intelligence had arrived from Scotland that Mary had not only "looked through her fingers" but was also obstructing justice to bring Bothwell to trial. Elizabeth demanded to know the truth and sent the experienced Henry Killigrew northward as her ambassador. When Killigrew arrived in Scotland days later, he found a "very doleful" Mary. She seemed, so he reported back to Elizabeth, more interested in who was publishing the defamatory placards against her and Bothwell than in finding her husband's murderers. By the end of the month, Killigrew and those loyal to the Earl of Moray had persuaded Mary that she must allow Lennox to pursue a private prosecution in Parliament against Bothwell as the murderer of his son.

Incomprehensibly, Mary flatly refused to be a coplaintiff with her father-in-law. In fact, she upheld the decree that Lennox could only come into Edinburgh with six armed men, while it was widely known that Bothwell had over four thousand adherents swarming in the town. Lennox shrank from entering Edinburgh without men to protect him. Bothwell, deprived of facing his accuser, was acquitted.

Disgusted with his sister, Moray headed for London. He told the English court that Bothwell "had always been his enemy" and was now in a position of absolute power. He also said that he would not return to Scotland unless and until Mary punished those responsible for her husband's murder. By mid-May, Mary was positively courting disaster. She married the Earl of Bothwell on May 15, only days after he divorced his wife.

Elizabeth immediately offered asylum to the young Prince James as pandemonium broke out in Scotland. Cecil himself wrote, "Scotland is a quagmire . . . The most honest desire to go away, the worst tremble with the shaking of their conscience."[5] Maitland remained loyal to Mary and was in constant correspondence with Cecil detailing the events as they unfolded. Arms were taken up by the Protestant Lords against Mary and her third husband, who were summarily defeated at Carberry Hill only one month after their wedding day. Bothwell escaped overseas, while Mary was taken through the streets of Edinburgh to the cries of "burn the whore" and "burn the murderess of her husband." Mary spat back at them that she would crucify the lot of them.[6] Two days later, she was bundled off to her island prison at Lochleven Castle. The Earl of Moray returned home to join Maitland and the other Lords of the Congregation in restoring order.

Before leaving England, Moray had asked Elizabeth for help, and she flatly refused. Though she recognized the dire state of Scotland's affairs, Elizabeth explained, she could never set herself up against an anointed queen in favor of those who had seized her throne. Nonetheless, she sent Sir Nicholas Throckmorton to Scotland to see if he could smooth the way for Mary's restitution and bring Prince James to England for safety. Throckmorton was too late to be of any real value aside from warning Elizabeth and Cecil of their "great peril" in abandoning the Protestant Lords to their cause. By the end of the summer, the Scottish Parliament had decided to establish a regency of nine nobles, naming Moray as regent, and procured Mary's abdication and her consent to the coronation of her son. Mary would remain indefinitely imprisoned at Lochleven Castle.

Elsewhere, another regent sat uncomfortably next to her son, the king. Catherine de' Medici, for her part, was deeply concerned about the "iconoclastic fury" on her border with the Netherlands. Worse still, her son, Charles IX, had grown desperately fond of the Huguenot leader, Admiral Gaspard de Coligny, who had also become the king's mentor. With the Huguenots in ascendance in France, and the Netherlander Calvinists standing their ground against the might of Spain, the situation for France's Catholic established order seemed grim. Nonetheless, Catherine could be happy that Mary's Guise uncles had withdrawn from court and were temporarily cut off from their niece.

Of course, the French Huguenots pressed home their advantage with the young king in the absence of the Guises. Coligny tried to persuade Charles that if they successfully ejected Philip from the Low Countries, it could only serve France's national interest. Catherine wisely resisted. The very last thing she cared to do was to alienate Philip and bring down the wrath of Spain on France. Nevertheless, Philip tested her mettle, requesting that Alba be able to march his crack troops the length of France to the Low Countries, as it was the most convenient route for his invasion forces. Catherine, naturally, failed Philip's test, unequivocally refusing an outlandish suggestion that would "set fire to the kingdom."[7]

The route was changed, but not without Catherine fearing reprisals from Philip's soldiers in the future. After all, with most of the Low Countries in revolt in the south, the Spaniards would be billeted on France's border. Catherine ordered a reinforcement of the northern defenses and hired six thousand Swiss mercenaries as a deterrent against potential Spanish aggression. Garrisons along the Netherlands borders in Piedmont, Champagne, Toul, Metz, and Verdun were reinforced.

In 1567, these tensions coincided with the burning issue from England's viewpoint. Would the French return Calais in accordance with the treaty of Cateau-Cambrésis? Catherine's response came soon enough. Since Elizabeth had broken the peace between France and England by taking Newhaven in 1562–63, France was quite content to maintain its current and natural borders. Calais would never be returned.

While Catherine was battling to save the fragile peace of France, Cecil's spies and ambassadors in Ireland discovered that Shane O'Neill, that bellicose Ulster chieftain who had kept his territories in a state of perpetual war, had appealed for five thousand troops from France to fight the English. He was politely refused. Simultaneously, O'Neill donned a diplomatic mantle and traveled from southern Ireland to Edinburgh and on to Rome, seeking aid for his cause while claiming to be saving Ireland for Roman Catholicism.[8] Naturally, Mary was in no position to offer succor to O'Neill at a time when her very throne was crumbling beneath her. Nonetheless, Pius V in Rome was prepared to lend a ready ear.

Sometime in the spring of 1567, the disreputable papal appointee, Armagh's Archbishop Magrath, wrote to Pius V for the establishment of the Holy Inquisition in Ireland. He urged the pope to grant this most serious request since Ireland's heretics "under form of sound doctrine yet by merry tales and pretty conceits disseminate many and diverse empty and profitless matters repugnant to the Catholic faith . . . [and] utter derisive and unseemly words even against God's holy church." Naturally, the pope agreed that such a Holy Inquisition should be established under the "sway and jurisdiction of the Most Illustrious and Catholic Prince O'Neill."[9]

This seemingly earnest plea was an outright lie. The number of "heretics" in Ireland was small, even ten years after Elizabeth's Act of Settlement. Shane's Catholicism was more a political tool to elicit support from Scotland, Spain, or the papacy than a matter of faith. The Anglo-Irish settlers professed the religion more or less as decreed by Elizabeth as the head of the Church of England. Not surprisingly, no pope had appointed any Catholic archbishop or bishop to any Pale diocese in Elizabeth's lifetime.[10] The Pale dioceses of Dublin, Kildare, Meath, and Armagh were fully Anglo-Irish in worship. Other Pale dioceses in Limerick, Cork, Ferns, Tuam, and Clonfert acknowledged Elizabeth's Royal Supremacy but continued to worship as traditional Catholics, with Elizabeth's full knowledge. Yet Ireland was rapidly becoming a battleground for religious and political tensions.[11]

Though a thief, bully, murderer, and cheat, Shane O'Neill maintained an iron grip on Ulster. Leicester, taking charge of the degenerating situation there, persuaded Elizabeth without too much argument that his brother-in-law, Sir Henry Sidney, would make an ideal Lord Lieutenant to replace Sussex. A tall, elegant, and likable man, Sidney had always been popular with Elizabeth's nobility. That he was also Leicester's favorite made his initial popularity with the Palesmen, Anglo-Irish, and Celtic chieftains (who called him "Big Henry of the Beer"), even more remarkable. Having only taken up his post in 1566, Sidney found that his support to stop O'Neill was nearly universal. Perhaps this groundswell of support for the English Lord Lieutenant is not so strange when considering that O'Neill had been terrorizing the Irish for over fifteen years—burning fields and villages, pillaging livestock and valuables, kidnapping whosoever stood in his way, and murdering at will.

Still, deciding to eliminate Shane O'Neill was one thing; succeeding was quite another. As the weeks became months, Sidney's obsession with routing O'Neill grew. Stuck between the divergent demands of the Celtic chieftains, the faction-ridden Anglo-Irish, the power-hungry Palesmen, and the English merchant adventurers, Ireland seemed more akin to a "Wild West" of native warring tribes and con men than a civilized nation. Sidney found his position as governor rapidly eroded, and by the spring of 1567, he had had enough. "For God's sake," Sidney begged Cecil by letter, "take me out of this world."[12]

Sidney hadn't been able to provide the Irish with a quick-fix solution to O'Neill. At the end of the day, it was the O'Donnells, who dominated Tyreannell in northwest Ulster, who handled matters. Though Elizabeth had voted Sidney a staggering £35,000 to mount a devastating force against O'Neill, few in Ireland had confidence that this time Sidney would prevail. As Sidney made his way northward from Dublin, the O'Donnells set aside their internal differences and joined forces with one another to repel O'Neill. Attacking Shane's encampment at Farsetmore, the O'Donnells literally forced O'Neill's men back into the swollen River Swilly. Hundreds of men drowned, while others willingly abandoned the once omnipotent O'Neill. Nonetheless, Shane had somehow escaped.

O'Neill desperately needed new allies. Unable to count on his own clan, who were already vying to take over from him on his death, O'Neill knew he would have to surrender to Sidney or make peace with the other Scotsmen in Ireland, the MacDonalds. Shane opted for the MacDonald solution, as he had already kidnapped their chief, Sorley Boy. On May 31, negotiations were opened in a large field in County Antrim, far away from their armies. Shane offered Sorley Boy's release in exchange for Scottish mercenary reinforcements. The MacDonalds pondered and said they'd consider the matter. Two days later, the MacDonalds gave Shane O'Neill their reply. They cut his throat and hacked him to pieces.

When Edmund Campion, the Oxford student who had so impressed Elizabeth, compiled his *History of Ireland* in 1569–70, he wrote, "Thus the wretched man ended, who might have lived like a Prince, had he not quenched the sparks of grace that appeared in him with arrogancy and contempt against his prince."[13]

Shane's body was buried at Glenarm initially. Yet Sidney remained dissatisfied that O'Neill was indeed dead. To placate Sidney, the chieftain's body was exhumed and his head sent "pickled in a pipkin" to the Lord Lieutenant, who promptly had it mounted on a pole over Dublin Castle as a lesson to all the "wild" Irish.

By the end of the summer of 1567, Mary Queen of Scots was imprisoned at Lochleven Castle; Shane O'Neill was dead; Philip's crack commander, the Duke of Alba, had marched into Brussels; France teetered on a fresh outbreak of religious violence; and England knew that to recover Calais it would need to go to war. It is little wonder Elizabeth felt the international situation was grave.

At home, the universities remained hotbeds of discontent, whether from Catholic or Protestant factions. Though Cambridge was emerging as the more "churchy" of the two universities, Oxford was seemingly overrun with the more conservative or Catholic society. While Cambridge

William Cecil, First Lord Burghley, painted around 1585. He was the longest serving and most trusted adviser to Queen Elizabeth.

Robert Cecil, the younger son of William Cecil, was his father's chosen heir. Constantly at loggerheads with the Queen's later favorites, Raleigh and Essex, he forged the succession of James VI of Scotland to Elizabeth's throne.

Sir Francis Walsingham came to the fore as Elizabeth's Principal Secretary, having honed his skills on the Continent as an emissary and ambassador in the 1560s. His network of informants became crucial in the unmasking of Fifth Columnists in the "wars of religion."

Robert Dudley, Earl of Leicester, was Elizabeth's trusted friend and greatest love. When she died, a letter from Leicester was found at her bedside, marked "his last letter."

Catherine de Medici was the single greatest influence in France during the reigns of her three sons Francis (François) II, Charles IX, and Henry (Henri) III.

Mary, Queen of Scots, queen of Scotland since the age of one week, grew up in the French Court, destined to marry the sickly Francis II. Upon his death, she determined that she would return to Scotland and vie for Elizabeth's throne.

The Duke of Alba (pictured at the right) instituted a Spanish-style Inquisition in the Netherlands known as the "Council of Troubles" to the Spaniards and the "Council of Blood" to the Netherlanders.

Philip II of Spain, once Queen Mary I's king consort, never ceased to try to return England to the Roman Catholic faith by whatever means were expedient until his death in 1598. He was often called "holier than the Pope" in his desire to save Catholicism from the Protestant threat.

Margaret, Duchess of Parma, Philip II's half-sister, was launched into the troubled Netherlands as its governor on behalf Philip II. She was respected, but, in the end, ineffectual in stopping the bloodshed.

Alessandro Farnese, Duke of Parma and son of Margaret, eventually became governor of the Netherlands himself, and ruled more fairly than the Duke of Alba, but by then the Eighty Years' War with Spain was already in its second decade.

Hercule-François de France, Duke of Alençon, the youngest of Catherine de Medici's sons was betrothed to Queen Elizabeth I and led an army on behalf of England into the Netherlands to help liberate them from Spanish oppression.

King Henry (Henri) III of France had also been engaged to Elizabeth I when he was the Duke of Alençon. Known for a degenerate court that wavered on religious matters, he would be assassinated nine months after he had ordered the murder of Henry (Henri) de Guise.

Henry (Henri) I (1549–88) de Lorraine, also known as Henry (Henri) de Guise, was related to Mary Queen of Scots and the leader of the powerful Guise family who stood in frequent opposition to the French Crown.

Gaspard II de Chatillon, also known as Admiral Coligny, was the leader of the Huguenot opposition. His murder unleashed the bloodbath on St. Bartholomew's Day in 1572.

Edmund Campion, the eloquent Jesuit divine, had once been a champion of the Elizabethan settlement and a protégé of the earl of Leicester.

Robert Persons was the administrative leader of the Campion Jesuit mission to England, escaping back to Rome then Spain. He is one of the suspected authors of the virulent attack on the Earl of Leicester in Leicester's Commonwealth.

Henry Garnett headed up the Jesuit mission to England after Robert Persons and Edmund Campion, staying in hiding for several years.

P. ROBERTVS SOVTHVELL, Soc. Iesu Londini pro Cath fide suspensus et secutus .3. mar. 1595.

Robert Southwell was the Puritan divine gentleman whose gift for prose was admired by all.

Edward Dering was the Puritan divine who dared to compare Elizabeth's Church to a decaying state to her during her private devotions.

Thomas Cartwright was the Puritan divine who was deprived of his status by William Cecil. Cartwright eventually went into exile, writing scathing pamphlets and tracts against the Elizabethan Settlement.

John Rogers was the prebendary of St. Paul's in London and the first Protestant martyr burnt at the stake by Queen Mary I, Elizabeth's half-sister.

This is the gruesome image of the execution of Edmund Campion, Alexander Briant, and Ralph Sherwin that was sold to the general public to commemorate the event.

Edmund Grindal was the moderate Archbishop of Canterbury who refused to allow the Elizabethan Settlement to overshadow his view of the Anglican Church.

John Knox, the Presbyterian Scottish religious leader, who was intimately involved in plots against Mary whilst queen regnant of Scotland.

Pope Pius V doggedly hounded Elizabeth and England to return to the Catholic fold, setting myriad plots and traps internationally, and failing miserably.

Pope Gregory XIII who decided to excommunicate Elizabeth without consulting Philip II of Spain or any other Catholic leader, pinning the document demanding her assassination "Regnans in Excelsis" to the door of Lambeth Palace in London.

King James I of England and VI of Scotland, son of Mary Queen of Scots, at the height of his powers as king of both countries.

Sir Walter Raleigh as painted in miniature for Queen Elizabeth. Her nickname for him was "Water," and she would frequently mimic a person dying of thirst when he came into her presence.

Robert Devereux, Second Earl of Essex, as he looked just before going to Ireland to head Elizabeth's army of occupation there.

English ships and the Spanish Armada battling in the English Channel, presumed to be off the coast of the Isle of Wight.

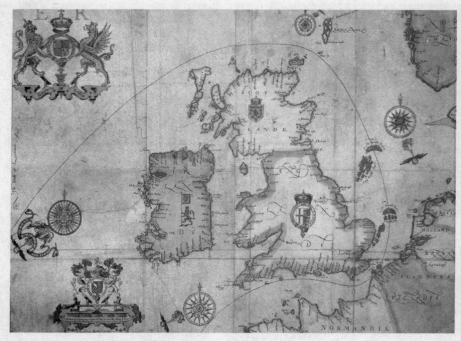

This is one of eleven charts showing the track of the Spanish Armada around Britain made contemporaneously with the attempted invasion of England.

The St. Bartholomew's Day Massacre was a watershed in Europe between Catholics and Protestants. It encompassed in a single week all the hatred, intolerance, and bloodshed that had been rife for decades throughout the northern European countries.

Henry (Henri) of Navarre, later Henry (Henri) IV of France was the Protestant heir to the French throne. Despite becoming king, the only way he could unite his country was to famously convert to Catholicism, insisting that "Paris is worth a Mass."

This image is widely believed to be the young Christopher Marlowe from his days at Cambridge. Marlowe worked as a counterfeiter and spy.

Queen Elizabeth I: These four images of Elizabeth show the evolution in her iconography from the young Virgin Queen at her coronation to the mature queen and the all powerful Gloriana.

overwhelmed Oxford in the sheer numbers of godly preachers, Oxford more than made up for the town's Catholic leanings with its own extreme ministers among its graduates in men like John Field and Thomas Wilcox. Both men, after just a few months in London, had already found themselves exiled.[14]

Cecil from his base at Cambridge and Leicester at Oxford instituted their own miniature secret services to provide intelligence to the queen for potentially serious threats. The most useful "agents" of both men within the universities invariably changed with the passing years, but more often than not, it was the students themselves that proved the most fruitful path for discovering dissident attitudes. After all, Elizabeth and her privy councillors knew that the Catholic students and their professors found refuge in the classrooms and universities at Louvain and Mechlin. Though these university spy networks had their roots in the controversies of the 1560s, they would continue until the end of Elizabeth's reign, with consequences far beyond the sphere of religious upheaval.

In the autumn of 1567, there were over twenty-seven Catholic exiles at Louvain from New College Oxford alone.[15] Their writings and books sent back illicitly to England had done "incalculable good in spreading the growth of the Faith," the Spanish ambassador wrote to Philip. The Spanish king's reply was a resounding endorsement for the "Apologetic School of Louvain," urging the ambassador to explore any opportunity to encourage the work of the Catholic English exiles.[16]

Yet, despite numerous warnings, Elizabeth refused to believe that these men represented a clear threat to her or England. Her preoccupation remained with the civil wars on the Continent. With thousands of *tercio* troops in the Low Countries led by the world's most competent general threatening to murder its Protestants, naturally, she was right.

The arrival of the Duke of Alba and his army on September 1 in Brussels heralded a new era. His first act was to demobilize those "Lutheran" mercenaries whose loyalty Margaret of Parma had purchased to quell the fury of the Calvinists. Only five days later, Alba issued his patent creating the tribunal he called the "Council of Troubles." Before long, it would be known as the "Council of Blood." Orange, Egmont, George de Lalaing, count of Hoogstraten, and Horn had all traveled to Germany in the summer to regroup, but by September 9 Horn, Egmont, and their secretaries had returned at Margaret's specific invitation.

The moment they arrived, the Spanish soldiers swooped, and they were arrested. All their papers were seized. Margaret, though still regent, had not only lost the confidence of Philip but was now directly implicated as Alba's accomplice. Bewildered and disgusted, she resigned her post on December 30, but not before swearing in the Duke of Alba as captain-general of the Spanish forces and governor-general of all the Low Countries. Undaunted by Margaret's sudden resignation, Alba wrote to Philip that "there is a new world to be created here."[17]

Over the next six months, Alba terrorized the country. He transferred executive power to his own trusted Spanish and Italian ministers from the local nobility. Spanish and Italian lawyers represented the Low Countries internationally, even running the chief towns as magistrates, or *corregidors*. Whenever a Netherlander died or resigned, a Spaniard took his place. What mattered was loyalty, or, as Alba called it, "a spotless character," and to possess such a thing one had to be either Spanish or Italian.

That was only the beginning. By Lent 1568, thousands of people had been arrested, tried, and executed for their part in the "fury." The swiftness and efficacy of the Council of Troubles was awe-inspiring. Those who had signed the petitions against Cardinal Granvelle in 1563 were hunted down. Albert van Loo, a revenue collector for the king, tried to commit suicide, fearing he would be blamed for the disorders in his jurisdiction. Orange, Culemborg, and Hoogstraten were summoned to appear before the court in January that year. They refused. They were, of course, tried in absentia, and all their property and possessions remaining in the Low Countries were forfeit. In all, over twelve thousand people were tried, and nine thousand condemned to lose most of their worldly possessions. Over one thousand were executed.

Orange and his followers were left no alternative: To recover their lost lands and property, they would need to invade the Low Countries at the head of an army. With Egmont and Horn imprisoned and other leaders under house arrest or dead, William of Orange emerged as the undisputed leader of the opposition to the Duke of Alba and his Council of Troubles.

Alba's forced forfeiture of his hereditary title was illegal; and as the ruler of the principality of Orange and all its possessions, Orange was constitutionally within his rights to enter his lands to wage war on his enemies. Alba, suspecting reprisals, kidnapped Orange's eldest son, Philip William, then studying at Louvain. Orange, however, remained undaunted, vowing to rid the Low Countries of its scourge, Alba. The Calvinist movement had won over its unwilling leader, who also happened to be a Catholic. Orange would never see his son again.

That autumn and winter, Catherine de' Medici, too, faced a new rebellion. Catherine's nerves hadn't been the only ones to have jangled at the thought of Alba marching through France and settling on its northeastern border. The Huguenot leaders, the Prince de Condé and Admiral Coligny, had become convinced that Catherine was in league with Philip to exterminate them as part of the plan to eradicate the Calvinists from the Low Countries. When Charles IX and Catherine refused to either attack Alba or release their mercenary soldiers, suspicion erupted into conflict. Word of savage attacks by Huguenots against Catholics surged in from the countryside. Near Toulouse, monks were reportedly killed and Catholics beaten or run out of town without any possessions.

Yet despite Catherine's best efforts to assuage the Huguenot leadership, France was heading for its second religious civil war in five years. Moving the court to the fortified town of Meaux in late September, Catherine had sent word for her Swiss mercenaries to come to their aid just as the towns of Melun and Péronne were attacked by rampaging Huguenots. When the Swiss troops arrived, Catherine and the king escaped amid a "forest of Swiss pikes" along with the senior members of the court and made a dash for Paris. Finally Catherine saw that the days for reconciliation were over. As the city of Paris was surrounded by the Huguenot army, and supplies blockaded along roads and by the River Seine, Catherine sent out appeals to those she hoped would send help, including Philip and Pius V. Under the signature of Charles IX, Elizabeth received a letter "praying and exhorting her to make no move, and show the Huguenots no favor."[18]

Elizabeth knew that England represented the strongest (albeit still weak) Protestant realm. She also recalled that it was the Huguenot desertion of the English at Newhaven in 1563 that lead to England's rout. Where only four years earlier they had abandoned the English and joined forces with the French Catholics, the Huguenots would now pay for their betrayal by her tacit support for Catherine. Moreover, Elizabeth would refuse exit visas to English Protestants sympathetic to their cause.

After all, Elizabeth could hardly argue with Moray in Scotland that subjects should not rise up against their anointed monarch, then say the opposite to Charles and Catherine in France. In Cecil's acknowledgment of Catherine's plea to the English ambassador in France, Sir Henry Norris, he confidently wrote, "Her Majesty much mislikes of the Prince of Condé and the Admiral."[19]

In reality, Elizabeth breathed more easily when France was in turmoil. Not only would France be unable to undertake any foreign enterprise against England while tackling its own divisions, but it had to be vigilant on its northeastern border with the Low Countries against incursions by Netherlander Calvinists seeking to help the Huguenots. At the back of Catherine's mind was Parma's malevolence.

Consequently, during that harsh winter of 1567–68, Paris froze and starved. The Huguenots had received succor from German *Reiter* (mercenary cavalry), yet even their resources had dwindled to precarious levels. Condé had taken Chartres but had to halt his campaign due to lack of supplies and money to pay his mercenaries. The countryside had been laid waste, with the land ravaged and its peasantry starving. With both sides unable to continue, peace was the only solution. This was signed by Condé and the king at Longjumeau on March 23, 1568. Still, the Protestants refused to leave all the towns they had taken, mostly for fear of reprisals. They had burned churches, destroyed religious ornaments and statues, and desecrated relics. Similar barbarity and murder had occurred where the Catholic government forces had taken towns. Though peace had broken out, Catherine would never again follow the road of clemency with the Huguenots.

TWELVE

An Ill-Conceived Escape and Rebellion

❧

Within this realm a practice [is] in hand for the
alteration of religion and the advancement of
the Queen of Scots to the crown.

—Franchiotto, an Italian spy,

to Francis Walsingham, 1568

S o, by the spring of 1568, England was the most peaceful country
in northern Europe. Though friction existed between Protestant
and Catholic, and the godly were on the increase in London, England seemed a relative haven when compared to the "hot wars"
affecting Norway, Sweden, Denmark, France, the Low Countries, Ireland, and Scotland.

Then, on May 2, everything changed. Queen Mary escaped from her
gilded prison at Lochleven. The Scots Queen immediately prepared for
battle, having written to her Guise cousins and Elizabeth on May 1, signing, "Have pity on your good sister and cousin."[1] Cecil had heard of Mary's
escape through his well-honed network of agents within a few days and
sent a messenger by return with a simple statement to Moray—deal with
Mary decisively and quickly.

Moray had hardly needed Cecil's urging. Within five days, Mary had
raised an army of some six thousand men to help her reclaim her throne,
many from the loyal Hamilton clan. Moray mustered his men, meeting
Mary's at Langside. The queen's forces were utterly routed. Over a hundred were slain and three hundred taken prisoner. Moray suffered very

few casualties. Meanwhile, Mary rode off from the battle with a few loyal supporters, hoping initially to reach Dumbarton and from there board a ship bound for France. However, Moray's men had swept ahead, blocking her way. Forced to flee across desolate passes in the Glenkens along the River Ken, Mary and her followers rested at the head of the valley of the Tarff, now called "Queen's Hill." At their final resting place of Maxwell Castle at Terregles, the decision was taken, for good or ill, to flee farther southward instead, across the Solway Firth and into England.

In borrowed clothes, covering her shorn head with a cloak, Mary made her way by fishing boat toward the small port of Workington. It was seven in the evening when her party of some twenty people stumbled ashore. Lord Herries, one of the four noblemen who had accompanied her, sent word to Sir Henry Curwen of Workington (whom he knew) claiming that he had eloped with a Scottish heiress and hoped to find refuge there. Fortunately, Curwen's servants replied that though Sir Henry was away, the group would be most welcomed. Still, despite her disguise, Mary was immediately recognized by one of the servants. The following morning the deputy governor of the region, Lord Sheriff, Richard Lowther, greeted the party with four hundred horsemen to take Mary to Carlisle. There she was installed in Carlisle Castle to await Elizabeth's pleasure.

The north of England had a large Catholic population, and the presence of the Scots queen there, hotly pursued by Scotland's regent, was far from a pleasurable prospect. Elizabeth swiftly called an emergency council meeting to discuss the unprecedented matter. Cecil and Leicester feared that Elizabeth's loyalty to her cousin Mary would win out over the political and religious imperatives of the past ten years.

For the council, leaving Mary in the north of England was nonsense, as she would be seen as England's future Catholic queen. Moving her south suggested coercion and possible long-term imprisonment, which would offend France, Spain, and the pope. Then, of course, there was the open question of why she had been imprisoned on the island fortress of Lochleven in the first place. Had Mary knowingly conspired with Bothwell to murder her own husband, the king of Scotland and an English subject? It was a tricky situation.

Much of their discussion centered on how Elizabeth should react. Mary requested a face-to-face meeting with England's queen to set out her woes. Moray insisted that Mary should be returned to Scotland and prison. Cecil led the council discussions. Was Mary guilty of conspiring to kill Darnley? It seemed to him that only by answering this query in the Scots queen's favor should Mary be restored to her throne. Yet if Mary were guilty, then her treatment must be commensurate with the crime. The only way to determine the way forward, Cecil argued, was to evaluate the evidence supporting her guilt or innocence. Only then could a popular uprising in the north be avoided.[2]

The council agreed to send Sir Francis Knollys, Elizabeth's cousin by marriage, and the Duke of Norfolk northward to parlay with Mary. There they would be joined by the warden of the West Marches, Lord Scrope, to deal with Mary and her advisers. They proposed that there be no formal trial or judgment, merely an airing of the evidence both for and against the Scots queen. Reluctantly, Mary agreed; it was obvious she would not be allowed the freedom to continue to journey onward to France, as she maintained she wanted to, unless she did. Elizabeth doubted Mary would be welcomed in France, after the near-cataclysm of the second religious war.

Time rumbled on. It was mid-July before it was decided to keep Mary in England. Elizabeth insisted that all allegations against Mary must be proven false before she could be released. Moray traveled south and produced the Casket Letters—named after the gilt and silver casket-shaped box holding them—which the Privy Council and Elizabeth read. Mary claimed that these were forgeries perpetrated by Moray. Of course, she would, wouldn't she? The evidence in these letters seemed to compromise Mary beyond doubt. Mary, to prove her innocence, would have to refute their authenticity in a manner that would convince the English.

Instead, Mary first tried to bribe Cecil. She sent word to him that if he helped her regain her throne, she would agree to the establishment of a Protestant church in Scotland "after the English pattern."[3] It was an act of desperation too far and rebounded against her. So, in an about-face, Mary withdrew from the proceedings. She refused to acknowledge the jurisdiction of the Privy Council to judge her in the matter as Scotland's anointed queen and refused to participate any further in the process.

Elizabeth wrote to Mary that the proceedings were merely examining the evidence to help her regain the throne. Of course, Elizabeth added, this could only occur if Mary were innocent of killing Darnley. Moray, too, received a letter allaying his fears that England's queen had been swayed to Mary's cause. Still, Mary would not be dissuaded. She rejected Elizabeth's viewpoint that in not responding, the stain would remain on her honor. Mary simply refused to plead.

By mid-October, it seems, Elizabeth had made up her own mind as to Mary's innocence. "The Queen's Majesty is now at the pinch so careful of her own surety and state as I perceive the Queen of Scots shall not be advanced to greater credit than her cause will serve. And I think," Cecil added conspiratorially, "that is rather to put her back than to further her."[4]

So the last opportunity Mary would have to speak out in her own defense passed. Elizabeth refused to sit in judgment on her cousin without Mary's answer to the charges set forth by Moray. The result was that the Scots queen was sent to the Earl of Shrewsbury at Tutbury for safekeeping, and supposedly out of harm's way.

Once again, Elizabeth underestimated the pull of the international Catholic League initiated all those years before at the Council of Trent. Luckily for England, by the end of 1568, France had erupted once more into civil war between the Huguenots, the Guise family, and the court faction.[5] Charles IX, fearing the intervention of Alba and the unwanted support of the Huguenots by Calvinist Netherlanders now living in France, found himself fighting extremists on all fronts.

Spain, though preoccupied with its own internal troubles from the Moriscos in the south and saber-rattling from the Ottoman Turk in the Mediterranean, remained committed to reconverting northern Europe to the true faith. What was needed in England was a man who could carry out any Machiavellian plan devised to that end. Incredibly, Philip chose this precise moment to replace his affable and intelligent ambassador Guzman de Silva with the archplotter Guerau de Spes.[6] Of course, de Spes lost no time inserting himself into the captive Queen Mary's network of servants and informants, zealously rooting out weak spots in Elizabeth's regime. By October 1568, he was regularly transmitting correspondence from Mary to Philip.

De Spes's ardent desire to be in the thick of things was plain from the outset. "In the neighborhood [where Mary is kept], which is the part of the country where there are most Catholics," de Spes wrote shortly after his arrival in London, "she has many sympathizers, and it will not be difficult to release her, and even raise a great revolt against this Queen [Elizabeth]; but it will be more prudent that your Majesty should not appear in this, and I will do nothing unless I receive orders from your Majesty or the Duke [of Alba]."[7]

De Spes's correspondence with Spain and Alba in the Low Countries proved to be a source of illumination and controversy, aimed at deposing Elizabeth and enthroning Mary as queen of England. Nonetheless, at the end of November, when four small coasters from Spain were forced by storms and "French pirates" into harbor at Plymouth, de Spes requested that the cargo be brought to safety by Elizabeth. As the Channel had been teeming with pirates of all nationalities for some time, Elizabeth ordered the cargo ashore, initially in good faith, to transport to Dover overland. It transpired that the "cargo" was £85,000 in gold—about one-third of the amount Elizabeth had received from her last parliamentary subsidy—and was destined to be used by Alba to pay his troops for enforcing the Council of Troubles in the Low Countries. To ensure its safe arrival in the Netherlands would result in the death of many Protestants; to keep it might result in war.

Yet on closer examination, it seemed that the money still belonged to the Genoese banker based in London, Benedict Spinola, and not the king of Spain. Spinola, when approached, agreed readily that Elizabeth represented a better credit risk than Philip and Alba. Papers were drawn up quickly for the loan of the money to Elizabeth instead.[8]

Naturally, de Spes was incandescent with rage. So much so that he had forgotten the first rule of an Elizabethan ambassador: to write only in guarded terms. He fired off a ranting missive to Alba at the end of

December saying that the queen "wishes to declare herself openly against his Majesty [Philip], in the belief that if she makes herself mistress of the sea, and another army goes by land to attack the States, the task will be easy . . . I pray your Excellency do not doubt this determination . . . This is the reason that has moved me to write so urgently that you should seize all English property and advise the King, in order that the same step be taken in all his dominions."[9] The letter was intercepted.

At the heart of Elizabeth's supposed desire to declare herself "openly" against Spain was de Spes's mistaken belief that both Cecil and Leicester were itching to become involved in the religious affairs of the Low Countries. Unfortunately for Spain, the Netherlands, and England, de Spes's advice was heeded by Alba, and all English property was seized. Five days later, on January 10, 1569, Elizabeth retaliated:

> *Her Majesty commands all and every, her justices and officials within her towns, cities, ports, and other places under her government, to take steps to detain and arrest with all their goods, chattels, and ships, all subjects born in the dominions of the King of Spain, in order that they may be held as security and pledges for the damages and loss received, without just or apparent cause, by the subjects of Her Majesty, and for other reasons which may appear.*[10]

Further letters were intercepted, leading to de Spes's house arrest. Within two weeks, Alba realized that he had acted precipitously and sent his own ambassador, Christophe d'Assonleville, to try to patch things up. While the queen and her councillors were more than happy to avert open war with Spain, Cecil's spies warned him of an even more treacherous plot involving de Spes and the Catholic earls of the north of England. The plan was for them to rise up against their anointed queen. The year 1569 began as momentously as it would end.

The following month, de Spes, still under house arrest, received a message in "a safe cipher" from the Duke of Norfolk and the Earl of Arundel, assuring the Spanish ambassador that they were biding their time to free him from "Cecil's impertinences" while they garnered their resources. "They will be able to turn out the present accursed Government," de Spes wrote to Alba on February 29, "and raise another Catholic one, bringing the Queen to consent thereto. They think your Excellency will support them in this, and that the country will not lose the friendship of our King . . . I have encouraged them."[11] The plot was intended to dethrone Elizabeth and imprison Cecil in the Tower. The messenger delivering the "safe cipher" was a long-term resident of London, the Florentine banker Roberto Ridolfi.

As the spring wore on, Norfolk's aspirations to marry the Scottish queen became generally known and gained momentum in the council, with Leicester cited as its foremost champion.[12] Moray, as Scotland's regent, thought that the marriage had a great deal to commend it. Mary herself was evidently in favor of anything that would release her from her drafty prison at Tutbury. Leicester thought it was an elegant solution to Mary's perpetual imprisonment that should satisfy both Spain and France. The only problem was that the plan became a "plot" with each week it remained carefully concealed from Elizabeth and especially Cecil. By June 1, it was no longer a secret.

It was September before Elizabeth broached the subject hotly with Leicester. It seemed Norfolk's plans had progressed to the stage where Bertrand de Salignac de la Mothe Fénélon, the new French ambassador, and de Spes had heard that if Elizabeth did not agree to the match, Norfolk intended to liberate Mary willy-nilly.[13] Yet none of them seemed to be troubled by the fact that Mary was still the wife of the Earl of Bothwell. Though Bothwell had escaped the wrath of Moray and "the king's party" in Scotland, he had been a political prisoner in increasing squalor in Denmark since Mary's defeat. Nonetheless, Bothwell was alive and for now remained Mary's husband.

Another point Elizabeth's councillors seemed to discount was that the Protestant heir to the throne, Catherine Grey, had died fifteen months earlier. Catherine's younger sister, Mary, had been in disgrace since 1564, putting the Protestant succession in disarray. Queen Mary's proposed remarriage to a Protestant English nobleman made the specter of the Scots' queen as an "acceptable" Catholic queen of England both a real possibility and alarming. Elizabeth was not amused that the issue of her successor should be raised again in such an oblique way.

So Elizabeth made inquiries that autumn. Leicester admitted on bended knee that it was a plan, not a plot, to find a resolution to indefinite imprisonment for Mary, which also threatened Her Majesty personally. Elizabeth was infuriated. Mary's papers were searched, specifically for material proof against Leicester and Norfolk's friends on the council, Arundel and Pembroke (William Herbert, 1st earl of Pembroke, Leicester's man in the council). None was found. Even Cecil was censured for not advising her earlier about the proposed marriage. Norfolk was her maternal cousin and England's only duke. It was sedition for him to marry without her approval, and just the sort of plotting she abhorred.

Elizabeth felt personally threatened, seeing once trusted friends within her council through betrayed eyes. She angrily decamped to her fortress of Windsor. From there Elizabeth commanded Norfolk to attend her. He refused, pleading sickness. Elizabeth insisted. Still he refused. Finally, on October 2, 1569, Norfolk was taken to Paul Wentworth's house in Burnham and from there to Sir Henry Neville's home.[14] Cecil called upon a man who had helped him a few years before on other "silent" endeavors of a clandestine nature to investigate the affair. It was the first official assignment Francis Walsingham would take on behalf of the government.

Walsingham had written his first significant political pamphlet in the spring of 1569, evidently with approval from Cecil and possibly Elizabeth. In the pamphlet, he described Mary as "an evil papist vying for the English throne" and a leading member of the league for the destruction of Protestantism. His dedication to the Protestant cause was unshakable, making him the perfect man to discover the truth behind the veil of lies.

Without delay, Walsingham concentrated on the Florentine banker, Roberto Ridolfi, who had been on the fringes of the court's financial affairs. Under the respectable cloak of banking, Pius V had made Ridolfi's services available to Mary, effectively as his secret nuncio in England. What Pius had been unaware of was that the charming Italian was also in the pay of Spain and France, reporting back regularly to their monarchs. Walsingham made Cecil aware that Ridolfi was receiving large sums of money from abroad and that much of this was destined to help finance rebellion in the north of England aimed at freeing Mary. The money, he suspected, came from the pope.

Ridolfi was put under watch. Walsingham, meanwhile, discovered that further funds were paid out to the bishop of Ross and other of Mary's loyal servants, including those in the pay of the Duke of Norfolk. The order was sent out for an arrest on October 7 signed by Leicester and Cecil "for the apprehension of Roberto Ridolfi, whom her Majesty would have remain in your house without conference until he may be examined of certain matters which touch her Majesty very nearly."[15] Ridolfi immediately and willingly confessed to Walsingham his funding the northern earls, Mary, and even Norfolk.

On October 8, Norfolk was transferred from Sir Henry Neville's home to the Tower. After Norfolk's initial interrogations and protestations of innocence, Elizabeth determined with Cecil that they had to "deep search" just how the plot ran. In what seems like a bizarre twist, Ridolfi pleaded for his liberty in return for his honesty. Amazingly, this was granted with a bond of £1,000 in security paid on the promise that he would no longer meddle in matters concerning the state, except by Elizabeth's consent.

Why was Elizabeth so generous to Ridolfi in face of proof that there had been several plots against her? The only reasonable explanations are either that the pliable Ridolfi promised he would faithfully serve England for an appropriate payment—just as he had done the pope, Philip, and Charles IX—or that Walsingham and Cecil deemed he would be of greater value to England left in place where his machinations could be followed.[16]

Clearly, Mary presented a serious threat. Cecil had little difficulty in persuading Elizabeth that so long as Mary lived, she would "always be a dangerous person to her estate." While Mary remained restrained, that danger could be contained; if she were at liberty, then the threat she posed would increase. What was needed was reliable information regarding the Catholic nobility, including Norfolk, whose Protestantism was seen as unsafe, and a clear idea of the type of defense a muster of the non-Catholic nobility and gentry could generate. Cecil wrote to the Earl of Sussex, now president of the Council of the North, directing him to be on the lookout for "lewd persons uttering seditious speeches or any attempting unlawful actions."[17]

Though the first reports back declared that there was no danger, Elizabeth remained mistrustful of Sussex, as he was one of Norfolk's dearest friends. It didn't help that Leicester loathed Sussex as well and that Elizabeth's favorite never missed an opportunity to whisper some poisonous remark about him into her ear. Yet, setting these petty squabbles aside, Elizabeth was right to fear her northern Catholic nobility. These were the men who guarded the borders between Scotland and England, and her first line of defense from a northern invasion. She now had proof that the pope had been funding rebellion among them.

The northern counties of Yorkshire, Northumberland, Durham, Cumberland, and Westmorland were a natural refuge for brigands and malcontents. Each county was dominated by a fortified cathedral city that had carried out the law of the land for centuries. With Chester on the west, Newcastle-upon-Tyne to the north, and York rising above the dales of York and Pickering, the only road north was through the Tyne Gap toward Scotland, and the way south stretched via the Great North Road. Lancashire (within Cumberland) was administered by a separate duchy under Elizabeth's control.

Yet it was the sheer isolation and distance from London as well as the mountainous terrain scarred with deep glacial valleys that made it a natural frontier for the local gentry and nobility to call their own. For centuries, this country had been dominated by the Earls of Northumberland (Percy) and Westmorland (Neville) and the Dacres, who ruled as its virtual princes. Elizabeth's great error was in ignoring the local magnates while favoring her southern "new men" like Sussex instead.

With her Act of Settlement came the need for these lords to outwardly conform. The locals, however, chose instead to embrace the Scottish Catholic priests who fled Knox's Reformation. As the books and pamphlets arrived from Louvain and elsewhere, Sir Ralph Sadler, Elizabeth's special envoy to the north, remarked that fateful December in 1569, "There be not in all this country ten gentlemen that do favor and allow of Her Majesty's proceedings in religion, and the common people be ignorant, full of superstition, and altogether blinded by the Popish doctrine."[18]

While the nobility in the north were not in favor of the Norfolk match, it did afford them the opportunity to rise up to free Mary and determine what they could do with her afterward. Though this was an unclear war aim, preparations were made nonetheless to carry Mary north to Scotland by Leonard Dacre's skilled horsemen.[19]

By November 1569, contact between the northern nobles and Rome had been made. As early as November 3, Pius V wrote a short note to Alba in the Netherlands, "exhorting him to do what he may in aid of insurgent Catholics in England, and for the liberation of the Queen of Scots and her restoration to the throne of Scotland."[20] The "insurgency" had yet to take place.

Meanwhile, Elizabeth made her feelings known. She would have felt better if the northern earls were under lock and key at the Tower. While the queen's musters outnumbered the northern earls by five to one, the earls represented a formidable threat of civil war. That November, Sadler wrote again to the queen that "if the father be on this side, the son is on the other, and one brother with us, the other with the rebels."[21] Elizabeth sent the final order to remand the earls into custody, but they were already on the move.

On November 13, the earls rode into the hilly cathedral city of Durham, forced their entry into the cathedral, destroyed the Communion table, and tore up the Bible. Three days later, on the steps of the Market Cross at Ripon, they raised the cross of the Crusades and read out their proclamation:

We, Thomas Earl of Northumberland and Charles, Earl of Westmorland the Queen's true and faithful subjects, To all the same of the old Catholic religion know ye that we with many other well-disposed persons as well as of the nobility as others have promised our faith in the furtherance of this our good meaning. For as much as divers evil persons about the Queen's Majesty have by their subtle and crafty dealing to advance themselves overcome in this our realm the true and Catholic religion towards God, and by the same abused the Queen, disordered the realm and now lastly seek and procure the destruction of our nobility. We therefore have gathered ourselves

*together to resist by force . . . with restoring of all ancient customs
and liberties to God's church and this noble realm.*[22]

The response to their call to arms was huge. If a gentleman was demanded by the queen to call ten men to muster against them, the same
gentleman would often send his son with twenty men to the earls. Others
hid in the woods rather than fight against their brothers for the queen.
Still, things looked grim for the rebels. Money was in short supply, and as
their army gathered around them, word came that Mary had been taken
southward and inland to Coventry in the Midlands. Knowing that they
would be unable to fight and win against the crown's superior forces, the
earls dispersed, fleeing across the border into Scotland.

Retribution for those who remained in England was swift. Over eight
hundred were executed under martial law in January 1570. Those who survived were rendered destitute, with their lands and property confiscate to
the crown for their insurgency. Their leaders, the northern earls, were at-
tainted by Parliament and all their lands and possessions forfeit. Moderate
Catholics who had not participated in the uprising fled into exile, knowing
full well that matters had become extremely grave. As they packed their
worldly goods, the English armies rode across the borders into Scotland,
burning over three hundred villages; taking those who helped the earls to
escape into custody or murdering them, razing ninety strong castles and
houses to the ground, and wreaking biblical devastation wherever they
went.[23] A new law called the Act Against Fugitives over the Sea ordered the
new Catholic exiles to return within six months or forfeit any and all profits
from their lands and businesses.

This was the Elizabethan equivalent to the Dissolution of the Monasteries perpetrated by Henry VIII, the suppression of the guilds under her
brother, Edward VI, and the burning of Protestant heretics by her sister,
Mary I. In straightforward government terms, it was the spoliation of the
north to ensure that they could never rise again against their anointed
queen. From Pius V's and Philip II's viewpoint, it was an act of war.

THIRTEEN

Regnans in Excelsis

We . . . lay before you . . . certain matters of urgent
importance in regard to the redressal of the Queen of
Scotland's wrongs, and the aid to be extended to the effort
being made on behalf of religion by the Catholics
in England and their forces.

—Pius V to Philip II, February 22, 1570

From her captivity, Mary, too, raised her standard against Elizabeth. On January 23 at Linlithgow, the Earl of Moray was shot and killed. His assassin, James Hamilton of Bothwellhaugh, had been appointed by his clansmen for the task. Moray had long been aware of his precarious position as James's regent so long as Mary lived. Financially ruined and weighed down by feuding factions at home, Moray had sent his envoy, Nicholas Elphinstone, weeks before to plead with Elizabeth to recognize Mary's son as James VI of Scotland and himself as regent. Scotland now stood on the brink of civil war. It would be nearly five long months before a new regent acceptable to England would be appointed.

In Rome, the pope fulminated. All of his efforts on behalf of the northern earls had seemingly failed. Nonetheless, a few rays of hope remained. Northumberland, Westmorland, and Dacre had all escaped into Scotland. What he didn't know was that the English commanders were marauding at will in the Borders to capture the rebellious earls and make an example of them.

Then, just as Moray was assassinated, welcome news came to Rome that Philip had resolved to send the "insurgent Catholics" in England 200,000 ducats, "and an English gentleman, who is secretly opposed to the Queen, is being sent hence to seek out those insurgent lords . . . 10 or 12,000 ducats, ready money, on the part of the king, and to tell them that the 200,000 ducats are at their disposal if they will be in time and required."[1]

On February 4, 1570, Pius V penned a letter to Alba: "In view of the confusion into which English affairs have been thrown by the Catholics in antagonism to the heretics and by consequence to her who plays the part of Queen of England . . . We, upon whom rests the burden of Apostolic servitude, must needs be in daily anxiety and solicitude as to their safety who have taken arms no less holy than just for the restoration of the Catholic religion in that kingdom."[2]

Pius V goes on to exhort Alba to lend the rebellious northern lords whatever armed forces he can to prevent them from being "overwhelmed by their adversaries, or dispersing of their own accord," and emphasizing that the outcome of this gargantuan battle rests solely in Alba's hands. Only Alba had the power to return England to Roman Catholicism, the pope claimed, "and if by God's help, supplemented to the best of your ability by your efforts, this should come to pass you must yourself see how great, how lasting, how true a glory you must thereby win."[3] However, by the time Pius V had written these unambiguous words urging Alba down the path of Holy War against England, the Northern Rising, as the rebellion became known, was over. By February 11, word officially reached the Pope.

Mysteriously, on February 20, Pius V responded at considerable length to a letter received from Thomas Percy and Charles Neville, the earl of Northumberland and Westmorland respectively, written on November 8, 1569. Knowing that their cause was lost, Pius V lamented, "We grieve that it should be in our pontificate rather than in any other that the Christian commonwealth should be invaded by so many and so potent poisons of wicked heresies, and afflicted with such deadly wounds." Then, after another full page of anguish, he signals to the northern earls that he is "forthwith granting you such sum of money as our present resources may enable Us to furnish you withal, as our dear son Roberto Ridolfi will give you more clearly and fully to understand, it being also our purpose to endeavor to grant you somewhat more than the slenderness of our resources may warrant, and with a willing and cheerful mind to lend your pious enterprise all the assistance that with the means at our disposal We by God's grace may."[4]

Seemingly, Ridolfi was back in business as the pope's spy and knew where to deliver the money to the exiled earls.

Two days later, Pius wrote to Philip to say how proud he was of the Spanish king and all he was personally doing to relieve the plight of England's Catholics. Still, for reasons that remain a mystery to this day, Pius did not make Philip privy to his innermost thoughts. Three days after this gentle and kind missive to Spain's king, on February 25, 1570, Pius V published a papal bull entitled *Regnans in Excelsis*, the damning paragraph of which is below:

> *We declare the said Elizabeth heretic and fautress [patroness] of heretics and her adherents, to have fallen under sentence of anathema, and to be cut off from the unity of the Body of Christ, and her, Elizabeth to be deprived of her pretended right to the said realm and of all and every dominion, dignity and privilege; and also the nobles, subjects and peoples of the said realm, and all else who in any manner have made oath to her, to be forever absolved from such oath, and all duty of liege-fealty and obedience, as by the authority of these presents We absolve them, and deprive the said Elizabeth of her pretended right to the realm and of all else aforesaid, and lay upon all and singular the nobles, subjects and peoples, and others aforesaid, our injunction and interdict, that they presume not to yield obedience to her, or her admonitions, mandates and laws; otherwise We involve them in the like sentence of anathema.[5]*

After years of threats, Elizabeth had been excommunicated. Any English man, woman, or child who continued to recognize her as queen would fall under the same anathema. Any Englishman who fought against her would be pardoned by the pope, Christ's representative on earth. No word of the excommunication had been discussed with Philip or Catherine de' Medici or Charles IX or Alba in the Netherlands or Emperor Maximilian II in Vienna. Why should it? Philip remained preoccupied in repelling the Ottoman Turks from Sicily after their victory in Tunis. He was also keeping his rebellious Morisco population in check in the south of Spain. France was yet again in the midst of civil war—its third in eight years. Alba had quite enough on his hands, and Maximilian hadn't handled his Protestant German princes to Pius's satisfaction. In the absence of leadership from the Catholic monarchs, Pius V had acted as so many popes had done before him, as a temporal leader.

For the time being, Elizabeth and her councillors were blissfully unaware that Pius V had proclaimed his papal fatwa on England's queen. In February 1570, word had reached them of several Guise plots to assassinate Elizabeth, with Sir Henry Norris, the English ambassador to France, warning Cecil once again of "the great danger the Queen is in through the machinations of the cardinal of Lorraine." As Huguenots increasingly sought, and were granted, refuge in England, detection of potentially undercover French Catholic assassins became ever more difficult. Norris's solution was for Mary to be "further out of the realm, as she being there the Cardinal daily devises some mischief here [in France] to be practiced by the Papists there [in England]."[6]

That spring, the council was split on how to address the Catholic threat that Mary continued to represent. Councillors Cecil, Bacon, Bedford, Sadler, Mildmay, and Knollys advocated rigorous enforcement of the existing legislation against the Catholics. Leicester and Arundel strongly disagreed and called for conciliation with France and Spain and advocated a mild attitude toward the English Catholics, who had failed at the end of the day to rebel with the northern earls. Three main points were discussed: the impending hostility of France and Spain, widespread Roman Catholic sympathy at home, and Mary Stuart.

Naturally, it was Mary who preoccupied them more than any other subject. To resolve the question of Mary would solve the other burning issues, or so they thought. In late May, Elizabeth believed she had reached an agreement with the French ambassador, La Mothe Fénélon, on how to restore Mary to her throne. First, the French king would need to induce the Hamiltons to surrender the northern earls or at least abandon their cause. Next, France and England would work together to get the warring sides to lay down their arms. English troops could then be safely withdrawn from Scotland, providing, of course, that the French would not send any more troops, and would withdraw those which were already there aiding the Hamiltons. Finally, Mary could proclaim that negotiations were at the ready for her release and restoration on the basis of Elizabeth's offer.

The devil was, as always, in the details of the offer. Essentially, Mary would need to renounce all pretended rights to the English succession, forbid any foreign troops in Scotland, surrender England's rebels, continue the men who led the king's party in Scotland in their offices, and maintain Scotland in its Protestant religion. Failure to do so would result in a joint and immediate condemnation by the English and Scottish parliaments, resulting in Mary's automatic forfeit of her Scots crown to her son.[7]

Fénélon dutifully sent off the proposed agreement to the French king in his dispatches of May 27, in the hope that he had brokered the release of Mary and lasting peace between England and Scotland. Unfortunately, Fénélon, like all of Britain, was utterly unaware that Pius V's bull excommunicating Elizabeth and absolving the English from their allegiance to the queen had been pinned to the door of the bishop of London's house in St. Paul's Churchyard two days earlier. The choice facing English Catholics between Pope and Queen would henceforth become known as "the Bloody Question."

The sense of surprise and outrage was complete. In England, ballads were swiftly composed and printed. Proclamations and pamphlets were posted in London and at the market crosses throughout the realm. London's Bishop Jewel gave a stirring sermon at St. Paul's. Cecil wrote a pamphlet, *England Triumphant*, outlining how England had never admitted papal supremacy on its shores. Philip, ensconced in his palace at the Escorial, was incensed. "What I have to say now is," he wrote to ambassador de

Spes on June 30, 1570, "I received from you . . . the two briefs (bulls) dispatched by his Holiness . . . His Holiness has taken this step without communicating with me in any way, which certainly has greatly surprised me, because my knowledge of English affairs is such that I believe I could give a better opinion upon them and the course that ought to have been adopted under the circumstances than anyone else . . . His Holiness allowed himself to be carried away by his zeal, he no doubt thought that what he did was the only thing requisite for all to turn out as he wished."

Philip knew better. "I fear that, not only will this not be the case, but that this sudden and unexpected step will exacerbate feeling there, and drive the Queen and her friends the more to oppress and persecute the few good Catholics still remaining in England."[8]

The immediate backlash against the papal bull was, of course, that Mary could not be released. On this, the once divided council was absolutely united. Fénélon reluctantly passed along Elizabeth's change of heart to the French king, cursing the papal timing. Mildmay and Knollys were selected as Elizabeth's representatives to enlighten Mary about the regrettable, but necessary, change of plan. "I am thrown into a maze at this time," Francis Knollys wrote to Norris in Paris, "that I know not how to walk from dangers. Sir Walter Mildmay and I are sent to the Scottish Queen . . . God be our guide for neither of us like the message."[9]

Despite "not liking the message," the decision was proved right. Before Elizabeth's emissaries had left court, two coded letters from Maitland to Mary and the bishop of Ross were intercepted by Lady Margaret Lennox, whose husband had at last been appointed as Scotland's new regent in place of the murdered Moray.[10] Cecil had these quickly decrypted, to discover to his horror that the promise of goodwill and amity from the Scots queen was nothing but a sham. The proof, in Maitland's own handwriting, was the coded instruction to Ross to accept any conditions during the negotiations with Fénélon and Elizabeth, regardless of their harshness. The only purpose of these negotiations was for Mary to regain her liberty, for "if she were once at liberty I fear not that means shall be found to make both England and Scotland loathe to enterprise far against her."[11]

Mary had been unmasked as a cuckoo in the nest, watching and waiting to steal England from beneath Elizabeth. The pope had declared any

English person loyal to Elizabeth a traitor to the Catholic faith. If they obeyed the pope, Elizabeth would declare them political traitors to the future peace of their country. What neither Mary nor Pius V had counted on was the "Englishness" of Elizabeth's island people. Yet it was precisely to this audience that Elizabeth had been playing her "middle of the road" tunes for the previous twelve years. At the end of the day, she had to believe, English interests would prevail above the religious issues of the day.

So Elizabeth began this new era of "warming" warfare as she meant to go along. Mary had sealed her own fate, in spite of the papal bull. She could never be released, since she had been proven, yet again, untrustworthy. Before the year was out Thomas Norris was recalled from France, to his huge relief, and Sir Francis Walsingham—a noted Puritan—took his place as ambassador at the French court. What Elizabeth already knew was that Walsingham was not only a loyal and highly intellectual Puritan but also had the ability, through his language and social skills, to ferret out the far-flung secret Catholic plots against her and England.

Her back was against the proverbial wall. Elizabeth had no choice but to fight "godly" Puritans, Catholics, or anyone else who threatened her realm, and she would do it on her terms. Her prayer composed that fateful year urges "Father most high" in these troubled times "to implant piety and root out impiety . . . to destroy superstitious fear . . . to spy out the worship of idols; and . . . to gain release from the enemies of religion as well as those who hate me—Antichrists, Pope lovers, atheists, and all persons who fail to obey Thee and me. With all these things, omnipotent Lord, favor me, and after death my kingdom will be the kingdom of heaven. Amen."[12]

FOURTEEN

The English State, Plots and Counterplots

The friendship of princes is adapted
to their convenience.
—Elizabeth quoting Machiavelli
to Fénélon, June 1571

On the very day that Pius V affixed his seal to the papal bull against Elizabeth, the queen fidgeted through a sermon in her private chapel delivered by the acclaimed Protestant divine Edward Dering. Though Dering had begun his career as the foremost Greek scholar of his day at Cambridge, he had already exhibited the unmistakable signs of Puritanism in his open criticisms of Cecil and Archbishop Parker. Yet, at the very end of this crucial sermon, Dering ventured beyond the pale. He took Elizabeth on a "progress" of her Church of England, just as Ezekiel did with God, to show her the corruptness of her creation:

> I would first lead you to your benefices, and behold, some are defiled with impropriations, some with sequestrations, some laden with pensions, some robbed of their commodities. And yet behold more abominations than these. Look after this upon your patrons, and lo, some are selling their benefices, some farming them, some keep them for their children, some give them to boys, some to servingmen, a

very few seek after learned pastors. And yet you shall see more abom-
inations than these. Look upon your ministry, and there are some of
one occupation, some of another: some shake bucklers, some ruffi-
ans, some hawkers and some dumb dogs and will not bark. And yet a
thousand more iniquities have now covered the priesthood. And yet
you in the meanwhile that all these whoredoms are committed, you
at whose hands God will require it, you sit still and are careless, let
men do as they list. It toucheth not belike your commonwealth, and
therefore you are so well contented to let all alone.[1]

It was an accurate picture of the very real concerns of the pious, who
had once upheld the Elizabethan settlement. It was also the death knell of
Dering's once promising career. Twelve years earlier Elizabeth knew that
she would never be able to address everyone's spiritual needs to their satisfaction; nonetheless, she tried to appease her own inner conscience
through tolerance. At the end of that fateful year of 1570, there was no
longer any need to reconcile the warring English Protestants. They were
English above all else. The Catholic declaration of war had been heard.

Still, the ultimate litmus test of loyalty to their sovereign over God, as always, was Parliament. Elizabeth feared a repeat performance of her Parliament of 1563–67, since she had failed to either marry or assure the
succession. Yet by January 1571 she needed to recall her troublesome
members for a much-needed injection of cash to the exchequer. The
Northern Rising or Rebellion had cost the crown dearly. Further, Mary's
predicament needed debating and resolving. Then there was the matter
of the official response to the papal bull.

It came as no surprise that the Parliament of 1571 was entirely comprised of Protestants. Paul Wentworth had retired, but was replaced by his
equally obstreperous and colorful brother Peter.[2] The grandson of Henry
VIII's great minister Cromwell also sat for the first time. Even three of
England's most intrepid seamen—Richard Grenville, John Hawkins, and
Humphrey Gilbert—prepared to take their parliamentary seats. Joining
the Lords for the first time was William Cecil, raised to the peerage as

William, Lord Burghley, on this first anniversary of the papal bull. He was only the fourth man elevated to the peerage since the beginning of Elizabeth's reign.

London's Bishop Edwin Sandys delivered the opening sermon at Westminster Abbey, acknowledging that there would inevitably be debates at the sessions about the church, which "must be purged from all false doctrine, from all idolatry and superstition," since "the Pope hath polluted and burdened the Church" with heathenish rites.[3] It was his rousing appeal to patriotism that made the most lasting impression:

> If we, linked together in the fear of God and in true concord and amity among ourselves, put to our helping hands, every one dutifully in his calling, to the supporting of this State and defending thereof, doubtless no enemy, no foreign power can hurt us, no bull of Basan[4] shall prevail against us . . . we and our Commonwealth . . . [in] despite of all . . . shall be strengthened and established forever.[5]

Members responded favorably. Not only did Parliament concentrate on the issues consuming the Church of England, but it voted further money for Elizabeth's government and agonized over what to do about Mary.

Unbeknown to Parliament, Burghley's silent vigilance combined with Walsingham's intelligence from France and the Low Countries revealed the next plot against Elizabeth. John Leslie, bishop of Ross and Mary's closest confidante, was being followed. Early in April, two men were apprehended at Dover as they arrived in port from the Low Countries. One of them was known to Burghley's agents as Charles Bailly, a close associate of Ross. Bailly was searched and his portmanteau examined.

Inside a number of prohibited books were discovered, along with a packet of letters in code for Ross. Bailly was dispatched to London to the care of Lord Cobham, warden of the Cinque Ports, for further questioning. The portmanteau was forwarded to Burghley. What Burghley had not initially realized was that Cobham had hidden the existence of the coded letters. Nonetheless, having had ample warning from Walsingham that something quite serious was afoot, Burghley placed William Herle—a

Welsh dissipated cousin of Lady Northumberland—as an informant in Bailly's cell.[6]

Herle proved expert at his task. He not only learned about the coded letters withheld by Cobham but also discovered that there had been a codebook in Bailly's possession, which he used to encrypt letters to Ross. Burghley set a bigger trap and allowed further letters to be exchanged with Ross. Bailly, meanwhile, was removed to the Tower and tortured to persuade him to reveal where he had hidden his cipher key. Cobham's duplicity was exposed, and he was placed under house arrest at Burghley's home. Still, the real breakthrough came from Bailly's admission that the coded letters "concerned a plot inviting the King of Spain, the Duke of Alba and the Pope to cause war in this realm and to have a force of strangers" invade England. Two unknown Englishmen were implicated, and Elizabeth ordered "the bishop [Ross] should be charged . . . and forced to disclose what he knew."[7]

A coalition representing opposing views within the Privy Council was sent to interrogate Ross, who lay in bed, pleading illness. At the same time, Bailly confessed, after a stint on the rack, that he was bringing letters from Roberto Ridolfi to the queen of Scots (code number 40) and de Spes (code number 30). Mary and de Spes were questioned, but both denied any knowledge of the letters or Ridolfi's whereabouts. Without the encoded letters and codebook, the only alternative to uncover the truth was to bring Ross to London for questioning. He was incarcerated at the bishop of Ely's palace and left to sweat, without any interrogation.

By now Parliament had recessed. Disappointingly for the Puritan right wing, no church reform bill was passed. Parliament did, however, pass crucial legislation to deal with the rebellious northern earls and papal bulls. The new law was essentially a treasons bill containing a statute in its final clause making it high treason to "imagine or practice the death or bodily harm of the Queen, to practice against the Crown or to write or signify that Elizabeth was not lawful Queen, or to publish, speak write, etc. that she was an heretic, schismatic, tyrant, infidel, or usurper."[8] It was harsh and purposely mirrored Henry VIII's treasons act of 1534. Royal assent was given to some forty-one bills, with Elizabeth vetoing all bills relating to church reform. Taking no further chances on her lucky escape from admonishment on her failure to marry or assure the succession, Elizabeth dissolved Parliament on May 29.

Still, Elizabeth knew that the entire plot against her had not been fully uncovered. So, instead of venturing widely throughout the southeast as was her custom on summer progress, Elizabeth only went to "safe havens." She visited her errant cousin the Duke of Norfolk at his Audley End home to determine if he was sufficiently contrite after his earlier plan to marry the Scottish queen. Atonement for his actions would mean he would be welcomed back at court in the autumn. Seemingly, Elizabeth was delighted with her stay and impressed that the duke had mended his ways. She naturally told Burghley.

Then something quite unexpected happened. A Welsh draper urgently demanded to see Burghley, claiming he had a disturbing tale to tell. It seemed Norfolk had asked the draper, Thomas Browne, if he could deliver a package with some fifty pounds inside to his steward, Laurence Bannister, in Shrewsbury. As Norfolk's earlier transgressions were well known, and Shrewsbury was the home of Mary Stuart's jailer, Browne decided to peek into the package. Inside were six hundred pounds in gold—not fifty in silver as pretended—as well as a packet of encrypted letters and others that had been deciphered.

A man named Robert Highford (or Higford) had signed the correspondence to Norfolk's steward, Bannister. As it turned out, Highford was none other than Norfolk's secretary. Burghley now had his "two Englishmen" who Bailly had claimed were involved in the plot. Highford was immediately examined, and crumbled. Norfolk's hapless secretary deciphered the letters shown to him haltingly before he remembered that the codebook itself was "under a mat, hard by the window's side where the map of England doth hang" at Howard House in London.[9] With the decoded letters in hand, Norfolk was once again placed under house arrest, naturally denying any involvement. Yet as soon as he was transferred to the Tower, Norfolk broke down, telling all without his jailers needing to resort to torture.

Norfolk explained how he had sent money to Scotland and was in correspondence with Mary again, despite promising Elizabeth only weeks earlier that he had abandoned the Scots queen. Among the encrypted letters, one was incriminating above all others. In February 1571, Mary had written to Ross saying that she knew Ridolfi was leaving the country. She proposed that the Florentine banker would be a most trustworthy envoy for them to send to Spain for help. Mary averred she would leave such decisions, nonetheless, to Norfolk.

Elizabeth seethed. Norfolk had lied to her face. Everything, despite Mary's continued imprisonment, was precisely as it had been two years earlier, only this time there were fresh plans to embroil Spain directly. She ordered both Norfolk's secretaries, Highford and Barker, to be put to the rack. In the three weeks that followed, the complete story was revealed. The plan was far wider than anyone in government had suspected.

Norfolk claimed that a servant of the Earl of Arundel had developed a plan to steal Mary from her captivity. Sir Henry Percy, brother of the disgraced Earl of Northumberland, who was rotting in prison, was implicated in a separate plan to overthrow Elizabeth. Still, Norfolk denied any dealings with Ridolfi.

Despite Norfolk's protestations, Burghley discovered that the Spanish Council of State had agreed to fund the plotters and invade England with a force of ten thousand soldiers from the Low Countries—if the English conspirators succeeded in deposing Elizabeth. Philip had written on September 14 to Alba, "I am so keen to achieve the consummation of this enterprise . . . I am so attached to it in my heart, and I am so convinced that God our Savior must embrace it as his own cause, that I cannot be dissuaded from putting it into operation."[10] Alba's spies informed him that Elizabeth had uncovered the plot. He quickly wrote to Philip that her discovery would *not* be the end of the matter.

So the bishop of Ross was examined at long last by a select committee of the Privy Council. He was afforded this honor as he held the rank of ambassador to Mary. Ross, apparently scared out of his wits, willingly spoke of the various plots and counterplots should the grander scheme fail—some involving Lord Stanley as well as Sir Henry Percy and scores of others sympathetic to Mary. Still, Ross went further than was strictly necessary. He claimed that Mary was "not fit for any husband, that she had poisoned the French King, her first husband, had been a party to the murder of her second and that she would not have kept faith with the Duke even if she had married him."[11] The mention of Mary's third husband, James Hepburn, Earl of Bothwell, still rotting in his Danish prison, stirred the hot embers of rebellion in everyone's mind.

Elizabeth had ordered her councillors investigating the conspiracies (later known as the Ridolfi Plot) to concentrate their efforts on the English turncoats. Ridolfi himself was overseas, presumably licking his wounds at the Vatican. All those implicated were arrested, and Norfolk's trial date was set for January 1572. Philip had communicated to de Spes that "the thread of the business now being cut, there is no more to say to you about it."[12]

Elizabeth was still outraged. De Spes would have to go—before Christmas. On December 15, 1571 she wrote to Philip and Alba in French, "We need not much repeat to you how long we have misliked Guerau de Spes . . . sent hither in place of Signor Guzman de Silva . . . so as we can no more endure him to continue than a person that would secretly seek to inflame our realm with fire brands, and hereupon we have given him order to depart."[13]

De Spes skulked away at last on December 26, escorted by Henry Knollys to Canterbury where he was met by England's most intrepid sailor, Sir John Hawkins, who would see him off English soil at Dover. The delay beyond Christmas, it seemed, was due to yet another plot—this time by de Spes—to murder Burghley. It was Burghley's agent, Herle, who had detected the two young men de Spes had captivated with the idea, claiming that it would save the life of Norfolk. According to the testimony of one of the men arrested, Edmund Mather, it was actually de Spes's secretary, Venturini Borghese, who had devised the means with which to carry it out. Borghese was stopped from journeying on with de Spes at Canterbury and returned to London for questioning. The two hapless young men, Kenelm Berney and Mather, were executed on February 10, 1572. Borghese was eventually allowed to rejoin his master, as he, too, was immune from prosecution.

While unraveling the Ridolfi Plot, Elizabeth was plotting as well. Negotiations had been opened with Catherine de' Medici for the marriage of Elizabeth to her younger son, Henry, Duke of Anjou. It was deemed to be such an important matter of state, particularly as Parliament was in session, that the garrulous French ambassador, La Mothe Fénélon, was to be kept out of the loop on Elizabeth's express command. Catherine readily agreed and selected her trusted councilor Paul de Foix to handle the preliminaries in Paris with Walsingham.

Still, Elizabeth had acquired a shady reputation when it came to marriage. Catherine impressed on Walsingham the necessity of concluding this marriage treaty swiftly, for she knew full well that marriage was Elizabeth's way to promise much and deliver little. Though Catherine was aware of the tactic, she remained anxious to see the negotiations come to fruition. She saw this as France's best means of quelling disgruntled Huguenot voices and obtaining peace within her realm. Walsingham had to agree with her. Within weeks of the discussions commencing, England's enemies were at work to stop the talks.

Philip dangled the leadership of his league against the Ottoman Turk in front of Henry of Anjou's eyes, even though Henry had only acquitted himself marginally in France's third civil war. The papal nuncio urged the nineteen-year-old to reflect on how life would be, married to a heretic, and an old, barren woman of thirty-seven. The Guises, of course, had hoped Henry would marry the Scots queen, who was after all some ten years younger than Elizabeth. They even worked hard to persuade Henry that it would be a straightforward matter to invade England and free Mary.

In the end, the marriage plans faltered, as anticipated, on the grounds of religion. Henry refused any compromise regarding his devotions remaining a private affair, and so negotiations stopped. Two days later, it was a desperate Catherine who proposed her youngest son, sixteen-year-old Francis, Duke of Alençon, in his brother's stead. This time, it was Elizabeth who refused to entertain the marriage, imagining everyone mocking her for marrying a boy less than half her age. The most influential person against the match with the youngest Valois prince was Leicester.

In fact, Leicester and Walsingham had been exchanging correspondence about how the Protestants in England might prevail without Elizabeth marrying a Catholic prince—an anathema to them both. On August 3, 1571, Walsingham wrote to Leicester that the main stumbling block to creating a Protestant League against Spain, the papacy, and the Hapsburgs of Austria was "our ancient league with the House of Burgundy," of which Philip was duke. With Philip's cousin as the Holy Roman Emperor in Vienna, and Austria acting as "the Pope's champion," Leicester and Walsingham agreed that courting the anger of both the Austrian and Spanish Hapsburgs simultaneously was too dangerous to contemplate.

Worse still, the French heir was no great catch since most of England's overseas trade still took place at Hamburg or Antwerp. What France did offer, however, was an "advancement of the Gospel there but also elsewhere, and therefore though it yieldeth not so much temporal profit, yet in respect of spiritual fruit that thereby may ensue, I think it worthy the embracing."[14]

As the wedding plans crumbled, both Elizabeth and Catherine agreed that a Protestant League would resolve many of their mutual problems on religious matters. The odd thing was that the French Catholic "war party" was *not* opposed. They viewed the struggle with Spain and Austria in dynastic terms of Valois against Hapsburg, as in the bad old days of the first half of the sixteenth century. So the *politiques* and the Huguenots at court presented Charles IX with a comprehensive policy against Spain through a Protestant League with England.

Fortuitously, William of Orange's younger brother, Louis of Nassau, had fled to France for asylum and was at the French court at the time of these discussions. He had fought on behalf of the Huguenots during the third civil war and settled at La Rochelle. From there, Nassau had been successfully launching piratical raids against Spanish shipping with his small fleet of Beggars. Just as Walsingham hatched his plan, Nassau had been attempting to entice Charles IX into an invasion of the Netherlands by sea. When Nassau heard that the English were contemplating an intervention, he addressed his heartfelt appeal to Walsingham instead. As Spain had just received Irish rebels at Philip's Escorial palace, Walsingham grasped how through Nassau's plan Elizabeth might be "revenged for the pretended troubles in Ireland by keeping the King of Spain occupied in Flanders."[15]

For Walsingham, all else would flow from the resolution of the prickly religious issues surrounding the queen of Scots. That meant the establishment of an effective Protestant League—both offensive and defensive—against the pope and Spain and not directly embroiling England in a ragtag invasion force in Flanders.

When the breakthrough in negotiations occurred at last, it seems to have been due to Walsingham's silent ability to read people and situations. Unexpectedly, Admiral Coligny returned to Charles IX's side at court in the autumn, leaving the disgraced Guise faction exiled from power. Within days, word came that the papal nuncio desired an audience with the king to present a sword blessed by Pius V and, more significantly, to prevent the negotiations succeeding with England. Philip had empowered the nuncio to speak on his behalf to entice Anjou into accepting his earlier offer to head up the Catholic League.

Just as all appeared to be lost, Walsingham could see by Catherine's demeanor that religion and, especially, the queen of Scots had become less important than the treaty. Walsingham had pressed Catherine on the issue of Mary and Scotland several times after the queen mother's private conferences with her son the king. Each time, Catherine admitted freely that she had forgotten to mention Mary. It was the breakthrough the English commissioners, Walsingham and Sir Thomas Smith, needed. What Walsingham hadn't known was that Catherine did discuss Mary's latest shenanigans with Charles, who said, "Alas, the poor fool will never cease until she loses her head . . . It is her own fault and folly."[16]

In the end, an offensive league was dropped from the treaty negotiations, and Charles IX provided a private side letter to Elizabeth promising to come to her aid in the event of an attack or invasion of England for religious reasons. Significantly for Elizabeth, the commissioners had obtained two further major concessions. First, France and England would join together to bring Scotland under the rule of one government. This concession may have been cemented by the unwelcome news that a band of Mary's followers had attacked Stirling Castle, murdering the regent, Lennox. Second, France would provide a secure base for England's cloth trade, which had become semi-itinerant since the loss of Calais in 1557. The establishment of Anglican churches in France for the English merchant community was an essential part of this provision. The Treaty of Blois was finally signed by the French and English commissioners on April 19, 1572.

The treaty held great promise for the future. It resolved the issue of a French or English partisan Scotland, created a home for the cloth trade, and provided a framework for both countries to work together for each other's defense. Above all, it strengthened the Protestant position in Europe, and in particular, Huguenot influence in France. Although it was an imperfect treaty, relying as so many do on the goodwill of the signatories to it, no one could foresee that a few short months later, all would be lost.

FIFTEEN

Massacre in Paris

And with this weight I'll counterpoise a crown,
Or with seditions weary all the world.
—*The Massacre at Paris*, act 1, scene 2
by Christopher Marlowe (1592)

While negotiations were under way for a marital alliance with England, Catherine de' Medici was also aiming to catch a Protestant bridegroom for her daughter Marguerite. The man in her sights was Henry of Navarre, First Prince of the Blood of France.[1] If only she could manage a Protestant League with Elizabeth in the north, covertly fund William of Orange's invasion of the Low Countries from Germany in the northeast, and seal a wedding to the southwest with Navarre, Catherine would, at a stroke, neutralize the Huguenot and ultra-Catholic Guise factions in France and secure her borders against the pope and Philip.

The plan had already been partially implemented. Catherine had succeeded in winning Elisabeth of Austria, daughter of Maximilian II, for her son Charles IX to protect her eastern flank. With Charles increasingly unpredictable in his behavior, Catherine was determined to take control of her own and France's destiny. Seemingly, she chose to side with the Protestants in the religious wars rumbling through Europe without openly breaking with either Spain or Rome.

Yet to win over Henry, Prince of Navarre—the tall and handsome but as yet uninspiring leader of the Huguenots—Catherine needed to persuade his mother, Jeanne, queen of Navarre, that she was sincere in her support and that the Huguenot population of France would be protected. Coaxing Jeanne out of her fortress stronghold at La Rochelle (which had its own government and laws) needed to be done subtly, with just a soupçon of menace, particularly as Jeanne had been unwell. France remained a Catholic country and, in matters of religion, loyal to Rome. Naturally, Pius V opposed any marriage linking Navarre and France and would require little persuasion to declare the queen of Navarre's son Henry illegitimate, since he was the child of Jeanne's second marriage "of questionable validity."[2]

Like so many menaces made in the French court, it was whispered to Jeanne with a velvet voice. The attraction to such a political marriage from Navarre's viewpoint was obvious. The more the ailing Jeanne thought about it, the more appealing it seemed. So Jeanne traveled to meet privately with Catherine de' Medici under a safe conduct signed by Catherine, Charles, *and* the Duke of Anjou to lay down her terms. Jeanne, who had been in long and amicable correspondence with Elizabeth, was taking no chances. While Walsingham and Smith were negotiating on behalf of Elizabeth, Jeanne was in talks with Catherine.

In mid-March, Jeanne invited Walsingham and Smith to a private dinner, where she discussed her concerns quite openly with the two English commissioners. After dinner, they adjourned to another room where twelve men "of religion" greeted them—men who were Jeanne's closest advisers. Many were Calvinist ministers whose hearts palpitated at the thought of a frocked priest performing the wedding ceremony, as it could "not but breed general offense to the Godly." Jeanne agreed. She feared she would "incur God's high displeasure" if the ceremony was a Catholic one. Walsingham calmly gave advice on how matters could be resolved for the good of all by use of a proxy bridegroom within the cathedral precinct of Notre Dame. When the proposed marriage seemed lost to all others, Walsingham wrote to Burghley "that hardly any cause will make them break; so many necessary causes there are why the same should proceed."[3] Once again, Walsingham was right. The marriage treaty was signed on April 11, 1572, only eight days before the Treaty of Blois united England and France.

• • •

That April proved momentous in other ways, too. Pius V became grievously ill. The pope, who had begun life as a shepherd before becoming a Dominican priest, then promoted through the ranks to cardinal, was not expected to survive. His pontificate had revised the catechism, breviary, and missal; reinstituted the Inquisition against "northern heretics"; set up a permanent Congregation of the Index, which would oversee and update the list of banned books; and issued numerous decrees against blasphemy, sodomy, adultery, and clerical marriage.[4]

April 1572 was also the month when the Dutch Sea Beggars who had been expelled from England's shores in February retook Brielle, one of two deepwater ports in the Netherlands, from the Spanish. Two months earlier Elizabeth and Alba had begun to discuss a resumption of trade between the Low Countries and England, interrupted since Elizabeth had sequestered Alba's pay ships in November 1568. The precondition to any agreement was for the queen to exile the Sea Beggars from her shores.[5] She readily complied, knowing it was a cunning deceit that would cost Spain dearly. It was also the "green light" for Louis of Nassau to press home his desire with Charles IX to invade the Netherlands.

Still, Elizabeth was not the only queen capable of cunning deceits that spring and summer. Catherine de' Medici, having secured the marriages of two of her children, proceeded to insinuate her younger and ambitious son Henry, Duke of Anjou, into a crown of his own. Anjou and his elder brother Charles loathed one another, with Anjou constantly taunting the king. Alençon and Marguerite also detested Anjou for his malicious nature (he was a remorseless teaser), but both were powerless to rebel against him, as he was Catherine's favorite child. On hearing from one of her favorite dwarves that Sigismund-Augustus II, king of Poland and Lithuania, lay dying, and without issue, Catherine sprang into action, bribing, cajoling, and bullying everyone who would make the decision on the king's elected successor. For her, only Anjou was fit to wear Poland's crown.[6]

By mid-May, Rome had elected Cardinal Ugo Boncompagni as Pope Gregory XIII. Where previously the pope was believed to be infallible and worshipped as the "sundial of the Church," by the end of his papacy Gregory XIII (1572–85) would be hailed by Catholics as a "Vice-God . . . greater and more excellent than a man."[7] For now, all that mattered to Catherine de' Medici was that the new pope give his dispensation to allow Henry of Navarre to marry Marguerite, his cousin in the third degree. With assurances from Catherine to Gregory XIII that the union was part of a master plan she had devised to keep Charles IX from going to war against Spain, the Pope assented to the marriage. It was the first important international action of his papacy.

Meanwhile, Louis of Nassau prepared to expand the Sea Beggars' bridgehead beyond Brielle. In the late spring, he approached Walsingham to ensure that Elizabeth would do no more than "allow Walloon refugees in England to buy provisions and to come over to him" in the Netherlands. No money was required. Walsingham had reported separately that Charles IX would be providing Nassau with all that he could wish.[8] Burghley replied that "we have suffered as many of the strangers (Netherlanders) to depart from hence as would, but that is but a simple help."[9] Burghley was alluding to Elizabeth's adventurers who were itching to become involved in the fray.

Then, on June 9, shortly after arriving in Paris to assist with her son's wedding plans, Jeanne, already ravaged by illness, died aged only forty-four. Though there was talk of poison, the autopsy result seemed to indicate that she had been suffering from tuberculosis and most likely breast cancer. Prince Henry was now King Henry of Navarre. Despite losing his mother, great protector, and mentor, Henry agreed to proceed with the wedding as planned by treaty in August.

In early July, Sir Humphrey Gilbert, armed with a passport personally endorsed by Elizabeth, crossed the Channel with a large company of English volunteers to help liberate the Netherlands. If confronted, Elizabeth would, as was her custom with all her adventurers, disavow any knowledge of his actions. Notwithstanding, Gilbert's "instructions" were quite clear—occupy Flushing and Sluys, the two remaining significant coastal towns. Above all, Gilbert was to prevent Admiral Coligny from possessing them. So much for the Treaty of Blois. Elizabeth was finally up for a fight. What had provoked Elizabeth into action was the clear eye with which she viewed Catherine's machinations across Europe. What the desired reaction to Alba's tyranny against the Calvinists had failed to provoke, Catherine's insatiable ambition did.

The beauty of the Gilbert plan was that to ambitious French eyes, Elizabeth was simply carrying out the terms of the Blois Treaty. Smith reported back to London that everyone at court was pleased. "Matters in Flanders begin to wax hot," Smith wrote later that month, "and the beginning of next month . . . the brood hereabouts will be fledged."[10]

Leicester had been told that Nassau's forces numbered around five thousand foot soldiers, most of them from Gascony, and twelve hundred horsemen. William of Orange, who had over four thousand horse, would be invading from the east. Meanwhile, Charles prevaricated. The official story was that he would not loose Coligny on the Low Countries until the Turks had been attacked in the eastern Mediterranean. Yet both Anjou and Catherine were dead set against France appearing to take part directly in the invasion. Meanwhile, Anjou in the wings, ever more attached to the fanatical Catholic creed and the Guise faction, seethed at Coligny's increasingly unbreakable influence on his brother the king. Catherine, too, allowed her mother's jealousy at being usurped by Coligny to rise. She saw the growing danger in the aging admiral's hold over her son.

Walsingham saw through all these factors and Charles's ruse. "The King is so far forward in this matter," Walsingham wrote to Burghley in early July 1572, "that no disguising will serve."[11] Within the week, Orange had crossed the Rhine with seven thousand horse and fifty ensigns of foot. Even the Ottoman Turks wanted to ally themselves to Charles IX. After their devastating defeat at Lepanto in October 1571, they offered to take to sea in force, and give France phenomenal sums of money to wage war on Spain.

While Walsingham pinned his hopes on Charles IX prevailing, Catherine de' Medici watched, apparently helplessly, as the Huguenot forces poured across the border into the Netherlands. On July 17, the Seigneur de Genlis invaded, under the orders of Coligny, who remained at Charles's side. The French were ambushed just outside Mons by the Spanish, who had been alerted well in advance. Within ten days it was all over. The Huguenots were slaughtered, with only a few hundred barely escaping alive. Had Catherine betrayed them and sent word to Alba as proof of her good faith? Or was it Anjou? Either is possible, since they both loathed Coligny and feared the mesmerizing hold he seemed to have over Charles.

Coligny, in a race against time, urged Charles to strike openly in the Netherlands with a new French force. Catherine, who had been away from Paris to meet her daughter Claude near Châlon, railed against Charles's stupidity on her return on August 4. Anjou, meanwhile, sought the advice of the Duke of Guise. Incandescent with rage, Catherine threatened to retire from her son's court, taking Anjou with her. After all she had done for Charles, she let him know in no uncertain terms that he had spat upon her work to make France strong again. He had invaded Spanish territory. It was an overt act of war against Spain, by far the mightiest empire of their day. Though too little, too late, Charles penned and sent a hasty letter congratulating Philip on his success. The thought of losing his mother's knowledge and influence made Charles fear for his very life and crown. The thought of losing his precious Coligny did not bear contemplating.

A series of emergency council meetings was held on Saturday and Sunday, August 9–10, 1572. Charles humbly kissed his mother's hand, begging her forgiveness in his greatest hour of need. At first Catherine refused, leaving Charles desolate. He sought solace and advice from his council members. They were united in their criticism of Coligny, recalling "the disloyalty, the audacity, prowess, menaces and violence of the Huguenots . . . magnified and exaggerated by such an infamy of mingled truths and artifices that from being the friends of the king, His Majesty was led to regard them as his enemies."[12] Charles would have to accept this version of the truth or lose his mother's guiding hand.

Once the charade led by Catherine was successful, and Charles meekly reined in, she resolved with Anjou on a plan to deliver France from "all future apprehension" by Coligny. They agreed the admiral must die. Charles, of course, would need to be kept out of the loop, since he was too malleable. The moment to strike would be at the wedding of Marguerite to Henry of Navarre.

As the wedding approached, Catherine whispered more poison in her son's ear. Henry of Navarre was a Protestant. The capital would become overrun with Huguenots and a potential killing field if they were allowed to go about armed. Charles of course concurred, and a royal proclamation forbidding arms and the molestation of any foreigner or Navarre follower was issued. Protestants throughout Europe, including Elizabeth, took this as an act of great kindness and reconciliation in keeping with the marriage treaty and the Treaty of Blois signed only four months earlier.

On the morning of Friday, August 22, 1572, a week after the wedding of Henry to Marguerite, Coligny wended his way back to his lodgings in rue de Béthisy after watching the king play tennis at the Louvre Palace. Just as an assassin took aim and fired from a third-floor window, Coligny stooped down to adjust his shoe. The first shot blew off most of Coligny's right-hand index finger. The next lodged in his left arm, and the third missed altogether. Coligny was rushed to his lodgings while the king was advised. Charles, seemingly outraged, sent his personal physician to attend the admiral and vowed to find his would-be assassin.

Coligny's wounds were not considered grievous. The Huguenots who were standing vigil in the street below rejoiced to "see the king so careful as well for the curing of the admiral, as also for searching out the party that hurt him."[13] To show full support for the convalescing Coligny, the king, his brothers, and his mother visited the admiral later that day. Yet Henry of Navarre and his uncle the Prince de Condé smelled danger.

As they calmed their Huguenot supporters, a man named Maurevert hired to assassinate the admiral was caught along with an accomplice. The man who had held the would-be assassin's horse for a quick getaway was a veteran servant of Henry, Duke of Guise. His weapon, a harquebus, had been "borrowed" from the personal armory of Francis, Duke of Alençon, the proposed bridegroom for Elizabeth. The link between Henry of

Anjou, his brother Francis of Alençon, and Henry, Duke of Guise, was unmistakable. Having come so close to regaining favor at court, Henry of Guise was not going to allow power to slip from his grasp once again.

At four in the morning, Guise and his Swiss mercenaries forced their way into the admiral's lodgings. Coligny was already on his knees in prayer. While he knelt, the mercenaries stabbed him repeatedly, then tossed his bloodied body out the window. In an orchestrated action throughout the capital, Huguenot houses were attacked. Men, women, and children were slaughtered, their bodies thrown into the streets or the River Seine. Huguenots to whom Charles had granted asylum at the Louvre were murdered, their two hundred corpses piled high in the splendid palace courtyard. Catherine seemingly lied to Charles that the Huguenots had planned to seize his throne and kill them all.

According to the Spanish ambassador Zuñiga, fanatics had entered the English embassy, where Francis Walsingham resided. Other English notables like the young poet Philip Sidney and Thomas Smith hid within the embassy from the mob. Some Dutch, German, Italian, and even French Protestants fled to the comparative safety of the English embassy. Yet only once the danger had passed was a royal guard posted outside Walsingham's ambassadorial home. In the first blood orgy of St. Bartholomew's Day, a conservative estimate of Huguenots slain exceeded two thousand.

This was the first such massacre of Christian against Christian. The suddenness, viciousness, and ferocity stunned all of Europe. Elizabeth, after long, hard reflection, wrote to Walsingham in December 1572:

> We are sorry to hear, first, the great slaughter made in France of no-
> blemen and gentlemen, unconvicted and untried, so suddenly (as it
> is said at his [the king's] commandment), did seem with us so much
> to touch the honor of our good brother as we could not but with lam-
> entation and with tears of our heart hear it of a prince so well allied
> unto us . . . We do hear it marvelously evil taken and as a thing of a
> terrible and dangerous example; and are sorry that our good brother
> was so ready to condescend to any such counsel, whose nature we
> took to be more humane and noble.
>   . . . Women, children, maids, young infants, and sucking babes

were at the same time murdered and cast into the river, and that liberty of execution was given to the vilest and basest sort . . . without punishment or revenge of such cruelties done afterwards by law upon those cruel murderers of such innocents . . . It doth appear by all doings, both by the edicts and otherwise, that the rigor is used only against them of the religion reformed . . . At the least, all the strangers of all nations and religions so doth interpret it, as may appear by the triumphs and rejoicing set out as well in the realm of France and other.[14]

In the months following the massacre, Elizabeth learned how her embassy had been invaded by the Parisian mob, how Walsingham and the others were reduced to hiding within the house to prevent their own murders, and just how much Walsingham's life was in danger. In his official correspondence on the massacre, he requested to be recalled to London. Elizabeth responded kindly but told him he might have to wait until 1573, when a replacement could be found. Only when messengers came to tell Elizabeth just how much Walsingham was risking his life in staying on did she officially recall him. Walsingham received the letter from Burghley on September 17, advising "you have been presently revoked and only a secretary left there."[15]

On September 21, Walsingham met with Catherine.[16] She didn't want to discuss ambassadorial recalls, or the massacre, but rather the continued negotiations for the marriage of Queen Elizabeth to her dwarfish son, Francis of Alençon. Walsingham stuck to the point. Elizabeth, he said, marveled that Charles could have countenanced the unadulterated violence by a Parisian mob, led by royal courtiers, particularly as the Huguenots had come to Paris under the king's express protection. Catherine wove a yarn of sundry Huguenot plots to kill the royal family and said she had needed to act swiftly. Walsingham countered immediately by asking, if they were so formidable, why were they unarmed and so easily killed? The queen mother answered that there was no time for due process of law, as the plots had been set in motion on the very evening they were discovered.

The audience with Charles hardly went any better. He was outraged that Elizabeth would dare to withdraw her ambassador, claiming some

sleight of hand by Walsingham. So Walsingham showed the king her letter. Charles stormed about, threatening to recall his ambassador from
London, too, shouting that if he did that, then where would they all be?
Walsingham said that it had happened before, and yet there he was; so in
the end, things do eventually sort themselves out. Charles threatened if
Walsingham told anyone else about his plans to leave that he would consider it an act of war. If Walsingham remained silent, then he would have
the king's protection.[17] It is unlikely, given what had occurred weeks earlier, that Charles's promise provided Walsingham with any solace.

For England and all other Protestant nations, the St. Bartholomew's Day
Massacre in Paris was a watershed. Without any viable Huguenot leadership their cause was temporarily in abeyance at best, at worst ultimately
lost. Much would depend on the leadership of Henry of Navarre. The
ultra-Catholic, pro-papal, pro-Spanish, pro–Mary Stuart Guise factions
were once again in the ascent, with Henry of Guise playing the part of
Catherine's and Anjou's new best friend. Guise was a shallow, self-serving
adventurer, and his fervent Catholicism was based on power and becoming Philip's and the pope's instrument in France—for a price. Nowhere is
this better stated than in Christopher Marlowe's *The Massacre at Paris*:

> *To burst abroad those never-dying flames*
> *Which cannot be extinguish'd but by blood.*
> *Oft have I levelled, and at last have learned*
> *That peril is the chiefest way to happiness,*
> *And resolution honour's fairest aim . . .*
> *For this I wake, when others think I sleep;*
> *For this I wait, that scorns attendance else.*
> *For this, my quenchless thirst, whereon I build,*
> *Hath often pleaded kindred to the King;*
> *For this, this head, this heart, this hand and sword,*
> *Contrives, imagines, and fully executes,*
> *Matters of import aimed at by many,*
> *Yet understood by none.*

For this, hath heaven engender'd me of earth . . .
For this, from Spain the stately Catholic
Sends Indian gold to coin me French écues;
For this, have I a largess from the Pope,
A pension and a dispensation too;
And by that privilege to work upon,
My policy hath framed religion.
Religion: O Diabole![18]

This was the man who would determine French policy regarding the queen of Scots in the coming years. Is it any wonder that Gregory XIII, pope for a mere three months, celebrated a *Te Deum* and struck a special medal commemorating the massacre in Paris in honor of the king?

SIXTEEN

The Puritan Underworld of London

It is no small comfort brother . . . to brethren of
one nation to understand the state of the
brethren in other nations.

—Letter to John Field, 1572

The killing fields of France did not stop at the Parisian sub-urbs. As word of the massacre spread, so did the violence. Crisscrossing the country, religiously motivated genocide continued at La Charité, Meaux, Bourges, Saumur, Angers, Lyon, Troyes, Rouen, Bordeaux, Toulouse, and Gaillac. Those who carried out the atrocities believed that they did so in the name of the king. While Charles IX had eventually admitted to the planned murder of Coligny and the Huguenot leadership, he cowered before the prospect of yet another rise into civil war and the ire of his formidable mother. Naturally, his heir and firebrand brother, Henry of Anjou, prolonged the bloodshed by urging the governor of Saumur and others to help the mobs kill Protestants.[1]

What of the bridegroom King Henry of Navarre? The shock and awe of the massacre in Paris was followed up by the forced conversion to Catholicism of both Henry and his younger brother. For the next three and a half years (until February 1576), both would be held virtual prisoners at court. Navarre was, as Charles IX knew full well, only third in line to the throne behind the king's two brothers. By forcing Henry of Navarre's abjuration, Charles not only deprived the Huguenots of their last vestige of credible leadership but also took away any excuses for the ultra-Catholic Guise faction to murder Navarre.

Unsurprisingly, by the autumn of 1572, religious war broke out once more. Those who could escape the carnage did, fleeing to Orange-held Holland and Zeeland in the Low Countries or to England. Those who went to the Dutch provinces did so to fight against Spain for the Calvinist cause. Huguenots fleeing to England simply hoped to resume some vestige of their previous lives. In exiling themselves from France, the court believed it had vanquished the Huguenots. Nothing could have been further from the truth.

One of the most spectacularly overlooked aspects of the Dutch and French civil wars was the part these exiles played in the affairs of their home countries and their adopted ones. As early as 1560, the French church in London had a blinding brilliance when Nicholas des Gallars, who would soon serve as chaplain to the queen of Navarre, took up his role as senior pastor there. Indeed, when John Calvin released des Gallars from Geneva to go on his mission to England, he wrote to Edmund Grindal, bishop of London, that "I deplore wholeheartedly that the Churches of the entire realm [of England] have not been organised as the godly people would have wished it at the outset."[2] By the time des Gallars left, Bishop Grindal wrote to Calvin that he had found des Gallars "of great use both to myself and our churches."[3] It was the personal relationship between des Gallars and Grindal, built on friendship, mutual trust, and common beliefs, that catapulted the reputation of the French church to rise even further.

The history of the "stranger," or foreign, churches stretched back to the reign of Edward VI (1547–53), when the Polish reformer John à Lasco received generous church privileges from the king.[4] It was a natural consequence of these good relations between the stranger French church and the English crown that several thousand Huguenot immigrants flooded into London seeking asylum, both before and after August 1572. After all, the status of their church and the welcome they would receive from its superintendent, Edmund Grindal, had been widely known.

The truth was that England needed these immigrants. They were no idle or economic asylum seekers. They were skilled merchants, courtiers, civil servants, printers and stationers, shipwrights, lawyers, accountants, or doctors who fled the seemingly unending waves of genocide. Elizabeth knew that in opening her arms to the "poor and hungry masses yearning to be free" she would strengthen England economically and politically.

Edmund Grindal, the superintendent in charge of "looking after," or perhaps better phrased as "looking into," his stranger churches and their flocks, was a moderate bishop. Grindal assured the leaders of these churches that he would not interfere with their ceremonies or rites but would remain available to them should they require his guidance for disciplinary purposes. While this may seem extraordinary, Grindal had been a Marian exile and was well acquainted with the Geneva doctrine. He also remained sympathetic to its teachings.

Consequently, it became natural for the heart and soul of the exiled Calvinist and Huguenot community in England to be centered on London. Émigrés from Spain, the Netherlands, France, Italy, and Austria all made their homes there and were allowed to worship in their own form of Protestantism under special license from Elizabeth, denied to them in their countries of origin. As the 1570s progressed, the time was ripe to proliferate their beliefs on the winds of change blowing throughout the realm. Arguably, nothing could be more natural than for their organizations and liberties to create an overwhelming urge among English Protestants to strive for their golden example.

The role of women in the new religious communities was even more often overlooked. Yet within both the English and stranger framework, women played an unusually significant role. Just as London was the center for exploring different Protestant forms of worship, the home and hearth dominated by women became the crucible for Protestant church reform. While the role played by Catholic women, such as the ladies of the Vaux family, has long been acknowledged, the contribution of godly women to the Protestant cause has by and large been ignored.

This may be in part due to bishops like John Whitgift who felt that their influence was exaggerated, with many women preachers being of the "lower sort." However, Bishop Grindal harkened back to the Vestments Controversy of the 1560s when women "hooted at" him with cries of "wear horns" at St. Anne's Blackfriars. It was a bitter memory. At times, the moderate Grindal recalled that he had had to distance himself from the "eagerness of their affection, that maketh them, which way soever they take, diligent in drawing their husbands, children, servants, friends and allies in the same way."[5]

Yet women believed themselves to be the "weaker vessel," the descendants of Eve, who brought man down from the Garden of Eden. They were the perpetrators of the Original Sin, or so at least the Bible said and everyone believed. Most of these "activist" women found the Church of England perplexing and nonresponsive to their needs. With the Puritan emphasis on personal preaching and their public prophesyings, where laity and clergy were taught and exchanged ideas openly, suddenly women were able to ask meaningful questions and receive answers. Women like Lady Elizabeth Russell, Lady Walsingham, and the Countess of Sussex (foundress of Sidney Sussex College at Cambridge) all sought private as well as public solace from their male preacher counterparts. The Puritan preacher Thomas Wilcox wrote to one of his lady correspondents who was in the "fearful tempest of her perplexities . . . most heartily" beseeching her to go "forward and faint not in the course of godliness."[6] These were no wayward innkeepers' wives or strumpets. They were well-educated women who reflected an overwhelming need to communicate directly with their preachers on a highly personal level. Among the most notable activist women was the exceptional Anne Locke.

Born the daughter of Stephen Vaughan, who was Henry VIII's factor, merchant adventurer, and diplomat at Antwerp, Anne abandoned her mercer husband, Henry Locke, with his permission, to go live in Geneva with their two children, to learn at the knee of John Knox.[7] When Locke died in 1572, she swiftly married Edward Dering, the godly preacher who had shown the queen the state of her church, and who was ten years her junior. Dering's correspondence is replete with his earnest teachings to Lady Mary Mildmay, Lady Golding, Mrs. Mary Honeywood, and Mrs. Catherine Killigrew, sister-in-law to both Sir Nicholas Bacon and Lord

Burghley. His Puritanism showed an unlimited concern with the concept of sin and its remedy through practical and plain preaching. His congregation was large, helping not only these influential women but hundreds of faceless others.

Dering's female following of "spiritual patients" was not at all uncommon. Wilcox corresponded with the Countess of Bedford, Lady Fielding, and Lady Anne Bacon, among others, preaching "little but godly, plain and necessary exhortations and directions for the exercise of godliness."[8] Like Catholic wives, Protestant wives seemed deeply committed to their religion as the guardians of the faith through their children and homes. There is no doubt that English Protestant wives frequently looked to their counterparts in the stranger churches for ways in which they might be able to improve the religious education of their families and servants.

Still, there was one woman who remained distinctly unimpressed. By the summer of 1572, Elizabeth had already been preached to by the spellbinding and godly Edward Dering about the parlous state of her church. Thomas Cartwright, who had argued against the motion *Monarchy is the best form of Republic* at the Cambridge debates of 1564 during Elizabeth's progress, had gone on to stir up more trouble. In 1570, Cartwright had angered the Cambridge hierarchy when, from the dignity of his Lady Margaret Chair, his devastating oratory on the early chapters of the Acts of the Apostles condemned the Church of England on Episcopal and hierarchical grounds. Worst of all, *An Admonition to Parliament,* written by John Field and Thomas Wilcox, and inspired by Cartwright's words, marked the point of no return.[9] The queen was not amused.

It all began shortly after the Duke of Norfolk's delayed execution for treason in the Ridolfi Plot, two months after the signing of the Treaty of Blois with France. Parliament was in session, pressing for sweeping religious reforms of the Anglican Church. Even before the cause had been lost, an anonymous popular diatribe entitled *An Admonition to the Parliament* was published from a secret printing press. The *Admonition* had moved on from attacks against the vestiges of "popery" and the dress of

Anglican bishops, concentrating instead on the new Puritan issue of whether the church needed bishops or a group of elders and an entirely different hierarchy.

For them, this was the crux of the problem with the Anglican settlement. Elizabeth had changed the prayer book but not the way in which the Anglican Church worked. This was true. From the queen's viewpoint, by retaining the framework of the Catholic Church, it was easiest to spread her religious solution with the least upheaval. She had retained the system of bishops and archbishops and all the trappings of their offices just as it had existed in her father's time. The main change had been the reinstitution of the prayer book substantially in the form of her brother's. The privileges and superiority of the bishop's office were seen as "rather granted by man for maintaining of better order and quietness in commonwealths, than commanded by God in his word."[10]

Two years earlier, Thomas Cartwright had called for the abolition of the titles and offices of the archbishops, bishops, deans, and archdeacons, suggesting instead that the government of the church should be restored to the primitive church with ministers elected by their congregation and presbytery at the local level. This was precisely what John Field and Thomas Wilcox called for in their *Admonition* attack on Parliament.[11] It was how the stranger churches were run in England, just as it had been the experience of the English Protestants in Geneva, Frankfurt, and Strasbourg when they had once been in exile, too.

It was the younger of the two authors, the curate of All Hallows Honey Lane, Thomas Wilcox, who wrote the penetrating and fiery tirade at the beginning of the *Admonition*: "We in England are so far off from having a Church rightly reformed according to the prescript of God's word, that as yet we are not come to the outward face of the same." Field later admitted that he had added the malicious and rabble-rousing "view of popish abuses yet remaining in the English Church." In fact, Field took sole responsibility for its "bitterness of style," particularly the really memorable phrases about the Book of Common Prayer like "an unperfect book, culled and picked out of that popish dunghill, the mass book, full of all abominations"; and "reading is not feeding, but as evil as playing upon a stage, and worse too"; and "they toss the psalms in most places like tennis balls"; and even "the commissary's court, that is, but a petty little stinking ditch that floweth out of that former great puddle."[12]

The church elders rapidly distanced themselves from the new extremism of Wilcox and Field. John Whitgift, master of divinity at Trinity College Cambridge and future archbishop of Canterbury, who had recently stripped Thomas Cartwright of his fellowship at the university on the technicality that he had never been ordained, was proud to take up the cudgels against the Puritans with his *Replye*. Meanwhile, Burghley, desperately ill with a recurrence of gout, was hell-bent on finding the illegal printing press and the printer of the pamphlets.

Whitgift was appointed to the task. The investigation led to the Huguenot printing presses of London, but when no proof could be found, Burghley became convinced that the Puritan aldermen of London were sheltering the printer. One of the names put forward was Thomas Vautrollier, an exiled Huguenot printer who had been established in the Stationers Company only two years earlier.[13] Elizabeth seethed at the lack of progress in finding the culprit press. What the queen hadn't immediately realized was that the actions of Field and Wilcox had split the Puritan wing in half.

Field and Wilcox were swiftly sentenced to a year's imprisonment at London's notorious Newgate Prison. Though they were feted by the younger and hotter gospellers, effectively keeping an "open house" at Newgate, older, calmer heads like Laurence Humphrey and a host of others visited them in prison to deplore "such Admonitions as are abroad . . . for that in some points and terms they are too broad and overshoot themselves."[14] In other words, they had done more harm than good and had "with unreasonableness and unseasonableness . . . hindered much good and done much hurt."[15] Even staunch Puritan sympathizers within the Privy Council—men like Leicester, Bedford, Sir Francis Knollys, Sir Walter Mildmay, Warwick, and Burghley—were aghast. Still, Leicester and Huntingdon—the most left wing in the council and consummate politicians suspected of duplicity by Burghley—watched and waited.

The damage that *An Admonition* had wreaked was done, however. It spelled the ultimate failure of the religion bill proposed in Parliament that spring that bore all the hallmarks of the most devoted Puritan members. Sir Francis Knollys defended the outrageous preamble to the bill, which claimed that "divers orders of rights, ceremonies, and observations" had been allowed since the Act of Settlement in 1559 and had been "permitted in respect of the great weakness of the people, then blinded with superstition."[16] The bill proposed one law for Protestants and another for Catholics. The Act of Settlement would only remain in force against "Papistical services, rites, or ceremonies," while all Protestant services would be allowed, with the consent of the bishop in each diocese, to omit certain forms of the established service or to use the form of service as the French and Dutch congregations were permitted in England.[17]

The bill was, of course, an anathema to the queen. On its third reading, its backers finally realized they would need to amend it. The offensive preamble was omitted, and varying services would be allowed only by the consent of a majority of bishops. Still, it was not enough. Elizabeth sent the Speaker of the House a message that no bills concerning religion were to be put before the House, unless the bishops "liked it" and the originally proposed bill and any amendments were shown to her first. Those who had spoken out about the "liberty of the House" at the previous session said nothing this time, thanks in large part to Field's and Wilcox's handiwork.

All this happened before the fateful genocide on August 24, 1572, in Paris. By the time of the St. Bartholomew's Day Massacre, three editions of the Puritan pamphlets by Field and Wilcox had been printed, including *A view of Popish abuses yet remaining in the English Church for the which godly ministers have refused to subscribe* and a smaller one entitled *An exhortation to the bishops to deal brotherly with their brethren*, in which Field and Wilcox compared the bishops to "galled horses that cannot abide to be rubbed."[18] Where a few short months earlier the Puritans had sought to bind the crown and the papacy through intolerable and intolerant legislation, their militancy was suddenly seen as having great foresight against the evils of the Catholic League.

Leicester and Huntingdon saw their moment to help the authors of *An Admonition* and especially the cause of reform of the church. Together they pleaded for the release of Field and Wilcox with the Privy Council. Their timing was perfect. Naturally, there had been a great furor and uproar from the pulpits, in broadsides, and in ballads against the St. Bartholomew's Day Massacre. By October, when the pair was released early, there was an added complication. They were "esteemed as gods" by the London mob, with Archbishop Parker lampooned as the "last" archbishop of Canterbury if the Puritan manifesto were adopted.[19] By Christmas, Thomas Wilcox was touring the Puritan strongholds in Leicester's and Huntingdon's lands in the Midlands, returning to his London home by early February 1573.

Interestingly, John Field disappeared without trace for nearly three years. Vanished, too, were his scathing manifestos against the church establishment. The question is, where had Field gone? The answer is we don't know for sure. In any event, his three-year silence seems to have been broken from the printing press of Michael Schirat at Heidelberg, where Thomas Cartwright had been languishing. Could it be that Field hadn't *wanted* to be silent but rather had been silenced by the lack of a clandestine press or printer in England willing to risk everything for him?

The printed word—whether in cheap print or as a work of art in books— had become a powerful tool, which Field had wielded with aplomb, but a printer or stationer who would take on these high-profile and dangerous projects in Elizabethan England would have to be a brave man indeed. Given Field's return to London in the late 1570s, his absence from the manifesto scene seems reasonable if his former printer refused further contact.

Yet in the intervening years, Puritan ballads had proliferated, with lessons of ungrateful children, the constant Susanna, and the return of the prodigal son sung on street corners, at public prophesyings, or in the home. Printed pages were torn out of cheap ballad chapbooks and adorned the walls of homes and taverns alike. Unlike the Protestant ballads that treated biblical subjects with humor, theirs considered such levity as pure blasphemy. Elizabeth had become convinced that the godly people were no longer interested in obedience to the crown despite the fact that she had not disfavored any "repugnant or mislikers of her religion."[20]

By June 1573, Elizabeth had had enough. The international Catholic

League had pushed long and hard against England's door, and now more and more Englishmen were deserting *her* church to worship at public Puritan prophesyings or in stranger churches. Even her beloved Leicester attended the French church from time to time. With her middle way seemingly eroded daily, Archbishop Parker wrote to Burghley that he must warn the queen that "both papists and precisians [Puritans] have one mark to shoot at, plain disobedience." In response Elizabeth issued a proclamation commanding her subjects to use only the Anglican prayer book and hand over all Puritan writings in their possession to their bishop or diocese or to the Privy Council.[21] When virtually none were returned by October 1573, she issued another proclamation to bishops and magistrates condemning them for lax enforcement of her June law, threatening imprisonment of anyone who spoke out against the Act of Settlement and Uniformity.

Elizabeth had managed to keep the chaos of religious civil war that plagued so many countries on the Continent at bay, but she feared in the first half of the decade that she would lose control. In her personal prayer for wisdom in the administration of the realm, she prayed:

> *Send therefore, O inexhaustible Fount of all wisdom, from Thy holy heaven and the most high throne of Thy majesty, Thy wisdom to be ever with me, that it may keep watch with me in governing the commonwealth, and that it may take pains, that it may teach me, Thy handmaid, and may train me that I may be able to distinguish between good and evil, equity and iniquity, so as rightly to judge Thy people, justly to impose deserved punishments on those who do harm, mercifully to protect the innocent, freely to encourage those who are industrious and useful to the commonwealth.*[22]

Whether she believed it was possible for those prayers to be answered at the beginning of 1574 remains a mystery.

SEVENTEEN

Via Dolorosa

*It is so difficult in these times to know the
difference between seeming and being.*

—Elizabeth to Anjou, 1580

A new wave of religious exiles now joined the old. Many of those Puritans in London's underworld who had turned to the printed word to build their reformed church were hunted down and thrown unceremoniously into its prisons. London's Bishop Sandys, attacked alongside Archbishop Parker and others in these Puritan manifestos, described Newgate, the Marshalsea, and London's other jails as "filthy and unclean places, more unwholesome than dunghills, more stinking than swine sties."[1] Many of the godly succumbed to the infections rampant in London's prisons, becoming pestilential martyrs to their cause. Of course, whatever happened in London was replicated throughout the realm a hundredfold.

Somehow, the preacher Thomas Cartwright escaped to Heidelberg, most likely with the assistance of one or more of the wives of the privy councillors who corresponded regularly with him. During his time at Heidelberg, the printing presses worked overtime disseminating the Word, as the city and its university had become the throbbing crucible of a Calvinist state welcoming French, Dutch, and now English Puritan refugees demanding to be heard.

Others were not so lucky. Edward Dering and others remained behind in London, suffering prolonged interrogations by the council's feared Star Chamber for sedition. Dering wrote of his relief that his wife, Anne Locke, had remained untouched despite her long devotion to the godly cause. He himself eventually escaped rough justice through the good offices of the Earls of Huntingdon and Leicester, possibly as it was widely known that he was dying of tuberculosis.

Where the godly like Dering had champions within the Privy Council—despite the witch hunts against others of their ilk—English Catholics had none. Their steady exodus from England's shores throughout the first twenty years of Elizabeth's reign is etched in history as a catalog of admirable faith and strength, impossible heroism and foolhardiness, tremendous sadness, and misguided political will.

Perhaps the most stirring of all the individual stories among the English Catholics is that of Edmund Campion. The Oxford graduate who had so impressed Elizabeth and Leicester during her 1564 progress had taken Holy Orders in the Church of England and was a deacon of Elizabeth's church. Leicester had recognized Campion's exceptional talent and oratory skills since that time and made the young man his protégé. Tall and well built, with a commanding yet soft voice, Campion inspired those around him as a man of great promise with a gift for language. When he left England in the summer of 1569 to visit his Oxford friend Richard Stanihurst at the family home in Dublin, even Leicester had no idea of Campion's troubled soul.

Campion's apparent attraction to the Stanihurst home was its library. He browsed its shelves with the intention of dedicating his history of Ireland to Leicester. Though he never completed it, Campion's work would be finished and eventually included in the great history of the British Isles undertaken by Ralph Holinshed entitled the *Chronicles of England, Scotland and Ireland*. The work would be authored under Richard Stanihurst's name. Whether Campion knew at that stage that it would be a history of Britain as seen through Tudor propagandist eyes is probable. Whether this influenced what was to follow is not.

From August 1569 until March 1570, Campion toiled away on his history. He knew his host family had served the Tudors for generations with distinction. In fact, Richard's father, James Stanihurst, had been the Speaker of the 1560 parliament that passed the Acts of Supremacy and Uniformity that consigned Catholicism to the past. Campion's friend Richard seemed to be following in his father's footsteps and was poised to propose marriage to Janet Barnewall, the daughter of another great Anglo-Irish family noted for serving the English crown faithfully. There was nothing to indicate that Campion's choice of host family or the timing of his visit was in any way nefarious to the crown. The only blot on Campion's record so far was that he had recently engaged himself as tutor in the household of Lord Vaux, the notoriously Catholic peer, before leaving England.

Though relatively insignificant, this was enough to raise the suspicions of Ireland's Lord Lieutenant, Sir Henry Sidney. After Campion had been with the Stanihursts for seven months, the Dublin Pale authorities suddenly came to interview him but found he had already decamped. What they hadn't realized was that Campion had found shelter with the Barnewalls, some dozen miles distant from the Stanihursts in Dublin. In thanking James Stanihurst for his hospitality and excusing his sudden need to escape, Campion wrote quite openly that he had been in danger from "the heretics of Dublin."[2] Weeks later, Campion was spirited out of Ireland through Drogheda and back into England. It was 1571. Within a few months, he left England to join his friends at the Catholic seminary in Douai in the Netherlands.

Campion's remark about "heretics" to Stanihurst was odd for a deacon of the Church of England to make to a loyal subject of the crown, but he knew what few in London did. The Stanihursts and the Barnewalls had turned to Catholicism, as many families of the Irish Pale had also done. Though their homes were built from the bricks of the dissolved monasteries, and both families had supported the Royal Supremacy, they were in the growing majority who felt that England's influence had become destructive to Ireland. Nowhere was that more apparent than in the alteration of church policy. Remote from London and court, these staunchly Anglo-Irish families felt that they and Ireland had been swept aside for the furtherance of the Protestant cause.

• • •

Campion's joining the exiled Catholic community at Douai was not an unusual thing for a young man of conscience to do. Since the early days of Elizabeth's reign when Sir Francis Englefield emigrated, thousands of others had joined him. Their primary concern was for the survival of English Catholicism. Just as Elizabeth felt that the only way to make the English understand her "middle way" was to educate the population and teach them to read and write, so the exiled Catholics felt that it was only by proper training of priests in seminaries that they could continue to carry the Word to the people.

Still, the first concern was how to clothe and feed these penniless Catholic nobles, academics, and gentry émigrés. As early as 1561, Margaret of Parma wrote to her half brother Philip II for a Spanish pension and money to erect religious houses.[3] By 1568, Dr. William Allen had founded his English College at Douai with money garnered from the pope and Spain. When Edmund Campion joined their ranks, the college hosted over one hundred young men. Within that number "it is well worthy of remark how very large a proportion of the early members of the college were graduates of the English Universities, especially Oxford . . . They brought with them the traditions of English University and collegiate life, and among these a high esteem for learning."[4]

Remarkably, despite this grand exodus from England and its universities, Elizabeth and her government had paid little heed to these exiles in the first ten years of her reign. What changed her attitude was the papal bull of 1570 and the certain knowledge that many received *ayudas de costa,* or Spanish pensions. Elizabeth recognized the danger in these men becoming pensioners of the Spanish state, particularly as the northern rebel lords Dacre, Neville, Northumberland, Westmorland, and their families were now among them.

The queen had no wish to create Catholic martyrs while she was attacking the ever-present threat posed by the brazen godly and their print campaign inside England. However, Elizabeth's wishes were the last concern on the minds of all those who practiced apostasy. Their separate paths along a Catholic and Puritan Via Dolorosa to the hanging tree at Tyburn were already etched in the activists' souls.

The year 1575 proved a decisive turning point. After nearly ten years of uncertainty, peaceful trade was restored between the Spanish Low Countries and England. The replacement of the Duke of Alba two years earlier by Don Luis de Requesens, who had previously been the governor of Lombardy in Italy, was crucial to the resumption of trade. Requesens, prematurely aged by fulfilling his duties for Philip in northern Italy, had hoped for a quiet retirement, but Philip wouldn't hear of it. Alba's strong-armed political policies in the Low Countries had been seen at last as bankrupt, and only a diplomat of Requesens's skill might be able to put things right, Philip believed.

An equally important factor to the peace was that without English trade, Philip's available treasury to maintain a steady state of war in the Netherlands and elsewhere was clearly diminished. Only a year earlier Philip wrote to his ministers, "I think that the Netherlands will be lost for lack of money, as I have always feared . . . We are running out of everything so fast, that words fail me."[5] What Philip had also failed to understand was that another threatened royal bankruptcy would do little to endear him to the Netherlander merchants.

Elizabeth grasped the nettle for resumption of trade and peace with Spain, quickly sending Dr. Thomas Wilson to resolve any outstanding obstacles. Requesens was taken off guard when Wilson put forward Elizabeth's demand that the English Catholics taking refuge in the Spanish Netherlands should be expelled prior to any final agreement being reached on trading matters.

It was an apparent masterstroke. Not only was Elizabeth about to conclude a peaceful trading relationship once again with the Spanish Netherlands, but she could appear to ensure that through this rapprochement, Spain would stop harboring her wayward Catholics, whom she regarded as rebels as well. Eventually Requesens agreed to expel the English Catholics from the Low Countries, but on condition that Elizabeth would no longer give shelter to Dutch rebels in England. Requesens kept his end of the bargain. Elizabeth did not, despite issuing a proclamation against Orange and his followers.

At the same time, William Allen recognized that the college at Douai could not continue without the political and financial aid of Spain and the Holy See. On April 5, 1575, Gregory XIII granted the college an annual pension of 1,200 crowns—increased to 2,100 crowns six weeks later—to safeguard its future. Nonetheless, the seminarians were literally starving. Much of their suffering was caused by Elizabeth's squeeze on all forms of apostasy at home, which in turn had been brought on by the plots hatched by Mary Queen of Scots and her followers. The series of penal laws that followed made it illegal to send cash to all Catholics overseas.

By 1575, the business of England's Catholic émigré community in the Netherlands had become a primary government concern. Indeed, a proposal was made in the Privy Council to open and copy all correspondence between Catholic exiles on Spanish pensions and their friends and families at home.[6] Though impracticable, the idea was gleaned from several successful networks of informants, spies, and traitors living among the exiles who had proved valuable intelligence sources about the exiles' correspondents in England.

Despite Gregory XIII's seeming generosity, it was too late to save the college in its current incarnation at Douai. On March 1, Requesens gave the order for the exiles to withdraw from the Spanish Netherlands. Though the people of Douai were mainly Catholic, they joined in the government's efforts to rid the city of the seminary. It is understandable why. Commerce had been ruined by the religious wars that now divided the country, and in the Spanish-held, Catholic territories. Reprisals against the general population were only a heartbeat away from the latest show of boldness from dissidents. Those who demonstrated against the seminarians did so for self-preservation in this life, perhaps at the risk of their eternal souls in the next.

Many of the students dispersed finally to Cambrai and Liège on the border with France. Yet finding themselves in a small, powerful diaspora, these men of the cloth were surreptitiously approached with sudden offers of money and full restitution of their lands and possessions in England by those working in the Elizabethan spy community. The price they would have to pay for the newfound English generosity would be to inform on their fellow seminarians.[7] Few accepted.

Requesens was as good as his word. The expulsion from Douai was only the beginning. Brussels, Antwerp, Mechlin, and Louvain soon followed. Those exiles who wished to remain in the seminary were forced to remove themselves to Rheims, where under the protection of the new French king, Henry III (formerly Duke of Anjou), they could be assured of a warm, if at times difficult, welcome. As the Huguenots saw the mass immigration of Catholics to the northern French city, their disquiet grew. They had not forgotten Henry's role in the St. Bartholomew's Day Massacre. Thus the sparks of the seventh French civil war were ignited.

Meanwhile, a tense situation also developed in England. Archbishop Parker, who had helped Elizabeth carry out her vision for the Church of England, was dying by April 1575. Burghley immediately proposed the noted moderate archbishop of York, Edmund Grindal, to replace him. After all, Grindal had had ample experience of dealing with crypto-Catholics in the north and was widely thought to be able to speak in a language familiar to the Puritans in the south, which would help these firebrands to "keep the humble and straight course of a loving . . . minister of Christ's gospel."[8]

In other words, Grindal was a transparently good man who could traverse the hot rhetoric on both sides of the religious divide. Though Parker died that May, it would take Elizabeth until December to name Grindal in his place. Whether the queen had a sixth sense about what would follow shall forever remain a mystery, but certainly she had her doubts about Burghley's favourite candidate, Grindal.

No time was lost, however, in trying to win over the seventy-first archbishop of Canterbury. Grindal received a letter from a privy councillor, thought to be either Sir Walter Mildmay or Sir Francis Walsingham, that was most revealing of the Puritan view of the Anglican Church:

It is greatly hoped for by the godly . . . that your lordship will prove a
profitable instrument . . . in removing the corruptions of the Court
of Faculties which is one of the greatest abuses that remain in this
Church of England . . . I could wish your lordship to repair hither
with as convenient speed as ye may . . . that there may be some con-
sultation . . . [on] how some part of those Romish dregs remaining . . .
may be removed.[9]

Like the Catholics in exile, Elizabeth and her councillors Leicester, Walsingham, and Mildmay were fully cognizant of "the unlearnedness of the Anglican ministry, abuses of excommunication, want of discipline, dispensation and tolerations for non-residency and such like."[10] By the time Parliament convened in 1576, legislation had been written to deal with these abuses. Those bills touching the regulation of ordinations, admissions to benefices, and licenses to preach, as well as educating the inferior clergy, would take priority. Elizabeth wanted to end the dissemination of any literature that attacked her church and the regular use of godly prophesyings involving both the local clergy and the laity. For Grindal, and to some extent Elizabeth, a further abuse existed in the Court of Faculties of the Anglican Church. Grindal was adamant that it must stop all Romish abuses like holding incompatible plural offices, nonresidency in the parish, receiving orders under canonical age, or marrying people in the forbidden seasons.[11]

Yet Grindal refused to halt reform there. He directed four leading members of the laity and ecclesiastical judges to look into abuses in the three other church courts: the Court of Audience, the Arches, and the Prerogative Court of Canterbury. In this, he had the full support of Leicester, Walsingham, Huntingdon, and Mildmay. Unusually, he also asked the panel of judges to suggest workable reforms. Unwittingly, Grindal had set out on his journey along his personal Via Dolorosa.

For Elizabeth, this smacked of the reforms proposed in 1571, reforms she had vetoed. Now, five years on, the bishops took the initiative once again and introduced Grindal's proposals to the House of Lords. Among the intended reforms was one to enforce church attendance, including the levying of fines. It would be another five years, however, before the recusancy laws would be enshrined in the 1581 Parliament.[12]

While the 1576 Parliament debated legislation, Elizabeth surveyed the state of religion throughout the realm as portrayed to the Privy Council. Public and church prophesyings were on the increase. By this time, they were a regular part of life in England's market towns, where Puritan preachers not only taught the gospel to the clergy but also invited the laity to join in. After these conferences, or classes, there would be a group supper, where the Puritan teachings were allowed to take root in the natural setting of dinner-table conversations.

It was these prophesyings that Elizabeth feared most. For her, these were not a means to better educate the clergy but smacked instead of public gatherings that could easily turn into public demonstrations of discontent. By 1576, reports reached court that there were civil disorders in the Midlands as a result of these prophesyings, or conventicles, as they were also known. Seeing that the wind was blowing in the direction of the godly among her most trusted advisers, Elizabeth decided single-handedly she was having none of it. So on June 12, she summoned Grindal to her presence and demanded he put a halt to them.

From that moment on, Grindal tried, not unlike Elizabeth herself, to plow a middle way through the religious quagmire. He felt it was his duty to protect the prophesyings not only from the Puritans' abuse but also from the unwanted though well-intended attentions of the queen. He collected testimonies about the prophesyings, wrote a scholarly treatise called *Tractatus de exercitiis,* and finally composed his *Orders for reformation of abuses about the learned exercises and conferences among ministers of the Church.*[13] This six-thousand-word manifesto defended preaching as the crucible of faith and civil order, for "where preaching wanteth, obedience faileth," and fear of the prophesyings was "only backward [to] men in religion [who] do fret against it." Grindal took the final step onto his Via Dolorosa with his conclusion to the queen:

> *I am forced, with all humility, and yet plainly, to profess that I cannot with safe conscience, and without the offence of the majesty of God, give my assent to the suppressing of the said exercises: much*

less can I send out any injunctions for the utter and universal subver-
sion of the same . . . Bear with me, I beseech you Madam, if I choose
rather to offend against your earthly Majesty than to offend the heav-
enly majestey [sic] of God.[14]

Grindal should have known that the best way to pacify Elizabeth was
not to oppose her openly. His friends on the council tried to protect him,
but to no avail. Elizabeth, as Supreme Governor of the Church of England,
felt compelled to send out the order directly to the bishops, ordering the
suppression of the prophesyings. Her command was even obeyed in
Grindal's own diocese. His Privy Council friends arranged for the archbishop to make an appearance before the council in the hope that he would
recant his stance. Grindal attended but disappointed everyone when he replied that he couldn't recant since "a second offence of disobedience, [is]
greater than the first."[15]

Grindal was sequestered at Lambeth Palace in May 1577. By November Elizabeth had refused his choice of "sufficient persons" to take his place
to fulfill his duties. He would never again officiate fully as archbishop of
Canterbury yet never ceased hoping to do so. Though he did carry out
some minor church functions, and acted as an arbitrator between Queen's
and Merton colleges, Grindal remained in disgrace. Yet while he did, Elizabeth's church seemingly crumbled around them.

In Sussex, Norfolk, and Suffolk, the queen's bishops engaged in political and religious wrangling with the gentry—both Catholic and Puritan.
London's Bishop Sandys quarreled openly with his successor, Bishop
Aylmer, whom he described as "coloured covetousness, an envious heart."[16]
Grindal's failing was not to see the political dimensions to the Puritan
cause. Elizabeth's was going into battle with the moderate and tolerant
archbishop.

What Elizabeth failed to understand in her extreme anger against
Grindal was that at the time when her church needed strong, personal, and
moderate leadership while it was under threat from Puritans and Catholics alike, she had effectively cut off its spiritual head. This was, however,
no personal vendetta or skirmish. Far more was at stake. Grindal, like
Leicester, cringed at the prospect of the proposed marriage of Elizabeth to

Francis of Anjou (formerly Duke of Alençon) and, like Leicester, did not hesitate to make known his views on the potential disastrous consequences of such a match.

Why had Elizabeth reconsidered marrying the runt of Catherine de' Medici's litter after refusing him so many times in the past? Though she was cooed at and wooed by Anjou's envoy, followed hotly by Anjou himself, Elizabeth hadn't lost her touch for the political imperatives of the day. Privately, she recognized that she had made a mistake only a few years earlier when she ignored William of Orange's pleas for military and financial assistance in his war against Spain.

Despite Orange's phenomenal successes in taking back his provinces of Holland and Zeeland from Alba, Elizabeth had misjudged her options and chosen the surer, safer policy decision of a rapprochement with Spain and an agreement with Requesens. Naturally, her hidden reason for the Spanish option was to have her rebellious English Catholics expelled from the Spanish-held Low Countries. Similarly, Elizabeth's unwillingness to help Orange compelled him to find an ally elsewhere. Only one man, however, appeared over the horizon with military and financial aid: Francis of Anjou, heir to the throne of France.

Despite Leicester's jaw-dropping spectacle at Kenilworth given for Elizabeth during her summer progress of 1576, where he implored the queen through weeks of feasting, allegorical plays, and set pieces not to marry Anjou, Elizabeth held fast to her French "frog," as she called him.[17] This was not for love, as the queen would have everyone believe. It was for politics. Anjou had emerged from nowhere as a force to be reckoned with, and William of Orange, in his desperation for an end to the bloodshed and restoration of the Dutch to their ancient liberties, was willing to make Anjou effectively king of Holland and Zeeland. With the death of Requesens in March that year and the announcement of the new governor in September as Don John of Austria (Philip II's only brother and the victor against the Turks at Lepanto in 1571), Orange needed a powerful ally—quickly. Anjou was his man.

This was the point when politics and religion collided as strange bedfellows. Though Elizabeth was minded to assist Orange and his fellow Beggars, she could not do so without risking war with Spain. The sham of a love match between the queen and Anjou served a treble purpose. Elizabeth could seemingly have lost her senses to love. She could give sustenance to Orange underhandedly through Anjou. Yet most significantly from her perspective, she could dissimulate with Philip, who feared a rapprochement with France would result from her love for her "frog." Philip would need to think twice if he went ahead with his proposed Catholic League with Pope Gregory XIII against England, as France stood geographically, militarily, and politically between them. With Anjou—heir to the throne of France—as Elizabeth's fiancé, France would need to remain neutral.

Rumors of this Catholic League had begun to trickle back to England through Walsingham's network of ambassadors and informers in Italy as early as the end of 1575. When the seminary at Douai had been forced to close its doors that year, Dr. Allen and Francis Englefield traveled to Rome to present an enticing prospect to Pope Gregory XIII. In their written memorial they demonstrated that England could easily be won back to Rome by a mere five thousand musketeers under the command of the renegade adventurer Thomas Stukeley (who just happened to be exiled in Rome). The invasion force could sail from Italy direct to Liverpool, which was a known stronghold of English Catholicism.

Gregory XIII embraced the bold plan and termed it "the Enterprise of England." He discussed it with the Spanish ambassador to the Holy See, Juan de Zuñiga, who thought it a marvelous undertaking; particularly as it would only cost the Spanish crown 100,000 ducats and the king's blessing. Though Philip sent half the subsidy required, he realized that the convoy needed to bring the ships engaged in the Enterprise out of the Mediterranean would vastly weaken Spain's fighting force there and risk the rise once again of the Ottoman Turks. To make matters worse, it was frankly an imprudent financial exercise, as Philip was about to declare bankruptcy yet again.

Still Gregory XIII bombarded Philip with pleas to persevere with the

Enterprise. Philip's ministers sang the same tune. "The worst is that the queen now knows," Zuñiga lamented, "what we had planned and feels the same indignation as if the enterprise had taken place."[18]

Zuñiga was absolutely right. Philip II and Gregory XIII were playing a treacherous game with Elizabeth. For years she had refused to offer financial and military assistance to William of Orange. She had consistently suggested that she act as a mediator between Spain and its rebellious subjects in the Low Countries. It was a suggestion Philip and his governors persistently ignored. When she had heard that Don John of Austria was giving sustenance to the exiled seminarians and allowing them to return to the Low Countries, she toyed with the prospect of helping the Calvinists under Orange. Yet on hearing that Allen, Englefield, Stukeley, and the pope had hatched this Enterprise of England she feared that the time to resolutely take sides might have come at last. Nonetheless, she made one final effort to mediate between the warring parties. On December 20, 1577, she wrote to Philip:

> The sorrow we feel for the calamities and miserable events which have befallen your Serenity's Netherlands, the excessive and terrible shedding of Christian blood, and our desire in all sincerity to promote your honour and advantage . . . As the destruction and desolation of dominions hinders kings themselves from founding their power and glory on the opulence of prosperous citizens, and the diminution of public wealth strikes at the basis of the power of those who govern, so is it unworthy of the regal office and dignity to judge harshly those who love and strive for us . . . our object being to endeavour to arouse in your breast the same compassion for your subjects which has been aroused in ours, and to testify how sincerely and straightforwardly we desire to act.[19]

Most likely, before this letter was sent to the Spanish king, Elizabeth had already chosen sides. Through Anjou, she would help Orange and his Calvinists. After all, Dr. Allen and Francis Englefield had been the first to draw blood with their scheme for the Enterprise of England. Now the security of the realm depended on destroying them.

PART III

The Years of Religious Terror,
1580–1591

EIGHTEEN

God's Outriders

The expense is reckoned.
The enterprise is begun.
—Edmond Campion, 1580

D r. William Allen and Francis Englefield believed heart and soul in the pope's right to depose Elizabeth. With the expulsion of the seminary from Douai, Allen had procured papal approval for a second seminary at Rome where students reportedly flooded, "daily coming, or rather flying to the college." Many were said to be the "best wits in England," with several plucked from Oxford University.[1]

The seminarians' sentiments were hardly a secret. What Elizabeth and her councillors needed to analyze, however, was the role that Gregory XIII, Philip II, and even the queen of Scots had planned for these missionaries in training. Allen's correspondence with the pope and Philip had already been detected, but as yet, his friendship with Mary Stuart had only been widely assumed. After considerable consultation with Elizabeth, it was agreed that the threat to the realm was so palpable that infiltrators would need to be sent to the new college in Rome.

Walsingham was the natural person to be put in charge of the exercise, as he had received full credit for unveiling the Italian side of the Ridolfi Plot in 1571. The very people who had worked for him then were still available all these years later. The two most influential of "Walsingham's moles" in Rome were a former stationer's apprentice, Anthony Munday, and his friend Thomas Nowell. They were welcomed into the English College in Rome on the feast of Candlemas on February 2, 1579, joining forty-two other seminarians. Among their number was a young and as yet unknown would-be priest named Robert Southwell.[2]

While at the college, Munday kept a diary, the first surviving record of a memoir of a spy. In it he claimed that the seminarians held competitions for who could utter the worst insults against Elizabeth and her ministers. Francis Bacon appears in the diary as "the Butcher's son, the great guts, oh he would fry well with a Faggot."[3] On the surface this was a pun for "frying bacon" coupled with the meaning that Francis Bacon was a great Protestant, since to "fry a faggot" meant to burn a heretic alive at the stake. However, Bacon was a person of precisely no significance at the time. He was not a minister, or even in the pay of the crown. So why mention him at all?

The only possible reason must be that Munday had come across the sons of Sir Nicholas Bacon—the elder Anthony and younger Francis—during his travels in France and disliked Francis intensely. While his own diary brings much of what Munday wrote into disrepute on the one hand, it also shows that he might well have been aware of another thorn in the papal side, a spy code-named "Fagot." The elusive Fagot was a mole in the French ambassador's household in London in the late 1570s and early 1580s who leaked intelligence back to Burghley and Walsingham, including damning information against Mary Stuart.

Munday's diary may well have been embellished to discredit men against whom he held grudges, like Bacon, but his descriptions of the dedication of the seminarians to their faith nonetheless rings true today. Munday wrote about self-flagellation as part of the toughening up of the seminary priests. The penitent, who could have been anyone within the student body, would dress in a long canvas robe with a hole cut in its back. The hood of his garment would be raised over his head to shield his identity. He would then walk up and down in the dining refectory whipping himself with a short-handled whip with "forty or fifty cords at it, about the length of half a yard: with a great many hard knots on every cord . . . and some of the whips have through every knot at the end crooked wires, which will tear the flesh unmercifully."⁴ The crooked wires, much like fishhooks, would make the blood run quicker, tearing at the flesh of the penitent's back. This form of self-scourging was a popular means of mortification among the more ascetic orders of the Catholic Church and highly reminiscent of the Flagellants, who sprang up in the aftermath of the Black Death in the thirteenth century.

As early as 1576, Allen's missionaries had begun to take the Catholic Word back to England and reinfiltrate the land of their birth. Cuthbert Mayne was one of the eighteen chosen to make the journey back home in this first wave. They were warned by Allen that it would be a mistake to underestimate the dangers they would face. Organized shire watches scoured the countryside for signs of sedition, religious or otherwise. Catholic families were under surveillance by their servants and neighbors. If the forces supporting the government did not apprehend the missionaries, there were always sturdy beggars and an army of vagrants who thronged the highways and byways eager to undertake the task for a paltry reward. Highway lawyers, footpads, rufflers, or upright men—all names for highway robbers—were commonplace. For a lone priest, as each of the seminarians was meant to be, officiating at his peripatetic Mass was a very precarious life, as Cuthbert Mayne would soon discover.

When Richard Grenville, the pirate adventurer and high sheriff of Cornwall, rode with a hundred men to the home of Sir Francis Tregian, Cuthbert Mayne was asked to identify himself. Defiantly, Mayne responded, "I am a man." Grenville was furious. He ripped open the priest's doublet and found an Agnus Dei case hanging from his neck. These were wax disks made from Easter candles, and each had the image of a paschal lamb pressed into it. Most significantly, they were blessed by the pope. The penalty for possessing one in England, since the Parliament of 1571, was death.

Rather than swear that Elizabeth was head of the Church of England to avert his punishment, Mayne chose death. Just before his execution in early December, he asserted that England would be restored to the true faith by the "secret instructors" of Douai, and should "any Catholic prince . . . invade any realm to reform the same to the authority of the See of Rome, that then the Catholics in that realm . . . should be ready to assist and help them."[5] Despite his defiance, Mayne's executioner showed him mercy, sixteenth-century-style. He was hanged and allowed to die before he was disemboweled and quartered. Sir Francis Tregian, as punishment for harboring Mayne and hearing Mass, was held in captivity for twenty-five years, and his lands were forfeit to Sir George Carey, the queen's cousin.

Seven months later, on June 21, 1577, the bishop of London wrote to Walsingham: "I have had conference with the Archbishop of Canterbury, and we have received from divers of our brethren, bishops of this realm, news that the Papists marvellously increase both in numbers and in obstinate withdrawing of themselves, from the church and the service of God."[6] A conference of bishops and councillors was summoned that July to discuss how to address recusancy. The result was a government paper proposing that known ringleaders, the old diehards upon whose advice "consciences of recusants depend," should be banished or imprisoned, "corrupt schoolmasters" should be removed, and obstinate offenders of the laws of England should be restrained, isolated, and punished.[7] This is the first paper written by the government on how to deal with the perceived threat of recusancy in England. Its author was Francis Walsingham.

For Elizabeth, it was one thing to hold fast to Catholicism; it was quite another to pray for an invasion by a Catholic prince as Mayne had done. What she had perhaps hoped was that Mayne's death would serve as a reminder to her people that as long as they quietly followed their faith and did not "intermeddle" in politics, she would remain true to them by not making "windows into their souls." She could not allow or forgive priests who were uncommonly well versed in politics to pronounce upon her steering at England's helm.

What Elizabeth had forgotten was her church history: Mayne and the hundreds of others who would soon follow him to England would delight in wearing their martyrs' crowns. Until the Mayne mission, Burghley's primary concern had been recusancy among the gentry. Catholic priests in England were by and large old men of the Marian period, too old to become crusaders once more.

• • •

The first inkling that Burghley and Elizabeth had that the pope might import younger, more vigorous priests came with the ill-fated voyage of Thomas Stukeley from Civita Vecchia to Ireland under the papal banner in 1578. Fortunately, Stukeley never got any nearer than Portugal.[8] With Stukeley's mission came the broader realization that the Enterprise of England, though somewhat hazy, contradictory, and convoluted, was already under way.

Nonetheless, the alarm was sent out in Ireland, fearing that Stukeley's stop at Lisbon was only to take on more men and arms. The Lord Deputy of Ireland sent frantic appeals to Burghley for money, men, and ships, but Elizabeth shrugged off Stukeley's invasion as a pipe dream and refused to allow it to be discussed in the council's meetings. She was right to do so. Stukeley was a swashbuckler, not the admiral of an invading army, as Elizabeth had already found out to her cost through his misadventures as a tax collector in Berkshire, her spy in Ireland, and leader of her expedition to Florida.[9] Before leaving Lisbon as a captain in King Sebastian's army for Morocco, Stukeley, characteristically iconoclastic, said that Ireland provided nothing for anyone but poverty and lice.[10] Given that Gregory XIII's plan was to crown his "nephew" Giacomo Boncompagni king of Ireland, Stukeley had proved more than a bitter disappointment.[11]

Within the year, the pope and Philip II found a more suitable replacement for the untrustworthy Englishman. The exiled James Fitzmaurice Fitzgerald, first cousin of Gerald, fifteenth Earl of Desmond, was selected by His Holiness to head up the Irish invasion. James Fitzmaurice had become the putative head of the Fitzgerald clan in Ireland when his cousin the earl had been imprisoned in the 1570s. The Desmonds, also known as "Geraldines," under the command of James Fitzmaurice, were responsible for much of the unrest in Ireland in the 1570s as they struggled for supremacy in Munster against the Earl of Ormond's Butler family.

The pope had chosen his man well. James Fitzmaurice was a man of great faith and courage and a bitter enemy of English rule in Ireland. In line with the brutality that scarred Ireland forever, James Fitzmaurice looted towns, slaughtered garrisons, and stripped civilians (including housewives) of the clothes on their backs and sent them literally naked into the enemy's camp.[12] Fitzmaurice had been a fine choice indeed, made even better by the selection of the Englishman Dr. Nicholas Sander as the papal envoy for the mission. Sander had been Elizabeth's nemesis since he had been one of the few exiled Englishmen to defend Pius V's bull of excommunication in his work *Regnans* (1570). Fearing unspeakable reprisals against the college at Douai, William Allen demanded that *Regnans* be suppressed. Sander seems to have agreed, though in 1571 he printed the papal bull in full in his *De visibili monarchia* and praised as a martyr John Felton, the man who nailed it up on the doors of Lambeth Palace in London.[13] With the valiant Fitzmaurice arrayed alongside the pulpit and eloquent pen of Sander, both the pope and Philip had every reason to believe in their collective victory in Ireland. From there, England was only a stone's throw away.

Though English, Dr. Sander had long reflected on the suffering of the Irish under English rule, believing that many of their ills were due to its unlucky geography at England's "postern gate." In fact, Ireland had been in Sander's heart as early as 1573, when as papal envoy he endeavored to sway Philip II to the Enterprise of England. Four years later, he wrote to William Allen, "The fate of Christendom depends upon the stout assailing of England."[14]

Then, in April 1579, the Spanish ambassador to England, Bernardino de Mendoza, the suave archplotter and key player in much of what was to come to pass, wrote to the Spanish ambassador in Paris:

> *An Englishman has arrived here . . . to tell the Queen that his Majesty had ordered the stopping of all ships on the Biscay and western coasts, and that Dr. Sanders [sic] and a brother of the earl of Desmond, James Fitzmaurice, Irishmen [sic], were fitting out ships. This has aroused some suspicion, because she has seized a letter written by some of the principal people in Ireland . . . telling James Fitzmaurice how glad they will be for him to come.*[15]

On July 17, Fitzmaurice and Dr. Sander sailed into Dingle Bay in the far southwest of Ireland. Together Fitzmaurice and Sander proclaimed the inspiration and purpose of their invasion: to fight against the "she-tyrant which refuseth to hear Christ, speaking by his vicar [the Pope]." Within days, an English privateer, Captain Courtenay, had seized and led away Fitzmaurice's tiny fleet. Burghley's man in Ireland, the Earl of Ormond, agreed to send five hundred men to meet Fitzmaurice and his troops. Though valiantly fought, it was all over by the end of October, and Fitzmaurice was dead. Despite a two-year-long relentless pursuit, Dr. Sander escaped capture, only to die alone in a wood, starved and frozen with his breviary and Bible under his arm. The "Second Desmond Rebellion" unleashed by Fitzmaurice and Sander turned into tribal warfare, which only ended with the death of the Earl of Desmond, Gerald Fitzgerald, in 1583.

A third attempt to invade England through its postern gate of Ireland was hatched in January 1580. An English merchant, John Dunne, who was trading in Bayonne, France, at the time, bribed a Spanish monk into telling him that Spanish forces were being raised for Ireland with the pope's blessing. He informed Walsingham at once. On verification by Walsingham's own agents, the secretary of state learned that eighteen ships were made ready, carrying twenty thousand men. With the pope's financial aid, this force grew to at least forty ships.

Elizabeth responded by sending reinforcements and her rapscallion adventurer William Winter with four ships to guard the Irish coast. At the end of the day, only two invasion ships made landfall at Smerwick and attempted to make a bridgehead. Within three days, they laid down their arms and surrendered. Nearly all were slaughtered in cold blood.[16]

The three failed papal-sponsored invasions did have one unintended success. Elizabeth's steady policy of balancing European power that had prevailed for the first twenty years of her reign now wavered. The Catholic Enterprise of England had failed so far, and it was obvious that there would be other attempts. England needed the protection of a stronger partner, and so Elizabeth sought a new rapprochement with France and a reopening of the marriage treaty with Henry III's brother, Francis, Duke of Anjou.

Of course, Elizabeth's desire to withstand all attacks by Catholic powers through a marriage to Anjou was, to say the least, deeply unpopular
with the vast majority of her people. When it was added to the perceived
slackening of measures against English Catholics, law-abiding citizens became understandably uneasy. It was the devil of a situation: Elizabeth
needed to reassure Anjou and France that she could moderate hostile reaction against the English Catholics, while masking her personal aversion
to the godly Puritans and maintaining the full force of the Anglican
settlement.

In the event, Elizabeth couldn't hold out against the storm of popular
opinion, nor are we sure she wanted to. Before the end of 1579, around the
time of Cuthbert Mayne's execution, Elizabeth wrote to Anjou breaking
off their engagement. "We poor inhabitants of the barbarous isle must be
careful in appearing for judgment," Elizabeth wrote Anjou, "where such
ingenious judges of our knowledge hold their seat in so high a place."[17]
For the pope, it was a pyrrhic victory that left the "she-tyrant" exposed,
albeit still in power.

Then, in 1580, it seemed that a turning point in the fortunes of the pope's
single-minded desire to overthrow Elizabeth finally arose. Until now,
William Allen had resisted the involvement of the Jesuits in the English
struggle. The execution of Cuthbert Mayne for treason, followed by two
further executions, changed whatever reservations Allen seemed to have
had. We shall never know for certain if it was Allen's aversion to call upon
Loyola's men as his holy warriors or the Jesuit Society's fourth superior
general Everard Mercurian's reluctance to become involved in the English cause. Mercurian had grown up in the Low Countries and had seen
all sorts of obstacles to Jesuit missions that hinged on the successful conversion of a religious flock in conjunction with the politics of the times.

For Mercurian, English Catholicism had become so opaque in the previous twenty years of Elizabeth's reign that fulfilling Jesuit goals seemed
impossible. Jesuit priests would need to live "in secular men's houses in
secular apparel." He fretted that they would founder "as how also their
rules and orders for conservation of religious spirit might there be

observed." More damning still was that the Jesuits had far-flung operations from Argentina to Japan at the coalface of Christian conflicts with
"heathen peoples," and Mercurian feared a face-off with Protestants within
Europe would damage their greater cause. Yet Mercurian finally buckled.
The arrival in Rome in 1579 of the Oxford exile Robert Persons gave Allen
the ally he needed to move Mercurian. Together with another priest, Edmund Campion, the two men were destined to bring Catholicism back to
England.

This was the same Edmund Campion who had so impressed Elizabeth
and Leicester at Oxford in 1566 and had escaped prosecution in Ireland in
1574. By 1580, Campion was a graduate of Douai and a Catholic priest.
Still, his successes within the Catholic exile community were not enough
for this exceptional young man, of whom Cecil lamented it was "a very
great pity to see so notable a man leave his country."[18] After his ordination,
Campion took the final step onto the ladder to martyrdom. He walked
from Douai to Rome and became a member of the Society of Jesus. It was
their founder, Ignatius Loyola, who reportedly said "Give me a boy at the
age of seven, and he will be mine forever." Campion proved to be a late
bloomer.

Like Campion, Persons had not always been an avowed Catholic.
While at Oxford, he had dabbled with the more defined theological posi-
tions of Calvinism before switching his allegiance to Catholicism. It was
his initial indecision that allowed him to obtain his first degree at Oxford
by taking the Oath of Supremacy on May 31, 1568. In 1570, however, on
seeing the deprivation of another Balliol College fellow and Catholic,
Richard Garnet, Persons became so distressed that he "temporarily" left
Oxford. Persons's initial desire to conform, then recant, was a common
story for independent thinkers of the day. His father converted to Rome
much later; one of his brothers became a Protestant clergyman, the other
a Catholic. His mother sheltered among the recusant underground, end-
ing her days at the notorious Enfield home of Anne Vaux at White Webbs.[19]

No one knows with certainty why Persons finally resigned his fellowship at Balliol College in February 1574. Though charged by the master at

Balliol with fiddling the accounts while he was the college bursar and dean, Persons most likely had already shown his own special blend of cussedness combined with a strong sense of right and wrong. Given leave to stay at the college through Lent, he was summarily expelled, as traditional stories would have us believe, by the "ringing of bells backwards, as for a fire" when he tried to enforce the Lenten fast. By 1581, he would be depicted as a screech owl by the Puritan preacher John Field in his religious tract *A Caveat for Parsons Howlet*.[20] Through this tract, it is easy to imagine how Persons's voice sounded to those who disagreed with him, and how his reputation as a "fierce-natured" fellow became part of his legacy.

As a result, toward the end of 1579, the final conversion of Superior General Mercurian to the English cause seems to have been due to a combined onslaught of Persons's reasoned arguments and Allen's reassurances that they could succeed in a truly Jesuit mission to reconvert England to Catholicism.

While they planned the final details of the mission in Rome, an earthquake hit London on April 6, 1580. Stones rained down from St. Paul's Cathedral; an apprentice was crushed by falling masonry at Newgate; the great clock bell at the Palace of Westminster struck against itself repeatedly, "shaking the earth"; the seas foamed; ships tottered, and a portion of the White Cliffs of Dover tumbled into the sea. For a people who believed that natural phenomena were "nothing but the very finger of God working his creatures" it was a portent of some unseen calamity to come. Some astrologers like Dr. John Dee sought to calm jangled nerves by claiming that the movement of the earth and celestial bodies was predictable by astrology and science rather than at the pulpit, but they were soon silenced by Puritans and Anglicans alike.[21] When ghostly castles or ships, the haunting cries of invisible hounds, "skulls of dead men," or other such terrifying visions appeared in the skies, it is little wonder that many feared God's retribution for the execution of the priest Cuthbert Mayne.

Mayne's execution for treason also moved Mercurian to take somewhat unusual measures. His orders to Persons and Campion stipulated that they were to avoid heretics at all costs. In fact, Mercurian went a step further. They were to "behave that all may see that the only gain they covet is that of souls" and not to entangle themselves in the affairs of the heretic English state. As Edmund Campion made his way back to Rome from his rhetoric teaching post in Prague to join Robert Persons for their joint mission, Mercurian stressed that neither man was to have about his person anything of a forbidden nature in English law: no papal bulls, no Agnus Dei.

Theirs would be a mission solely to reconvert the lapsed English to Catholicism. Unlike Judaism, which had over centuries adapted itself successfully into the home for its survival, English Catholicism, so the argument ran, needed a priest officiating to ensure correct adherence to the Word. Persons, though the younger of the two, was appointed leader of the mission; Campion his lieutenant. As they left Rome in April 1580, traveling on foot and using aliases to escape detection, a letter was sent from a well-wishing seminarian who witnessed their departure, describing what he felt was assuredly a turning point in history. That letter was intercepted by an English spy and its contents forwarded to Sir Francis Walsingham. The "secret" mission was awaited eagerly in England, long before the pair had crossed the Alps into France.

One of the great mysteries of their mission to England was whether Persons and Campion had recognized the political dimension instigated by the pope and Spain to overthrow Elizabeth the "she-tyrant." Given the pressures on English Catholic exiles and the pair's experiences and presence in Rome over several months, as well as the failed attempts to invade Ireland, both men would have needed to be the "least informed Englishmen in Europe" to remain unaware of the bigger picture.[22]

Having withstood three "invasions" with equanimity, in June 1580 Elizabeth became alarmed when she learned that Persons and Campion had crossed into England under assumed names. Burghley immediately issued a proclamation in the queen's name, which unfortunately ran to two folios. This was no punchy piece of propaganda. While it held some stirring messages about the pope and the king of Spain seeking to "dispose of the Crown" and the queen striving to "maintain her honour and glory by retaining her people in the true profession of the Gospel and free from the bondage of Roman tyranny," its sheer tediousness was enough to anesthetize the most well-wishing reader.[23] As a result, the plan to seg-regate recusants from the general population went nearly unnoticed by many as a key part of the proclamation.

It was the oratory of Edmund Campion that awakened them. At St. Mary Overie (Southwark Cathedral today) Persons and Campion swore publicly that they had been ignorant of the pope's Irish invasion plans and even read out Mercurian's orders forbidding them from dabbling in "matters of state." Some were persuaded; others feared government retri-bution against England's Catholics. In one church, on one day, the two opposing English Catholic worldviews were laid bare. It was Campion's oratory that swayed those who had conformed, claiming that if they were to worship in an Anglican service, it would be a final victory for the Elizabethan settlement.[24] He won the day. Just.

The meeting broke up shortly before a former student from Rome—now a government informer, Charles Sledd—led an official searcher to St. Mary Overie. Persons and Campion were already on the Great North Road, heading for the relative safety of Hoxton (Hackney in London to-day), where they spent the night.[25] The following morning they were surprised by the arrival of Thomas Pound, a recusant prisoner who had bribed his way out of the Marshalsea prison. As a loyal follower of theirs, Pound had been deputized by his fellow recusants to ride through the night to talk to Persons and Campion. His mission was to persuade the priests into writing a declaration of the purpose of their mission, which Pound would safeguard in prison and only publish in the event of their capture. It would, at the very least, protect them from the malice of a propaganda coup by the government branding them as political agitators. Both men agreed and duly wrote out their declarations. Persons sealed his; Campion left his open for anyone to read.

Having returned to the Marshalsea with his mission accomplished, Pound couldn't resist reading Campion's statement. He was so moved that he showed it to his fellow recusant prisoners. Addressed to "Her Maj-esty's Privy Council," one of the most stirring paragraphs still echoes through time: "Many innocent hands are lifted up to heaven for you daily by those English students, whose posterity shall never die, which beyond seas, gathering virtue and sufficient knowledge for the purpose, are determined never to give you over, but either to win you heaven, or to die upon your pikes."[26] In no time at all, copies were circulated throughout the jail, then on to the prisoners' visitors and out into London and beyond. What had been intended as a document to be read only in the event of capture had become a political manifesto to defend the liberties of English Catholics.

Unlike Burghley's boring and tedious prose, Campion's reached the hearts of the downtrodden reader. He had returned home to his "dear Country" for the "glory of God and the benefit of Souls," as he had been strictly forbidden to deal in matters of state. Since Campion knew that capture meant death, the streak of the martyr that had grown quietly within exploded to the surface in this declaration, soon to be known as *Campion's Brag*. According to Campion, the Catholic League and "all the Jesuits in the world . . . cheerfully . . . carry the cross you shall lay upon us, and never to despair your recovery, while we have a man left to enjoy your Tyburn."[27]

As copies of *Campion's Brag* proliferated, the two men split up. Persons traveled the highways of the Home Counties, while Campion sought the relative safety of the Catholic north for the next six months. Their letters back to Rome spoke of their mental and physical privations, with Campion complaining that "I cannot long escape the hands of the heretics . . . [because] the enemy have so many eyes so many tongues, so many scouts and crafts." Persons wrote, "We never have a single day free from danger."[28]

It was Persons who described the violence he saw about him best: "Everywhere there are being dragged to prison, noblemen and those of humble birth, men, women and even children . . . There comes a hurried knock at the door, like that of a pursuivant—all start up and listen,—like deer when they hear the huntsmen; we leave our food and commend ourselves to God."[29] Thus it was when Ralph Sherwin, the junior seminarian who accompanied Persons and Campion on their mission, was captured. Another seminarian, Edward Rishton, also a former Oxford undergraduate who had studied at Douai, was captured at the Red Rose Tavern in

Holborn when the pursuivants raided it. The searchers had expected to find Persons there, but the Jesuit had lost his way, only arriving after Rishton's arrest.

For over twenty years, Elizabeth could appear to staunchly support her laws in theory, so long as she could mitigate them in practice. The papal invasions and the seminarian priests put an end to that pretense. If Elizabeth and the realm were to remain secure, Parliament needed to act decisively. So, in early 1581, the "Act to retain her Majesty's subjects in their Due Allegiance" was passed. It was the beginning of the fight back against the external Catholic League in defense of the Elizabethan settlement. Its functional shortcoming was that it omitted to make it an offense to *convert* to Catholicism. Its result was the beginning of decades of terror for loyal subjects who happened to be born Catholic. That the bill was introduced by the member of Parliament Thomas Norton, also known as the "Rackmaster," and passed without opposition by both houses shows that the pope, Philip II, and the seminarians had achieved what Elizabeth had failed to do: unite the English against the enemies at their gates.

NINETEEN

The Ungodly Witch Hunts

❧

It is obvious enough that nowadays the whole of
Christendom is split in two, and that princes and peoples
are divided and in such a state of mistrust and hostility
to one another on account of religion that it is impossible
to make any serious arrangement between those
whose religion is different.

—La Mothe Fénélon in London to Catherine de' Medici

Edmund Campion had decided that he would die in the land of his birth, a martyr to all those souls he so fervently wished to save. With the publication of *Campion's Brag* had come a government-sponsored reply, written by the Puritan divine William Charke, who had been expelled from Cambridge University for nonconformity. When it was shown to Campion, he quite rightly claimed that it was a vituperative answer to his reasoned arguments and arranged for five hundred copies of his *Decem Rationes* to be made available in early 1581 for a scholarly debate at Oxford. Printed on a clandestine printing press, Campion's "Ten Reasons" was so precisely and pithily penned that many more wavering souls made the leap back to Catholicism.

Then, on Tuesday, July 11, on his way north to Lancashire to retrieve some papers he had left at Houghton Hall, Campion sought permission from Persons to stay at Lyford Grange near Wantage in Oxfordshire with the staunchly Catholic Yate family. He had not been to Lyford Grange before, despite having received several invitations. Advised that he would not preach but merely stay the night, Persons agreed to let Campion go. The next day, Campion said his good-byes and headed north. What he hadn't realized was that his time at Lyford had caused a fervent desire to hear him preach and such dismay among the community that a rider was dispatched to find him and bring him back to Lyford Grange for that purpose. The rider caught up with Campion at an inn just outside Oxford, and the Jesuit was persuaded to return.

For several days, all was peaceful. A steady stream of students and local residents came to hear the inspiring words of the famous scholar. Campion, a man of tremendous wit and charm, held the people spellbound. On the morning of Sunday, July 16, unbeknown to the priest, among his listeners were George Eliot—a Catholic, convicted murderer, and rapist-turned-informant—and his friend David Jenkins. Neither man had intended to stop at Lyford, but when they spied a servant keeping watch on the roof of the house, they recognized the telltale signs of a secret Mass. It would prove fortuitous for Eliot and Jenkins, ruinous for Campion.

Eliot and Jenkins left Campion's service along with the others, thanking their hosts for allowing them the privilege of listening to the great scholar. By one o'clock in the afternoon, Eliot and Jenkins had returned with the local magistrate, Mr. Fettiplace, riding beside them. They searched the house for the rest of the day, finding nothing. Fettiplace apologized for the inconvenience but listened to Eliot and Jenkins and placed a night guard on watch. The following day, the hunt for Campion resumed. It was Jenkins who finally saw the "chink in the wall of boards" over the stairwell. Taking a crowbar to it, he tore the boards off the wall, breaking through to the cramped room beyond where Edmund Campion and two other priests were concealed.

Campion was immediately brought to London for questioning. The terms of his early imprisonment are unclear, with Campion himself speaking of an interview with the queen. On August 6, 1581, Burghley wrote to Shrewsbury, Mary Queen of Scots' jailer, that Campion had been taken to Leicester. Despite the near hysteria on both sides of the religious divide and wild rumors that Campion had recanted Catholicism to become archbishop of Canterbury, at his trial the Jesuit priest made it clear that he had been merely offered his liberty if he would attend Anglican services. Whether he liked it or not, Edmund Campion had become a renowned political prisoner.[1]

That August, Campion appeared at a public discussion in the chapel of the Tower of London flanked on either side by the dean of St. Paul's and the dean of Windsor. What might have been a useful debate about the lawfulness of imposing the Anglican Church on England as a whole became an emotional harangue about the Jesuit mission to breach the country's national security and commit murder. Nonetheless, with Archbishop of Canterbury Grindal still under effective house arrest, it is difficult to see how Elizabeth's rudderless church could be in a position to look at the Jesuit threat in any other way.

At this first public appearance, the obvious injuries to Campion's shoulders and arms indicated he had been put to the rack. On August 10, Burghley wrote to Walsingham, who was in France on business: "We have gotten from Campion knowledge of all his peregrination in England, as in Yorkshire, Lancashire, Denbigh, Northampton, Warwick, Bedford, Buckingham . . . We have sent for all his hosts in all countries [counties]."[2]

On November 20, 1581, Campion's trial was convened to a packed courtroom. The Jesuit priest showed further signs of torture. Though the statute of 1581 had already been passed into law, Campion was tried under the old treason law of Edward III, presumably to avoid making him a religious martyr, which trying him under the new law of 1581 might do since the Jesuit "conspiracy" had been the motivating factor in the law's inception. The charges brought forward were "for conspiring to compass the death of the Queen and raise sedition within the realm."[3] Implicated, though not specifically named in the indictment, were Philip II and Gregory XIII. Campion was tried along with the other Catholic priests currently in custody—Ralph Sherwin, Edward Rishton, Robert Johnson, Thomas Ford, John Collington, and William Filby. The last two of these had been mere local priests who had come to hear Campion preach at Lyford. Robert Persons and William Allen were tried in absentia.

Those who had been instrumental in Campion's undoing testified for the government. Charles Sledd, who had led the pursuivants to the Red

Lion Inn hoping to capture Robert Persons, testified that while in Rome and Rheims, before he recanted Catholicism, he had learned about the invasion plans from William Allen. George Eliot, who had been instrumental in Campion's capture, told the court that the Jesuit had preached of "a great day" soon to come and that it was general knowledge amongst the prisoners that there was an invasion planned. The real drama was reserved for the soon-to-be playwright Anthony Munday, who recited from his diary about the seminarians schooled in treason. The guilty verdict had been decided long before the testimonies were complete. No sound evidence was produced to show that Campion had been part of any plot to assassinate the queen. For Burghley and Walsingham, all that mattered was the security of the realm, the queen, and the Protestant faith. Campion had been a threat to all three.

Edmund Campion was led from the Tower through a driving rain to the scaffold at Tyburn. There he was hanged, drawn, and quartered in the time-honored tradition for traitors. Father Ralph Sherwin and Father Alexander Briant also met their traitors' deaths that day. Seven other priests followed within the year.

As for Persons, he eluded capture, escaping to the Continent with a wave of Catholic refugees fleeing the new persecution. He would never see England again, but would devote his life to "the Enterprise" so dear to the pope's and Philip's hearts.

Elizabeth could not know that Campion's execution had imperiled the Jesuit mission to England. On the contrary, fear of a coup d'état loomed large in the government's mind, and further steps were deemed necessary for the security of the realm. Diplomacy and international trade had long formed a primary strand for England's financial security; "adventuring" with the likes of Drake—newly returned from his voyage of circumnavigation with enough looted treasure to keep the government in funds for years—was another. "Planting," or colonization, in North America by Sir Humphrey Gilbert represented a bold, if tentative, strike against Spain, declaring that England intended to be a world power. Elizabeth rebelled against Philip's or the pope's authority to rule the world as it had done for the previous one hundred years.

The political landscape was changing rapidly, however, and all England's efforts to ensure its security were mere pinpricks in the sides of her enemies. Philip II had successfully invaded Portugal in 1580, after the death of King Sebastian at Alcazar in Morocco, and was now king of both countries, uniting their empires. Gregory XIII remained determined to demonstrate papal supremacy over England and pushed once more for Philip to consider his "Enterprise of England."

Political Catholicism was growing daily. Mary Stuart's cousin Henry of Guise was gaining strength once more against the increasingly unpopular Henry III. The French king was seen to be weak and effeminate, mocked by contemporaries for his fastidiousness and his young male favorites, called *mignons*. Henry viewed both the Duke of Guise and his heir Anjou as potential enemies of the crown.

Meanwhile, the French people were literally starving by the interruption to farming and hyperinflation from decades of war. Shipping had been interrupted by English, Dutch, and Huguenot corsairs. Anarchy was prevalent, with local nobles acting like regional warlords. Guise and his brand of ultraorthodox Catholicism offered a downtrodden people hope.

In Scotland, Walsingham remained exercised by the sudden appearance of the French claimant to the defunct title of the Earl of Lennox. The handsome, dashing, and violently Catholic Esmé Stuart, Count or Seigneur d'Aubigny, was escorted personally by Henry of Guise to Dieppe to see him off on his adventure to Scotland and the court of his cousin James VI. On May 3, 1580, Walsingham wrote to the English representative in Scotland, Robert Bowes, that he feared "some great and hidden treason not yet discovered."[4] Naturally, d'Aubigny had been sent by Guise at Mary Stuart's behest to reconvert her sixteen-year-old son, James, to Catholicism and send intelligence back to Guise for a planned invasion. Their scheme was only uncovered and foiled by Walsingham's newly set up network of informants in 1582–83 as part of the unraveling of what became known as the Throckmorton Plot.

As for Spain, Philip remained deeply committed to his recovery of the Netherlands. Worse for Elizabeth, he made no secret of his desire to turn his eye to England once his rebellious Dutch provinces had been brought to heel. Something, Walsingham and Burghley agreed with the queen, needed to be done. So once again, Elizabeth pulled out her ancient, dog-eared marriage card and dealt it to Anjou in the autumn of 1578. Henry III and Catherine de' Medici were delighted as it helped them maintain a balance of power against Spain that a weakened France desperately needed. What they hadn't realized was that Elizabeth's true motive was to assist Anjou—newly acclaimed by the Dutch rebels as their "Duke of Brabant"—to rule the rebellious Dutch provinces for himself. No wonder Henry III had branded his brother a "common criminal."[5] Anjou's leadership of the Dutch rebels only served to anger Philip, who retaliated against France by supporting the designs of Henry of Guise.

For England, it was an explosive situation. Jesuit missionaries, the enmity of the pope, Philip II, and now the Guise faction once more in France, meant that the realm was in grave jeopardy. Since Walsingham had proved so effective in the past and had acted as a foreign minister to the queen, the task of masterminding resistance to the powers seeking to destroy England fell to him. Walsingham would not only look to diplomacy as his standard tool but would also use his proven skills covertly. In effect, Francis Walsingham had become head of the English secret services and the foreign ministry, and it was these final nine years of his life that would determine his legacy, for good or ill.

Despite this, Walsingham was not in charge of ferreting out English priests, though both Sledd and Munday had been in his pay to destroy Campion.[6] That duty fell to the local authorities. The bishops, lords, and even the county lord lieutenants all had their own network of spies and pursuivants. Nevertheless, it was hardly a well-oiled machine. Often, strangers were picked up on the high roads by chancers in the hope that they would prove to be someone worth something to the authorities.

At home, detection of priests, whether Jesuit or not, was seen to be the primary danger. Their capture usually depended on the boring job of keeping watch on houses of known recusants, since the change in legislation in 1581 imposed a fine of twenty pounds on Catholics not attending Anglican services. Over the next three years, a large number of recusants were imprisoned, and the courts were overwhelmed with cases relating to their failures to pay fines. Instead of the fines contributing positively to the exchequer, they were becoming a liability to the state. By 1585, the recusancy fines would be farmed out by the crown in much the way customs duties were for sweet wines or spices.

Of course, on a human level, the situation had become intolerable. Letters from recusants—though undoubtedly written to stress their hardships—remain poignant today. Richard Tremayne told the Privy Council that he was willing to pay twenty-five pounds in additional fines but begged "for pity's sake to be absolved from paying since all his lands had been seized" as he had defaulted on his original recusancy fines. Tremayne's ready cash had been eaten away by his long journeys back to Cornwall to answer the indictments against him.

Another victim of the Draconian law, Nicholas Tichborne, wrote that he was the younger son of a younger son and only possessed a small farm holding to support his wife and children; that is, until it had been seized by royal officers for his inability to pay his recusancy fines. He wrote to the council from prison, pleading to be set free so that he could beg or borrow enough money to pay all that he owed and keep his family from starving.

Others, like James Welsh, a scholar of Magdalen College Cambridge, earned his living as a spy against Catholics in the pay of the bishop of London. His reason for spying against his friends was simple. As a Catholic, he could not find work as a schoolmaster.[7]

Yet there were those, more entrepreneurially minded, who found a more original way of dealing with the heavy burden of being a Catholic in England. Sir George Peckham had been imprisoned in the roundup of "hosts" to Jesuit priests in 1581. Once released, Peckham and the Catholic merchant Sir Thomas Gerard became actively involved in financing the second voyage of Sir Humphrey Gilbert to colonize North America. The plan to resettle the Catholic population in the American colonies met with favor from Walsingham; so much so that his stepson, Christopher Carleill, was one of the investors in the scheme. They raised the money, but Sir Humphrey sank with his ship during the voyage. Walter Raleigh, Gilbert's half brother, took up the gauntlet and enticed the gentlemen to invest in his "plantation" in Roanoke.[8]

Recusancy on the local level was simply not Walsingham's focus. He saw his duties as discovering fifth columnists from the Continent—be they English or foreign—and bringing them to justice. Some would be left in place for several months or years in order to discern if they could lead Walsingham to bigger fish. For these covert operations, he had several levels of sources available to him. Aside from the local authorities, Walsingham also learned a great deal about the movement of priests from England's ambassadors overseas. Sir Henry Cobham, ambassador at Paris from 1579 to 1583, was a mine of information about English priests living in France. The official reports from ambassadors like Cobham were often supplemented with informal accounts from merchants or even itinerant actors and semiofficial secret agents scattered throughout Europe.

Among these agents was the secretary of the French ambassador in London, Jean Arnault. In 1582, Arnault went to Rome to plead the case of Fabrizio Pallavicino, brother to Elizabeth's financier, Horatio, who had converted to Protestantism and hired Protestant armies for Elizabeth on the Continent. Fabrizio, who had remained resident in the Papal States, had crossed swords with the Inquisition—not for any religious breach but because he was involved with a financial syndicate competing with the pope's for the export of alum to northern Europe. Arnault stayed with the French ambassador to Rome, Paul de Foix, whose systematic policy had been to alert Walsingham of planned attacks against Elizabeth.[9]

These informants, whether official or casual, were the tip of the army of small-time yet infamous "spies" in Walsingham's employ. Many were used occasionally for a specific purpose. Fewer would be trusted with long-term projects. At the port towns in England, Walsingham had his own searchers stationed to scrutinize every traveler coming into the country. Often, the searchers would make random requests to examine letters and their baggage. The only problem with his searchers was that they were notoriously corrupt and could be bought cheaply. In addition, a determined priest or infiltrator could readily pay a foreign ship's captain to set him ashore on one of England's lonely beaches to avoid detection.

Still, Walsingham wasn't the only privy councillor with a network of spies. Lord Burghley had used the services of servants in embassies, couriers, courtiers, actors, and linguists in his employ since the outset of Elizabeth's reign. Nor were all of these spies used to detect subversives. Privy councillors like Leicester and Burghley were not above spying on one another, too, and those who did the spying often found lucrative employment with the adversaries of their former employers.

Swimming in these murky waters, Walsingham focused at first on apprehending priests or others entering England illegally for the purpose of overthrowing the queen. Four names of men who assisted the secretary throughout stand above the rest. In the order in which they entered Walsingham's service, these men were Robert Barnard, Walter Williams, Thomas Rogers, also called Nicholas Berden, and Maliverny Catlyn.[10] Walter Williams, though not officially in Walsingham's pay at the time, would prove pivotal in uncovering the greatest prize of all in the witch hunt for England's enemy: proof of Mary Stuart's complicity to overthrow Elizabeth.

Williams had been one of Walsingham's agents placed in Rye jail in 1582 to extract treasonable intelligence from a Catholic prisoner. On his release in February 1583, he was sent on a similar errand to Paris, where Ambassador Edward Stafford described him as devoted only to the "holy bottle": drink. Whether this was part of an elaborate subterfuge is difficult to say. Whatever the truth, Williams soon found himself at the hub of operations forwarding Mary's secret correspondence to France from within the French embassy in London.[11]

The thirteen-month intelligence operation at Ambassador Michel de Castelnau's residence was launched by Walter Williams and the "mole" Henri Fagot, whom some experts believe to have been Castelnau's clerk, Laurent Feron.[12] Fagot sent a report to Walsingham that Francis

Throckmorton had dined with the ambassador and that he had recently sent Mary Stuart the sum of 1,500 crowns, "which is on the ambassador's account."[13] A month later Fagot informed Walsingham that the queen of Scots was directly involved in some sort of a conspiracy and that the chief agents were Throckmorton and Henry Howard, both enemies of Leicester. Walsingham set his watchers onto Throckmorton and on November 5, 1583, arrested him for the Throckmorton Plot. Among his seized papers was a list of names of "certain Catholic noblemen and gentlemen" and details of harbors "suitable for landing foreign forces."[14]

Mary's involvement in clandestine correspondence with Castelnau was pretty convincing. What made it so galling for Elizabeth was that she had recently opened discussions to release the Scots queen from her captivity in June 1583 in return for assurances about Mary's future conduct. In all, Fagot passed along forty-odd letters from Mary to Castelnau. Throckmorton was named as one of Mary's postmen; George More was the other. Henry Howard, brother of the disgraced Duke of Norfolk, was later confirmed as also receiving letters from Mary.[15]

In the first letter, dated July 3, from Castelnau to Mary, the French ambassador reported his discussions with Bernardino de Mendoza, the Spanish ambassador. Castelnau believed that Anjou could be induced to change sides and sketched out how Mary might help. The next letter leaked was Mary's reply, written on July 14. She made it clear that she had always detested the "pox ridden" Anjou and that she doubted his prowess. In the third letter that July, Mary asked Castelnau to try to push Henry III to send troops to Scotland in support of her son, who had recently escaped to St. Andrews from the Protestant Lords who had been holding him captive. She let Castelnau know, in no uncertain terms, that if Henry III would not intervene, plans were well advanced for her cousin Guise to intervene on her behalf—with or without the French king's authority. Castelnau's personal dream of reconciliation between the two queens lay in tatters.

As Mary's scheme unfolded, the government discovered that Henry of Guise planned to personally lead a small invasion force of five thousand men to land near Arundel in Sussex. Simultaneously, Philip II would send twenty thousand Spanish troops to Lancashire to raise the Catholic north of England. The purpose of the invasion was to liberate Mary, defeat

Elizabeth's forces, then overthrow her to put Mary on England's throne.[16] Yet in his confession, poor Throckmorton had only revealed the details of the southern invasion.

Walsingham soon had the verification he needed. Spies across Europe warned that Guise's army was at the ready, and Philip II would pay for half the invasion. Francis Throckmorton and his brother Thomas, along with Ambassador Mendoza, were to organize a welcoming committee of Catholic gentlemen to greet the French when they landed. Walsingham made further arrests, although most of those in the plot, including Thomas Throckmorton, had had time to make good their escape. In the end it was only Francis who was executed as a traitor at Tyburn in July 1584, dying "very stubbornly," refusing to ask Elizabeth's forgiveness.

Mendoza had been expelled earlier that year for "conduct incompatible with his diplomatic status."[17] He immediately took up his next posting as Spain's ambassador in Paris. Meanwhile, Mary's clerk and keeper of her secret correspondence there, Thomas Morgan, remained undeterred in preparing another "notable Service for God and the Catholic Church"—the assassination of Elizabeth.

TWENTY

Frustrating the Designs of Our Enemies

❧

The worst is that the Queen now knows what
we had planned and feels the same indignation
as if the enterprise had taken place.
—Ambassador Zuñiga to Philip II

Shortly before the execution of Francis Throckmorton for treason, Elizabeth's "frog," Francis of Anjou, died of complications of a tertian fever (malaria). His failure to win back territory for the rebellious Dutch, however, had broken him long before the disease did. Anjou's death was a mixed blessing to Spain. Though ineffective as a military commander, Anjou had been a moral boost to the beleaguered Dutch. Now that he was dead, the Protestant Henry of Navarre was next in line for the French throne.

In recent years, reversals for the Dutch in the Low Countries had been terrifying. Certainly, it was thought they would not be able to hold out much longer against the "iron fist in the velvet glove" approach inflicted on them by the brilliant commander Alexander Farnese, Duke of Parma. William of Orange pleaded with Henry III to send money and men, thus taking the place of his dead brother, Anjou, but Orange's pleas were met with stony silence.

Less than four months later, at the end of June 1584, an unknown soldier of fortune, Balthasar Gérard, made an appointment to see William of Orange at his home in Delft. As William left the dining room to go upstairs, Gérard shot the beloved Orange at close range, killing him. Gérard tried to make good his escape to collect the 25,000-crown reward that Philip II had placed on William's head, but the assassin was captured before he could leave Delft. In an age of gruesome executions, Gérard's figures among the worst. The magistrates sentenced him to death, but first his right hand should be burned off with a red-hot iron; his flesh should be torn from his bones in six places; and only then should he be quartered and disemboweled, his heart torn from his body and thrown in his face.

The assassination of William of Orange changed everything. If the Dutch Revolt failed, then Philip would once again possess the Netherlands and its ports facing west toward England. Once Holland fell, Philip's invasion of England could not be far behind. Orange's untimely death instantly ignited the long-standing cold war between England and Spain into a hot one, and thereby changed the course of European history. With the breakaway seventeen Dutch provinces more determined than ever to remain free from Spanish rule, and Henry of Navarre powerless to intervene on their behalf, Elizabeth was now under tremendous pressure from Leicester, Hatton, and Walsingham—the "hawks" of her council—to become the putative leader of the Dutch Revolt.

As Walsingham saw it, the Dutch needed protection from "a potent prince."[1] Burghley, like Elizabeth, favored a combined approach with France against Spain but worried at the same time that France would then become the occupying army of the breakaway provinces. Leicester and Walsingham concurred with any *action* as opposed to *inaction*, simply because they feared the Dutch "ere Christmas next, to become Spanish."[2]

Henry III had his own pressing problems. The ultra-Catholic Guise faction was demanding that Henry do something—anything—to prevent the handsome, daring, and Protestant Henry of Navarre from becoming king of France. Henry III tried to persuade Navarre to convert to Catholicism against the promise Navarre would become Henry's official heir.[3] Navarre naturally refused. Then, by the end of 1584, the Guise faction agreed to form a Catholic League with Philip II "for the preservation of the Roman Catholic religion, the extirpation of heresy both in France and the Low countries, and the exclusion of the heretic of Navarre from the throne of France.'⁴ Philip would be its paymaster, with 50,000 crowns disbursed each month to support the league in exchange for the restoration of the town of Cambrai to the Spanish king.

To compound matters further, the exiled former king of Portugal, Dom Antonio da Crato, was now demanding succor in France. He wanted French men and arms to help him recapture his crown from Philip, strewing vague promises about as if they were confetti. Elizabeth's hope that the weakened Henry III would agree to give joint sustenance with England to the Dutch provinces ebbed away daily.

Since 1563, Elizabeth had viewed foreign wars as an utter waste of men, munitions, and money. Still, as the negotiations for a joint response with France dragged on, it was obvious that something would need to be done rapidly, or Holland would fall. Leicester and Walsingham urged Elizabeth repeatedly to move swiftly, or the enemies would all too soon be at England's gates. Finally, she felt obliged to send the "wise person" of William Davison to open discussions with the Dutch for her.

Then, in March 1585, the plans of the French-Spanish Catholic League were revealed to Elizabeth. Out of sheer anger, she acted decisively, sending Edward Wotton to Scotland to invite James VI to cooperate with England in a Protestant League. Frederick II, king of Denmark, and the Protestant German princes were invited to join by Sir Thomas Bodley. Arthur Champernowne, Walter Raleigh's uncle, was dispatched to Henry of Navarre to extend the queen's invitation to him personally as well.

A month later, the Dutch States-General wrote to Elizabeth asking her to become their sovereign queen and requesting she send four to five thousand men to relieve Antwerp from Parma's nearly yearlong siege. She had never approved of taking arms up against a sovereign lord, and yet, if she allowed the Dutch to fall, England, she had been persuaded, would be next.

In the meantime, Parliament had been convened to ask for a subsidy for the Dutch adventure. As before, Parliament retained its strong and vociferous Puritan membership. The revelation of the Throckmorton Plot and the dangers it represented to the realm, hot on the heels of the Jesuit missions, had the honorable members in an uproar. Though the Dutch subsidy was granted with the minimum of fuss, their main purpose was to ensure Elizabeth's safety. They, like Burghley, were worried about the strengthening of the Catholic threat. Elizabeth only cared to have the subsidy bill discussed and once more began to obfuscate on religious matters. Parliament, yet again, would not be cowed.

A bill called the Oath of Association to bring to justice anyone who plotted to kill the queen was debated and entered its third reading before the House when Dr. William Parry, a new member and one of Burghley's agents in France, rose to protest, denouncing "the whole bill" as it "savoured treasons full of blood, danger, despair and terror to the English subjects of this realm." When challenged, Parry exclaimed that he would tell his reasons for objecting "only onto Her Majesty."[5] Parry was censured for trying to gag Parliament and was only readmitted on Elizabeth's order after the Christmas break.

By mid-February 1585, Edmund Neville, Parry's accomplice in a plot formed the previous summer to assassinate Elizabeth, reported it to the authorities. Leicester and Walsingham were sent immediately to interrogate the egregious MP. Parry confessed that it was young Edmund Neville who had hatched the conspiracy. Parry's defense was that he was merely acting as an undercover agent for Burghley. It was his job, after all, to infiltrate the exiled English Catholic community in Paris. The only problem with Parry's argument was that he hadn't told Burghley about the plot. Unsurprisingly, Burghley did not come to his rescue, and so Parry met a traitor's death.

The renewed attempt on Elizabeth's life resulted in a compromise in the wording of the Oath of Association: Only those who were "assenting or privy" to the offense of attempting any harm to the sovereign could be tried under its provisions. Though framed in an atmosphere of terror, the Oath of Association stood the test of time and was only repealed in the reign of Queen Victoria.[6] That March, Elizabeth wrote to Mary, "In open Parliament motion has been made . . . to revive the former judicial proceedings against you, which . . . was only stayed at that time by us."[7]

...

Yet religious tensions continued to rise. The year 1585 dawned with Gregory XIII making yet another proclamation against England's heretic queen, calling her people to arms for Catholicism. The bellicose pope had agreed to give Philip II nearly 2 million crowns annually over a five-year period to eradicate the "heretical state" of England. Proceeds would be collected from the papal concessions to the crown of Spain and collected in special chests at Madrid's mint for the king's personal use against Elizabeth. Before the year was out, Philip raised an additional 900,000 crowns for his Enterprise.[8]

Then Philip struck a brilliant blow. Early that spring the Spanish king had called for help from the English, Danish, and northern German merchants to relieve the starving Spanish people after a harsh winter. The specific invitation to the English merchants was to send cargoes of corn. In these troubled times, Philip's call for help was accompanied, of course, with a personal promise of safe conduct. Payment for the corn would be made by bills of exchange payable to the City of London in Antwerp at fair-market prices. The ships dutifully arrived en masse laden with food.

Then, without warning, on Wednesday, May 26, 1585, Philip II ordered all Protestant shipping in Spain's harbors to be boarded and sequestered in a coordinated attack. Only one ship escaped, the English bark *The Primrose*. It would return to England with the terrified Spanish magistrates and harbormasters aboard, to catalog the disaster to the Privy Council. Naturally, the starvation of the Spanish people was pure fiction.

The response to Philip's underhand dealing with the English was swift and complete. In June, Elizabeth let loose Sir Francis Drake, the bane of the Spanish, on yet another voyage to "singe the King of Spain's beard." Walsingham drafted his "Plot for the Annoying of the King of Spain," in which ships of war would be dispatched against the Spanish fishing fleet just as it arrived at the Newfoundland banks for its spring fishing expeditions. Ships were to be captured and cargoes taken to pay for the Spanish depredations against England. Walsingham's idea was that the Spanish should now starve in fact, rather than in fiction.[9] Walter Raleigh, heir to his half-brother's lands in North America, received his commission and executed his duties to the letter. He captured the Spanish fishing fleet along with six hundred mariners.[10]

Henry III's reaction to the renewed Spanish threat against the Protestant countries was not surprising. He and his mother abandoned Henry of Navarre in favor of the Guise faction. Navarre, already proving himself to be a great military commander, retaliated by announcing his support for the Protestant League. By the middle of July, Catherine de' Medici and her son had signed the Treaty of Nemours with the ambitious Henry of Guise. Mary Stuart's star was once again in the ascent.

Though Henry of Navarre appealed to Elizabeth for money to raise a mercenary army in Germany, and Elizabeth initially agreed, she was rightly afraid of lifting her head too high above the parapet with both Spain and France simultaneously. To complicate matters further, while Navarre's envoy was still in London, a deputation of Dutch nobility arrived to offer Elizabeth sovereignty of the Low Countries. Navarre's man left empty-handed, while the Dutch stayed on, haggling with Elizabeth. Walsingham wrote to Sir Henry Wotton, "This cause of the Low Countries doth at this present wholly entertain us. Her Majesty's own natural inclination to peace is not unknown . . . Entering into a war with so puissant a prince as the King of Spain, especially . . . that things in France take such a course, may seem an enterprise of dangerous consequences."[11]

Finally, two months later, on August 10, the Treaty of Nonsuch with the Dutch was signed. Essentially, the queen was bound to provide four thousand foot, four hundred horse, and seven hundred men for garrison duty to serve at her cost until the end of the war. In exchange, the States would make over to the English the towns of Brielle, Flushing, and Rammekins as security until the monies spent on their behalf could be repaid. Elizabeth also agreed to send a "nobleman of great quality not only to take charge of our forces but to assist you by his advice and council [sic]." Leicester would be her general.[12]

Virtually every nobleman in England put together his own forces under the queen's banner in the month that followed, and over three hundred noble gentlemen adventurers led thousands into Holland and war by the end of the year.[13] Leicester would command the armies to prevent "the King of Spain to grow to the full height of his design and conquests."[14]

Sadly, Leicester was never a great military commander, and in the autumn of 1585, he had reason to have his mind elsewhere. Leicester had suffered the loss of his only legitimate son and the hope of perpetrating the family line through the boy's marriage to Arbella Stuart, another putative heir to Elizabeth's throne. To make matters worse, while Leicester prepared to leave for the Low Countries, a ferocious attack against him appeared in a scurrilous pamphlet entitled *Leicester's Commonwealth*. It became an instant bestseller. This work of Catholic propaganda against Elizabeth's greatest favourite became a cause célèbre with Protestants and Catholics alike. It proved Sir Francis Englefield's assertion that "instead therefore of the sword, which we cannot obtain, we must fight with paper and pens, which cannot be taken from us."[15]

Fortunately, others were more able than Leicester. Drake had an ambitious plan that could rip apart the Spanish Empire as a diversionary tactic. He planned to attack the Galician coast of Spain before heading westward to capture Santo Domingo, Cartagena, Nombre de Díos, Río de la Hacha, and Santa Marta in the West Indies. After that, Drake would head north to provide sustenance to Raleigh's stranded colonists in Virginia. Though Drake would bring twenty-three hundred men with him, the truly daring part of the voyage was his intention to free around five thousand Cimaroon slaves from the Spanish to fight alongside his own men as their equals.[16] Drake felt that he owed these slaves his very life and fame, for it was a group of slaves who had shown him the Pacific and inspired his voyage of circumnavigation.

Though Elizabeth had had intelligence about Philip's Armada plans, she hadn't realized that the Enterprise had been under way in all seriousness since the autumn of 1583. By the autumn of 1585, most of the pieces on the chessboard had been moved into place for the coming military conflicts between Spain, England, France, the Low Countries, the German princes, Rome, and Navarre. Gregory XIII had died and was replaced by Pope Sixtus V, who would prove equally hostile to England's queen.

As mountains of official papers piled higher on Philip's desk, among them was Santa Cruz's plan for the Armada, or the Enterprise of England. Philip himself had become physically twisted with arthritis and old age. Yet nothing came to pass in Spain without his personal stamp of approval and margin comments on each and every letter. The king of Spain would pore over his papers into the small hours of the morning by candlelight, attempting to find some magic strategic solution that would rid him of the overwhelming Protestant threat.

Admiral Santa Cruz wrote to Philip that he would be ready to sail for England before the year was out, but how could Philip allow his admiral to sail without the backup he had planned from Parma in Holland? Surely until the Dutch provinces were conquered, the Armada could not risk the voyage? None of his papers told him where Drake—nicknamed El Draco, the Dragon—had sailed to. As indecisive as Elizabeth may have been, Philip truly dithered. For a king who only had six months without armed conflict in his entire thirty-year reign thus far, indecision was an anathema.

For good or ill, it was Sixtus who would crystallize his thinking. The pope urged Philip to strike before England could land its forces in the Netherlands. Philip hastily disagreed and wrote to his ambassador in Rome: "Let His Holiness judge whether I can undertake new enterprises, with this one [the Dutch war] in its current state . . . because the war is fought against heretics . . . I am so busy with the war in the Netherlands, which is as holy as a war can be, I could not (even though I wish to) find the money for the others."[17]

At long last, Leicester landed in the Netherlands in December 1585 to serve as Elizabeth's governor-general of the Dutch provinces. Philip's enormous desk was piled ever higher daily with official memos about the English in Holland and their admiral Drake wreaking devastation in the Canaries, the Cape Verde Islands, and the Caribbean, where he had sacked Santo Domingo, Cartagena, and finally St. Augustine in Florida.

Horatio Pallavicino, now Elizabeth's envoy to Germany, whose brother had been held hostage by Gregory XIII, gloated that "it is most certain that one year of war in the Indies will cost the Spaniards more than three years of war in the Netherlands." Pallavicino, a clever merchant banker, was the master of understatement. In Madrid, Philip's friend and the former cardinal of Brussels, Cardinal Granvelle, expressed the outrage for all Spain when he said, "I keenly regret that the queen of England makes war on us so boldly and dishonestly."[18]

History is all about your point of view.

TWENTY-ONE

A Long-Awaited Execution

My end is my beginning.

—Mary Stuart's motto

The Throckmorton Plot had made Elizabeth fear that Mary Stuart would never stop scheming. Oddly enough, what cemented this perception was the negotiation with James VI to take charge of his mother and repatriate her to Scotland. Elizabeth and Walsingham had been in finely poised discussions with James for nearly two years before the Scots king finally refused to countenance Mary's return. James ordered his envoy, the devilishly good-looking Patrick Gray, in March 1585 to write to Elizabeth to inform her that "the Association desired by his mother should neither be granted nor spoken of hereafter." If the son acted thusly to his own mother, how could Elizabeth be wrong about Mary's character?

From James's lofty perch, his mother had abandoned him before he held any memory of her. Further, he had had it drummed into him by his various regents that Mary had arranged for the murder of his father. Quite enough had happened since his birth to ensure that James held no filial love for Mary. So when the renewed approach came in 1584 for James to take charge of the mother he never knew, and upon whom much of his realm's woes had been heaped, James understandably felt no personal emotion for her. As Mary's excitement at being reunited on Scotland's throne with her son dawned, James cooled on the idea. Mary hadn't remotely considered James's feelings. Why should she? Her natural expectation was to rule alongside her son. James's had been quite the reverse.

The tragic figure in the piece was, of course, Mary herself. Now in her early forties, Mary held the delightful vision of being set free from her fourteen-year captivity to be reunited with both her son and her crown. In the negotiations for her freedom she gave away everything that she had fought for—from renouncing her pretensions to England's throne to any determination of Scotland's religious future—all to be set free and meet the son she had been forced to abandon around her first birthday.[1]

However, Mary had become detached from reality after all her years of imprisonment, as is so common. She hadn't "known" her son's mind or indeed that she represented the very threat that he feared most: loss of his crown of Scotland that he had worn since he was a year old. Even sadder, Mary hadn't seen that James saw himself as Elizabeth's putative heir and did not want his mother to ruin his chances of succeeding the childless Elizabeth, now in her early fifties. Of course, when Mary read her son's callous reply, that he would not countenance negotiating with his mother so long as she remained a prisoner of England, the old flame of rebellion flashed once again, as Mary penned her reply to James, "I am so grievously offended at my heart at the impiety and ingratitude that my child has committed against me."[2]

Mary concluded by threatening to "disinherit" James and bestow Scotland upon his greatest enemy. The same day, she wrote to Elizabeth that Patrick Gray was a troublemaker—*ce petit brouillon*—and James was an ungrateful, badly brought-up child. Mary rightly felt her freedom torn away from her, not by Elizabeth this time but by her own son. The shock of it was nearly too much to bear, and so Mary tried to rationalize how James could treat her so shabbily. Perhaps it was the sinister advice of his unwise counsels? It must be Patrick Gray, or James's new favorite, Captain James Stewart, newly created Earl of Arran, surely. Yet slowly, the stark and horrid truth dawned on her. James had repudiated the "Association" that would ensure Mary's release to maintain his own position and power. He had turned his back once and for all on his mother.

Was Mary's threat of disinheriting James entirely idle? Her murdered husband, Lord Darnley, had a younger brother, Charles Stuart. Charles married the daughter of Bess of Hardwicke, Elizabeth Cavendish, and the young couple had a little girl, Arbella. Elizabeth, on discovery of the marriage, imprisoned the couple for marrying without royal approval just as she had done with Catherine Grey all those years earlier. Yet when Arbella's father died in the spring after Arbella's birth, the baby and her mother went to live with the formidable Bess. Could Arbella, an English-bred Stuart, granddaughter of the ambitious Margaret Lennox and Bess of Hardwicke, be the enemy that Mary sought to release against James? As Bess of Hardwicke was Arbella's sole caretaker after the girl's mother died in 1582, and Bess was increasingly estranged from her husband, Shrewsbury, Mary's keeper. The situation was potentially volatile.

There is little doubt that there was right and wrong on all sides of the issues surrounding Mary's continued imprisonment. Nonetheless, Walsingham's primary consideration remained security of the realm, and Mary, since the Throckmorton Plot, had put England on a heightened state of alert. Bess of Hardwicke, in part to keep the stain of any closeness with Mary away from her beloved granddaughter Arbella, sharpened her notoriously vituperative tongue and spread rumors about Mary to her husband, Shrewsbury. Bess declared that Shrewsbury and Mary had had two children together during her captivity. Shrewsbury was outraged; Mary, apoplectic. Bess and Shrewsbury separated, with Shrewsbury's reputation in tatters, while Bess wove further fairy tales to an incredulous court. In the end Elizabeth had Bess examined by the Privy Council, and the stories were seen for the fabrications they were.

Of course, it was impossible in these circumstances for Shrewsbury to remain with his wife and maintain Mary as his prisoner. With all this fresh notoriety Mary would, in the council's view, once again become a magnet for Catholic plots even if she did not instigate them. The only "winner" in the sad state of affairs would be Shrewsbury himself. By Elizabeth's deep-searching for the truth, the hapless earl had been freed from the two women who had ruined his life—his wife and Mary—but who could take Shrewsbury's place and under what conditions?

Mary was quickly removed back to Tutbury Castle and the custody of Sir Ralph Sadler in January 1585. Elizabeth did not want the loyal Shrewsbury to be more offended than he had been already by the allegations leveled at him, so she created a thin veil of unknown but suspected Catholic threats and the sudden need to keep Mary in the custody of Puritans.

While Bess of Hardwicke ranted and testimonies were given before the Privy Council, Mary became more and more isolated in her dour prison at Tutbury, as well as increasingly impoverished. Henry of Guise, as Mary's financial adviser, was busily feathering his own nest in France and was guilty of either severe maladministration or simply pilfering Mary's marriage settlement from her days as queen of France. Before that, Henry III, under the ever-watchful Catherine de' Medici, had forced Mary to swap her valuable estates in Touraine for loss-making ones elsewhere. In no time at all, her ambassador James Beaton, archbishop of Glasgow, was obliged to raise a mortgage to the value of 33,000 crowns against these. Beaton, who was the only man still answerable to Mary, shouldered the entire blame for her poverty, though it is difficult to see how he could have avoided a royal order for the exchange of lands—an exchange that benefited Francis of Anjou, and ultimately the French crown. The only person to escape her thoughts of wrongdoing was Shrewsbury's former secretary, Thomas Morgan, who now served in the powerful position of Beaton's chief cipher clerk. It was Morgan who sent Gilbert Gifford to Mary in December 1585 with letters that would foreshadow Mary's own end.

Unfortunately for Mary, she had trusted Morgan. Though he had constructed over forty cipher alphabets for Mary and held virtually all of her foreign correspondence with Spain, Rome, and France, as well as having been at the heart of the Throckmorton and Parry plots, Morgan had also become sloppy. When Gifford presented himself to Morgan as a former student of William Allen's at Rheims, Morgan took Gifford into service as a courier within weeks, without carrying out adequate checks. Gifford was given a letter of introduction to Mary, recommending him in the warmest terms as a trustworthy Catholic gentleman who had "offered to do all the friendly Offices he may do."[3]

The glowing reference for Gilbert Gifford did not stop there. Morgan wrote that he had given Gifford specific instructions to establish correspondence with Mary. "This," Morgan added confidently, "he promised to put into execution with care and I hope he will show his good will and diligence in the cause. He required my letters to your Majesty, thereby to give him credit and a mean to enter into intelligence with your Majesty."[4]

On Gifford's landfall at Rye, the port searcher apprehended him straightaway and took him to Walsingham. There is no record of their interview. Though it is possible Gifford had always been in Walsingham's service, it is only after they met that we know for certain Gilbert Gifford had agreed to betray Mary and all his Catholic friends to enter Walsingham's pay.

Obviously Walsingham knew Gifford was coming and a further Catholic plot was already under way. In fact, at the time Gifford approached Morgan in Paris, Walsingham had finally succeeded in moving Mary to the Earl of Essex's home, Chartley Hall. To Mary's chagrin, her jailer, the staunch Puritan Sir Amias Paulet, tightened her security even further. Though Mary complained bitterly to Elizabeth about Paulet's stern treatment, prohibiting her from even taking fresh air, he had been acting on orders of Walsingham himself. All discussions between Mary and the castle servants, as well as those serving in Mary's household, could only take place with Paulet in the room. None of Mary's servants were allowed to leave the grounds without a guard. No stranger was allowed admission on any pretext. Laundresses, coachmen, or other seemingly innocuous tradespeople were put to the closest scrutiny possible.

Mary's isolation was near complete, and the more isolated she became, the more desperate her plight. The only correspondence allowed was through the French ambassador, though even then diplomatic privilege was suspended. All packets, whether incoming or outgoing, were carefully examined by either Walsingham or his unquestionably zealous secretary and cryptographer Thomas Phelippes. Walsingham had devised a method of opening Mary's letters without disturbing their seals so that neither the ambassador nor Mary knew the letters had been searched for hidden meaning. After three short months of this charade, Walsingham wrote to Paulet to tell him that Mary should be informed that all her letters for France would need to be sent directly to Walsingham before they could be forwarded. Mary's last vestige of privacy had been removed with her transfer to Chartley.[5]

The success of Gifford's mission as Walsingham's spy depended entirely on his ability to get letters to the information-starved Mary. The man who made this possible was none other than Thomas Phelippes. Around Christmastide 1585, Phelippes was dispatched to Chartley to arrange a plausible means by which letters could be passed to Mary without arousing her suspicions that her loathed jailer was facilitating her communications.

Phelippes saw at once that Chartley, unusually for a Tudor manor house, had no private brewery. Considering that England's population of around four million people drank eighteen million barrels of beer annually, with over three-quarters of it brewed domestically, the answer to Walsingham's dilemma was obvious. The beer casks brought to Chartley could feasibly serve as mailboxes for Mary's correspondence. They could be delivered "full" with inward letters to the Scots queen and returned "empty" with Mary's replies inside. A watertight casket needed to be built and hidden inside the casks, and Chartley's brewer taken into Walsingham's confidence. Mary was no fool; if the casks were delivered by someone other than the proper person, the elaborate ploy could fail.

While these preparations were made, Gifford remained in London among the closed world of the Catholic community. When the time was ripe, around January 12, 1586, Gifford made himself known to the new French ambassador, Châteauneuf, to lay before him a cunning plan. Gifford claimed full credit for the "brewery plan" and insisted that all was ready. Though deeply mistrustful, Châteauneuf gave Gifford a letter for

Mary, without any matters of importance discussed therein. Gifford went straight from the ambassador's London residence to Chartley's brewer. Within four days, the letters were safely in Mary's hands. How Mary knew about the first casket letters, or indeed that the beer casks would provide a new conduit for her to the outside world, remains a mystery.

After nearly a year cut off from any external contact, Mary clearly felt hopeful once again. She set to work to let those who were faithful to her know that she had a secret means by which she could write and receive letters. Once her letters were written, the method for placing them into the casket was simple. Mary would dictate to her secretary, Claude Nau. He transcribed the letters into code, wrapped them securely in a leather packet, and handed it across secretly to the Chartley brewer. The brewer placed the packet into the corked tube in the bung of the cask. The "honest fellow," as Paulet nicknamed the brewer, then took out the leather packet and handed it over to Gifford. Gifford would redeliver the letters that same evening to Paulet back at Chartley. The code in the letters was easily decrypted and the contents noted for the government's use; then the packet was resealed, and Gilbert Gifford rode off to London to give the letters to the French ambassador. The first letters arrived with Thomas Morgan in Paris by mid-March.[6]

This first packet contained letters to Morgan and James Beaton in Paris, a letter to Henry of Guise, and one to Châteauneuf. All that was to be learned from this first group of letters was Mary's elation at being able to communicate with them once more. In her instructions on how to reply, Mary told Châteauneuf to send all packets that had been held for her at the embassy via Gifford. At last Walsingham knew that the plan had worked. All he needed now was to ensure that the chain of control wasn't breached.

They didn't have long to wait. In the twenty-one packets sent through to Mary were all the letters written since the discovery of the Throckmorton Plot. Morgan, Charles Paget, a noble exiled Catholic, and James Beaton all wrote from Paris. Sir Francis Englefield and Robert Persons wrote to her from Spain. From the Low Countries two other correspondents wrote of developments there—albeit a year out of date. The vindication Walsingham must have felt at being able to read at one sitting *all* the foreign correspondence relating to the Throckmorton Plot should have been tremendous.

How Mary had pinned her hopes and prayers on the empty promises of Henry of Guise for years, how she had turned to Philip of Spain, and how Philip with Parma had planned her escape, as well as how all these schemes had failed, were laid before Walsingham. He could see with absolute clarity where the chinks in Mary's armor were: whom she trusted and how she thought over the previous two years. Among this treasure trove, two of the letters demonstrated beyond any doubt that Mary had full knowledge of the Throckmorton Plot encompassing the Guise and Spanish invasion plan and she approved of it. Based on those two letters alone, Walsingham could have presented an open-and-shut case against Mary for treason based on the Oath of Association. Still, Walsingham wanted more.

To protect the secret nature of the organization against Mary, Walsingham told Paulet to give a pay raise to the "honest brewer" when he demanded it. Walsingham also had other plans for Gifford back in Paris. Before his man went on to pastures new, Gifford wrote to Mary to commend his "cousin," who was a man, apparently, "of honest credit, good wealth, good understanding and a servant of the earl of Leicester." It was Gifford's substitute who would hand over the return correspondence from the French embassy to Mary in dribs and drabs, in part to allow time for the complete deciphering of the letters, in part because they were too numerous to fit into the casket within the cask.[7]

It is at this point that an entirely separate conspiracy to assassinate Elizabeth, coupled with a romantic ideal to free Mary and put her on England's throne, merges. A priest named John Ballard had been part of a plot in 1584 to murder Elizabeth along with his friend and fellow priest, Anthony Tyrrell. The pair later claimed that they had gone to Rome to seek Gregory XIII's blessing. Gregory may have been favorable to Ballard's request (so long as it didn't interfere with his own plans), but the Jesuit rector of the English College in Rome, Alfonso Agazzari, was not. This should not have come as any surprise. The Jesuits, he said, had been clear from the outset that they had no wish to become embroiled in England's politics.

On their way back from Rome, in the spring of 1586, Ballard and Tyrrell stopped in Paris. There they met Charles Paget, Mary's long-standing
servant. Ballard, reportedly an unstable man, bragged to Paget that he
knew all the leading Catholics in England and Scotland and that he had
been sent to the Continent to declare their readiness to take up arms
against Elizabeth. When Ballard later repeated his story to the Spanish
ambassador Mendoza, he added that the time was ripe to invade, as England's finest soldiers were engaged in the Low Countries with Leicester.
So far, Ballard had said nothing that Mendoza hadn't already known. He
was thanked for his attention and sent on his way.

Before Ballard and Tyrrell left Paris, Charles Paget told them they must
visit Anthony Babington in London. En route, and certainly not suspecting to unite their plot to Babington's, the pair met with an ex-soldier in
Parma's army, John Savage. Together with Gilbert Gifford's cousin William Gifford, Savage had planned to murder Elizabeth as well.[8] Unknown
to all of them, Walsingham was following their every move.

Anthony Babington, after whom the notorious Babington Plot is named,
became an admirer of Mary Queen of Scots when he was a boy, most
likely when he had served as a page to the Earl of Shrewsbury. Like many
other young Catholics, he saw Mary in the romantic guise of the spirit of
the Counter-Reformation and Elizabeth as England's "she-tyrant." In his
letters to Mary, his flowery language revealed how she could fulfill his
Catholic vision for England. Originally from Derbyshire, the twenty-five-
year-old was typical of well-to-do Midlands Catholic youths, like Charles
Paget, who prayed for a change in their religious fortunes.

Ballard met Anthony Babington at his lodgings in London late in May
1586 but seemingly had known him for at least two years before that. Ballard, true to form and full of braggadocio, gave Babington an overblown
account of the preparations under way and the great Catholic League that
was at hand against Elizabeth.

To an intelligent and sensitive young man like Babington, this was not
the good news that Ballard had believed it to be. On June 7, 1586, Babington met with his close circle of friends: Sir Thomas Salusbury, a ward of

the Earl of Leicester and heir to Lleweni in Denbighshire in Wales; Edward Abington of Worcestershire, Elizabeth's cofferer; Chidiock Titchborne from Southampton, a known Catholic; and Charles Tilney, cousin of Edmund Tilney, Master of the Queen's Revels and censor of all plays. When Babington told his friends what Ballard had said, he lamented, "We seemed to stand in a dilemma . . . On the one side lest by a massacre . . . the magistrates here would take away our lives . . . and on the other side lest the stranger should invade and sack our country, and bring it into servitude to foreigners."[9] The only course open to them, Babington felt, was to flee England.

As a result, Anthony Babington applied to an acquaintance of his, Robert Poley, who was, of course, in Walsingham's pay. Poley and Nicholas Skerres had just returned from their spying mission on Frederick II of Denmark, along with some of Leicester's company of actors, Leicester's Men.[10] Babington was not to know about Poley's double life, since he had also fooled Thomas Morgan. On March 11, Morgan wrote to Mary that they should, in fact, use Poley to their own advantage as it was known that he "is placed with the Lady Sidney, the daughter of Secretary Walsingham, and by that means ordinarily in his house and thereby able to pick out many things to the information of your Majesty."[11]

It was then that the Babington plotters thought better of fleeing. What if they freed Mary and placed her on the throne without the foreign intervention of Spain? Meanwhile, Babington himself had been recommended to Mary through two distinct channels: Morgan in Paris and her former emissary Fontenay, who was her secretary Nau's brother-in-law. This seemingly made Babington trustworthy. Fontenay wrote that Babington had a dispatch for her from Scotland. So Mary wrote to Babington on June 25 to convey the letters through her trusted messenger. Babington's indiscreet reply began "I write unto her touching every particular of this plot" and continued by revealing the entire plan of rescuing her and "despatching the usurping competitor" by six of his closest friends to place Mary on her English throne at long last.[12] Walsingham noted down every detail before forwarding the letter on to Mary, who received it on July 14, 1586. Though the Scottish queen didn't know it, she was at a crucial crossroads. If she had written disapprovingly to Babington or, better still, informed her jailer, who knows how the outcome could have changed? The fact remains, she did neither.

Mary replied on July 17. It was a lengthy letter that left no doubt regarding her attitude. Mary wholeheartedly approved of Babington's scheme. Throughout her reply Mary stresses the practical considerations of what must be done. The conspirators must have horsemen at the ready to advise her when Elizabeth was dead. She let Babington know in no uncertain terms, too, that failure could only bring the most dire consequences for them all. To rescue her, Babington would need "a good army, or in some very good strength"; otherwise, she would remain Paulet's prisoner. She wrote to Sir Francis Englefield that same day that she "fear[ed] they may ruin themselves in vain," meaning that she would never be successfully rescued.[13] After the letter was decrypted, Thomas Phelippes drew a gallows on the outside of it before handing it across to Walsingham.

This was still not enough for Walsingham. He penned a forged postscript, also in Mary's cipher, to ask for the names of the six gentlemen who would rid her of Elizabeth:

> *I would be glad to know the names and qualities of the six gentlemen which are to accomplish the designment; for that it may be I shall be able, upon knowledge of the parties, to give you some further advice necessary to be followed therein . . . As also . . . particularly how you proceed: and as soon as you may, for the same purpose, who be already, and how far everyone, privy hereunto.*[14]

Twelve days before her reply to Babington, Mary heard that a full treaty between James and Elizabeth had been signed at Berwick, excluding Mary's interests entirely. All Mary wanted to do now was escape her captivity. On Tuesday, July 19, "the gallows letter" was in Walsingham's hands. Gilbert Gifford fled to the Continent the following day to avoid the fallout from the impending arrests. By July 29, Babington had received the gallows letter and deciphered it with Tichborne. By August 4, Ballard was in custody, with Babington fleeing north to St. John's Wood. Ten days later, Babington, too, was captured and brought through jeering crowds to the Tower of London. By the end of August, they had all confessed.

• • •

Mary remained at Chartley, ever hopeful of her release, ever ignorant of events. On August 11, Paulet suggested that Mary join him for a buck hunt. Mary was unused to any kindnesses from Paulet and took particu‐ lar care over her toilette under the assumption that they would be meeting the local gentry. As they rode out, a group of horsemen thun‐ dered toward them. Could this be Babington's men come to rescue her? If Mary had thought this, she was mistaken. The lead horseman, Sir Thomas Gorges, wearing the queen's colors, dismounted and approached Mary. "Madame, the queen my mistress finds it very strange that you," Gorges warned Mary loudly, "should have conspired against her and her state, a thing which she could not have believed had she not seen proofs of it with her own eyes and known it for certain."[15]

Mary's servants were immediately dragged from her side for their im‐ plied guilt in the plot. A bemused Mary was taken with her physician to Tixall, still dressed in her fine riding clothes, utterly abandoned. She hadn't worn her usual gold cross so that she could kneel in prayer as was her cus‐ tom. Mary would stay at Tixall for a fortnight while Paulet searched every inch of her apartments and household at Chartley. The inventory of Mary's possessions shows a queen who had had to sell all her jewels of great value, with her greatest possessions being miniatures of her son, James, and Elizabeth.

When Mary was taken away on September 21, 1586, at gunpoint, her ser‐ vants were locked in their rooms, their windows guarded so they could not witness a martyr's departure for posterity. Mary was taken to Fother‐ ingay Castle in Northamptonshire to stand trial.

Forty-two commissioners were appointed to take part, with thirty-six arriving at Fotheringay by early October. The trial took place on October 14 and 15. The case against Mary was based upon the testimony of Mary's secretaries and her own correspondence. Her July letter to Babington— the gallows letter—was the most important document to be produced. Mary objected, claiming that the gallows letter was a forgery, just as the ciphers and sequence of events were fictitious. She added that this was all Walsingham's work, as he had always sought her death.

Walsingham sprang to his feet: "I call God to witness . . . that as a private person I have done nothing unbeseeming an honest man, nor as I bear the place of a public man, have I done anything unworthy of my place."[16] The Tudor concept of the public and private person lived on in Elizabeth's servants. Walsingham's ambiguous phrasing leads us to conclude that he did what he had to for the state, no matter how personally distasteful.

Though the verdict and sentence were intended to be immediate, Elizabeth hesitated. In the small hours of the morning of October 13, she summoned Davison to her, demanding he write to the commissioners to deliberate and adjourn the commission until such time as she could personally review the results, prior to pronouncing sentence. Elizabeth knew a guilty verdict was a foregone conclusion. Ten days after the trial was ended, the commissioners reassembled in the Star Chamber at Westminster. "Considering the plainness and evidence of the proofs," Walsingham wrote that day, ". . . everyone [sic] of them after this gave their sentence against her, finding her not only accessory and privy to the conspiracy but also an imaginer and compasser of her Majesty's destruction."[17]

All that remained was for Elizabeth to sign Mary's death warrant, something that all Elizabeth's ministers believed would be difficult to obtain. For a month, they cajoled and devoted themselves to the task, but to no avail. All the confessed plotters had been executed as traitors. Parliament presented the queen with a petition on November 12, "for the speedy execution of Mary, late Queen of Scots, according to the just sentence which had been pronounced against her." Elizabeth delivered her famous reply:

> If I should say unto you that I mean not to grant your petition, by my faith I should say unto you more than perhaps I mean. And if I should say unto you that I mean to grant your petition, I should then tell you more than is fit for you to know. And thus I must deliver you an answer, answerless.[18]

Nonetheless, Parliament's petition had the desired effect. Elizabeth knew full well that she could not keep the verdict against Mary a state secret forever. On December 3, 1586, she consented to proclaiming the sentence. Of course, special embassies from Spain, France, and Scotland choked the court to plead for Mary's life. Mendoza, who knew how Elizabeth thought, had rightly predicted that the embassies alone would provide a stay of execution for the Scots queen. Elizabeth had a heartfelt aversion to harming a hair of an anointed monarch, and Mary was no exception. So while Elizabeth delayed, Walsingham, in particular, was at his wits' end.

Finally, on February 1, after a long discussion with Lord Admiral Howard, Elizabeth sent for William Davison. He was to bring Mary's as yet unsigned death warrant. Davison had no sooner entered than Elizabeth commanded him to pass her pen and ink, and she signed it without hesitation. She then told him to take it to the Lord Chancellor to have him affix the Great Seal of England. As he was leaving, utterly stunned, Elizabeth added that he should stop in to see Walsingham at his home, where he had been ill for some while. She asked Davison to tell him what had just transpired, adding with a wicked smile, "The grief thereof will go near to kill him outright."[19]

With the queen's signature and Great Seal affixed to the death warrant, Burghley moved quickly to carry out the sentence. On the morning of February 8, 1587, the final act in the twenty-year drama between the two British queens was played out. As Mary mounted the scaffold in the Great Hall at Fotheringay, her sentence was proclaimed across England. She would serve as a symbol to all Catholics that "stubborn disobedience . . . [and] incitement to insurrection . . . against the life and person of her Sacred Majesty" would never again be tolerated.[20]

Elizabeth, of course, recanted her signature on the death warrant. Davison was summarily taken to the Tower, entering through its notorious Traitor's Gate. Yet eventually, for Davison, Traitor's Gate swung both ways. He was later released on an eye-wateringly high bond of £10,000. Elizabeth had heavily scripted her reaction to Mary's demise, and Davison was a much-needed scapegoat. A dynamic performance, lasting all of three weeks, was put on at court by the queen, where she cried loudly, shouted her anguish for all to hear, and significantly wrote a heartfelt letter of apology and explanation to James, blaming Davison and begging

James's forgiveness. James may have been many things, but he was no fool. If Elizabeth begged forgiveness, he would gladly comply. With the throne of England dangled before his eyes, how could he refuse?

When Mary's head with its elaborate auburn wig was held aloft for the executioner to say the customary words for traitors, "Long live the queen," in Elizabeth's name, war with Spain became inevitable. After all, Philip—once king of England—held his own fair right to the throne through Edward III. Now that Mary was dead, the time had come for him to reclaim it for Catholicism.

TWENTY-TWO

God's Obvious Design

*Let tyrants fear . . . that under God I have
placed my chiefest strength and safeguard in the
loyal hearts and goodwill of my subjects.*
—Elizabeth I, Armada Speech, August 9, 1588

The news of Mary's execution reached Elizabeth the following day, just as Elizabeth had mounted her horse and headed off for her daily hunt. She did not take any heed of Shrewsbury's son or his apparent haste to speak to her. Instead, Burghley received the official confirmation, for which he thanked young Shrewsbury, and then did precisely nothing with his knowledge. All of Greenwich Palace buzzed with the news—as did London, where bells of deliverance were rung out from the churches, before Elizabeth herself registered the momentous turn of events. Elizabeth promptly embarked on a three-week-long grief-stricken harangue, punctuated with sobs and accusations launched at her ministers that would have made her father seem even-handed. Still, the facts were the same. With Mary dead, Philip would most certainly invade.

News of Mary's execution at Fotheringay took longer to arrive on other shores. Channel storms prevented word reaching Paris until ten days later. Of course, the scheming Spanish ambassador Bernardino de Mendoza was the first outside the English embassy to hear the reports. His immediate reaction was to call upon the Paris Committee of Six-teen, who were fashioning the Paris mob into a revolutionary force to back Guise in his ultra-Catholic and antiroyalist conspiracy against Henry III. Among those who would fight by Guise's side were exiled Catholic Scots, Irishmen, and Englishmen. They listened intently to the report of Mary's demise. Mendoza's next stop was his own embassy, where an army of devoted emissaries convened to spread the word that the queen of Scots had been beheaded, murdered on the order of England's heretic queen. Before Elizabeth's official proclamation had arrived in the French capital, the Catholic League had made their verdict against the "English Jezebel." Elizabeth had committed judicial murder of her Catholic rival, and Henry III was her accessory and accomplice.

The friars of Paris preached fanatical and treasonous calumny against their king. Rumors flew about crypto-Protestants close to the throne, their poisonous heresies and witchcraft devouring the French king's court. Priests warned of ten thousand secret Huguenots, lurking in the shadows of Parisian cellars and alleyways, armed to the teeth, just waiting to slit the throats of the city's Catholics. Libelous pamphlets and ballads fluttered across the Channel, back to England. Yet Henry III seemed oblivious to the dangers.

In Brussels, Parma had heard of Mary's execution long before Mendoza's letter had reached him. A thoughtful man and phenomenal military leader, Parma immediately assessed what the news would mean for the war in the Netherlands. For the commander of an army of largely heterogeneous mercenaries, it was a sensible time-out to take. History would judge Alexander Farnese, Duke of Parma, as the chief architect of modern Belgium. His reconquest of the southern ten rebellious "Dutch" provinces had brought a period of reconstruction to the south, and he was not about to jeopardize his years of hard-won gains by taking his eye off the military map of the Netherlands.

Parma already knew that the English intervention was doomed in 1586. In his eighteen months in Holland, Leicester had managed to achieve the inconceivable, alienating and infuriating his friends and the Dutch by his arrogance and incompetence, and he had made Parma warm to him. Sir John "Black Jack" Norris, who had faithfully served under

William of Orange for years, had been relieved of his command by Leicester and shipped back to England. Leicester's ablest field commander after Norris was the mercenary Count Hohenlo. Within months of Leicester's appointment as governor-general, Hohenlo's closest friends claimed that if he met Leicester again, blood would be shed. So Parma, learning about Mary's execution and assessing the situation, penned a letter to Philip saying that he fully supported the Enterprise of England, which must happen sooner rather than later, since this murder of the Scots queen was an offence against Spain's honor and the Catholic faith.

Enrique de Guzmán, Count of Olivarez, Spain's ambassador to Rome, only received word from Mendoza on the morning of March 24 when Mendoza's courier rode into the courtyard of the Spanish embassy. Olivarez lost no time in digesting Mendoza's message. Mary, the primary hope of salvation for English Catholics, had died a martyr to her religion. His Holiness should also know that Mary had rejected her heretic son, James VI, and willed her claim to the English throne to Philip II of Spain. As for France, His Holiness should be aware that Henry III was Mary's enemy, and thereby the enemy of His Holiness and Spain. Mendoza's last suggestion was for William Allen to be made a cardinal at once so that he could be the religious leader of the invading army. English Catholics would, of course, rush to his standard.[1]

Mendoza's message betrays a certain concern that Felice Peretti, Pope Sixtus V, would not share his own zeal for the English Catholic cause. It was a mistake even Philip II made. Despite the veritable gushing of accolades Sixtus V heaped upon Elizabeth, calling her "his worthy opponent" and sighing, "Ah, if only she were a Catholic," Mendoza should have looked to his actions rather than words. They spoke volumes. Though he made withering remarks about Philip, Sixtus V was nonetheless yoked to the Spanish king's slow-moving wagon to restore the breakaway northern European Protestant dominions to Catholicism. Certainly Dr. William Allen, resident in the small house adjacent to the English College in Rome, never doubted Sixtus for a moment.

. . .

Still, the Roman Catholic world waited for Philip's reaction. The news reached him in his lofty palace of San Lorenzo de El Escorial nestled in the Guadarrama Mountains near Madrid. The Escorial, as it became known, was more of a retreat or monastery than a royal palace. As far as the eye could see, there was no other human habitation. Philip, it is believed, had the news for over a week before he was stirred into action. Where Elizabeth had gained a reputation for hesitation and prevarication, Philip's motto was *festinare lente*—hasten slowly.

Mendoza's letters had been followed swiftly by Parma's and the pope's. Santa Cruz, Philip's able admiral in charge of the Armada fleet already assembling at Cádiz and Lisbon, demanded 150 great galleons (the battleships of their day), 40 *urcas* (tubby vessels that were used to store provisions), and 320 auxiliary craft, from dispatch boats to cruisers. Santa Cruz demanded a total of 510 ships at sail besides 40 galleys and 6 galleases to be manned by 30,000 sailors, carrying 64,000 soldiers. In other words, the largest force by far ever to be assembled at sea.

Parma, on the other hand, urged Philip *not* to use his navy but to allow him to attack instead, using the 30,000 infantry and 4,000 horse at his disposal from the Low Countries. Above all else, Parma stressed, the element of surprise would be crucial to success. Philip must have shaken his head in dismay at such a thought while he scrawled his reply across the page: *"Hardly possible!"*

Just as Parma stressed the importance of the element of surprise to Philip, so Drake urged Elizabeth, "The advantage of time and place in military action is half the victory."[2] Drake, like Hawkins, itched to spring into action, to embark on some naval endeavor to cripple Spain's worst-kept secret—its Armada. The wisdom of a preemptive strike against Spain depended largely, however, on England's ability to mobilize as many ships as possible into the Channel when the winter of 1587 allowed. "Her Majesty shall also make preparation of all the strength that she can make by sea . . . ," Burghley wrote to Leicester, "that her own ships shall be removed to Portsmouth in March next and a great number of her subjects' ships shall also be made ready . . . as by further intelligence of the King of Spain's preparations shall be requisite."[3]

By March, the plan had been pieced together. On March 27, 1587, Drake set sail with a total of forty-two vessels for his secret mission to "singe the beard of the King of Spain." Drake's secret plan was to use Dom Antonio, the dethroned Portuguese king, as a decoy for his mission to destroy as much of the fleet at Cádiz as time would allow. Drake met with Walsingham to agree on the spread of disinformation. Traitors to England and Philip's various English spies were well known to Walsingham by now but had been left in place for this very purpose. Most prominent among these was Sir Edward Stafford, the English ambassador in Paris. Philip's own machinery of espionage was left to do the rest. Stafford's acceptance of 8,000 crowns from Philip as a pension only weeks earlier had been known to Walsingham and Elizabeth on the very day it occurred.

Before Drake set sail from London, Stafford passed the intelligence to Mendoza. "The Queen of England's secretary writes to the new confidant [Stafford] telling him," Mendoza scrawled to Philip urgently, "to be careful what reports he sends from here . . . The Queen had not decided anything about sending out the fleet, as the intelligence sent by the ambassador here had cooled her."[4] Ten days later the "true advices from England" were in Mendoza's hands. It was too late. Drake, the feared El Draco, had set sail two weeks earlier. Aside from a storm off Finisterre where one ship was lost, the voyage had gone swiftly. Within eighteen days of sailing, Drake stood in the roads off Cádiz.

Philip had been crippled by gout and self-doubt for the previous six months. Nonetheless, orders for his ships to finally set sail went out. As ever well informed, Philip fulminated while envying the swift and intrepid English navy. Raleigh and his inconvenient Virginia colony had been troubling his planned conquest of North America. That mariner Davis had already attempted two voyages to discover the Northwest

Passage to Cathay (China) and would soon be making a third. Now another captain, called Thomas Cavendish, had set sail for Peru in his ship *Desire*.

Though the Spanish king toured his gardens at Aranjuez—his oasis of calm—he found no peace from the English. They always had at least two hundred ships at sea plundering his empire. Even the English Admiralty took a share of the registered plunder. While Philip shambled through his perfumed gardens in the sunny April afternoons of 1587, he was said to muse repeatedly about Elizabeth, "Clearly God must be allowing her waywardness on account of her sins and unfaithfulness." Even the pope's offer of a million ducats toward the Armada had only been conditional on the successful invasion of England, with the stipulation that Philip "would not maintain the throne" for himself. When Sixtus V's spies reported back to Rome that this was precisely the king of Spain's goal, Sixtus thundered threats of divine vengeance aloud unless Philip "repented of his great sin, and obeyed the Vicar of Christ."[5] When an urgent dispatch arrived from Mendoza while Philip reflected on the sorry state of his affairs, he ignored it, turning one last time to shuffle as best he could through those gardenia-scented gardens he so adored. The message, of course, carried momentous news regarding Drake's intentions.

Unbeknown to Philip, Drake had already seized the port of Cádiz while the townspeople celebrated a local fair in the central town square. Cries of "El Draco!" rang out. As the people of Cádiz fled toward the castle for protection, the castle gates were shut behind the first wave of the panicked crowd. In the next seconds, there were shrieks and screams from the far side of the closed gates. Twenty-five people were trampled before the guard had the wit to reopen them.

There were sixty-eight ships in harbor, but Drake only sank twenty-four before he was forced to weigh anchor as the Spanish soldiers opened fire. As Drake's fleet sailed west he learned from his prisoners that Juan Martínez de Recalde, Spain's most respected naval officer after the Marquis of Santa Cruz, was somewhere off Cape St. Vincent with a squadron half the size of Drake's carrying gold from the Indies. After their ten days in an orgy of plunder in and around Cádiz, Drake's fleet set sail toward Recalde. What Drake had perhaps not realized was the devastating impact this skirmish in

Cádiz had on the Spanish. The losses were not great, in Philip's own words, "but the daring of the attempt was very great indeed."[6]

Of course, neither Cape St. Vincent nor Recalde was on the agreed strategic map Elizabeth had approved. Still, Drake was conscious that another strategic objective of his mission was to make it "pay for itself." So far, he had failed to inflict a death blow to the Spanish fleet or capture adequate plunder. While Drake missed Recalde, the English fleet did destroy a squadron of coasters and fishing boats bringing barrel staves for the Armada's water barrels.

From Sagres on the Portuguese coast, Drake weighed anchor, and ships carrying his dispatches and the disabled turned to the north, homeward bound. Drake had had news that the king's own carrack, the massive *San Felipe*, was bound for Seville with its annual treasure of spices, jewels, and other luxury goods from the East. It was a treasure too great to let pass by. Drake spied the *San Felipe* at São Miguel in the Azores and engaged the carrack, easily seizing her. The value of the booty was £114,000, not to mention the ship itself worth 3 million reals and the blow to Philip's pride.

Yet it was the sinking of the small fleet carrying barrel staves that would prove the most profitable to England. This unplanned and seemingly petty rout, from a twenty-first-century viewpoint, delayed the Spanish Armada for over a year. Without the barrel staves, the fleet would have no fresh water. More staves would need to be forged, and the Armada would have to wait.[7] The other real benefit to the delay could not have been foreseen by anyone at that point. The long-suffering Marquis of Santa Cruz died unexpectedly, only to be replaced by the soldier and hero of Cádiz, the Duke of Medina Sidonia.

By the time the Spanish Armada finally left the Iberian Peninsula in July 1588, it was doomed to fail. It did not comprise the 510 ships that Santa Cruz had wanted. It had not taken into consideration Parma's plan. Instead, Philip II, an armchair general, merged the Armada plan with Parma's. The fleet, he ordered, would rendezvous with the Spaniards in the Netherlands and be shepherded to England's shores in the Narrow Seas. Even by today's standards, it was a tricky feat to complete successfully. Then there was the matter of money. Sixtus hadn't given his million ducats, and the Indian fleet had been ordered not to sail for fear of capture. Philip's coffers were completely empty.

Elizabeth, too, had her problems, mostly in assuaging bruised egos. Raleigh, who considered himself a maritime genius, was relegated to the Admiralty of the West Country, while Drake was vice admiral of the entire fleet under Lord Admiral Howard. William Burroughs, Burghley's man in Drake's Cádiz raid of 1587 who had mutinied, had been passed over. Henry Knollys resented the upstart Drake's prominence. Leicester, to his credit, backed Admiral Howard in his choice of Drake as his vice admiral. He knew how the mere mention of Drake's name threw the Spaniards into paroxysms of fear.

Elizabeth, despite repeated criticism by strategists and historians for her intrusive and contradictory orders to her fleet, allowed her admirals to do what they did best: fight. While the fleets prepared for invasion, all England was made ready in its own way. Villagers developed strategies in case the Spaniards made landfall; barricades were erected and roads readied to be blocked or ambushed. Across the entire south coast of England, bonfires had been erected on all the high peaks leading from Land's End to London.

As the vast crescent-shaped formation of the Spanish Armada lumbered into view off the Cornwall coast at the Lizard at 4:00 P.M. on the afternoon of July 29, 1588, the first beacons were lit. By 4:15 P.M., Elizabeth and all London knew that the Armada had come. Much of what followed is hazy and contradictory, typical of the fog of war.

The Armada of 132 Spanish ships made a formidable sight. The fleet stretched two miles in breadth. With their huge fore- and aftercastles, the ships towered like giants over the faster, sleeker English ships. The English fleet of some 182 ships and 15 victualing ships was far lighter than the Spanish, but it outgunned the Armada and had no disgruntled convict rowers powering it as the Spaniards had.

In the first battle, at Eddystone, the heavy fighting was frustrating for both sides. The English had run rings around the Spanish defensive crescent formation but hadn't been able to penetrate it. The English long-range bombardment had merely annoyed the Spanish. Whenever Recalde took an action, Drake seemed to anticipate him and canceled it out. When Drake took the offensive, Recalde read his mind. The day's fight could only be called a stalemate. "The duke," so the official log reads, "collected the fleet, but found he could do nothing more."

The English fleet chased the Armada past Plymouth to Start Point. Yet the Armada maintained its majestic, defensive formation. Howard and Drake were worried. They had to prevent the rendezvous with Parma at any cost. That night the Lord Admiral wrote to Walsingham: "We gave them fight [from nine o'clock until one and] notwithstanding we durst not adventure to put in among them, their fleet being so strong."[8]

At Portland Bill on August 2, neither side understood its weaknesses and strengths as yet. Two battles raged all day, with the Spaniards repeatedly attempting to draw the English in close to grapple and board. The English, while defending the coastline, tried to weather the Armada's seaward wing. Each side failed to disable the other. Nonetheless, it was a furious action with the roar of cannon thundering constantly while the men were nearly blinded by smoke and flames. It looked as though the second day of fighting would end in a stalemate, too, until the *San Salvador*, carrying the bulk of the Spanish powder and shot, exploded. It was a critical loss to the Spanish.

At dawn on Wednesday, August 3, disaster struck the Spaniards. The *Gran Grifon*, the flagship of the tublike *urca* supply ships, was straggling and listing badly. An English squadron broke off to attack, and before the Spaniards could maneuver to its defense, the *Gran Grifon* was beset on all sides, riddled with cannon and musket shot. Yet despite listing heavily, the *urca* somehow managed to rejoin Recalde's column. By afternoon, the wind had dropped altogether, and the two fleets drifted barely a mile apart, unable to move. The dead calm continued through the night. For the first time, heavy casualties were reported by the Spanish, with sixty men killed and another seventy wounded; most on the stricken *Gran Grifon*.

By the morning of August 4, the wind had picked up again, and the fleets engaged each other at the Isle of Wight. By now, the English recognized that they would need to move in closer. As the smoke cleared from the early battle, Drake spied Martin Frobisher in the largest English ship of the line, cornered by the Spaniards. *The Triumph* raced to his rescue. Frobisher was saved.

That night, Howard called another council of war. It seemed to him that no matter how they changed tactic, they looked unable to sink ships decisively. Somehow they must stop the Armada before it reached Parma in the Netherlands. He needn't have feared. Though the Armada was anchored a mere two leagues off Calais, within spitting distance of Parma, Spain's great general never gave the order to "join hands" with Medina Sidonia. The only explanation that Drake could imagine for Parma's standing down was that the winds had picked up again to a moderate gale, and they must have only had Dutch flat barges for moving cattle to join the Armada. It was the wind that gave Drake his brainstorm—fireships.

Drake laid his plan before Howard and his council of war. He volunteered to be the first to set fire to his own ship. Five other commanders followed, and that night they sailed into the tightly formed Spanish ships at anchor. The six fireships entered the anchored Armada, ramming the Spanish. The cracking of wooden hulls, screams from the wounded, and fire and smoke punctuated the night sky. In the chaos, Medina Sidonia slipped his cables and stood out to sea. This time, the Armada fleet couldn't follow. The fireships—nicknamed hellburners—swept through the crowded anchorage. By the morning of August 7, what remained of the Armada had scattered and the English were once more in pursuit.

The last fight between the fleets off Gravelines was never fully recorded by either side, making the usual fog of war impenetrable. The English drew in nearer to the Spaniards but not near enough. The Spaniards fought back, struggling desperately to board the English ships, while the English ducked and weaved between them. Toward the end of the battle, Medina Sidonia saw that although he had called his ships back into their crescent-shaped defensive formation, they were too badly disabled to maintain it. His ships were being drawn inexorably onto the Flanders shore and doom. Neither the English nor the Spaniards had understood that a new age of naval battle had dawned in which speed and cannon could outweigh strength and grappling.

Just as it seemed that it might only be an hour or so before the entire Spanish fleet foundered, a violent squall with blinding rain and swirling winds blew up. The English had to maneuver quickly to keep from crashing into each other. By the time they had regrouped, standing away northward, they saw the lumbering Spanish fleet out of range once again, reforming slowly into their crescent formation.

The English instinctively knew that the battle was over, won for them by a "great wind." The Armada fleet lumbered on northward, around the north of Scotland, then due south hugging the western coast of Ireland. Of the thirty thousand soldiers and crew, over twenty thousand lost their lives, most to starvation and disease. Contrary to the fairy tales, many were executed as they tried to seek refuge in Ireland, killed for whatever plunder could be had, by locals or by English soldiers.

Of the ten thousand Spanish survivors, many more died of their wounds or privation once they returned to Spain. It was commonly murmured there that every noble family had lost a son in the Spanish Armada. Mendoza's prediction to Philip that it had been "God's obvious design" to bestow upon him the crown of England had been proven utterly false.

PART IV

A House Divided,
1591–1603

TWENTY-THREE

The Norfolk Landing

... *this young scholar, that hath been long studying
at Rheims, as cunning in Greek, Latin, and other
languages, as the other in music and
mathematics ... Pray, accept his service.*
—The Taming of the Shrew, II.i.76–80

On August 9, 1588, Elizabeth rode out to Tilbury, flanked by Leicester, to deliver her Armada Speech to the army, gathered to fight the invasion that never came. Bedecked in shining armor, brandishing her sword, England's queen was more reminiscent of a young Boudicca than a fifty-five-year-old, beleaguered monarch. The lines "I know I have the body but of a weak and feeble woman, but I have the heart and stomach of a king, and a king of England, too" resound in history classes and beyond through the ages. The second part of that sentence is less known: "and take foul scorn that Parma or any prince of Europe should dare to invade the borders of my realm."[1] Whether Elizabeth realized it or not by August 9, the danger from the Grand Armada had passed.

However, other perils were brewing. In early November 1588, long after the Armada celebrations had abated, Fathers John Gerard and Edward Oldcorne secretly landed on the marshy and desolate Norfolk coast. They had come to join the cheerful and scholarly thirty-three-year-old Father

Henry Garnet, who had been thrust forward as the superior of the English Jesuits in July 1586, only weeks after he had returned home to England from Rome. Garnet's companion on the road back to England was Robert (or rather St. Robert since 1970) Southwell. Though Gerard and Oldcorne had been expected since the spring of that Armada year at Garnet's Finsbury cottage, the English headquarters of the Jesuit mission to England, it had been unsafe for them to land and make their way to London.

Garnet had witnessed the roundups of suspected foreign Catholics and potential troublemakers before the Armada came. All had been incarcerated as enemies of the state. Before that, he had been studiously informed about the Parliament of 1586–87 where the Puritan radical and turbulent baiter of Anglican bishops, Dr. Peter Turner, MP, followed up his statement from the 1584 session that "no Papist can be a good subject" with a call for Catholics to "by some token be known." Turner attempted to pass into law the principle that Catholics should be obliged to wear a badge for all to see. Turner's friend Richard Topcliffe, MP, had further stirred the house with stories of "weapons and all massing trumpery, with books papistical . . . in the very next house joining the Cloth of Estate by the Parliament House," where he found "prayers for King Philip." Topcliffe had demanded a search of "certain houses in Westminster suspected of receiving and harbouring Jesuits, seminaries, or of seditious and Popish books and trumperies of superstition."[2] Garnet's Finsbury home, complete with its hiding place for six or seven men, was never searched, as it had long been assumed to be vacant.

Though Turner and Topcliffe had failed in 1587, the earlier Parliament of 1584–85 had prevailed. Legislation had been passed to transform the collection of recusancy fines into an efficient tax collection system for the exchequer. The theory behind the law was to stop the steady overcrowding and overwork in England's courts. Recusants would continue to be convicted in absentia on the sole evidence of informers. Few, if any, judges troubled themselves to discover if the informers were relatives or disgruntled neighbors or former friends of the defendants.[3] Indeed, as many were to learn, their nearest family were often their worst enemies, especially when a juicy inheritance was the prize.

That same Parliament passed a new Treason Act, specifically aimed at

Jesuit priests and those who harbored them, providing that any layman who "shall wittingly and willingly receive, relieve, comfort, aid, or maintain any such Jesuit, seminary priest . . . shall . . . for such offence be adjudged a felon." The penalty was, naturally, death. The reaction among the Catholic gentry was immediate. A secret and urgent meeting was called at Hoxton, to the west of the City of London, where the leading Catholic gentry including Sir Thomas Tresham, Sir William Catesby, and Lord Vaux were assembled. After much heated discussion, they agreed that "the priests shall shift for themselves abroad, as in inns or such like places, and not visit any Papists . . . except they be sent for." Lord Vaux agreed to pay a relief for priests who remained in the country of "one hundred marks" apiece.[4] Little did they know that Walsingham's most highly skilled spy, Nicholas Berden, was also present, taking copious notes.

This was only part of the unfolding drama for Catholics in 1588. The rise in executions—in all seventeen priests, nine Catholic laymen, and one woman, Margaret Ward, who was charged with providing the priest William Weston with rope to escape his prison at Bridewell—was shocking. Margaret Ward, crippled by her captors on the rack, generated tremendous sympathy. Elizabeth was so outraged by the effects of the torture that she "pardoned two other women who had borne themselves before the tribunal with singular courage," Garnet wrote to the superior general in Rome in the month before Gerard's Norfolk landing.[5]

In a way, the greatest threat to the Jesuit reconversion of England to Catholicism was the Jesuits themselves. Since Campion's and Persons's time, they had singularly been unable to establish a bridgehead anywhere in the country. It was Garnet's duty to reverse and revive their fortunes, and Norfolk seemed the best place to begin that task. Not only did the Norfolk coast provide a perfect landing station, but it had a skein of Catholic families, intertwined and interrelated, who would provide the close-knit network Garnet so desperately needed.

Garnet's companion from Rome, Robert Southwell, was a Norfolk lad, born at Horsham St. Faith. He grew up in the shadow of the Benedictine prior acquired by his grandfather, Sir Richard, in the time of

Henry VIII. Like many other good Catholic families, the Southwells had benefited personally from the Dissolution of the Monasteries. Besides, Southwell knew better than most just how Norfolk society worked. So when Henry Garnet issued instructions to concentrate their efforts on ministering to the Norfolk gentry in a first instance, he approved. After all, Robert's father still lived at Horsham St. Faith, though he had long before converted to the Anglican Church. After Norfolk, the plan was to knit their network throughout England to bind themselves to other Catholic gentry.

The Southwells knew the other great Catholic families in the county well. Southwells had married into the Bedingfields of Oxburgh Hall, and the Bedingfields had married into the Yelvertons. In the spring of 1589, it was time for John Gerard to put his new plan into place to secure the Jesuit toehold in Norfolk using this very family network.

Just south of Grimston lies the village of Oxborough and its hall, a magnificent moated manor house built in the 1480s, complete with decorative crenulations and battlements. John Gerard was brought there by Edward Yelverton, with whom he had lodged for the previous six months. The owner of Oxburgh Hall, Thomas Bedingfield, had given the Jesuit priests his blessing to make a minor alteration to his palatial home. Yelverton and Gerard were accompanied by an Oxford-born carpenter and joiner of remarkable talent, Nicholas Owen. It was Owen who would complete the desired works.

Owen, a small and wiry man, had grown up in the shadow of Oxford Castle in the parish of St. Peter Le Bailey at 3 Castle Street. Nicknamed "Little John" or "Little Michael" by Gerard, Owen had volunteered his exceptional services to Henry Garnet sometime in the autumn of 1588 or spring of 1589. Owen had completed his apprenticeship to William Conway, an Oxford joiner, four years earlier and in the intervening period had perfected the art of fine furniture making, which included virtually undetectable hides for priests. Yelverton had vouched for Gerard to Bedingfield, and Gerard did the same for Owen. The purpose of the visit was to build a hide at Oxburgh Hall that would escape the detection of the shire searchers.

Garnet best explained how it worked to Jesuit General Claudio Acquaviva. "When the priests first arrive from the seminaries, we give them every help we can. The greater part of them, as the opportunity offers, we place in fixed residences. This is done in a very large number of families through our offices." Gerard's job was to reconcile the gentry to this plan and have them take in a priest. Owen's was to build a virtually undetectable hide. Each hide would be different—like a bespoke piece of furniture specifically built for its space.

Still, Owen was but one man. After Oxburgh, it was quite clear that he was streaks ahead of any other "priest-hole" builder of his day. So it was quite natural that Owen would only build hides for the "Chiefest Catholic houses" and build up a thriving consultancy advising others in his art.[6] More exceptional still was Owen's utter silence about any of the places where he had worked.

At Oxburgh Hall, the hide still stands in the garderobe just off the King's Room. There is a small recess of door height against the interior wall that is common in the reuse of space. When one steps close to the recess wall and puts one's weight onto it, a portion of the wall swings open, revealing the hide beneath. The access cover is nine inches thick and cannot be detected from outside as a hollow space. Beyond, the L-shaped room measuring approximately three feet wide by seven feet high was where the priests would hide in the event of searchers arriving unexpectedly.

By 1590, Thomas Bedingfield was dead. His heir, Henry, aged eight, had been anonymously accused of "treasonable designs" with papists, and the Norfolk justice of the peace ordered Oxburgh Hall diligently searched. Nothing and no one was found. Owen's hide, where the priests took cover, had withstood its first test. So, from Oxburgh Hall, the Jesuit network grew. If priests were to minister to their flocks in the homes of the gentry, they would be provided with hides, preferably built by Nicholas Owen.

TWENTY-FOUR

Marprelate, Puritans, Catholics, and Players

The Martinists or Puritans were much more
dangerous for domestic broils, than the Span-
iards were for open wars.
—Archbishop Whitgift

The battle for the hearts and minds of Elizabeth's subjects was as alive in 1589 as it had been thirty years earlier when she ascended the throne. Father Robert Persons had strengthened his link with Spain to found a seminary at Valladolid. Within four years others would be founded at Seville, St. Lucar, and St. Omer in the Spanish Netherlands. Persons would never acknowledge that his actions upset a growing number of Catholics in England, known as the Appellants, who would remain steadfastly loyal to Elizabeth and abhor the threats of a Spanish or papal invasion.[1]

Persons's ensuing print war in the post-Armada period sought to defend the innocence of the Jesuit mission and priestly vocation. Naturally, the Puritans responded. Ballads, chapbooks, and other forms of cheap print proclaimed their authors' worldview, and Elizabethan censorship swung into high gear. Though Catholic texts had long been banned and seen as subversive, a new voice was raised that grabbed the reader's heart. The Jesuit cause in England had found a new poet, the first true wordsmith since Campion—Robert Southwell. His poignant

"Vale of Tears," only one of hundreds of poems, describes a forbidding landscape that could be England as much as a soul conscious of sin:

> *A vale there is enwrapped with dreadful shades,*
> *Which thick of mourning pines shrouds from the sun,*
> *Where hanging cliffs yield short and dumpish glades,*
> *And snowy flood with broken streams doth run.*[2]

Where Robert Southwell had become the new voice of Catholicism in England, another furtive writer emerged—Martin Marprelate. Martin Marprelate was, of course, a pseudonym, and the Marprelate tracts lacked the poetry and deep emotion of Southwell. To this day, no one knows for certain who the "Marprelate" author or authors were, though many have been suspected, from the Catholic Robert Persons to the playwrights John Lyly, Thomas Nashe, and Walsingham's man Anthony Munday. Martin's message was raucously Presbyterian in tone, unforgiving, racy, and, most dangerously, written in colloquial prose that appealed to the masses. In a society that had just begun to recognize the significance of the printed word, the Marprelate tracts were dangerous enough. They became positively seditious when they began to be performed on the stage.

By 1589, the Martin Marprelate controversy was racing ahead at full tilt. Eight tracts had been printed—none favorable to the Elizabethan settlement. The Master of the Revels, Edmund Tilney, became apoplectic with rage once these began to appear in London's playhouses. Unless and until someone could stop these outrageous sketches, Tilney would have to close the theaters. The Lord Mayor wrote his confirmation to Burghley that he understood "it was your honours [sic] pleasure, that I should give order for the stay of all plays within the city, in that Mr. Tilney did utterly mislike the same."[3]

A special censorship commission of three men was appointed with Tilney as its main member. Burghley evidently took a lively interest, as did Elizabeth, whose passions had long been the theater, music, dance, and pageantry. The Corporation of London was represented on the censorship commission, too, since it had a public duty to preserve public order from the "Martinists," as fans of the tracts were called. The third member on the commission was a divinity expert appointed by Archbishop Whitgift. The issue for the mostly Puritan corporation and aldermen of London was not so much the regulation of plays, as it remained for the crown and Tilney, but the suppression of plays altogether.[4]

Given that the players, actors to us today, were a crucial part of everyday entertainment at court and around the country, as well as a secret weapon in Elizabeth's arsenal of spies, ceding control of censorship of the theaters to the Puritan aldermen in London was an anathema to Elizabeth. Long before Walsingham came to power, William Cecil, as Lord Burghley was known in the 1560s, had used the services of playwrights like George Gascoigne and poets like Edward Dyer to report on activities of certain noblemen in whose homes they had entertained. This practice continued throughout Elizabeth's reign.

In the winter of 1585 when Elizabeth had dispatched Thomas Bodley to Frederick II of Denmark with the message "that [it is] the purpose of the Guise to force the king [of France] to deprive the King of Navarre of his succession to the crown," Walsingham had reinforced Bodley with two of his best spies, Robert Poley and Nicholas Skerres. The "English gentlemen" Poley and Skerres were met in Denmark by Leicester's Men, who had come to play at Elsinore Castle for the Danish king the following spring, reporting to them on the Dutch debacle.[5] Poley and Skerres brought the intelligence from both Holland and Denmark back to Walsingham.

Burghley had used the impoverished scholar Christopher Marlowe from the playwright's early Cambridge days as a spy, with the attraction from Marlowe's viewpoint being extra money and privileges. It was Burghley who had rescued the outspoken Marlowe in 1587 when he had been accused of defecting to Rheims. Burghley had been in charge of Marlowe's "mock" interrogation, and Burghley released Marlowe back to his duties on behalf of the crown.[6]

The links between the theater, the secret service, and political controversy would rumble on. Meanwhile, the censorship of plays was to be the commission's primary function, just as the Stationers' had been to license and censor all that was fit to print since 1559. The main reason for the thirty-year gap between print and performing censorship is attributable to the growing popularity of the new Elizabethan theater in the 1570s and the proliferation of companies of players with patrons from the queen through most of her top nobility. Elizabeth herself was quite willing to see representations of current political events staged, such as Marlowe's *Massacre at Paris* or John Lyly's *Endymion* and *Sappho and Phao*. The Marprelate plays were another matter entirely.

The controversial Martinist plays have not survived and have only come down to us by allusions to the portions most offensive to Elizabethans. However, over twenty tracts survive in print.[7] *Mar-Martine* and *A Whip for an Ape; or, Martin Displayed* were the first to be performed in the summer of 1589. Thought to have been written by John Lyly and Thomas Nashe, these plays were the beginning of the furor and are usually blamed for the rise in Elizabethan censorship of the stage:

> These tinkers terms, and barber's gests first Tarleton on the stage,
> Then Martin in his books of lies
> Hath put in every page.[8]

A Whip for an Ape, also thought to be by Lyly, identifies "Martin" as a performing ape, who attacks Lady Divinity. In later plays, the ape Martin appeared with "a cock's combe, an ape's face, a wolf's belly, cats [*sic*] claws." Full of scatological metaphors and imaginative insults against the established church, they simply had to be suppressed.[9] After all, "thinking" audiences couldn't always catch the full impact of the references during a performance, so they sought out the printed versions to which the plays referred. The only way to stop the proliferation of profanity was to find the clandestine Marprelate press and its printer and close down his business.

The Martinist plays were causing widespread disorder and generated myriad complaints from London's Puritan aldermen. As the irreverence toward the Puritans grew, so the objects of these raw satires fueled further public disorder. Thomas Phelippes, Walsingham's right-hand man, wrote, "The division between the Protestants and the Puritans is not other than it has been for a long time." Martin's words were in "every-man's mouth." The pamphlets were instant bestsellers.[10]

Burghley gave the order to find the Marprelate printing press, smash it, and bring in the printer for questioning before the Star Chamber. One man's name kept popping up in the investigations, the Worcestershire-born printer Robert Waldegrave. How the talented Waldegrave, by and large printer of Puritan pamphlets by divines like Laurence Chaderton, John Field, and John Knox became embroiled in the Marprelate Contro-versy remains a mystery. Perhaps there is a hint in his 1580s incarceration at the hands of Archbishop Whitgift? Seemingly, the archbishop had had Waldegrave imprisoned at least twice at the White Lion, the favored prison for obstinate Puritans.[11] Still, these Puritan divines had had their works legitimately published in London and registered in the Stationers Company without jeopardizing the livelihoods of their printers. So what had changed?

Was it the Armada threat? Was it the Jesuit missions? Whatever the reasons, Elizabeth's bishops were ill prepared for Martin's biting satire and upped the ante. On the first Sunday of the Parliament in February 1589, Bishop Richard Bancroft took to the pulpit at St. Paul's Cross—the official place to disseminate the government's take on current events and religious policy, and just around the corner from the churchyard, where most of the printers worth their salt had their stalls. Bancroft, of course, preached about the evils of Martin Marprelate's invective. The following Wednesday *A Proclamation against Certain Seditious and Schismatical Books and Libels* appeared with a particular message from the queen: "These secretly published schismatical and seditious books and defamatory libels and other fantastical writings . . . tended to the abridging or rather to the overthrow of Her Highness's lawful Prerogative allowed by God's law and established by the laws of the Realm."[12] Elizabeth had decided that Martin was calling the Anglican settlement into question, and she was unamused.

Shortly after the proclamation, someone on the hunt for the press no-ticed that one of the works of the Puritan divine John Udall had been printed on the "Marprelate press." The searchers, led by John Wolf, beadle of the Corporation of London, barged into Waldegrave's premises under the sign of the Crane in St. Paul's Churchyard, smashed his press, and took his cases of type and copies of John Udall's *State of the Church of England*. Fortunately for Waldegrave, he had had wind of the raid and had already escaped to the West Country and from there by sea to Scotland. Within the year, Waldegrave had become the official printer to the court of James VI.

The furor about Martin Marprelate was condemned by Francis Bacon, youngest son of Lord Keeper Nicholas Bacon, who had died a decade earlier. Francis had been seeking high office, without any success, and seemingly had not had the backing of his uncle Burghley. The controversy gave him a platform for speaking out. The ribald style was roundly condemned as "this immodest and deformed manner of writing . . . whereby matters of religion are handled in the style of the stage."[13]

Yet the Marprelate Controversy was nothing new to the world of theater. The Puritan aldermen of London had never made a secret of their view that theaters and stage plays were "an offence to the godly." They broke the Sabbath, and yet "two hundred proud players jet in their silks" under the protection of the queen. Since the formation of Leicester's Men in 1572, all playing companies had to be licensed by Elizabeth and wear the livery of their lord sponsor. This separated them from "masterless men" and vagabonds who clogged England's roads, making them quasi-servants of their lords' households. If the affiliation between the company and the lord who sponsored them became interrupted either by death or disgrace of the lord or any reportable misdeed of the company, then the license to play would be revoked, or worse.

Still, there were other threats to the world of theater and its influence on English hearts and minds. The "plague time" quotas had been instituted out of concern for public health, and once fifty deaths or greater per week due to plague were logged, the theaters were closed. Plague, however, never closed the other places where people congregated, most notably London's churches, Westminster Abbey, or St. Paul's Cathedral. When the plague didn't close the theaters as hoped in the long, hot summers, the Lord Mayor, as in 1586, closed them on the *presumption* that the warm summer *might* breed a plague.[14]

By 1590, censorship by the Master of the Revels on behalf of the commission was commonplace, with Tilney using his "learned judgment" to strike out or demand a redraft of "such parts and matters as they shall find unfit and undecent to be handled in plays, both for Divinity and State." Just in case the impresarios or the playwrights and players didn't understand the penalty, that, too, was spelled out: "Perpetual disabilities are threatened to those who produce any pieces not so allowed."[15]

Paul's Boys, the theater company of boy players of the cathedral, was dissolved in 1590, presumably for offenses similar to Marprelate. They only regrouped around 1600. Even Shakespeare had a brush early in his career with Tilney. When Shakespeare had been brought in as one of the "fixers" of the "stale" manuscript of the play *Sir Thomas More,* he soon discovered the sensibilities of the crown. The play remains officially anonymous to this day, though five playwrights seemingly comprise its authors. There were at least three sets of alterations, with the final and latest set believed to be one of the rare glimpses of William Shakespeare's handwriting—Hand D.[16] The problem with the play arose around the scene of the "ill May Day" of 1517 when Thomas More as Lord Chancellor refused to recognize Henry VIII's position as head of England's church while entertaining the Lord Mayor and the aldermen of London at his home. More is sympathetic and tragic throughout, since he had remained a figure of admiration in the public's psyche. The sympathy of the playwrights, as always, remained with their audiences.[17]

With prohibitions following each proclamation against the playhouses and inns situated within London's walls, it is little wonder that the entrepreneur impresarios like Philip Henslowe and Edward Alleyn took action. They decamped throughout the 1590s over the Thames River to that haunt of pleasure and vice, Southwark, which fell outside the Liberties of London. A large part of Southwark had been under the control of the bishop of Winchester for over half a century, and he happily derived much of his income from the brothels and the "Winchester Geese" (their prostitutes) within its boundaries. The words of Thomas Aquinas were often repeated to the bishop, that "prostitution in the towns is like the cesspool in the palace; take away the cesspool and the palace will become an unclean and evil-smelling place."[18]

To avoid such a catastrophe, the church provided a ready solution. The Episcopal Court required "stewholders" (brothel-keepers) not to detain any woman who wished to give up her "craft" and to prohibit any married women or nuns from partaking of their establishments' shelter. Further, whores could not solicit or "throw stones" at passersby to get custom. In this way, the bishop of Winchester's conscience was assuaged. Local burghers could happily run the bishop's businesses. The Thames wherry men were delighted with the increase in their trade, and the owners of the playhouses, Henslowe and his son-in-law Alleyn, joined in, finding brothel-keeping at least as profitable as the theater.[19] Soon, Francis Langley planned to build the Swan theater on the Bankside, much to the objection of the powerless Lord Mayor. Even Elizabeth's cousin Lord Hunsdon had taken on the farmed-out enterprise of the Paris Garden from the bishop of Winchester. While the Lord Mayor fulminated, sometimes more successfully than others, this happy solution ultimately provided us with the plays by Marlowe, his successor Shakespeare, and the flowering Renaissance of English theater.

There were other religious winds blowing against the theater and its players beside those of the Puritan aldermen in London. The Earl of Leicester, Elizabeth's "Sweet Robin," had died shortly after the failed Armada invasion in September 1588. Francis Walsingham followed in April 1590. William, Lord Burghley, was gnarled with arthritis and crippled by gout and old age. Though he remained her councillor until his death in August 1598, his voice in the affairs of state had become fainter. These pillars of Elizabeth's Privy Council had deserted her to death and infirmity.

The new generation of councillors, advising or alternatively coercing Elizabeth, was brash, ambitious, and looking toward their personal futures. Leicester had brought forward his bright, beautiful stepson Robert

Devereux, Earl of Essex, as his proposed successor in the mid-1580s. Elizabeth undoubtedly saw a young Robert Dudley in Essex, and a past long forgotten. Where Essex relied on his charm, talent, and wit, Burghley's chosen successor, his younger son, Robert Cecil, used his ambition, Machiavellian streak, and raw intellect in the service of the crown. Essex was born to a title and wealth; Cecil as the younger son was not. Walter Raleigh had come to court slightly before Essex and was one of the reasons for Leicester's bringing his stepson into the limelight when he did. Though Raleigh had begun without a personal fortune to his name, Elizabeth had made him one of the wealthiest men in England and the largest landholder by far in Ireland. Francis Bacon, most likely the brightest of them all and Robert Cecil's first cousin, had been barred from high office due to an unwise inaugural speech in Parliament, as much as by a lack of support from Burghley. Where Elizabeth had been adept in her younger days at keeping warring factions at bay, her royal will would be tested by the new dramatis personae.

If Essex represented Elizabeth's heart, Cecil stood up for her steely will. He knew he was dwarfish and misshapen, as over 25 percent of all Tudor children were due to the poor diets of their mothers while pregnant. He knew he would never win any beauty contests as Essex could. Nor did he have Essex's gift of verse-making. So Cecil made up for his lack of physical presence with a mind like a steel trap and a skill for oratory that would develop in the coming years.

Though Walsingham had died in April 1590, a year later, no one had been appointed to replace him. Essex had been spurned for the job. Not only had Elizabeth refused to consider him for Walsingham's vacant position, but she refused to appoint him to the Privy Council. When Elizabeth visited Burghley's home at Theobalds in May 1591, Cecil put on a not-too-subtle play for her in which a messenger delivered a dispatch for "Mr. Secretary Cecil." Three months later, with a strong shove center stage from his father, Robert Cecil, aged only twenty-eight, became a privy councillor. Essex fumed that the "elf" had been singled out for this exceptional honor. Raleigh was livid, and perhaps it was this that threw him into the arms of Elizabeth Throckmorton that year.

Still, Burghley wasn't dead yet. Nor was he quite ready to allow the baton of defender of the Elizabethan settlement to pass into the hands of his son. In October 1591 Burghley issued a royal proclamation "Establishing Commissions against Seminary Priests and Jesuits" as part of his *Declaration of Great Troubles Pretended against the Realme by a number of Seminary priests and Jesuits*. It was deliberately intended to accuse Philip of prolonging "the former violence and rigor of [his] malice" against England with renewed Armada threats.

Burghley, for once, wrote quite stirring words. He accused Philip, with the authority of the new Pope Gregory XIV "hanging at his girdle," of practicing "with certain principal seditious heads, being unnatural subjects of our kingdom . . . to gather together with great labours upon his charges a multitude of dissolute young men, who have, partly for lack of living, partly for crimes committed, become fugitives, rebels, and traitors, and for whom there are in Rome and Spain and other places certain receptacles made to live in and there to be instructed in school points of sedition."[20]

The new, and short-lived, Gregory XIV (Niccolò Sfondrati of Milan), was more concerned with the French wars of religion, which were not going well, despite his excommunication of the Protestant Henry IV. Nonetheless, both the pope and Philip were outraged by Burghley's accusation that they were guilty of fomenting disloyalty to Elizabeth. Burghley knew better, though. He had already learned that they were actively seeking a suitable heir to the English throne—a topic of discussion long outlawed by the queen.

Robert Persons became the Catholic strategist for a response to Burghley. With Richard Verstegan, his official in Antwerp, he drafted a reply with the catchy title *A Declaration of the True Causes of the great troubles, presupposed to be intended against the realm of England,* or *A Declaration* for short. While denying any close links with Spain, *A Declaration* was nonetheless printed with Philip II's money. When it was received by Anthony Bacon, the head of Essex's secret service, it came with a health warning: "a seditious vile book which . . . might be kept from any but such as were affected."[21]

. . .

As the war of words between Jesuit interests and Burghley became hot, there were other pressing issues at home. Burghley, the ultimate statesman, had ensured that Cecil became his natural inheritor, as well as the man in charge of the bulk of Francis Walsingham's network of spies and informants.

This is precisely where the trouble began. By May 1593, Robert Cecil was the most powerful man in all England. Though Essex had been admitted as a privy councillor that February, Cecil's grip on government had already tightened. Walsingham's papers had been "stolen"—presumably confiscated by Cecil, who now ran Walsingham's spy network. His ability to smooth himself into place as Walsingham's natural successor has long made him the "presumed thief" of Walsingham's papers.[22] Effectively, Cecil was now prime minister, home secretary, and foreign minister. With Burghley increasingly infirm, Cecil oversaw his own remit as well as his father's and did both jobs extremely well. In no time at all, Elizabeth had promoted Cecil in her esteem from her "pigmy" to her "elf."

This was the state of affairs in government when the theaters closed for most of 1592 due to a prolonged bout of plague. The economy shrank and times were hard. Shakespeare retired to his Stratford-upon-Avon home and wrote his two epic poems, *Venus and Adonis* followed by the *Rape of Lucrece*, both dedicated to Essex's young friend Henry Wriothesley, Earl of Southampton. Marlowe, too, hunted for a patron to supplement his lack of income from the stage. With years of outspokenness behind him and accusations of atheism common knowledge, Marlowe was unable to find paying work, other than for the government as an undercover agent.

To make matters more difficult for him, Henry Chettle's prefatory letter for a new pamphlet called *Kind-Heart's Dream* reopened the thorny issue of Marlowe's atheism, theoretically making him unfit as a playwright. Even Robert Greene's *The Groatsworth of Wit* had attacked both Marlowe and Shakespeare the preceding year. Shakespeare, now under the patronage of Southampton, received effusive apologies; Marlowe was only given insults as a diabolical atheist.[23]

Marlowe, to lick his wounds, retired to the manor house of his erstwhile "handler" Thomas Walsingham, first cousin of Francis, who had just been released from prison for debt. In January 1593, Strange's Men performed Marlowe's last play, *The Massacre at Paris,* about the gruesome St. Bartholomew's Day Massacre.[24] The play was even more newsworthy in 1593, as Henry III had murdered Henry of Guise in 1589, then been assassinated himself only nine months later. Catholic France now had a Protestant king, Henry IV, formerly Henry of Navarre, who was still battling for his throne with English aid.

It was the "show it like it is" violence of *The Massacre* that struck the audiences dumb. Marlowe was confronting the religious violence of his times. Elizabethans evidently loved it, as it was Strange's Men's best earner of the short winter season. In early spring, plague struck again, the worst outbreak in thirty years. It would claim 8 percent of London's population—but Marlowe's expression of violence in *The Massacre* would soon threaten all London.

On February 17, the remains of the separatist Roger Rippon were brought to the Cheapside home of Justice Richard Young. His coffin proclaimed that Rippon was the last of the seventeen great enemies "of God, the Archbishop of Canterbury, with the High Commissioners, have murdered in Newgate within these five years." Archbishop Whitgift had indeed been incarcerating separatists—the more orthodox of the Puritan shades of gray—to Newgate for the previous two years. There they rotted, without trial, in Newgate's infamous "Limbo," left to die.

John Penry, the Welsh pamphleteer and good friend of the printer Robert Waldegrave, was arrested on March 22. Separatist leaders Henry Barrow and John Greenwood were arrested the following day under the 1581 "Seditious Words" statute. What had once been a charge of blasphemy or heresy was now treason. They claimed they never intended the queen any harm. Only four days after Penry's arrest a new royal commission was created to hunt down Barrowists, Separatists, Catholic recusants, counterfeiters, vagrants, and anyone else who does "secretly adhere to our most capital Enemy the Bishop of Rome or otherwise do willfully deprave condemn or impugn the Divine Service and Sacraments."[25] Alien religions and atheism were one and the same.

By April, libels began to appear threatening the city's stranger population, mostly Dutch and French Huguenot, who had been living peaceably for decades within London's walls. Cardinal William Allen's view was that Elizabeth was repopulating England with strangers "of the worst sort . . . to the great impoverishing of the inhabitants, and no small peril of the whole realm."

Then, in May, a rhymester who called himself "Tamburlaine" after Marlowe's great play conflated the public hysteria against foreigners and Marlowe's great works with devastating results. Tamburlaine's verse is directed against foreigners, merchants, Machiavellians, and Jews and begins:

> *Your Machiavellian Merchant spoils the state,*
> *Your usury doth leave us all for dead*
> *Your artifex and craftsman works out fate,*
> *And like the Jews, you eat us up as bread.*

Twenty-six lines later, Tamburlaine finally gets to the point: "We'll cut your throats, in your temples praying."

Elizabeth was extremely worried. At the weekly Privy Council meeting on May 11, she demanded Cecil call a halt to the sedition. The Dutch churchyard had been smeared with libels, as had the Huguenot church. He was ordered to put the Lord Mayor under pressure to discover the heart of this outrage and examine *anyone* who might be suspicious.

Meanwhile, Cecil ordered the arrest of one of his former unruly agents, Richard Cholmeley, who he suspected of involvement in a plot to kill the queen. When Cholmeley had gathered some sixty armed thugs to his side as Cecil's recusant-hunter, he had gone too far. Cholmeley's elder brother, Sir Hugh, had been a great friend of Cecil's, and Richard's behavior was proving threatening. By the time Cecil interrogated Cholmeley that May, the rogue agent had embraced atheism, and Christopher Marlowe. No wonder Burghley found the matter a labyrinthine maze, easier to enter than to exit. When Cecil discovered that Cholmeley was associated with a new plot by the pope and Philip II, known as the Stanley Plot, which was already under way for another invasion of England through Scotland, the queen was informed. The date was May 26, 1593.

The playwright Thomas Kyd, onetime roommate and bedmate of Christopher Marlowe, had been arrested nearly two weeks earlier. Hidden among Kyd's papers were "vile heretical Conceits denying the deity of Jesus Christ." Cecil ordered Kyd to be taken to Bridewell and tortured. Bridewell's most feared feature was something called "the scavenger's daughter"—an iron ring tightened by the turn of a screw that brings the head, feet, and hands together until they form a circle behind the victim's back. Kyd held out in "the scavenger's daughter" as long as he could before he denounced his friend Marlowe, saying that "it was his custom in table talk or otherwise, to jest at the divine scriptures, jibe at prayers, and strive in argument to frustrate and confute what hath been spoke or writ by prophets and such holy men."[26]

Cecil's network reacted in much the same way it had done when Walsingham was in charge. It set out to entrap the conspirators. Burghley was brought into the inner circle and needed little prompting about his previous dealings with Marlowe. The last time Burghley had seen the playwright had been fourteen months earlier, when he shielded Marlowe from a charge of high treason for counterfeiting. The hazy question of whether Marlowe was a single, double, or triple agent loomed unanswered.

At the end of the day, like Cholmeley, Marlowe had become a severe liability. Two days later the playwright was arrested at Thomas Walsingham's Kent home. By May 20, bail had been posted.[27] So long as Marlowe checked in on a daily basis with Cecil, he could remain at liberty. In the meantime, executions of other separatists began. John Penry was removed to Surrey, where he was hanged at five in the afternoon.

On May 30, Marlowe joined a small feast in a private dining room at the home of Eleanor Bull at Deptford, less than a mile from the royal palace of Greenwich. The other guests at the private feast were Ingram Frizer, an operative of Thomas Walsingham's and known swindler, and Nicholas Skerres and Robert Poley, both veteran operatives of Francis Walsingham's network. Christopher Marlowe, the most talented playwright of his day, was stabbed in the eye by Frizer and killed. Frizer walked free on the testimony of Skerres and Poley.

The warning to playwrights from the government was clear. No one was above the law.

TWENTY-FIVE

Elizabeth's Eminence Grise and the Final Battles for England

> *The Queen in all her robes had fallen the first day of the*
> *parliament . . . The King [James] did fall without harm, the*
> *French King [Henry IV] with a great bruise; which proves*
> *that some great planet in this configuration was precipitate.*
> *But God is gracious.*

—Henry Howard to James VI, 1601

The world of the 1590s was a distinctly different place for Elizabeth's England. The war with Spain had been "hot" since 1585—ever since the queen had agreed to send Leicester at the head of an army to the Netherlands—but when Parma had taken Calais from the French, Henry IV, already financed by Elizabeth, needed more able men and supplies. Essex, who in Elizabeth's eyes was her ablest soldier, was sent with his "volunteers" to fight by Henry's side.

When Essex returned home from the siege of Rouen at the end of 1592, England was a plague-ridden country. The economy was suffering from a slowdown due to widespread death and illness. The exchequer was drained due to the prolonged war. For Elizabeth, the quickest and most efficient way to rebuild her dwindling financial resources was to send her adventurers to sea for plunder.

Raleigh and the Duke of Cumberland became the heroes of an action called the Islands Voyage of 1596, seizing the Portuguese carrack *Madre de Díos* and sailing her back to England. Its precious cargo of gold, spices, and gemstones had an estimated worth of £150,000.

The gossipy Venetian ambassador in Spain wrote in cipher to the doges that "never at any time in history has the West India fleet been so harried by the English . . . [than] at this present moment."[1] Nothing could be further from the truth. Philip was planning another Armada.

What worried Essex, however, was that England had fallen increasingly into the grasp of Robert Cecil. Only Robert and his father, Lord Burghley, shared the queen's overview of the world's affairs. Where his stepfather, Leicester, had been able to "pocket his pride," Essex could not. He needed to be "in the know" at all times. At first, when Essex became a privy councillor in February 1593, he threw himself into his work in the vain hope that he could supplant Cecil and Burghley as the queen's chief adviser. He knew as well as the next person that Burghley's hourglass had little sand left to filter down.

Direct means having failed, Essex's own "secret service" seemed to be the best way to achieve his ends. Discovered Catholic plots were always a popular means to win Elizabeth's heart; so, on the slimmest of motives, the queen's physician Roderigo Lopez was accused of attempting to assassinate her in 1594. Lopez was a Marrano Jew, who had been converted forcibly to Catholicism before fleeing to England. Elizabeth found the allegations incredibly difficult to swallow at first, but in the end relented when Cecil joined Essex's voice against the hapless, and most probably innocent, Lopez. Elizabeth's physician would lose his life to Essex's great designs.

It was also an agent in Essex's pay who informed the earl in June 1592 that Ferdinando Stanley (the future Lord Strange), the patron of the actors Strange's Men, had been in contact with Cardinal William Allen and was a crypto-Catholic. Fifteen months later, a Lancashire man named Richard Hesketh brought Ferdinando a message from his exiled cousin Sir William Stanley asking him to help advance his "friends" overseas. Stanley wanted Ferdinando to press his claim to Elizabeth's throne and promised his Catholic army from the Low Countries to back him. Ferdinando immediately informed the authorities. Hesketh was hanged as a traitor.

Six months later, by now Lord Strange, Ferdinando fell ill, dying within forty-eight hours of "cruel pains . . . frequent vomitings of a dark colour, like rusty iron . . . that stained the silver Basins in such sort, that by no act they could possibly be brought again to their former brightness." His body was said to run "with such corrupt and stinking humours that no man could in a long time come near the place of his burial."[2] The government presumed he had been killed by some Jesuit connivance. Catholics presumed it was the government. Still others believed it was Bess of Hardwicke, protecting her granddaughter Arbella's claim to Elizabeth's throne. Hugh Owen, Sir William Stanley's coconspirator in the plot, wrote to Thomas Phelippes, Cecil's code breaker, to clear Essex of any culpability in the death of Lord Strange, thereby implicating him. Cecil would not forgive Essex for his meddling.

The 1590s were marked by a change of tack between the warring parties. While one eye remained surely fixed on the present and the queen's safety, the other roamed freely, looking toward her successor. Everyone participated. Philip II sponsored another edition of Persons's work *A Conference about the Next Succession to the Crown of England* in late 1593. Going back to William the Conqueror, the book claimed that all English claimants were insignificant. James VI would still be a foreign monarch who would favor his fellow Scots. Only the Infanta Isabella could be regarded as the true queen of England. *A Conference* succeeded only in driving a further wedge between Catholics, with the pro-Elizabethan Appellants gaining ground.

What no one besides Robert Cecil knew was that James VI had also been soliciting Spanish aid for his bid to the English succession. The priest-turned-informer John Cecil had informed Robert that he had been charged with canvassing James's claim in Madrid. Cecil was keeping his superior knowledge to himself. From Cecil's viewpoint James was the most likely successor, and as he knew England was increasingly bankrupt with each passing year at war, Cecil sought some solution to the nation's financial, succession, and religious crises.[3]

Essex's reaction was to seek retribution against Spain for its audacity and martial glory for himself. As a man of "great designs," it was natural for him to cast himself in the role of England's savior. The Dutch, he reasoned, had resisted for over twenty years and still had a flourishing trade based out of Amsterdam in the 1590s. If England could cast herself in the Dutch model, then not only would England prevail, but the English—and in particular Essex—would prosper. The time was ripe to plan an excursion once again into Spanish waters.

While Essex pieced together his expedition with the Dutch, Cecil turned his eagle eye to the religious issues at home. Cardinal William Allen, who had coauthored the ill-conceived treatise with Robert Persons on the English succession, died in October 1594, leaving Persons vulnerable to attack from all sides. Since Allen had headed the Jesuit mission to England from the outset, and the papal and Spanish invasion plans had been deeply unpopular with English Catholics, Henry Garnet wrote to Superior General Acquaviva that year about the rapid growth in anti-Jesuit criticism in England.

Though Robert Southwell had remained faithful to his mission, he grew despondent that the Jesuits were failing in their task to save England for Catholicism. "I have been on horseback round a great part of England," he wrote to Acquaviva, "in the bitterest time of the year, choosing bad roads and a foul sky for my pilgrimage, rather than waiting for the fair weather when all the Queen's messengers are on the prowl, much worse than any rainstorm or hurricane."⁴ As yet unknown to the general public was Southwell's *An Humble Supplication to her Majesty*. Southwell had written this from the heart as a reply to the *Declaration* drafted by Burghley for Elizabeth's signature in 1591. Though not officially published until 1600, it casts a palpable shadow over the plight of the seminary priests in England at the time:

> We have been long enough cut off from all comfort, and stinted to an
> endless task of sorrows, growing in grief as we grow in years, one

misery overtaking another, as if every one were but an earnest for a harder payment. We had some small hope, that our continued patience, and quiet effusion of our blood at your Majesty's feet, would have kindled some sparkle of remorse towards us: But still we see that we are not yet sunk to the depth of our misfortunes.[5]

An Humble Supplication was an unwise move, making the melancholy priest Southwell the top priority of Richard Topcliffe, the Queen's pursuivant and Catholic-torturer. Southwell, Garnet, and other Jesuits had narrowly escaped Topcliffe at their conference at the resplendent moated manor of Baddesley Clinton in Warwickshire by hiding in a secret chamber constructed by Nicholas Owen in the sewer. On Sunday night, June 25–26, 1592, the much-admired Southwell was arrested at Uxendon Manor near London—the home of the Bellamy family—giving himself up so that others could escape.

Topcliffe set out his gruesome plan for Southwell in a letter to Elizabeth. The Jesuit would be made to "stand against the wall, his feet standing upon the ground, and his hands but as high as he can reach against the wall like a trick at Trenchmore [a dance of the period]." Though it sounds innocuous enough, Topcliffe was describing a new and specially devised form of torture in which the victim would be suspended by his wrists for hours, dislocating them. After an entire day suspended by his wrists, Southwell remained mute. Elizabeth, squeamish when it came to torture though not averse to using it when required, sent two clerks of the Privy Council to assist. After two further days of torture, Southwell still remained silent. Finally, Robert Cecil came to see the prisoner.

As Cecil came into the dark, dank cell to interview Southwell, the priest's father was petitioning Elizabeth directly to secure his release. Richard Southwell described how his son was lice-ridden, starved, and half dead from torture. He agreed that if his son had committed a crime for which the punishment was death, then he must die, but that in any event he was a gentleman and deserved to be treated as one.

Elizabeth was swayed. On July 28, the Privy Council wrote to the Lord Lieutenant of the Tower of London "that her Majesty's pleasure is you shall receive into your custody and charge the person of Robert Southwell, a priest whom Mr Topcliffe shall deliver unto you, to be kept close prisoner so as no person be suffered to have access unto him." For the next two and a half years, Robert Southwell would remain in solitary confinement, forgotten by his enemies.[6]

Cecil felt revulsion at Topcliffe's methods. After Robert Southwell's trial and conviction for treason in February 1595, he oversaw a prosecution of the queen's priest-hunter for maligning privy councillors (notably himself and his father) and ordered Topcliffe into the Marshalsea. Topcliffe naturally complained directly to Elizabeth that his disgraceful treatment would make "the fresh dead bones of Father Southwell at Tyburn . . . executed . . . since Shrovetide . . . dance for joy." Though he was released shortly after, and remained in the government's employ for a further four years, Topcliffe came under Cecil's vigilant eye once more in 1596 for his treatment of Catholic prisoners in the Gatehouse.[7]

The year 1596 brought further battles for the hearts and minds of the English. Essex led the raid on Cádiz with Raleigh and the Dutch. Despite landing and occupying the port, and wounding Philip's bruised pride once more, it achieved little to replenish the exchequer's coffers—a major aim of the exercise. Worse still, the chain of command had broken down; Raleigh and Essex were often at daggers drawn, and Cecil as well as Elizabeth had been disappointed not to receive their forecast profits from the expedition.

Nonetheless, Elizabeth and Cecil encouraged English pamphleteers like Henry Roberts to sing the praises of Essex and Raleigh to boost national pride in these troubled days. Though Drake and Hawkins had been killed in action in the Caribbean that year, the average Englishman could puff out his chest with pride that tiny, vulnerable England had taken on the greatest empire in the world—not once or twice but three times— with the second and third armada attempts dubbed the "invisible" armadas unlike the "invincible" Armada of 1588.

While Essex sailed to glory at Cádiz, Elizabeth formally appointed

Cecil secretary of state. He was put in charge of the Admiralty on behalf of the Privy Council and plugged the leaks wherever he found them. Cecil ensured that gold, spices, and jewels did not disappear to mud-larkers waiting to catch stolen riches from newly docked vessels.

The 1590s, though half finished, was already proving a decade of high inflation, failed harvests, and severe plague. Elizabeth was aging rapidly, though no one at court dared to remark on that demonstrable fact. The succession needed to be assured and a smooth transition put in place.

Nothing convinced Cecil more about the need for a smooth succession than the shock and sudden conversion to Catholicism of Henry IV of France, who famously remarked that "Paris is worth a Mass." The Franco-Spanish Treaty of Vervins concluded in 1598 brought peace to France at last, and a long overdue burying of the hatchet with Spain. Philip recognized Henry IV's kingship, and Henry, in turn, pronounced religious toleration with the Edict of Nantes.

That left England and the Dutch out in the cold, and Elizabeth reaching metaphorically for her sword. Ireland was in revolt against English rule once again—though this time for dynastic rather than religious differences. Essex was itching for intervention, albeit always suggesting someone other than himself to go fight.[8] Soon enough, Elizabeth would put him to the test and send him to Ireland to put down the rebellious province once and for all.

Then, at the beginning of August 1598, the most steadfast light in Elizabeth's firmament was extinguished. The death of William, Lord Burghley, who had advised the queen since she was a teenager, was a bitter blow to Elizabeth. He had, however, ensured his succession through his able son Robert. Though Cecil never became Lord Treasurer, he did obtain his father's office as Master of the Court of Wards, which in turn provided Cecil with his fortune. The only area in which Cecil was unable to maintain his father's influence was in the religious arena. Perhaps it was because

Archbishop Whitgift simply wouldn't accept the younger man's advice. The more likely reason was, however, that Cecil had not inherited his father's evangelical soul.

The Essex expedition to Ireland ended in disaster, despite being the best-equipped expeditionary force ever to cross the Irish Sea. His defeat at the Battle of Yellow Ford on August 14, 1598, where he lost over two thousand men, was proof positive that he was no military commander. Essex raced back to London after signing a six-week truce with the rebellious Tyrone so that he could explain himself to the queen. Sadly, Essex had become unhinged, and he forced his way into the queen's dressing room to tell her that his failure in Ireland was the fault of his enemies, and in particular Robert Cecil. Ranting that Cecil was in the pay of the Spaniards, Essex was eventually taken away and put under house arrest.

Cecil had, in fact, opened peace negotiations in June 1599 with Spain. Elizabeth's bitter enemy Philip II had finally died in 1598, only weeks after signing the peace treaty with Henry IV. Cecil's opposite number Dr. Jerome Comans, commissioned by Philip's heir, Philip III, arrived in London on August 20 to "treat the peace." The main condition imposed by the new king was that all English trade should return to the Spanish-held port of Antwerp from the Dutch-held port of Amsterdam. However, Cecil saw that such a compromise would permanently weaken England's Dutch ally, particularly as Dr. Comans also made clear that Philip III would never give in to religious toleration in the Dutch breakaway provinces. The negotiations were over before they began.

Meanwhile, James VI of Scotland was hedging his bets for his succession to Elizabeth's throne. Both Essex and Cecil had been taken into his confidence. By 1598, James had had copious correspondence with Essex, which would certainly have been considered treasonable by the queen had she known about it. Cecil, on the other hand, remained at one remove in his secret correspondence with James. On Essex's return from Ireland, there is little doubt that the king's representatives in London kept James fully informed of the earl's volatility. By 1601 James had steadily turned his attentions to Cecil, remarking to his envoy Edward Bruce in London, "Ye must so deal with Mr Secretary . . . if in these points I be satisfied, that ye have power to give them full assurance of my favour, especially to Mr Secretary who is king there in effect."[9]

The ill-fated Essex Rebellion of February 1601, which only lasted eight hours (thanks in part to the betrayal of Essex by his "friend" Francis Bacon), gave James great cause for alarm, as he had no idea what Essex had done with their correspondence. Visions of the queen's searchers poring over Essex's papers threw James into a panic. He dashed off a note to Bruce explaining that "things were so miscarried by that unfortunate accident [the Essex Rebellion] that I was out of all hope that ye could come any speed at the Queen and council's hand, anent [concerning] the main point: to give out a plain declaration, which must be enacted in her own records, that I am untouched in any action or practice that ever hath been intended against her, especially in this last [Essex]; wherein I wonder that, according to your former letter, ye have written nothing in this last."[10]

James needn't have feared. Robert Cecil had long before decided that only James should become England's next monarch. Any incriminating evidence against the Scots king was destroyed or put away safely. By April 1601, negotiations for the smooth transition from Elizabeth upon her death to James VI had been set in train, so long as their correspondence remained entirely secret. For Cecil, the thought of the Spanish infanta or Arbella Stuart as England's next queen sat badly after the half century of service his father had given to Elizabeth.

Significantly, Cecil had also won the trust of the Appellants, who had given him their potential solution to ally the forces of English Catholicism to the new English nationalism thus reducing the power of the papacy. The Cecil-influenced *Protestation of Allegiance* given to Elizabeth at the end of January 1603 was the result. It proposed that the Appellants would swear and acknowledge Elizabeth as their true and lawful queen and defend her life and England against any and all plots or invasions made in the name of the restoration of the "Romish religion."[11]

The potential solution came too late. Elizabeth was already ailing. At the beginning of March 1603, she took a turn for the worse. The sixty-nine-year-old Elizabeth, queen for over forty-four years, was dying. She had stood at her privy chamber window embrasure for two solid days, refusing food, running her index finger along her sore gums, staring blankly. Worn out by the burdens of office and age, disappointed by the loss of all those who had died before her, and stricken by the execution of Essex forced upon her, Elizabeth had simply given up the will to live.

In the gray morning hours of Thursday, March 24, 1603, Tudor England expired with Elizabeth. Too weak to name her successor, she pointed her hand to her head and nodded as the name of James VI of Scotland was read out by Sir Robert Cecil. James VI of Scotland, the only child of Mary Queen of Scots, was duly proclaimed James I of England. Satisfied, Elizabeth Tudor finally allowed herself to slip away.

TWENTY-SIX

Epilogue

The King of Scotland has succeeded quietly.

—Venetian ambassador to the doge

James VI of Scotland, now James I of England, waited until after Elizabeth's state funeral to make his progress into England. With him came his Danish wife, the daughter of Frederick II, Queen Anne, and his son and heir, Prince Henry. His younger son, Charles, remained at home in Scotland for the time being. Two months earlier, Father Henry Garnet, who had been the soul of the Jesuit mission to England since 1586, had written to James assuring England's new king that he would never have cause to distrust his fellowship or the Jesuits' "love, fidelity, duty and obedience."[1]

On April 19, 1603, James rewarded Thomas Gerard, Father John's brother, for the family's loyalty to his mother and bestowed a knighthood on him. Henry Percy, Ninth Earl of Northumberland, and Thomas Howard, heir to the executed Duke of Norfolk, were sworn in to James's Privy Council at Whitehall later that month. The Venetian ambassador wrote to the doge in Venice that "the King continues to support those houses . . . who were oppressed by the late Queen." William Weston, the former Jesuit superior, and other captured Jesuit priests were released from their captivity. There had been every reason for the Catholic population to hope for a new era of future royal favor.[2]

James saw a wealthy realm in England, impoverished by years of religious war. If only the Catholic population had known before he became king that he had written to Sir Robert Cecil, "Jesuits, seminary priests, and that rabble where England is already too much infected . . . I would be glad to have both their heads and their bodies separate from this whole land, and safely transported beyond seas."[3] James wanted peace, but he wanted the riches England could provide him with more.

Sir Robert Cecil would be the man to give these to him. Cecil maintained his iron grasp on government until his death in 1612, having been elevated to Earl of Salisbury in May 1605. It was to Salisbury that Lord Mounteagle brought word of a plot to blow up the houses of Parliament in October 1605, later known as the Gunpowder Plot. William Shakespeare had lampooned Cecil in 1593 when he wrote his *Richard III* using the Tudor myth of Richard's deformity and molding it to Cecil. Robert Cecil, Earl of Salisbury, died a hated, avaricious man, whose epitaphs proclaimed, among other things, that he had gone to hell to raise the devil's rent. Nonetheless, Cecil's great achievement was the arrangement of the smooth transition from Tudor to Stuart England.

Raleigh had remained Cecil's steadfast enemy and was imprisoned in the Tower for high treason against the new king, his lands confiscated in Virginia as well as Ireland, for allegedly plotting to put Arbella Stuart on the throne. Only the pleading of Queen Anne and Prince Henry succeeded in saving Raleigh's life—for a time. During his many dreary years in the Tower of London, Raleigh wrote his great work *History of the World* and some of his best poetry, including "The Lie." Desperate to find his freedom, he promised James that he would locate the fabled golden El Dorado. James allowed him one final chance to find America's riches. When Raleigh failed, he returned to England a broken man, ready for the executioner's block. As he readied himself for the ax to fall, he famously said, "'Tis a sharp remedy, but a sure one for all ills."

Cecil's cousin Francis Bacon, who had betrayed the Earl of Essex, went on to become a great Stuart statesman who by 1621 had risen to become Lord Verulam, Viscount St Albans. His dream of becoming Lord Chancellor was fulfilled in 1618.

The schisms in both the Protestant and Catholic faiths grew. The self-imposed exiles like the Brownists of Elizabethan England had returned from Leiden in the Netherlands from a lifetime abroad, hoping for a new start in Stuart England. James was not prepared to grant one. So these Puritan separatists, better known today as the Pilgrim Fathers, chartered a 180-ton merchant ship, the *Mayflower*, from a London merchant adventurer and sailed for the colony of "Northern Virginia" in Massachusetts Bay in 1620. Only thirty-seven colonists were "Leiden Separatists," with sixty-five additional passengers and crew seeking a life free from religious intolerance in the New World.

James's "transportation policy" for Catholics originally intended for Northern Virginia was moved farther south. During the reign of James's heir, Charles I, Lord Baltimore, founded the "great city" of Baltimore as a Catholic enclave promoting Catholic ideals. The state of Maryland was named after Charles's queen, Henrietta Maria, the youngest child of Henry IV of France.

The Catholic plea for toleration in England never faded. Peace was finally declared with Spain in 1604 at the Conference at Somerset House. The Catholics were betrayed not only by James but also by Spain. Economic imperatives at last took precedence over saving souls. Angered at their betrayal, a small group of men agreed that the only way to be rid of such traitorous leaders was to blow up the Houses of Parliament in the terror plot known as the Gunpowder Plot.[4]

By the end of the seventeenth century, it became illegal in statute for the reigning monarch to be Catholic after James's grandson, James II, was deposed. England preferred to import other distant and Protestant Stuart cousins, William III and Mary II, from the Netherlands as its rightful monarchs. The religious tensions rumbled on well into the twentieth century.

Is it possible that Elizabeth thought that a Stuart dynasty might be an untrustworthy and dangerous one for the English? Unfortunately, we shall never know. Still, James was the best choice for her successor. Just as religion haunted Elizabeth from the outset of her reign in 1558, so did the issue of the succession. It was a Tudor curse established in the reign of Henry VIII and laid to rest in Elizabeth's.

In her Golden Speech to Parliament on November 30, 1601, Elizabeth expressed her lifelong ambition for the legacy of her rule: that she had been God's "instrument to preserve you from envy, peril, dishonour, shame, tyranny, and oppression."

That is how she would have liked to be remembered.

NOTES

Abbreviations

BL   British Library

CSP   *Calendar of State Papers*

CW   Marcus, Leah, Janel Muller, and Mary Beth Rose, eds. *Elizabeth I: Collected Works*. Chicago: University of Chicago Press, 2000.

EEBO   Early English Books Online

ODNB   *Oxford Dictionary of National Biography*

SP   State Paper

Prologue: The Sacrificial Priest

1. James A. Galloway, Derek Keene, and Margaret Murphy, "Fuelling the City: Production and Distribution of Firewood and Fuel in London's Region, 1290–1400," *Economic History Review*, n.s., 49, no. 3 (August 1996): 447–72. Oliver Rackham, *The Illustrated History of the Countryside* (London: Weidenfeld & Nicolson, 2003), 32–45.

2. Norman Jones, "Living the Reformations: Generational Experience and Political Perception in Early Modern England," in "The Remapping of English Political History, 1500–1640," ed. A. J. Slavin, special issue, *Huntington Library Quarterly* 60, no. 3 (1997): 273–88.

3. Ben Weinreb and Christopher Hibbert, eds., *The London Encyclopaedia* (London: Papermac, 1983), 789–90. The quote "rich and strange" comes from Ariel's song to Ferdinand in Shakespeare's *The Tempest* (act 1, scene 2).

4. Lacey Baldwin Smith, "English Treason Trials and Confessions in the Sixteenth Century," *Journal of the History of Ideas* 15, no. 4 (October 1954): 471–98.

5. *CSP, Domestic, Mary*, no. 140.

6. *CSP, Spain, Philip and Mary*, ed. W. Turnbull (1861), undated letter thought to be late August 1553, 2: 196.

7. Linda Porter, *Mary Tudor: The First Queen* (London: Portrait, 2007), 280.

8. For further information on Elizabeth's imprisonment in the Tower and later at Woodstock, please refer to Lord Bedingfield's "Articles" on his custodianship of the princess in "State Papers Relating to the Custody of the Princess Elizabeth," ed. C. R. Manning (Norfolk: Norfolk and Norwich Archaeological Society, 1855).

9. John Dudley, Duke of Northumberland and Earl of Warwick, had seized power from Somerset during King Edward VI's minority and had been behind the disinheritance of Mary and Elizabeth in the succession. Lady Jane Grey, aged only seventeen, had been married off to Northumberland's son Guildford, to ensure that the duke would retain his position as the right hand of the monarch.

10. *ODNB*, "John Rogers."

11. David Knowles, *The Religious Orders in England*, vol. 3 (Cambridge: Cambridge University Press, 1971), 421.

12. Part of the battleground between the Vatican and the Protestant church was the notion that the Bible should remain solely in Latin and not in the spoken language or vernacular of the country. According to the Vatican, the people needed to hear God's word as "interpreted" to them through the priest.

13. *CSP, Spain, Philip and Mary*, 125.

14. *ODNB*, "John Rogers."

15. Gardiner was one of the most successful Tudor statesmen in the sixteenth century. His uncanny ability to survive earned him the nickname of "wily Winchester" from John Foxe in his *Acts and Monuments,* and he was undoubtedly a man of great intellect and guile. A staunch Catholic, Gardiner had found a way—except in the reign of Edward VI—to maintain loyalty to both the crown and the papacy.

16. John Foxe, *Acts and Monuments*, 3 vols. (London: George Seeley 1853–1855), 1: 249–251.

17. *CSP, Spain, Philip and Mary*, 139.

One: The New Deborah

1. John Nichols, *The Progresses and Public Processions of Queen Elizabeth (collected from original manuscripts, scarce pamphlets, corporation records, parochial registers etc.) 3 vols.* (London: London Society of Antiquaries, 1823), 1:34.

2. *CSP, Venice*, 7:12.

3. Nichols, *Progresses of Queen Elizabeth*, 1:60.

4. *CSP, Venice*, 12. See also Nichols, *Progresses of Queen Elizabeth*, 1:34–35.

5. *The Passage* is reprinted in A. F. Pollard, ed., *Tudor Tracts, 1532–88* (London: Constable, 1903), 365–95. See also Nichols, *Progresses of Queen Elizabeth*, 38.

6. Nichols, *Progresses of Queen Elizabeth*, 1:39.

7. Ibid., 39–40.

8. Ibid., 44.

9. Ibid., 49.

10. Ibid., 35, 50.

Two: The Realm and the Ministers of Lucifer

1. *CSP, Spain, Philip and Mary*, no. 152.

2. Toby Green, *Inquisition: The Reign of Fear* (London: Macmillan, 2007), 128. See also Salazar de Miranda, *Vida y sucesos prósperos y adversos de Don Fr. Bartolomé de Carranza y Miranda* (Madrid, 1788), 30.

3. Green, *Inquisition*, 128. See also Salazar de Miranda, *Vida*, 192–96.

4. J. E. Neale, *Elizabeth I and Her Parliaments*, 2 vols. (London: Jonathan Cape, 1958), 1: 22.

5. This illness recurred at irregular intervals and is thought to have been a type of influenza. It killed Henry VIII's elder brother, Arthur. It had returned with a vengeance in 1558–9, rivaling the worst plague years of Elizabeth's reign. Paul Slack, *The Impact of Plague in Tudor and Stuart England* (London: Routledge & Kegan Paul, 1985), 70.

6. Margaret Spufford, *The World of Rural Dissenters, 1520–1725* (Cambridge: Cambridge University Press, 1995). See also *Seventeenth Century Journal* 1, no. 1, 1986, p. 31.

7. *CSP, Foreign*, 1:51, no. 144.

8. Philip had discovered by January 1555 that Paul IV (Gian Pietro Carafa) had signed a secret treaty with France negotiated by the cardinal of Guise (maternal uncle of Mary Queen of Scots) to wrest the Kingdom of Naples away from the Spanish Empire in what would become known as the Carafa War of 1556–57. When the pope was told that his plan had been discovered, he sent his nephew Carlo, Cardinal Carafa, on a "peace mission." The Spanish representative at the talks, Francisco de Vargas, claimed that Carlo Carafa "has always been and always will be pure poison, an enemy of their Majesties [Charles V and Philip II] and a Frenchman body and soul, full of mischievous ideas." *CSP, Spain, Philip and Mary*, p. xviii.

9. *CSP, Rome*, 1:1, no. 2.

10. Mary Stuart had been married earlier in the year to the Dauphin Francis of France. As the future queen of France and the queen of Scotland, she embodied a formidable threat to Elizabeth.

11. Neale, *Elizabeth I and Her Parliaments*, 1:34.

12. Ibid., 35.

13. Ibid., 36–37.

14. Ibid.

15. J. E. Neale, *Elizabeth I* (London: Folio Society, 2005), 55.

16. Ibid. See also *CSP, Spain*, vol. 1, no. 37.

17. Neale, *Elizabeth I and Her Parliaments*, 1:54.

18. Ibid., 60.

19. Ibid., 64–67.

20. Ibid., 72. See also *Commons Journal*, 1:59.

21. Ibid., 74–75. See also *Zurich Letters*, 1:24, and *Parker Correspondence* (Parker Society), 66.

22. This was first tested by Sir Thomas More in 1523.

Three: Determined to Be a Virgin Queen

1. Conyers Read, *Mr. Secretary Cecil and Queen Elizabeth* (London: Jonathan Cape, 1977), 198.

2. Ibid.

3. Chris Laoutaris, *Shakespearean Maternities: Crises of Conception in Early Modern England* (Edinburgh: Edinburgh University Press, 2008), 62.

4. Ibid., 27. See also C. D. O'Malley, *Andreas Vesalius* (University of California Press: Berkeley and Los Angeles, 1964), 161–62 of the *Fabrica* (1543).

5. Ibid., 28.

6. Castiglione, Baldesar, *The Book of the Courtier*, tr. George Bull (London: Penguin Classics, 2003), 217.

7. It was deemed incestuous because Henry had slept with Anne's sister, Mary.

8. Read, *Mr. Secretary Cecil and Queen Elizabeth*, 138–39.

9. Her mother, Mary of Guise, had been regent of Scotland since she was a week old, her father having been slain at Flodden by Henry VIII's army.

10. Antonia Fraser, *Mary Queen of Scots* (London: Folio Society, 2004), 68.

11. Ibid., 69. See also Hume Brown, *Early Travellers in Scotland* (Edinburgh: James Thin, 1973), 75.

12. *CW*, 52.

13. Castiglione, *Book of the Courtier*, 216.

14. Mary Queen of Scots had been sent to the French court to live from the age of six as the future wife of Henry II's eldest son, Francis. Mary's mother was manipulated by her powerful Guise brothers in France—the cardinal of Lorraine and Francis, Duke of Guise—to do as they bid. Henry II never fully trusted the Guise family but appreciated them as a powerful force at court and was pleased to have such a crucial pawn as Mary Queen of Scots as his daughter-in-law.

15. Roger Collins, *Keepers of the Keys of Heaven* (London: Phoenix, 2010), 346.

16. Ibid., 386.

17. Neale, *Elizabeth I and Her Parliaments*, 1:86.

18. *CSP, Spain*, 1:1.

19. *CSP, Rome,* 1:15.

20. Ibid.

21. Pius IV was pope from December 25, 1559, to December 9, 1565.

Four: Many an Uneasy Truce

1. Collins, *Keepers of the Keys of Heaven,* 363.

2. Nicholas Crane, *Mercator* (London: Phoenix, 2003), 42–45.

3. H. de Vocht, "Thomas Harding," *English Historical Review* 35, no. 138 (April 1920): 233–44.

4. Robert Tittler, *Nicholas Bacon: The Making of a Tudor Statesman* (Athens: University of Ohio Press, 1976), 59.

5. Ibid., 235.

6. Collins, *Keepers of the Keys of Heaven,* 362.

7. Naturally, this process led to other abuses by other heads of state, with the Holy Roman Emperor demanding the same "sweetener" as his nephew Philip. Later, from the time of Henry IV of France (1589–1610), the French kings would join in as well, making an utter farce of the conclaves electing the pope. The practice was only abolished by Pius X after the conclave electing him in 1903.

8. Geoffrey Parker, *The Grand Strategy of Philip II* (New Haven: Yale University Press, 2000), 93.

9. Mary had two Guise uncles, Francis of Guise and Louis I of Guise. Francis was the military leader; Louis was the second cardinal of Guise. Both also adopted the title "of Lorraine," i.e., Francis of Lorraine and cardinal of Lorraine for Francis and Louis, respectively.

10. J. Lynch, "Philip II and the Papacy," *Transactions of the Royal History Society,* 5th ser., 11 (London, 1961): 24.

11. As part of the "deal" with Charles V, the papacy also relinquished the right to appoint the clergy to their benefices.

12. Lynch, "Philip II and the Papacy," 26–27.

13. See Parker, *Grand Strategy of Philip II,* chapters 1, 2. Also *CSP, Rome,* 1:21–26; Ronald, *Pirate Queen,* chaps. 1–4.

14. *CSP, Rome,* 1:20.

15. Ibid., 22.

16. Ibid., 24.

17. *CSP, Foreign,* 2:98, no. 229.

18. Ibid., no. 231.

19. Ibid., no. 246.

20. Ibid., 2:144, no. 334.

21. Ronald, *Pirate Queen,* 35. See also *CSP, Foreign,* 2:313, no. 623.

22. *CSP, Foreign,* 2:188 (excerpt from December 21 letter from the Duchess of Parma to Philip II from MS Paris. Angl. Reg. xxi Teulet, 1. 467).

23. France followed Salic Law, which automatically excluded any female issue from becoming a queen regnant.

24. Reputed to be why the French Protestants were called "Huguenots." Another interpretation is that they named themselves after Hugues Capet, father of the French Capetian Dynasty.

25. Leonie Frieda, *Catherine de Medici: Renaissance Queen of France* (New York: Fourth Estate, 2003), 135.

26. Ibid., 136. Also, N. M. Sutherland, "Queen Elizabeth and the Conspiracy at Amboise, March 1560," *English Historical Review* 81, no. 320 (July 1996): 474–89; J. Dureng, "La Complicité d'Angleterre dans le complot d'Amboise," *Revue d'Histoire Moderne et Contemporaine* 6, no. 4 (1904–05): 249–56. Note that this last article has created some furore and has often been quoted as a source proving that Queen Elizabeth was implicated in the plot. Having read the article, I agree with N. M. Sutherland that its research is questionable and conclusion spurious.

27. In Henry VIII's will, which was approved by Parliament, he effectively disowned his elder sister Margaret's descendants from her marriage to the Scots king in favor of his younger sister Mary's heirs by the Earl of Suffolk. Catherine was Lady Jane Grey's younger sister.

Five: The Battle for Hearts and Minds

1. Read, *Mr. Secretary Cecil and Queen Elizabeth*, 228.

2. Tracy Borman, *Elizabeth's Women* (London: Jonathan Cape, 2009), 244. See also *CSP, Spain*, 1:116.

3. *CSP, Foreign*, 4:312, no. 550 (5).

4. Castligione, *Book of the Courtier*, 199.

5. Read, *Mr. Secretary Cecil and Queen Elizabeth*, 229.

6. The second-largest city in England at the time was Norwich, followed by Bristol and the other port cities. Water remained the preferred mode of transport for goods and people whenever possible.

7. Gāmini Salgādo, *The Elizabethan Underworld* (London: Folio Society, 2006), 1.

8. Ibid., 8.

9. David Cressy, *Bonfires and Bells: National Memory and the Protestant Calendar in Elizabethan and Stuart England* (London: Weidenfeld & Nicolson, 1989), 26.

10. Ibid., 8.

11. *CW*, 665; *Twelfth Night*, 2.3.88–89.

12. See Dame Frances Yates's seminal work *The Art of Memory* (London: Pimlico, 2005).

13. Eamon Duffy, *The Stripping of the Altars* (New Haven: Yale University Press, 1992), 570.

14. Ibid.

15. Duffy, *The Stripping of the Altars*, 572–73, 566.

16. Ibid., 577–78.

17. T. Cooper, *Certaine Sermons* (London, 1580), 164. These sentiments were echoed by John Knox.

18. H. Holland, *A Treatise against Witchcraft* (Cambridge, 1590), 2.

19. Tittler, *Nicholas Bacon*, 59.

20. *CSP, Rome*, 75, no. 140.

21. The first councils attempted were in Mantua in 1537, then Vicenza in 1538. The first Trent council was called for 1542 but was boycotted by the French, meaning that the first time it met was in December 1545.

22. Ibid., 75–77.

23. Ibid., 79.

24. Read, *Mr. Secretary Cecil and Queen Elizabeth*, 234.

25. Ibid., 235. See also BL, Add. MSS 35830 f. 228.

26. *CSP, Rome*, 79, no. 153.

27. Ibid., 59, no. 126.

28. Frieda, *Catherine de Medici*, 159.

Six: Untrustworthy Allies

1. *CSP, Foreign*, 1561-1562 (London, 1865), 4:301, no. 598.

2. Read, *Mr. Secretary Cecil and Queen Elizabeth*, 245–46.

3. *CSP, Foreign*, 4:21–28.

4. SP 70/37 f., May 2, 1562.

5. *CSP, Venice*, 337.

6. *CSP, Rome*, 77–78.

7. Ibid., 82.

8. Horsey had been exiled from England ever since Mary Tudor's battle for her crown. He had been one of Robert Dudley's accomplices in the effort to put Lady Jane Grey on the throne. He had only returned from his French exile in 1561.

9. Read, *Mr. Secretary Cecil and Queen Elizabeth*, 248–49.

10. *CSP, Spain*, 259.

11. Read, *Mr. Secretary Cecil and Queen Elizabeth*, 257.

12. N. M. Sutherland, *Princes, Politics and Religion, 1547–1589* (London: Hambledon Press, 1984), 140–53.

13. *CW*, 142–43.

Seven: Christ's Soldiers

1. Patrick Collinson, *Godly People* (London: Hambledon Press, 1983), 11, attributed to John Huckford of Elmstead in the proceedings in the Archdeaconry Court in Colchester.

2. Ibid., 7.

3. Christopher Haigh, "Puritan Evangelism in the Reign of Elizabeth I," *English Historical Review* 92, no. 362 (January 1977): 30–31.

4. Neale, *Elizabeth I and Her Parliaments*, 108n.

5. Fraser, *Mary Queen of Scots,* 152–53.

6. SP 63/5/101.

7. The Scots were so-called "redshanks" because of their pale, red legs exposed by their kilts.

8. SP 63/1/79.

9. SP 63/4/22 viii.

10. SP 63/4/37.

11. *ODNB,* "Shane O'Neill." See also William Camden, *The History of the most renowned and victorius Princess Elizabeth* (printed by M. Flesher, London, 1688).

12. Shane O'Neill is the only Irish "freedom fighter" who was not resurrected in the twentieth century as a folk hero, though some have admired his military tactics.

13. Ciaran Brady, *The Chief Governors: The Rise and Fall of Reform Government in Tudor Ireland* (Cambridge: Cambridge University Press, 1994), 10.

14. Marcus Tanner, *Ireland's Holy Wars* (New Haven and London: Yale Nota Bene, 2003), 88.

Eight: The Great Catholic Threat

1. Read, *Mr. Secretary Cecil and Queen Elizabeth,* 315. See also James Melville, *Memoirs* (London, G. Scott Printers, 1683), 51.

2. Ibid., 317.

3. Fraser, *Mary Queen of Scots,* 228.

4. Read, *Mr. Secretary Cecil and Queen Elizabeth,* 340.

5. *CSP, Rome,* 180–81.

6. Ibid.

7. Ibid., 182–83.

8. Read, *Mr. Secretary Cecil and Queen Elizabeth,* 347–84.

9. Fraser, *Mary Queen of Scots,* 253.

Nine: Betrayal amid Dreamy Spires

1. *CSP, Rome,* 190.

2. Patrick Collinson, *The Elizabethan Puritan Movement* (London: Jonathan Cape, 1967), 72. Collinson does identify St. Stephens Cornhill but it is an error on his part.

3. Ibid., 78.

4. Ibid., 79.

5. Ronald, *Pirate Queen,* chap. 9.

6. SP 12/176/68.

7. Alan Crossley et al., eds., *Victoria County History: Oxfordshire,* vol. 4, *The City of Oxford,* "Roman Catholicism," 312, available online at British History Online, http://www.british-history.ac.uk/report.aspx?pubid-10.

8. Collinson, *Puritan Movement,* 62.

9. Alice Hogge, *God's Secret Agents* (London: HarperCollins, 2005), 37–38.

10. Ibid., 41.

11. *ODNB*, "William Allen." See also Allen, *Modest Defence* (London: Manresa Press, 1914), 104.

12. John Jewel, bishop of Salisbury's *Apology of the Church of England* (translated from the Latin *Apologia pro Ecclesia Anglicana*), written in 1561, was officially sponsored by the church and published in 1562. It intended to show a one-sided view that the Church of England faced no threats from any other Protestant quarter. In other words, it was a work of government propaganda. Jewel was a Marian exile bishop.

13. *ODNB*, "William Allen."

14. *ODNB*, "Paul Wentworth."

15. Read, *Mr. Secretary Cecil and Queen Elizabeth*, 364.

16. BL, MS Cotton Charter IV.38 (2), written in Elizabeth's hand and much revised. Her handwriting, normally extremely legible and quite beautiful, shows signs of anger and haste.

Ten: Iconoclastic Fury

1. Geoffrey Parker, *The Dutch Revolt* (London: 1977), Allen Lane, 30.

2. This payment was known as the "Nine Years' Aid."

3. G. Groen van Prinsterer, *Archives* (Leiden: 1835–37), 1st ser. 1:152, Granvelle to Philip II, March 10, 1563.

4. Parker, *Dutch Revolt*, 54.

5. Ibid., 63.

6. Ibid., 57. See also original sources in footnote 33.

7. Ibid., 58.

8. Jews who nominally followed Christian religions.

9. Ibid., p. 66. Margaret had defended this "usurpation" by the nobles, but the king never read her letter, issuing the abstract *Estado* 527/70 written by Gonzalo Pérez.

10. Alba became the Spanish governor-general in the Netherlands from 1567 to 1573 and was given the nickname of "the Iron Duke" for his harsh treatment of the local population.

11. *CSP, Spain*, 404, no. 285. Philip makes it clear here to Guzman de Silva, his ambassador to England, that this is only a family visit, and not a matter of state.

12. Ibid., 72.

13. Ibid., 76.

14. *CSP, Foreign*, 8:21.

15. *CSP, Spain*, 1:76.

16. Groen van Prinsterer, *Archives*, 2:364, Horn (Montigny) to Orange. In 1569, the Duke of Alba accused Philip's Flemish groom of the bedchamber, Jean Vandenesse,

of leaking this state secret to Horn and Orange. Fortunately for Vandenesse, he died before a verdict of his guilt could be confirmed.

17. C. V. Wedgwood, *William the Silent* (London: Phoenix Press, 1944), 69. See also Groen van Prinsterer, *Archives*, 1:440.

18. *CSP, Rome*, 214–15.

Eleven: Two Murders and Mayhem

1. Darnley's skull, now at the Royal College of Surgeons in London, has been analyzed and found to be pitted with traces of "a virulent syphilitic disease," according to the report by Karl Pearson, "Skull and Portraits of Henry Stuart Lord Darnley," *Biometrika* 20 (July 1928): 1–104. I thank Lady Antonia Fraser, DBE, for pointing out this reference in her *Mary Queen of Scots*.

2. Read, *Mr. Secretary Cecil and Queen Elizabeth*, 374.

3. *CW*, 116.

4. *CSP, Spain*, 1:397.

5. Read, *Mr. Secretary Cecil and Queen Elizabeth*, 378.

6. Ibid., 378–79.

7. Frieda, *Catherine de Medici*, 199.

8. *ODNB*, "Shane O'Neill."

9. *CSP, Rome*, 266–67.

10. The "English Pale" is defined as an area of English jurisdiction and colonization. The term "pale" on its own denotes a stake, fence, or boundary. The area "inside the Pale" became synonymous with the civilized English colony, as opposed to "beyond the Pale," where the local population was deemed to be savage or wild.

11. Tanner, *Ireland's Holy Wars*, 88.

12. SP 63/20/13, January 18, 1567

13. *ODNB*, "Shane O'Neill." See also Campion, "Ten Reasons," proposed to his adversaries for disputation in the name of the faith and presented to the illustrious members of the university (London, Manresa Press, 1914), 130.

14. Collinson, *Puritan Movement*, 129.

15. John Bossy, *The English Catholic Community, 1570–1850* (London: Darton, Longman & Todd, 1975), 12.

16. *CSP, Spain*, 1:418, no. 294; 432, no. 300.

17. Parker, *Dutch Revolt*, 106.

18. *CSP, Rome*, 260.

19. Read, *Mr. Secretary Cecil and Queen Elizabeth*, 394.

Twelve: An Ill-Conceived Escape

1. Fraser, *Mary Queen of Scots*, 347.

2. Read, *Mr. Secretary Cecil and Queen Elizabeth*, 399.

3. Ibid., 406.

4. SP 63/26/8.

5. The court faction was mostly *les politiques*. They were Catholic and possessed a political will to see beyond the religious questions that divided the nation.

6. Many believed Philip's choice of ambassador was in retaliation for Elizabeth's unfortunate choice of Dr. Man as her ambassador to Madrid, who decried publicly that Pope Pius V was nothing but a "canting little monk."

7. *CSP, Spain*, 2:75.

8. Ronald, *Pirate Queen*, 129–38. The incident is known as the Seizure of Alba's Pay Ships, and it set alight international diplomatic correspondence between England, the Low Countries, Spain, and Rome for months.

9. *CSP, Spain*, 2:91–92.

10. Ronald, *Pirate Queen*, 129.

11. *CSP, Spain*, 2:111.

12. The plan is thought to have come originally from Maitland. Norfolk appears to have hesitated initially but was influenced by Leicester, Arundel, and Pembroke as well as Mary in letters. He never met Mary.

13. Read, *Mr. Secretary Cecil and Queen Elizabeth*, 449.

14. *ODNB*, "Thomas Howard, fourth duke of Norfolk."

15. Conyers Read, *Mr. Secretary Walsingham and the Policy of Queen Elizabeth*, 3 vols. (Hamden, CT: Archon Press), 1:66. See also SP. Dom Eliz. lix. II.

16. Ibid., 65–68, for the entire Ridolfi incident in the 1569 plots against Elizabeth.

17. Ibid., 452–55.

18. R. R. Reid, "The Rebellion of the Earls, 1569," *Transactions of the Royal Historical Society*, n.s., 20 (1906): 184.

19. Ibid., 187.

20. *CSP, Rome*, 1:314.

21. Read, *Mr. Secretary Cecil and Queen Elizabeth*, 460.

22. Reid, "Rebellion of the Earls, 1569," 197.

23. Conyers Read, *Lord Burghley and Queen Elizabeth* (London: Jonathan Cape, 1960), 20.

Thirteen: Regnans in Excelsis

1. *CSP, Rome*, 323.

2. Ibid., 324.

3. Ibid.

4. Ibid., 326–27.

5. Ibid., 328.

6. *CSP, Foreign*, 9:196–97.

7. Read, *Lord Burghley and Queen Elizabeth*, 22–23. See also La Mothe-Fénélon, *Correspondance* (Geneva, Droz, 1999), 3:100.

8. *CSP, Spain*, 2:254.

9. Ibid., 27.

10. These were, of course, the parents of the murdered Henry, Lord Darnley.

11. Ibid.

12. *CW*, 163.

Fourteen: The English State, Plots, and Counterplots

1. *A Sermon preached before the Queen's Majesty*, EEBO, 27–28.

2. Peter Wentworth was married to Francis Walsingham's sister Elizabeth.

3. Neale, *Elizabeth I and Her Parliaments*, 1:185.

4. A mythological bird that breathes a ghostlike fire.

5. *Neale, Elizabeth and Her Parliaments*, p. 186.

6. William Herle had been acting as a part-time government agent since 1559. He was well educated and spoke Latin, Flemish, Italian, French, and Spanish. Working as a sometime "merchant," or more accurately pirate, he was able to make valuable contacts on behalf of Cecil in northern Germany and the Low Countries. His later official embassies were not successful, though he was used as a spy until his death in 1589.

7. Read, *Lord Burghley and Queen Elizabeth*, 39.

8. Neale, *Elizabeth I and Her Parliaments*, 1:226. See also Hooker, 490.

9. Ibid., 41.

10. Parker, *Dutch Revolt*, 124.

11. Ibid., 43.

12. *CSP, Spain*, 2:348.

13. Kervyn de Lettenhove, ed., *Relations politiques des Pays-Bas et de l'Angleterre*, vol. 5, (Brussels: Académie Royale, 1885), 230.

14. Read, *Mr. Secretary Walsingham and the Policy of Queen Elizabeth*, 1:142–43.

15. Ibid., 149.

16. R. J. Knecht, *Catherine de' Medici* (London: Longman, 1998), 234.

Fifteen: Massacre in Paris

1. If Catherine de' Medici's three remaining sons—Charles IX; Henry, Duke of Anjou; and Francis, Duke of Alençon—died without issue, then Henry of Navarre was next in line for France's throne. His mother, Jeanne d'Albret, queen of Navarre, had inherited the small kingdom on the Spanish border from her uncle Francis I, grandfather of the present king.

2. Knecht, *Catherine de' Medici*, 148. See also Abel Desjardins, ed., *Negociations diplomatiques de la France avec la Toscane* (Paris: Giuseppe Canestrini, 1859), 3:711.

3. BL, Cotton MSS, Vespasian F vi. Folio 4b.

4. Collins, *Keepers of the Keys of Heaven*, 366.

5. For more detail on these swashbuckling seafarers, see Ronald, *Pirate Queen*, 158–60.

6. Sigismund-Augustus had not only maintained the peace in Poland between Prot-

estant and Catholic successfully and united Poland and Lithuania, but he had also ensured the smooth succession through the Union of Lublin to elect his successor. There was probably no poorer choice than Anjou to replace him.

7. Collins, *Keepers of the Keys of Heaven*, 372.

8. Read, *Mr. Secretary Walsingham and the Policy of Queen Elizabeth*, 2:211.

9. Ibid., 212.

10. Ibid., 213.

11. Ibid., 215.

12. Frieda, *Catherine de' Medici*, 248.

13. Ronald, *Pirate Queen*, 160–61.

14. *CW*, 215.

15. Read, *Mr. Secretary Walsingham and the Policy of Queen Elizabeth*, 2:233. See also Sir Dudley Digges, *The Compleat Ambassador* (London: Thomas Newcombe for Gabriel Bedell and Thomas Collins, 1655), p. 250.

16. Due to her leading role in the assassination of Coligny, Catherine has been remembered by history as "the Black Queen" and whatever good she had done was completely undermined.

17. Read, Mr. Secretary Walsingham and the Policy of Queen Elizabeth, 234.

18. J. B. Steane, ed., *Christopher Marlowe: The Complete Plays* (London: Penguin, 1969), 300–301, 1.2.33–63.

Sixteen: The Puritan Underworld of London

1. R. J. Knecht, *The French Civil Wars* (London: Longman, 2000), 165–66.

2. Collinson, *Godly People*, 251, translated from the French by the author.

3. Ibid., 252.

4. Collinson, *Elizabethan Puritan Movement*, 114.

5. Collinson, *Godly People*, 275.

6. Ibid.

7. Locke was the brother of the merchant adventurer Michael Lok, who was ruined by the Frobisher North American gold scam. See Ronald, *Pirate Queen*, 210–13.

8. Collinson, *Godly People*, 316. See also Wilcox's *Works* (1624).

9. *ODNB*, "Thomas Cartwright."

10. Collinson, *Elizabethan Puritan Movement*, 101, 103.

11. The *Admonition* was made to Parliament rather than the queen as head of the Church of England because the archbishops sit, of course, in the House of Lords and all changes in legislation must be approved by them.

12. Collinson, *Elizabethan Puritan Movement*, 120.

13. Read, *Lord Burghley and Queen Elizabeth*, p. 116.

14. Collinson, *Elizabethan Puritan Movement*, 120.

15. Ibid., 121.

16. Neale, *Elizabeth I and Her Parliaments*, 298.

17. Ibid.

18. *An Admonition to Parliament* and *Certain Articles Collected and Taken by the Bishops*, EEBO.

19. BL, Lansdowne, 17, no. 43, f. 97.

20. Read, *Lord Burghley and Queen Elizabeth*, 110.

21. Ibid., 117.

22. *CW*, 142–43.

Seventeen: Via Dolorosa

1. Collinson, *Elizabethan Puritan Movement*, 152.

2. Tanner, *Ireland's Holy Wars*, 92.

3. Peter Guilday, *The English Catholic Refugees on the Continent, 1558–1795*, vol. 1 (London: Longmans, Green, 1914), 7.

4. Thomas Knox, The First and Second Diaries of the English College, Douay, 1868. xxxi.

5. Parker, *Dutch Revolt*, 166. See also Spanish SP IVdeDJ51/31, royal reply May 31, 1574.

6. Guilday, *English Catholic Refugees on the Continent*, 69n.

7. Ibid., p. 72.

8. Collinson, *Elizabethan Puritan Movement*, 160. See also P. Stubbes, *Second part of the anatomie of abuses*, ed. F. J. Furnivall (London: New Shakespeare Society, 1882) 100–102.

9. Ibid., 161.

10. Ibid., 162.

11. Ibid., 163.

12. A recusant is any person, especially a Roman Catholic, who refused to attend the services of the Church of England until 1791. The Act of Uniformity of 1558 first imposed fines on all nonattenders of a parish church, but Roman Catholics were the specific target of the Act Against Popish Recusants of 1592; subsequent acts through the seventeenth century imposed heavy penalties on Catholic recusants, the exaction of which persisted up to the Second Relief Act of 1791. Recusancy among Catholics was not common until 1570, when the papal bull *Regnans in Excelsis* excommunicated Elizabeth I.

13. Collinson, *Godly People*, 376.

14. Ibid.

15. Ibid., p. 377.

16. Ibid., p. 388.

17. In 1572 Elizabeth licensed his players as Leicester's Men, who rapidly became the premier actors and production company of their day.

18. Parker, *Grand Strategy of Philip II*, 164–65. Also quote from Zuñiga cf. letter to Philip II, August 9, 1576. *CSP, Spain*, 2.

19. *CSP, Spain*, 2:549–50.

Eighteen: God's Outriders

1. Hogge, *God's Secret Agents*, 55.

2. Robert Southwell was the third son of Richard Southwell, who was the natural elder son of Sir Richard Southwell, whom Mary Tudor had sent to ensure that John Rogers had been burnt at the stake as ordered.

3. Ibid., 57.

4. Ibid., 57–58. See also Philip Ayres ed., *Anthony Munday: A Roman Life* (Oxford: Clarendon Press, 1980), 21–27.

5. Ibid., 62.

6. Read, *Mr. Secretary Walsingham and the Policy of Queen Elizabeth*, 2:280.

7. Ibid., 281–82.

8. Stukeley presented himself to the court of the boy king, Sebastian of Portugal, and was sidetracked from his appointed mission to the invasion of Morocco against the "greater infidel" the Moors. Within the year, Stukeley, Sebastian, and the Moorish king all died at the Battle of Alcazar, which was later portrayed in a play in the 1590s by Thomas Kyd.

9. See Ronald, *Pirate Queen*, 59–60, 155–56.

10. Read, *Lord Burghley and Queen Elizabeth*, 240.

11. Boncompagni was thought to be the natural son of the pope.

12. Ibid., 241.

13. *ODNB*, "Nicholas Sander."

14. "Some Letters and Papers of Nicholas Sander, 1562–1580," *Miscellanea XIII*, Catholic Record Society pub., 26 (London: CRS, 1926): 1–57.

15. *CSP, Spain*, 2:665–66.

16. Read, *Mr. Secretary Walsingham and the Policy of Queen Elizabeth*, 2:365–66.

17. *CW*, 239.

18. Hogge, *God's Secret Agents*, 67.

19. Victor Houliston, *Catholic Resistance in Elizabethan England* (Burlingame, VT: Ashgate, 2007), 2–3.

20. Persons's name was often spelled "Parsons" by Protestants and posterity, though he always spelled it "Persons" himself.

21. Keith Thomas, *Religion and the Decline of Magic* (London: Weidenfeld & Nicolson, 1971), 80, 358. See also John Calvin's *An Admonicion against Astrology Iudiciall*, 1561, 106.

22. Houliston, *Catholic Resistance in Elizabethan England*, 25. See also John E. Parish, *Robert Persons and the English Counter-Reformation*, Rice University Studies 52 (Houston, 1966), 13.

23. Read, *Lord Burghley and Queen Elizabeth*, 244–47.

24. Evelyn Waugh, *Edmund Campion* (London: Longmans, 1961), 109.

25. It is thought that they may have sheltered at the home of Sir William Catesby, father of the Gunpowder Plotter Robert Catesby.

26. Ibid., 117.

27. Hogge, *God's Secret Agents*, 83–84.

28. Waugh, *Edmund Campion*, 127.

29. Hogge, *God's Secret Agents*, 86.

Nineteen: The Ungodly Witch Hunts

1. Read, *Lord Burghley and Queen Elizabeth*, 249.

2. Ibid. See also Digges, *The Compleat Ambassador*, 373.

3. Ibid., 250.

4. Read, *Mr. Secretary Walsingham and the Policy of Queen Elizabeth*, 2:368.

5. Knecht, *French Civil Wars*, 212–16.

6. John Bossy, *Under the Molehill: An Elizabethan Spy Story* (New Haven: Yale University Press, 2001), 145–51.

7. Read, *Mr. Secretary Walsingham and the Policy of Queen Elizabeth*, 2:298–299, 323.

8. Ibid., 308. *ODNB*, "Sir George Peckham." There is some minor controversy over whether Walsingham was the initiator of the plan, or Peckham, as a result of a letter from Ambassador Mendoza to Philip II dated July 11, 1582. On balance, I believe that Peckham was the author of the move to create a new home for Catholics in America.

9. Bossy, *Under the Molehill*, 26.

10. Read, *Mr. Secretary Walsingham and the Policy of Queen Elizabeth*, 2:313–22.

11. Bossy, *Under the Molehill*, 31–38.

12. In John Bossy's earlier book, *Giordano Bruno and the Embassy Affair* (New Haven: Yale University Press, 1991), he had believed Bruno to be "Henri Fagot." He claims in *Under the Molehill* that "Fagot" was Feron. Bruno, a defrocked Dominican priest with court connections across Europe, was highly influential in literary circles and loathed by Catholics as a traitor. He eventually returned to Rome, where he was tried for heresy and burned at the stake in front of a satisfied pope.

13. *CSP, Scotland*, 432.

14. *A Discoverie of the Treasons Practised and attempted . . . by Francis Throckmorton* (London, 1584), Harlian Miscellany, 3:192.

15. Apparently the correspondence didn't hold any great secrets, as Mary knew not to trust him. He was imprisoned five times in the 1580s, and only returned to favor under the patronage of the Earl of Essex in 1595. Howard's title was Earl of Northampton.

16. Bossy, *Under the Molehill*, 76; Read, *Mr. Secretary Walsingham and the Policy of Queen Elizabeth*, 2:395–96.

17. Parker, *Grand Strategy of Philip II*, 171.

Twenty: Frustrating the Designs of Our Enemies

1. Read, *Mr. Secretary Walsingham and the Policy of Queen Elizabeth*, 3:73.

2. Ibid., 76.

3. When Navarre, who had been forced to abjure his Protestant faith, escaped from his captivity in February 1576, he took on the mantle of the leader of the Protestant Huguenot faith and became a practicing Protestant once more.

4. Ibid., 94.

5. Neale, *Elizabeth I and Her Parliaments*, 2:39. See also D'Ewes, *A Compleat Journal of the Votes, Speeches and Debates, both of the House of Lords and House of Commons throughout the whole Reign of Queen Elizabeth, etc.* (London: Jonathen Robinson, 1693), p. 340

6. Ibid., 52–53.

7. Ibid., 50.

8. Ronald, *Pirate Queen*, 291.

9. Read, *Mr. Secretary Walsingham and the Policy of Queen Elizabeth*, 3:102.

10. *CSP, Foreign*, 19:572.

11. Read, *Mr. Secretary Walsingham and the Policy of Queen Elizabeth*, 3:108–9

12. *CSP, Foreign*, 20:6.

13. Ronald, *Pirate Queen*, 279.

14. Read, *Lord Burghley and Queen Elizabeth*, 310.

15. D. C. Peck, "Government Suppression of Elizabethan Catholic Books: The Case of *Leicester's Commonwealth*," *Library Quarterly* 47, no. 2 (April 1977), online reprint, www.dpeck.info/write/suppression/html (accessed January 12, 2012).

16. Ronald, *Pirate Queen*, 279.

17. Parker, *Grand Strategy of Philip II*, 179–80

18. Ibid., 181.

Twenty-One: The Long-Awaited Execution

1. Fraser, *Mary Queen of Scots*, 447–50.

2. Ibid., 450.

3. *ODNB*, "Thomas Morgan."

4. Read, *Mr. Secretary Walsingham and the Policy of Queen Elizabeth*, 3:2.

5. Ibid., p. 9.

6. Fraser, *Mary Queen of Scots*, 470.

7. Read, *Mr. Secretary Walsingham and the Policy of Queen Elizabeth*, 3:13.

8. *ODNB*, "Anthony Babington."

9. Ibid.

10. *CSP, Foreign*, 23:39; 19:415, April 17.

11. Read, *Mr. Secretary Walsingham and the Policy of Queen Elizabeth*, 3:21–22.

12. Fraser, *Mary Queen of Scots*, 475.

13. Ibid., 476.

14. Ibid., 477.

15. Ibid., 478.

16. Read, *Mr. Secretary Walsingham and the Policy of Queen Elizabeth*, 3:53.

17. Ibid., 55.

18. Ibid., 56.

19. Ibid., 63.

20. Ronald, *Pirate Queen*, 292.

Twenty-Two: God's Obvious Design

1. Garrett Mattingly, *The Defeat of the Spanish Armada* (London: 2006), 17–53.

2. Ronald, *Pirate Queen*, 306.

3. Read, *Mr. Secretary Walsingham and the Policy of Queen Elizabeth*, 3:219.

4. Ronald, *Pirate Queen*, 297.

5. Ibid., 296.

6. Ibid., 302.

7. Ibid., 303.

8. Mattingly, *Defeat of the Spanish Armada*, 274–75.

Twenty-Three: The Norfolk Landing

1. *CW*, 326.

2. Neale, *Elizabeth I and Her Parliaments*, 2:62, 112, 176.

3. Ibid., 58–72.

4. Hogge, *God's Secret Agents*, 114–15.

5. Ibid., 96.

6. Ibid., 118–19.

Twenty-Four: Marprelate, Puritans, Catholics, and Players

1. Houliston, *Catholic Resistance in Elizabethan England*, 47, 56–60.

2. *ODNB*, "Robert Southwell," from *The Poems of Robert Southwell, SJ: A Bibliographical Study*, James H. McDonald, ed., (Oxford: Clarendon Press, 1967), 41.

3. V. C. Gildersleeve, *Government Regulation of the Elizabethan Drama* (Westport, CT: Greenwood Press, 1975), 55. See also Hazlitt, *English Drama*, 34–35.

4. E. K. Chambers, *The Elizabethan Stage*, 4 vols. (Oxford: Clarendon Press, 1967), 1:277.

5. *CSP, Foreign*, 19:415, April 17; *CSP, Foreign*, 20:89–90; David Hohnen, *Hamlet's Castle and Shakespeare's Elsinore* (Elsinore, Denmark: Elsinore Castle Publications, 1982), 42.

6. David Riggs, *The World of Christopher Marlowe* (London: Faber & Faber, 2004), 334–35.

7. Joseph Black, "The Rhetoric of Reaction: The Marprelate Tracts (1588–1589), Anti-Martinism, and the Use of Print in Early Modern England," *Sixteenth Century Journal* 28 (Autumn 1997): 713.

8. Ibid., 714.

9. Ibid.

10. Gildersleeve, *Government Regulation of the Elizabethan Drama*, 91–92.

11. Katherine S. Van Eerde, "Robert Waldegrave: The Printer as Agent and Link between Sixteenth Century England and Scotland," *Renaissance Quarterly* 34, no. 1 (Spring 1981): 47.
12. Black, "Rhetoric of Reaction," 711.
13. Chambers, *Elizabethan Stage*, 1: 294.
14. Ibid., 293.
15. Ibid., 295.
16. BL, Harleian MS 7368.
17. Gildersleeve, *Government Regulation of the Elizabethan Drama*, 92–93.
18. Salgãdo, *Elizabethan Underworld*, 37.
19. Ibid, 37–38.
20. Houliston, *Catholic Resistance in Elizabethan England*, 50.
21. Ibid., 54.
22. Alan Haynes, *Robert Cecil: First Earl of Salisbury* (London: Peter Owen, 1989), 21.
23. Riggs, *World of Christopher Marlowe*, 308.
24. Ibid.
25. Ibid., 317.
26. Charles Nicholl, *The Reckoning: The Murder of Christopher Marlowe* (London: Vintage, 2002), 52–53.
27. The records remain silent as to *who* posted Marlowe's bail.

Twenty-Five: Elizabeth's Eminence Grise and the Final Battles for England

1. Ronald, *Pirate Queen*, 329–31.
2. Hogge, *God's Secret Agents*, 264–65.
3. David Loades, *The Cecils* (London: National Archives, 2007), 202.
4. Hogge, *God's Secret Agents*, 171.
5. Houliston, *Catholic Resistance in Elizabethan England*, 51.
6. *ODNB*, "Robert Southwell."
7. BL, Harleian MS 9889.
8. This was not due to cowardice but rather to a realization that if he left court, Cecil's influence would continue to grow, to his detriment.
9. Edmund Goldsmid, ed., *The Secret Correspondence of Sir Robert Cecil with James VI King of Scotland* (Edinburgh: Privately printed, 1887), 7–8.
10. Ibid., 7.
11. Hogge, *God's Secret Agents*, 292.

Twenty-Six: Epilogue

1. *CSP Domestic*, 14/xix, p. 11
2. Ibid., 41.
3. Ibid., 45.

4. The plotters, Robert Catesby, Thomas Winter, Robert Winter, John Wright, Christopher Wright, Thomas Percy, Guy Fawkes, Sir Everard Digby, John Grant, and Ambrose Rookwood were all executed. See Alice Hogge's fabulous book about the reasons for the plot, *God's Secret Agents* (London: HarperCollins, 2004) as well as Lady Antonia Fraser's excellent *The Gunpowder Plot: Terror and Faith in 1605* (London: Weidenfeld & Nicolson, 2002).

BIBLIOGRAPHY

State Papers and Manuscripts

Ashmolean MS 226, f. 233

British Library

  MS Cotton, Charter IV

  MS Cotton, Vespasian F

  MS Harley 416, f. 200

Bodleian Library

  MS Gough Eccl. Top. 3, f. 101

  Oxford Diocesan Papers, d. 14, f. 86

  Savile MS 42

Calendar of State Papers, Domestic, Mary, 1553–58. Rev. ed. Ed. C. S. Knighton. London, 1998. In notes: *CSP, Domestic, Mary.*

Calendar of State Papers, Foreign, Elizabeth, 23 vols. Ed. J. Stevenson, Sophie Crawford Lomas, et al. London, 1863–1950. In notes: *CSP, Foreign.*

Calendar of State Papers, Foreign, Mary, 1553–58. Ed. W. Turnbull. London, 1861. In notes: *CSP, Foreign, Mary.*

Calendar of State Papers, Rome, vol. 1, *1558–71.* Ed J. M. Rigg. London, 1916. In notes: *CSP, Rome.*

Calendar of State Papers, Scotland, vol. 6, *1581–83.* Ed. William K. Boyd. Edinburgh, 1894. In notes: *CSP, Scotland.*

Calendar of State Papers, Spain, Elizabeth. 4 vols. Ed. Martin A. S. Hume. London, 1892–99. In notes: *CSP, Spain.*

Calendar of State Papers, Spain, vol. 13, *Philip and Mary.* Ed. W. Turnbull. London, 1861. In notes: *CSP, Spain, Philip and Mary.*

Calendar of State Papers, Venice, vol. 7, *1558–80.* Ed. Rawdon Brown and G. Cavendish Bentinck. London, 1890. In notes: *CSP, Venice.*

Nichols, John Gough, ed. *The chronicle of Queen Jane, and of two years of Queen Mary, and especially of the rebellion of Sir Thomas Wyat: written by a Resident in the Tower of London.* 1850; rpt. New York: AMS Press, 1968.

Carier, Benjamin. *A Missive to His Majesty of Great Britain, King James. Written Divers years since by Doctor Carier. Conteining the motives of his conversion to Catholike religion. With a notable fore-sight of the present distempers both in the church and state of His Majesties dominions: and his advice for the prevention thereof.* Paris, 1649. Early English Books Online.

State Papers 12/176/68; 12/206/54; 12/208/2; 12/186/92

Rare Books

Aubrey, John. *Miscellanies.* London: printed for Edward Castle, 1696. Early English Books Online.

———. *Remaines of Gentilisme and Judaisme.* 1687–89. British Library, Lansdowne MS 231. London: Folklore Society, 1881.

Bacon, Francis. *Works.* Ed. James Spedding, Robert Leslie Ellis, and Douglas Denon Heath. 15 vols. Boston: Brown and Taggard, 1860. Available online at http://openlibrary.org/books/OL7117340M/The_works_of_Francis_Bacon.

D'Ewes, Sir Dudley. *A Compleat Journal of the Votes, Speeches, and Debates, both of the House of Lords and House of Commons throughout the whole Reign of Queen Elizabeth etc.* London: Jonathan Robinson, 1693.

Foxe, John. *Acts and Monuments.* London: Early English Books Online, 1563.

Gardiner, Stephen. *The Letters of Stephen Gardiner.* Ed. J. A. Muller. Cambridge: Cambridge University Press, 1933.

Laing, David (ed.), *Works of John Knox,* Edinburgh: Wodrow Society, 1864.

Nichols, John. *The Progresses and Public Processions of Queen Elizabeth (collected from original manuscripts, scarce pamphlets, corporation records, parochial registers etc.).* 3 vols. London: London Society of Antiquaries, 1823.

Nicholson, W., ed. *The Remains of Edmund Grindal.* Cambridge: for the Parker Society, 1843.

Roberts, A. *A Treatise of Witchcraft.* London: N[icholas] O[akes], 1616. Early English Books Online.

Scot, Reginald. *The Discoverie of Witchcraft.* 1584; rpt. [London]: John Rodker, 1930.

Topsell, E. *The Reward of Religion.* London: W. Stansby, 1596, Early English Books Online.

Vaughan, W. *The Golden-Grove.* London: Simon Stafford, 1600. Early English Books Online.

Books

Arnade, Peter. *Beggars, Iconoclasts, and Civic Patriots*. Ithaca: Cornell University Press, 2008.

Bate, Jonathan, and Eric Ramussen, eds., *The Complete Works of William Shakespeare*, London: Palgrave Macmillan, 2007.

Besterman, T. *Crystal-Gazing*. London: William Rider & Son, 1924.

Bossy, John. *The English Catholic Community, 1570–1850*. London: Darton, Longman & Todd, 1975.

———. *Giordano Bruno and the Embassy Affair*. New Haven: Yale University Press, 1991.

———. *Under the Molehill: An Elizabethan Spy Story*. New Haven: Yale University Press, 2001.

Brady, Ciaran. *The Chief Governors: The Rise and Fall of Reform Government in Tudor Ireland, 1536–1588*. Cambridge: Cambridge University Press, 1994.

Buckley, George. *Atheism in the English Renaissance*. New York: Russell & Russell, 1965.

Byrne, M. St. Clare. *Elizabethan Life in Town and Country*. London: Methuen, 1925.

Castiglione, Baldesar. *The Book of the Courtier*. Tr. George Bull. London: Penguin, 2003.

Chambers, D. S. *Popes, Cardinals and War: The Military Church in Renaissance and Early Modern Europe*. London: I. B. Tauris, 2006.

Chambers, E. K. *The Elizabethan Stage*. 4 vols. Oxford: Clarendon Press, 1967.

Collins, Roger. *Keepers of the Keys of Heaven*. London: Phoenix, 2010.

Collinson, Patrick. *The Elizabethan Puritan Movement*. London: Jonathan Cape, 1967.

———. *Godly People*. London: Hambledon Press, 1983.

Corbett, J. S. *The Successors of Drake*. London: Longmans, Green, 1900.

Duffy, Eamon. *The Stripping of the Altars: Traditional Religion in England, c. 1400–c. 1580*. New Haven: Yale University Press, 1992.

Du Maurier, Daphne. *Golden Lads: A Study of Anthony Bacon, Francis and Their Friends*. London: Victor Gollancz, 1975.

Elton, G. R. *England Under the Tudors*. London: Folio Society, 1997.

Fraser, Antonia. *Mary Queen of Scots*. London: Folio Society, 2004.

Frieda, Leoni. *Catherine de Medici: Renaissance Queen of France*. New York: Fourth Estate, 2003.

Gildersleeve, V. C. *Government Regulation of the Elizabethan Drama*. Westport, CT: Greenwood Press, 1961.

Goldsmid, Edmund, ed. *The Secret Correspondence of Sir Robert Cecil with James VI King of Scotland*. Edinburgh: Privately printed, 1887.

Green, Toby. *Inquisition: The Reign of Fear*. London: Macmillan, 2007.

Gristwood, Sarah. *Elizabeth and Leicester*. London: Bantam Press, 2007.

Guilday, Peter. *The English Catholic Refugees on the Continent, 1558–1795*, vol. 1. London: Longmans, Green, 1914.

Hammer, Paul E. J. *Elizabeth's Wars*. London: Palgrave Macmillan, 2003.

Harrison, G.B., ed. *The Letters of Queen Elizabeth I*. London: Cassel, 1968.

Hartley, T. E., ed. *Proceedings in the Parliaments of Elizabeth I*, vols. 1, 2, and 3. Leicester: Leicester University Press, 1981.

Haynes, Alan. *Robert Cecil, 1st Earl of Salisbury*. London: Peter Owen, 1989.

Hill, Christopher. *Economic Problems of the Church, from Archbishop Whitgift to the Long Parliament*. Oxford: Clarendon Press, 1956.

Hogge, Alice. *God's Secret Agents*. London: HarperCollins, 2005.

Houliston, Victor. *Catholic Resistance in Elizabethan England*. Burlington, VT: Ashgate, 2007.

Kamen, Henry. *The Spanish Inquisition: An Historical Revision*. London: Phoenix Giant, 1997.

Knecht, R. J. *Catherine de' Medici*. London: Longman, 1998.

———. *The French Civil Wars*. London: Longman, 2000.

Knowles, David. *The Religious Orders in England*, vol. 3. Cambridge: Cambridge University Press, 1971.

Lefranc, F. *Sir Walter Raleigh écrivain*. Paris: Armand Colin, 1968.

Lettenhove, Kervyn de, ed. *Relations politiques des Pays-Bas et de l'Angleterre*, vols. 4 and 5. Brussels: Académie Royale, 1885.

Loades, David. *The Cecils: Privilege and Power Behind the Throne*. London: National Archives, 2007.

MacCaffrey, Wallace T. *Elizabeth I: War and Politics, 1588–1603*. Princeton: Princeton University Press, 1992.

———, ed. *The History of The Most Renowned and Victorious Princess Elizabeth, Late Queen of England, by William Camden*. Chicago: University of Chicago Press, 1970.

Macfarlane, Alan. *Witchcraft in Tudor and Stuart England*. London: Routledge & Kegan Paul, 1970.

Manning, B. L. *The People's Faith in the Time of Wyclif*. Cambridge: Cambridge University Press, 1919.

Marcus, Leah S., Janel Muller, and Mary Beth Rose, eds. *Elizabeth I: Collected Works*. Chicago: Chicago University Press, 2000.

Marlowe, Christopher. *The Complete Plays*. London: Penguin, 1976.

Neale, J. E., *Elizabeth I*. London: Folio Society, 2005.

———. *Elizabeth I and Her Parliaments*. 2 vols. London: Jonathan Cape, 1957.

Nicholl, Charles. *The Reckoning: The Murder of Christopher Marlowe*. London: Vintage, 2002.

Owen, G.D. *Elizabethan Wales*. Cardiff: University of Wales Press, 1962.

Parker, Geoffrey. *The Dutch Revolt*. London: Allen Lane, 1977.

———. *The Grand Strategy of Philip II*. New Haven: Yale University Press, 2000.

Porter, Linda. *Mary Tudor: The First Queen*. London: Portrait, 2007.

Prescott, H. F. M. *Spanish Tudor: The Life of Bloody Mary*. London: Constable, 1940.

Rackham, Oliver. *The Illustrated History of the Countryside*. London: Weidenfeld & Nicolson,2003.

Read, Conyers. *Lord Burghley and Queen Elizabeth*. London: Jonathan Cape, 1960.

———. *Mr. Secretary Cecil and Queen Elizabeth*. London: Jonathan Cape, 1977.

———. *Mr. Secretary Walsingham and the Policy of Queen Elizabeth*. 3 vols. Hamden, CT: Archon Press, 1967.

Riggs, David. *The World of Christopher Marlowe*. London: Faber & Faber, 2004.

Ronald, Susan. *The Pirate Queen: Queen Elizabeth I, Her Pirate Adventurers, and the Dawn of Empire*. New York: HarperCollins, 2007.

Salgãdo, Gãmini. *The Elizabethan Underworld*. London: Folio Society, 2006.

Spufford, Margaret, ed. *The World of Rural Dissenters, 1520–1725*. Cambridge: Cambridge University Press, 1995.

Starkey, David. *Elizabeth*. London: Vintage, 2001.

Steane, J. B., ed. *Christopher Marlowe: The Complete Plays*. London: Penguin, 1969.

Stewart, Alan. *Philip Sidney: A Double Life*. London: Chatto & Windus, 2000.

Stowe, John. *A Survey of London Written in the Year 1598*. Phoenix Mill, UK: Sutton Publishing, 2005.

Sutherland, N. M. *Princes, Politics and Religion, 1547–1589*. London: Hambledon Press, 1984.

Tanner, Marcus. *Ireland's Holy Wars*. New Haven and London: Yale Nota Bene, 2003.

Thomas, Keith. *Religion and the Decline of Magic*. London: Weidenfeld & Nicolson, 1971.

Tittler, Robert. *Nicholas Bacon: The Making of a Tudor Statesman*. Athens: University of Ohio Press, 1976.

Waugh, Evelyn. *Edmund Campion*. London: Longmans, 1961.

Wedgwood, C. V. *William the Silent*. London: Phoenix Press, 2001.

Weinreb, Ben, and Christopher Hibbert, eds. *The London Encyclopaedia*. London: Papermac, 1983.

Wernham, R. B. *Before the Armada*. New York: Harcourt, Brace & World, 1966.

Yates, Frances. *Giordano Bruno and the Hermetic Tradition*. Chicago: University of Chicago Press, 1964.

———. *Theatre of the World*. Chicago: University of Chicago Press, 1969.

Youings, Joyce. *Sixteenth-Century England*. London: Pelican, 1984.

Articles

Black, Joseph. "The Rhetoric of Reaction: The Martin Marprelate Tracts (1588–89), Anti-Martinism, and the Uses of Print in Early Modern England." *Sixteenth Century Journal* 28, no. 3 (Autumn 1997): 707–25.

de Vocht, H. "Thomas Harding." *English Historical Review* 35, no. 138 (April 1920): 233–44.

Galloway, James A., Derek Keene, and Margaret Murphy. "Fuelling the City: Production and Distribution of Firewood and Fuel in London's Region, 1290–1400." *Economic History Review*, n.s., 49, no. 3 (August 1996): 447–72.

Haigh, Christopher. "Puritan Evangelism in the Reign of Elizabeth I." *English Historical Review* 92, no. 362 (January 1977): 30–31.

Jones, Norman. "Living the Reformations: Generational Experience and Political Perception in Early Modern England." In "The Remapping of English Political History, 1500–1640," ed. A. J. Slavin, special issue, *Huntington Library Quarterly* 60, no. 3 (1997): 273–88.

Josten, C. H. "Robert Fludd's Theory of Geomancy and his Experiences at Avignon in the Winter of 1601 to 1602." *Journal of the Warburg and Courtauld Institutes* 27 (1964): 327–35.

Reid, R. R. "The Rebellion of the Earls, 1569." *Transactions of the Royal Historical Society*, n.s., 20 (1906): 171–203.

Smith, Lacey Baldwin. "English Treason Trials and Confessions in the Sixteenth Century." *Journal of the History of Ideas* 15, no. 4 (October 1954): 471–98.

Sutherland, N. M. "Queen Elizabeth and the Conspiracy at Amboise, March 1560." *English Historical Review* 81, no. 320 (July 1996): 474–89.

INDEX